T0389575

The Role of Imagination in STEM Concept Formation

Cultural and Historical Perspectives on Science Education

DISTINGUISHED CONTRIBUTORS

Series Editors

Catherine Milne (*New York University, USA*)
Kathryn Scantlebury (*University of Delaware, USA*)

VOLUME 9

The titles published in this series are listed at *brill.com/psec*

The Role of Imagination in STEM Concept Formation

A Cultural-Historical Journey into Researching Play-Based Settings

By

Marilyn Fleer

BRILL

LEIDEN | BOSTON

Cover illustration: Photograph by Nicola Bailey for Monash Education (© Conceptual PlayLab)

All chapters in this book have undergone peer review.

The Library of Congress Cataloging-in-Publication Data is available online at https://catalog.loc.gov

Typeface for the Latin, Greek, and Cyrillic scripts: "Brill". See and download: brill.com/brill-typeface.

ISSN 2589-6202
ISBN 978-90-04-52004-2 (paperback)
ISBN 978-90-04-52005-9 (hardback)
ISBN 978-90-04-52006-6 (e-book)

Contents

Acknowledgements

Sincere thanks to the publishers who kindly agreed to re-publish the nine papers that are interspersed throughout this volume. Full citations are included for each re-published paper in the respective chapter that introduces each paper in turn.

Figures and Tables

Figures

Tables

CHAPTER 1

Beginning the Journey into Early Childhood Science Education Research

Beyond Alternative Conceptions

Abstract

This chapter time stamps a period in the development of early childhood science education research. The many chapters of this volume and the republished 9 journal papers collectively lay the historical landscape that led to an Australian Research Council (ARC) funded five-year programmatic study of: *Under what conditions does children's imaginative play promote the visualisation and imagination of abstract STEM concepts?* Through a personal narrative of one researcher, this chapter begins that journey into early childhood science education research, and the final 2 chapters conclude the journey by bringing together a theoretical model for teaching STEM in play-based settings and a suite of resources for continuing the legacy.

Keywords

constructivism – alternative views – children's science – first nation – early childhood – science

1 Introduction

The phone rings. I look at the clock in the hotel room where I am staying in Copenhagen, and it is 2 in the morning. Is it a nuisance call ... someone is getting the time zone wrong ... or is it something more serious?

The voice on the phone is strong, and fully awake – unlike me – saying she is calling from the Australian Research Council (ARC). She growls at me because I had not kept my phone details up to date in RMS (Research Management System) and she has had quite a time locating me. RMS is a web-based system used by eligible researchers to prepare and submit research applications and assessments. Researchers record their personal profile into the system.

Now I am fully awake. My brain is going into overdrive as I remember that almost 12 months ago that Monash University had asked me to prepare an application to the ARC for their Laureate Fellowship Scheme.

The ARC is the premier research funding body. It is the engine that drives quality research in Australia. It is highly valued because it funds blue skies research, and it underpins what constitutes research success in the academy. Funding is across all disciplines. But with only 27.5% of applications in 2019 by women, gaining a grant in one's lifetime is difficult – especially for women who only try once, whilst their male counter parts go again and again (ARC, 2019, 2020). Winning funds for blue skies research, means it is possible for an academic to progress their own research agenda through the discovery scheme, or if they are lucky, take their work forward in a linkage grant with a partner organisation who has the same research need.

Like many countries around the world, the ARC has its own prestigious award category known as the Australian Laureate Fellowship scheme. It is reported on the ARC website that the Australian Laureate Fellowship scheme aims to "supports world-class researchers to conduct research in Australia. The Australian Government is committed to attracting and retaining outstanding researchers and research leaders of international reputation. The scheme funds ground-breaking, internationally-competitive basic and applied research".[1]

Could my proposal named in 75 characters have been successful? Could there be an appetite across the disciplines for bringing forward programmatic research on: *Science and engineering concept formation in homes and play-based settings*? Could the meagre 175 characters I had available to summarise 3 decades of my research have traction with peer assessors?

The assessment panel made up of Laureate Fellows across disciplines assess and decide who gets up into the list of peer reviewed fundable proposals. Did they think the 10 pages of text to showcase the planned programmatic research would represent a stepwise change in research, as is expected in an application to the ARC at this level? This is what I wrote:

> This programmatic study aims to research conceptual play by examining imagination in play and imagination in science, engineering and technology. The project expects to generate new knowledge about concept formation of infants, toddlers and pre-schoolers in play-based settings and homes. The projected outcomes include understandings about how concepts can be intentionally taught in play settings and learned at home for particular age periods. Significant benefits include increased exposure to these concepts in the formative years, a model of intentional teaching of concepts suitable for early childhood teachers, and the building of world

class research program and research capacity in early childhood science, engineering and technologies.

So now I am wondering ... feeling some hope ... had I been successful? The Director of the ARC says to me, "Congratulations you have been awarded our most prestigious research accolade, the Laureate Fellowship". I am speechless, so she continues, "Actually you have additionally won the Kathleen Fitzpatrick Laureate Fellowship".

Kathleen Fitzpatrick is presented historically as a tireless advocate for women in the humanities and social sciences. Her illustrious career included being president of the Council for Women in War Work, a foundation member of the Australian Humanities Research Council, and the founding fellow of the later Australian Academy of the Humanities. She also engaged in visionary work, such as establishing the Melbourne University Women's College, and University House.

On the ARC website it shows why this award was named after her. The "Australian Laureate Fellowships include fellowships allocated to exceptional female researchers who will also undertake an ambassadorial role to promote women in research and to mentor early career researchers, particularly women, to encourage them to enter and establish a career in research in Australia".[2]

This additional award is really significant because it gives permission to take forward my agenda to support early childhood educators in STEM education and with research mentoring, become the next generation of researchers to continue that legacy. It makes visible in the academy that early childhood education can and does punch above its weight, despite the field having low status.

The early childhood education field and the academy are primarily women, who teach or study children and families. For most of my academic life, we have had limited support for scholarship. It was only in recent years that the ARC included a research category called *early childhood*. With a history of being invisible in research, it is rather ironic that I would be the first women in educational research in Australia to take out their top award.

But where did this all begin? This volume showcases through a set of published papers and their context (as chapters), a journey over time into the emergence of early childhood science education in Australia (1980s onwards) through the eyes of one researcher. By building on the shoulders of those who set the foundations of science education, notably represented in the Journal of the *Australasian Science Education Research Association* (ASERA), it becomes possible to show the path through which researching imagination in science, engineering and technologies in early childhood education was trodden.

Imagination in play is central for the early childhood institution. Imaginary play is the pedagogy of choice. Imagination is a key psychological function of the preschool child. But 30 years ago, it was absent in the science education research literature. The steps towards this contemporary research agenda (Chapter 9) had to be conceptualised through scholarly discomfort (Chapters 1–2).

In this first chapter with the re-published research Paper 1 that follows, I signal a deep discontent with the theoretical paradigm in which science education research was grounded. In so doing, I showcase what the field had to forge in inventing early childhood science education research. Although I didn't know it then, the field was in turmoil.

2   Beginning the Journey

"Educational research was making no difference to practice" said the most preeminent science education researcher at the time, Professor Peter Fensham from Monash University. It was 1988 and I had just been appointed to my first academic position. This gave the possibility that I could attend the *Australian Association for Research in Education* conference[3] to hear about the latest educational research in Australia. I chose to go to a symposium on Science Education research – an area I wanted to take forward in my PhD.

I was sitting in a room primarily full of white males listening to a group of white males. I later learned that this group was made up of the leading science education researchers in Australia and internationally, and had been nicknamed the Monash Mafia. So of course, I was determined **not** to pursue my PhD at Monash. But 12 years on, it was Peter Fensham who encouraged me to apply for a professorial position at Monash University. I am still at Monash today.

What was the discontent for me at that time? What was the disconnect? I was so fresh to the area of science education research that I gobbled up everything that was put in front of me to read, and everything I could find in the key science education journals. I engaged in as many conversations about science education research with colleagues as would dare to sit with me in the tearoom. This was in the time of the college-university binary system and before I had children and had become time poor. I began attending a really important conference hosted by the ASERA. The association published papers from that conference in a peer reviewed journal called RISE – *Research in Science Education*. But none of this work spoke to the field in which I had been teaching – early childhood education – and none of it seemed theoretically grounded in how I had come to understand the development of children, or the realities of teaching science in play-based settings. So how could I take my PhD forward?

I soon learned that there were few pioneers in early childhood science education research, and this meant working it out for myself. This was not a novel idea. At that time early childhood education in Australia had only one professor, and she was not interested in science education research. In fact, few of my peers were. The second chapter of the journey will tell that story.

What was the research that was going on in science education at the time when I began my PhD? What treasure trove of science education literature was available to support my study of early childhood science education? In the bibliography of my PhD thesis there was just one professional association practice paper with the word preschool in the title, and one UK journal paper that mentioned early years – which in that context means the youngest children in the school sector. Studying the contents pages of RISE prior to 1991 when my PhD was conferred, brought very little relevant literature. However, 2 papers by Valda Kirkwood and her co-authors were referenced. Even though I did not know it at the time, they were symbolic of a new way of thinking that was on the horizon.

The closest research context and associated empirical studies of the late 70s through to the early 1990s relevant to imagining in STEM and imagination in play, was associated with primary schools. The list that follows for the 1970s to the 1980s brings forward children's thinking in floating and sinking (Biddulph & Osborne, 1984), chemical change (Fisher & Kimber, 1975), and temperature (Appleton, 1985). It also looks at pedagogy in primary schools, such as, using children's drawings (Hayes & Symington, 1984, 1988; Symington, 1977), system level support (Cranston & McAllister, 1988), and discovery learning (Napper, 1976) and foundational research into primary preservice teachers (Skamp, 1988).

RISE 1970–1980s:

- Appleton, K. (1985). Children's ideas about temperature. *Research in Science Education, 15*, 122–126. https://doi.org/10.1007/BF02356533
- Fisher, J. W., & Kimber, R. L. (1975). Grade placement of physical and chemical change concepts in primary school science. *Research in Science Education, 5*(1), 177–187. https://doi.org/10.1007/BF02558622
- Hayes, D., & Symington, D. (1988). Purposes achieved by drawing during science activities. *Research in Science Education, 18*(1), 104–111. https://doi.org/10.1007/BF02356585
- Napper, I. (1976). The development of science concepts in primary children by discovery strategies. *Research in Science Education, 6*(1), 27–43. https://doi.org/10.1007/BF02558647

- Symington, D. J. (1977). Primary school pupils' ability to see scientific problems in everyday phenomena. *Research in Science Education, 7*(1), 41–49. https://doi.org/10.1007/BF02643111
- Biddulph, F., & Osborne, R. (1984). Pupils' ideas about floating and sinking. *Research in Science Education, 14*(1), 114–124. https://doi.org/10.1007/BF02356797
- Hayes, D., & Symington, D. (1984). The satisfaction of young children with their representational drawings of natural phenomena. *Research in Science Education, 14*, 39–46. https://doi.org/10.1007/BF02356789
- Skamp, K. (1988). Preservice primary teacher education in NSW: A comparative analysis of espoused science education curricula. *Research in Science Education, 18*(1), 71–82. https://doi.org/10.1007/BF02356582
- Cranston, N., & McAllister, R. (1988). Pupils' learning of science in primary schools: A system-level investigation. *Research in Science Education, 18*(1), 22–34. https://doi.org/10.1007/BF02356577

The limited number of works in RISE sat within the emergent international paradigm shift in science education where researchers were studying children's thinking in science. Alternative frameworks (Pfundt & Duit, 1991), intuitive ideas (Osborne & Freyberg, 1985), conceptual change (Carey, 1985), children's science (Driver, Guesne & Tiberghiene, 1985), cognitive conflict (Rowell and Dawson, 1977), naïve knowledge (Champagne, Gunstone & Klopfer, 1983) and misconceptions (Gilbert & Watts, 1983) were the buzz words emerging in the research papers from primarily three different parts of the world – the university of Waikato, Leeds University, and Monash University. The latter brought with it a network of researchers from across Australia who met each year at the ASERA conference.

In dealing with the problem of science education research not making a difference to practice, researchers influenced by the new ideas of Roger Osborne from New Zealand were putting attention on what children were thinking when engaged in science lessons. Strongly influenced by Piaget's research into the naïve thinking of children, Roger Osborne and a generation of science education researchers began to amass a huge corpus of data on children's thinking in chemical change (Driver, 1983), earth and beyond (Nussbaum, 1985a), electricity (Cosgrove & Osborne,1985), force and motion (Gunstone & Watts, 1985), heat and temperature (Erikson & Tiberghien, 1985), life and living (Carey, 1985), light (Guesne, 1985), matter (Nussbaum, 1985b), and so on. So why did researchers concentrate their efforts and resources on studying children's ideas in science? Driver, Guesne and Tiberghien (1985) insightfully gave a rationale for this question in the preface of their edited book:

> We hope that the chapters with their various emphases give an insight into the conceptual world of children in our classrooms; and insight which we hope will be helpful in making science teaching and learning more rewarding to teachers and children alike. (p. VIII)

But classrooms in schools are not designed in the same way as preschools and childcare centres.

What did we know from research into preschool children's thinking of science concepts? I had to wait until 1990s if I wanted guidance. The science education journals didn't tell a story about this until I submitted my thesis for examination. Staying with a focus on RISE, and the journal of ASERA which had now become one of the leading international journals with a new look cover, I could see some changes were afoot. As can be seen in the references that follow, different questions were being asked about researching children's thinking in science when the children were younger. Even though more papers were published that focused on primary science education, ten papers emerged in the journal over a ten-year period that were oriented to early childhood science education. As the list shows, gender had emerged as an area of research in early childhood and primary science education (Bearlin, 1990), new approaches to supporting early childhood teachers (Fleer, 1990; Kirkwood, Bearlin, & Hardy, 1989), new tools for measuring teacher attitudes (Coulson, 1992) and children's thinking in science were being published (Coulson, 1991; Fleer, 1991a, 1996; Fleer & Beasley, 1991; Fleer & Hardy, 1993). Other journals were also beginning to publish research in early childhood science education.

RISE 1990–2000s:

- Bearlin, M. (1990). Toward a gender-sensitive model of science teacher education for women primary and early childhood teachers. *Research in Science Education, 20*(1), 21–30. https://doi.org/10.1007/BF02620476
- Coulson, R. (1991). Preschool children's interests in science. *Research in Science Education, 21*(1), 345–347. https://doi.org/10.1007/BF02360490
- Coulson, R. (1992). Development of an instrument for measuring attitudes of early childhood educators towards science. *Research in Science Education, 22*(1), 101–105. https://doi.org/10.1007/BF02356884
- Fleer, M. (1990). Scaffolding conceptual change in early childhood. *Research in Science Education, 20*(1), 114–123. https://doi.org/10.1007/BF02620486
- Fleer, M., & Hardy, T. (1993). How can we find out what 3 and 4 year olds think? New approaches to eliciting very young children's understandings in science. *Research in Science Education, 23*(1), 68–76. https://doi.org/10.1007/BF02357046

- Fleer, M. (1991a). Socially constructed learning in early childhood science education. *Research in Science Education, 21*(1), 96–103. https://doi.org/10.1007/BF02360462
- Fleer, M. (1996). Fusing the boundaries between home and child care to support children's scientific learning. *Research in Science Education, 26*(2), 143–154. https://doi.org/10.1007/BF02356428
- Hardy, T., Bearlin, M., & Kirkwood, V. (1990). Outcomes of the primary and early childhood science and technology education project at the University of Canberra. *Research in Science Education, 20*(1), 142–151. https://doi.org/10.1007/BF02620489
- Kirkwood, V., Bearlin, M., & Hardy, T. (1989). New approaches to the inservice education in science and technology of primary and early childhood teachers (or mum is not dumb after all!). *Research in Science Education, 19*(1), 174–186. https://doi.org/10.1007/BF02356857

With this backdrop of science education research in Australia and New Zealand, we now turn our attention to the challenges researchers were facing in early childhood science education.

First the early childhood science education research needed to invent a method and theorise a methodology that could catch young children's science thinking in play-based settings. This was the focus of Ruth Coulson (1992). In keeping with the quantitative tradition, she presented a method paper on how to measure the attitudes of early childhood educators towards science. However, children's science was the buzz word then (Osborne & Freyberg, 1985). But there was a problem. *Very little science was taught in preschool settings. So how could I recruit participants if there was limited science being taught?*

The *second* related problem which emerged more fully over time, was teachers' knowledge of science concepts – this being the reason why early childhood teachers do not teach science – or so I was told by the literature then and now. But in the early days of conceptualising something that didn't exist – research in early childhood science education – it was hard to see why the assumption of blaming the victim for not teaching science was problematic. We will return to this problem later in Chapter 4. What was studied initially by researchers was primary teachers' scientific understanding, and as Fisher and Kimber (1975) point out, "One of the biggest problems with primary school science is in obtaining teachers who have the confidence to teach it" (p. 177). They solved the problem by bringing in a specialist science teacher into their research experiment, and then raised questions about the transferability of their results:

> A specialist science teacher was used in these studies. Would this method
> of instruction [semi-formal with procedural cards and discussion points

for small and whole groups] have been suitable for the normal class teachers? Would they have attained comparable results? Would the same teacher obtain similar results with students in other schools? These are a few of the many factors which plague researchers who investigate grade placement of concepts such as physical and chemical change in primary school science. (Fisher & Kimber, 1975, pp. 183–184)

This work sat in contrast with the research of Margaret Bearlin (1990) and later Valda Kirkwood and Tim Hardy, who saw the problem differently. They suggested that both primary and early childhood teachers had scientific knowledge associated with many of their personal practices, such as chemistry in cooking, and their research showed that with a gender-sensitive professional development (PD) program that unclaimed knowledge could be made conscious and used. *Years of gendered conditioning of girls and women as not good at science had resulted in a lack of confidence and not a lack of competence in science.* This was at a time when scholars worried about girls and science and technology (GASAT conference I 1990, Girls And Science And Technology) because research was showing problems with equity of access to resources and career opportunities in the sciences (Kelly, 1987; Smail, 1987). But this finding of Margaret Bearlin and later Valda Kirkwood and Tim Hardy didn't have traction in the science education community, despite a replication of their research showing the same results (Appleton, 1995).

Third, early childhood science education research literature was in its infancy, it needed to be built. There was so little out there to find and to read. Little guidance was available on how to set up a study in play-based settings or what might be the methods for finding out preschool children's thinking in science. Would early childhood science education research need to mirror the existing ways of researching so as to identify very young children's alternative views, their misconceptions and the alternative frameworks they were operating in? Could we also amass a body of static knowledge about their thinking and include this in the handbooks on children's thinking in science (Pfundt & Duit, 1991, 1994)?

Sitting in the office of one of my PhD supervisors at the University of Queensland I was given an article on the definitive thinking at the time in science education on secondary students thinking in science (Osborne & Wittrock, 1985). As a dutiful student I read this article but didn't really connect with it until I had read more of the literature described above. Returning to the same office 12 months later with data and this article in hand, and a bigger picture of children's thinking in science, I was asked to present a snapshot of video data to my PhD supervisor. As he looked at the 3–8-year-old children learning science with teachers who had participated in the PECSTEP program (Primary and Early Childhood Science and Technology Education Project) designed by Bearlin, Kirkwood and Hardy, he exclaimed: "But the children keep changing their mind". He meant that the children's conception of science concepts kept changing in one science lesson. Knowledge generated about very young children's thinking in science was not static or definitive after all.

Keeping with the misconception's literature, the children all displayed alternative models and explanations of how an electrical circuit worked. The diagram below is illustrative of what was in the literature and eventually in my thesis (Fleer, 1991a; Figure 1.1). The children could show this physically and give their theories. They could talk about a flat battery like a piece of paper – showing with their hands the flattening of a battery. But they could also use felt board pieces to show how a torch could be made and then create this with Lego or cylinders, batteries, wires, and switches (Fleer, 1991b). Like Fisher and Kimber (1975) had found, children could engage easily with abstract scientific concepts. But unlike Fisher and Kimber (1975), the children's teachers were not science specialists but rather early childhood teachers who had participated in the PECSTEP PD program. And additionally, unlike Fisher and Kimber (1975), I did not expect their views would be the same if I interviewed them on the next day.

I recall feeling bewildered at my supervisor's surprise – as this was the norm in early childhood education – children's thinking in science is not a static phenomenon. Children constantly contradict themselves, and you have to go beyond the individual, and study the societal, cultural and institutional context in which the individual is located and sharing their thinking. You have to

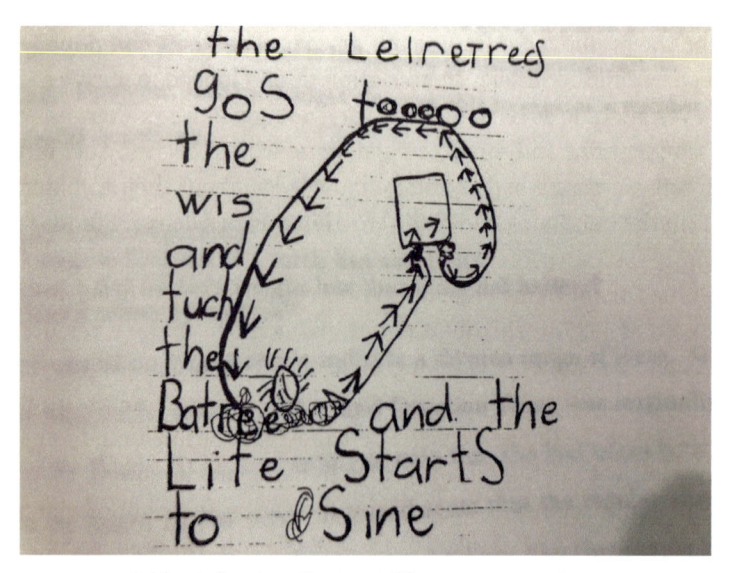

FIGURE 1.1   Bridget's drawing of a circuit (Fleer, 1991a, p. 292)

find the ways of capturing this. *But the methods to bring this forward in research were not yet there* (Chapter 5).

Fourth, what dominated the field was surveys and interviews. An interview about an incident was deemed at the time to be the most powerful way of creating a context in which to study students' thinking (Osborne & Freyberg, 1985). Looking at stick figures and line drawings about a science concept like light, where children are presented with a candle and asked to explain the light source and how it travels in an interview were common. But mostly students were given multiple choice questions with a range of explanations to select from. *However, the children I was researching could not read or write.*

Fifth, interviewing children about an incident was closer to what could work. Studies about children's conceptions of living and non-living, done with interesting approaches, such as classifying a series of cards and then asking children why they had categorised as they did (Bell & Freyberg, 1985), for instance, the Sun is living because it is yellow or because it has face drawn on it, provided a way forward. Or so I thought. But I found interviewing children as young as 3 and 4 years of age was challenging, because they are still developing their language. For example, using the word *smoke* to explain to the researcher their thinking about *steam* would be deemed to sit outside of the right explanation in science. How can children explain steam or condensation or other phenomena in their everyday lives if they don't yet have the words to name it? *They just have not been alive for long enough to build the necessary vocabulary.* But there were other problems.

Sixth, I had learned from my review of the behavioural sciences literature in my master's thesis (Fleer, 1987a, 1987b), that taking children out of their everyday life to interview them was problematic in many First Nation cultures. Asking questions as part of identifying children's thinking was viewed in some cultural communities as disrespectful, because asking 'why or what' suggests you are questioning the authority of the person speaking (Fleer & Williams-Kennedy, 2002). For some children, asking questions is not part of their cultural background. I had learned that in some communities, knowledge is collectively understood, shared only with permission from the elders, and is discussed in a distributed way. That is, knowledge could not be contained in the head of the individual but rather was socially located, kept alive through songs, storylines, lines in the sand, art, geographies etc. *This distributed rather than individual construction of knowledge was totally different to what was being presented in the constructivist literature from the mid 1980s right through until the beginning of 2000.*

Finally, I was theoretically worried about the constructivist literature, with its focus on the individual, because it named science concepts that 'were not aligned with the science community' as alternative. Driver (1983) recommended that "Alternative frameworks suggested by pupils offer teachers readily available opportunities to illustrate characteristics of the scientific pursuit through the appraisal of competing interpretations or concepts of events" (p. 82). By the late 1990s there were volumes and volumes of literature building on what individuals think about a range of science concepts. Most notably brought together in handbooks or other scholarly publications and updated every few years, such as that of Pfundt and Duit (1991, 1994). These were the *go-to works* on alternative conceptions for researchers in the science education community. But herein lies the problem. What is the alternative that is assumed? It seems *Western science was totally implicit in this construction of what children should think.* In the paper that follows, the epistemological arguments that worried me at the time are given. Whilst I could not solve this problem, the writing of that paper was cathartic. I could in a very small way object to what I was steeped in, be critical of what was being promoted at the time as the way to undertake research in science education. After many failures (Fleer, 1997, 1999; Fleer, Sukroo & Faucett, 1994), I was finally on the road to critiquing my own methods and assumptions about the nature of early childhood science education research.

3   Concluding Remarks and Future Directions

The paper that is discussed below sets the stage for questioning the theoretical lenses of the dominant research at the time. It sat within a suite of papers on children's thinking in science coming out of New Zealand (McKinley, 1992, McKinley & Waiti, 1995), but also spear headed in Australia by Christie (1991) and Aikenhead (1996) in Canada.

3.1   *Paper 1: Children's Alternative Views: Alternative to What?*
The critique was as much about my own research to that point, as it was about the context in which I was researching. What dominated my thinking was:

1.   *Worldviews and cultural meaning-making systems*: In order for individuals to begin to appreciate meaning systems and the processes of knowledge construction in another culture, the two cultures must come together and exchange world views. Ganma is a powerful metaphor for realizing this. Science curriculum development in Australia has the potential to provide an avenue for bringing together differing world views in science. However, to what extent are school children exposed to different knowledge systems, particularly in science? What world views do they experience? How differently would science curriculum look if it took into account the differing world views found in multi-cultural Australia?

Is indigenous knowledge in science considered? These are questions researchers, teachers and curriculum developers need to ask themselves and their colleagues (p. 121).

2. *Assumptions in the science education literature*: These studies do not discuss other world views or cultural knowledge construction in science. Western science is assumed as the norm (p. 24).

3. *Data collection bias*: ... the data elicited from such children when interpreted within a Western meaning framework may never reveal knowledge of the classification system or a representation of interrelated features of Aboriginal life and belief (p. 126).

4. *Gaps in the science education literature*: ... we know very little about the meaning systems of non-Western children in science (p. 127).

5. *Dominating methodology in science education*: What is interesting to note in these studies is the disparity between the methodology employed to find out what children think in a range of cultures and the theory which underpins it – constructivism. If constructivism "emphasises that science is a creative human endeavour which is historically and culturally conditioned and that its knowledge claims are not absolute" (Matthews 1994, p. 139), then why is only one cultural construction of science knowledge used as the benchmark for the analysis of children's responses (p. 128)?

6. *Supporting teachers in science education by having more inclusive research approaches and assumptions*: Teachers need to know more about other world views than the one they have been enculturated into, if they are to portray a view that science is socially constructed, and if they are to make sense of the range of children's scientific thinking and ideas that they bring to science lessons. If teachers only have one world view, they will consider the views of children from different cultural groups with different world views as alternative. It has been shown that this is indeed the term given in the science education literature to those views that are not considered by the scientific community (obviously Western) as right (p. 132).

But this agenda was not mine to take forward. That was the role of the First Nation peoples and those reconceptualising and broadening what counts as mainstream science education (see McKinley, 1992; McKinley & Waiti, 1995).

Notes

1 https://www.arc.gov.au/grants/discovery-program/australian-laureate-fellowships
2 https://www.arc.gov.au/grants/discovery-program/australian-laureate-fellowships
3 https://www.aare.edu.au/

References

Aikenhead, G. (1996). Cultural assimilation in science classroom: Border crossings and other solutions. *Studies in Science Education, 7*, 1–52.

Appleton, K. (1995). Student teachers' confidence to teach science: Is more science knowledge necessary to improve self-confidence? *International Journal of Science Education, 17*(3), 357–369. https://doi.org/10.1080/0950069950170307

Australian Research Council (ARC). (2019). *Gender and the research workforce. Excellence in Research for Australia (ERA).*

Australian Research Council (ARC). (2020, December 23). *Selection outcome reports.* https://www.arc.gov.au/grants/grant-outcomes/selection-outcome-reports

Bearlin, M. (1990). Toward a gender-sensitive model of science teacher education for women primary and early childhood teachers. *Research in Science Education, 20*(1), 21–30. https://doi.org/10.1007/BF02620476

Bell, B., & Freyberg, P. F. (1985) Language in the science classroom. In R. J. Osborne & P. Freyberg (Eds.), *Learning in science: The implications of children's science* (pp. 29–40). Heinemann.

Biddulph, F., & Osborne, R. (1984). Pupils' ideas about floating and sinking. *Research in Science Education, 14*(1), 114–124. https://doi.org/10.1007/BF02356797

Carey, S. (1985). *Conceptual change in childhood.* MIT Press.

Christie, M. J. (1991). Aboriginal science for the ecologically sustainable future. *Australian Science Teachers Journal, 37*(1), 26–31. https://search.informit.org/doi/abs/10.3316/aeipt.52383

Cosgrove, M., & Osborne, R. (1985). A teaching sequence on electric current. In R. J. Osborne & P. Freyberg (Eds.), *Learning in science* (pp. 112–123). Heinemann.

Coulson, R. (1991). Preschool children's interests in science. *Research in Science Education, 21*(1), 345–347. https://doi.org/10.1007/BF02360490

Coulson, R. (1992). Development of an instrument for measuring attitudes of early childhood educators towards science. *Research in Science Education, 22*(1), 101–105. https://doi.org/10.1007/BF02356884

Cranston, N., & McAllister, R. (1988). Pupils' learning of science in primary schools: A system-level investigation. *Research in Science Education, 18*(1), 22–34. https://doi.org/10.1007/BF02356577

Driver, R. (1983). *Pupil as scientist.* McGraw-Hill Education.

Driver, R. (1985). *Children's ideas in science.* McGraw-Hill Education.

Erickson, G., & Tiberghien, A. (1985). Heat and temperature. In R. Drvier, E. Guesne, & A. Tiberghien (Eds.), *Children's ideas in science* (pp. 52–84). McGraw-Hill Education.

Fisher, J. W., & Kimber, R. L. (1975). Grade placement of physical and chemical change concepts in primary school science. *Research in Science Education, 5*(1), 177–187. https://doi.org/10.1007/BF02558622

Fleer, M. (1987a). Using microcomputers to support early literacy learning. *Australian Journal of Reading, 10*(3), 177–182. https://search.informit.org/doi/abs/10.3316/aeipt.37640

Fleer, M. (1987b). The introduction of micro-computers into schools with Aboriginal students. *Journal of the Australian College of Education, 13*(2), 115–116.

Fleer, M. (1990). Scaffolding conceptual change in early childhood. *Research in Science Education, 20*(1), 114–123. https://doi.org/10.1007/BF02620486

Fleer, M. (1991a). *Early childhood science education: The teaching-learning process as scaffolding conceptual change* [Doctoral thesis]. University of Queensland. https://trove.nla.gov.au/work/31792423

Fleer, M. (1991b). *Why won't my torch work? Physics for 4 to 8 year olds* (Australian Early Childhood Resource Book Series, No. 1 March). Australian Early Childhood Association.

Fleer, M. (1996). Fusing the boundaries between home and child care to support children's scientific learning. *Research in Science Education, 26*(2), 143–154. https://doi.org/10.1007/BF02356428

Fleer, M. (1997). A cross-cultural study of rural Australian Aboriginal children's understanding of night and day. *Research in Science Education, 27*(1), 101–116. https://doi.org/10.1007/BF02463035

Fleer, M. (1999). Children's alternative views: Alternative to what? *International Journal of Science Education, 21*(2), 119–135. https://doi.org/10.1080/095006999290741

Fleer, M., & Beasley, W. (1991). A study of conceptual development in early childhood. *Research in Science Education, 21*(1), 104–112. https://doi.org/10.1007/BF02360463

Fleer, M., & Hardy, T. (1993). How can we find out what 3 and 4 year olds think? New approaches to eliciting very young children's understandings in science. *Research in Science Education, 23*(1), 68–76. https://doi.org/10.1007/BF02357046

Fleer, M., Sukroo, J., & Faucett, T. (1994). Determining young aboriginal children's scientific understandings: A pilot study. *Research in Science Education, 24*(1), 371–372. https://doi.org/10.1007/BF02356367

Fleer, M., & Williams-Kennedy, D. (2002). *Building bridges: Researching literacy development for young Indigenous children.* Australian Early Childhood Association.

Gilbert, J. K., & Watts, D. M. (1983). Concepts, misconceptions and alternative conceptions: Changing perspectives in science education. *Studies in Science Education, 10*(1), 61–98. https://doi.org/10.1080/03057268308559905

Guesne, E. (1985). Light. In R. Driver, E. Guesne, & A. Tiberghien (Eds.), *Children's ideas in science* (pp. 10–32). Open University Press.

Gunstone, R., & Watts, M. (1985). Force and motion. In R. Drvier, E. Guesne, & A. Tiberghien (Eds.), *Children's ideas in science* (pp. 85–104). Open University Press.

Hayes, D., & Symington, D. (1984). The satisfaction of young children with their representational drawings of natural phenomena. *Research in Science Education, 14,* 39–46. https://doi.org/10.1007/BF02356789

Hayes, D., & Symington, D. (1988). Purposes achieved by drawing during science activities. *Research in Science Education, 18*(1), 104–111. https://doi.org/10.1007/BF02356585

Kelly, A. (1987). Why girls don't do science. In A. Kelly (Ed.), *Science for girls* (pp. 12–17). Open University Press.

Kirkwood, V., Bearlin, M., & Hardy, T. (1989). New approaches to the inservice education in science and technology of primary and early childhood teachers (or mum is not dumb after all!). *Research in Science Education, 19*(1), 174–186. https://doi.org/10.1007/BF02356857

Klopfer, L. E., Champagne, A. B., & Gunstone, R. F. (1983). Naive knowledge and science learning. *Research in Science & Technological Education, 1*(2), 173–183. https://doi.org/https://doi.org/10.1080/0263514830010205

Kuhn, T. (1970). *The structure of scientific revolutions* (2nd ed.). University of Chicago Press.

Matthews, M. R. (1994). *Science teaching: The role of history and philosophy of science*. Routledge.

McKinley, E. (1992). Research issues in Maori science education. In B. Bell, A. Begg, F. Biddulph, M. Carr, M. Carr, J. McChesney, & J. Young Loveridge (Eds.), *SAMEpapers 1992* (pp. 1–22). University of Waikao.

McKinley, E., & Waiti, P. (1995). Te Tauaki Marautanga Putaiao: He tauira – The writing of a national science curriculum in Maori. In A. Jones, A. Begg, B. Bell, F. Biddulph, M. Carr, M. Carr, J. McChesney, E. McKinley, & J. Young Loveridge (Eds.), *SAMEpapers 1995* (pp. 75–94). University of Waikao.

Napper, I. (1976). The development of science concepts in primary children by discovery strategies. *Research in Science Education, 6*(1), 27–43. https://doi.org/10.1007/BF02558647

Nussbaum, J. (1985a). The earth as a cosmic body. In R. Drvier, E. Guesne, & A. Tiberghien (Eds.), *Children's ideas in science* (pp. 170–192). McGraw-Hill Education.

Nussbaum, J. (1985b). The particulate nature of matter in the gaseous phase. In R. Drvier, E. Guesne, & A. Tiberghien (Eds.), *Children's ideas in science* (pp. 124–144). McGraw-Hill Education.

Osborne, R., & Freyberg, P. (1985). *Learning in science: The implications of children's science*. Heinemann.

Osborne, R., & Wittrock, M. (1985). The generative learning model and its implications for science education. *Studies in Science Education, 12*(1), 59–87. https://doi.org/10.1080/03057268508559923

Pfundt, H., & Duit, R. (1991). *Bibliography of students' alternative frameworks and science education* (3rd ed.). University of Kiel.

Pfundt, H., & Duit, R. (1994). *Students' alternative frameworks and science education* (4th ed.). University of Kiel.

Rowell, J., & Dawson, C. (1977). Teaching about floating and sinking: An attempt to link cognitive psychology with classroom practice. *Science Education, 61*(2), 243–251. https://doi.org/10.1002/sce.3730610215

Skamp, K. (1988). Preservice primary teacher education in NSW: A comparative analysis of espoused science education curricula. *Research in Science Education, 18*(1), 71–82. https://doi.org/10.1007/BF02356582

Smail, B. (1987). Organising the curriculum to fit girls' interests. In A. Kelly (Ed.), *Science for girls* (pp. 80–88). Open University Press.

Symington, D. J. (1977). Primary school pupils' ability to see scientific problems in everyday phenomena. *Research in Science Education, 7*(1), 41–49. https://doi.org/10.1007/BF02643111

Vygotsky, L. S. (1998). *The collected works of L.S. Vygotsky: Child Psychology* (M. J. Hall, Trans.; R. W. Rieber, Ed., Vol. 5). Plenum Press.

Paper 1: Children's Alternative Views: Alternative to What?

This paper originally appeared as Fleer, M. (1999). Children's alternative views: Alternative to what? *International Journal of Science Education, 21*(2), 119–135. https://doi.org/10.1080/095006999290741 Reprinted here with permission from the publisher.

Abstract

The assumptions implicit within Western science education research and practices are considered in this paper. It is argued that it is Western science which underpins science teaching and that other world views, e.g., those constructed in Aboriginal cultures, are not foregrounded. The notion of alternative views positions knowledge construction in other cultures in ways which disallow different world views or understandings to emerge. Alternative implies alternative to Western science.

Introduction

The Western scientists censor out the intuitive, the ideas and traditions of uneducated people, and the folk wisdom of the past and confine themselves to empirical data. The metaphor building at the heart of Western science lies in its refusal to admit any but hard data, and it gives rise to a hard, mechanistic model of the world in which human appetites and weaknesses are out of the picture. (Christie, 1991, p. 27)

In recent years, the rational foundations of Western science and the self-perpetuating belief in the scientific method have come into question (Bleier, 1986; Kuhn, 1970). Western science and scientific activity has been perceived as context free, value neutral and objective (Barnes, 1985; Chalmers, 1988; Kuhn, 1970). It is thought that through experimentation and close observation truths will be revealed. Arguments have been put forward which question these basic assumptions (Bleier, 1986; Eisler, 1988, Kuhn, 1970; Wajcman, 1991; Woolgar, 1988).

Integral to Western science is the acclaimed scientific method. McCarl Nielsen (1989) states that the use of the scientific method assumes that nature and the social world are knowable. It is thought that through the process of recording observations of what appears as object reality by a subjective (independent) researcher, data can be derived, interpreted and used to build, confirm or refute theories. Hypotheses are proven through showing in a repeated fashion some kind of causal link. Yet as Bateson (1979) argues, this assumes the causal link will always be true across time and contexts. Consequently, science never proves something, but rather it probes and finds the best causal connection possible at the time. The notion of finding a truth for reality is highly questionable.

> ... science is a way of perceiving and making what we may call 'sense' of our precepts (Bateson, 1979, p. 29). ... science, like all other methods of perception, is limited in its ability to collect the outward and visible signs of whatever may be truth. Science probes; it does not prove. (Bateson, 1979, p. 30)

This paper brings together Western and Aboriginal science in the context of curriculum development in Australia, and questions the assumptions we hold about Western science in shaping science teaching. The first part of this paper discusses an Aboriginal world view in relation to science and science education. This is followed by a brief overview of the research which underpins curriculum development in Australia. Methodological implications for cross-cultural research also feature. Finally, recent curriculum development in Australia is explored with a view to ascertaining to what extent differing world views are presented to children.

An Aboriginal World View

An Aboriginal person in Australia is someone who identifies as an Aboriginal and one who is accepted as such by his/her community (Department of

Employment, Education and Training, 1991, p. 4). Across Australia, there are not just many regional groups of Aboriginal people with distinct languages and cultural practices, but individuals who vary in their traditional cultural affiliation. Consequently, great variability in traditional science knowledge is likely among Aboriginal people within and across communities. However, scholars, e.g., Christie (1991), Partington and McCudden (1992), Harris (1990), and Jones et al. (1995) have, in general terms, shown that a common world view is evident and manifests itself in many facets of everyday life for Aboriginal people, regardless of their traditional cultural affiliation.

In July 1990, Michael Christie presented a paper to 200 delegates at the annual conference of the Australian Science Teachers' Association. He said:

> When I say that there are two hundred people in this room, I am making in some ways, a rather bizarre metaphoric leap, by assuming that in one sense, we are all identical and therefore can be included meaningfully in a set of '200 people'. We are in fact, all quite different, so different that it would be impossible for me to actually define what a *person* is, but my scientific system allows us to assume that in some sense we are all alike, and to that extent, counting people is a meaningfully scientific process.
>
> Aboriginal scientists refuse to make such a huge metaphoric leap. They know each person is an individual, from a certain family, from a certain part of the land, from a certain totem, related to each other in particular ways. It is their relatedness and their affiliations which are significant in the Aboriginal system, and to quantify people would force us to ignore those metaphors which define out various modes of connectedness with the world and each other. (Christie, 1991, p. 27)

In the example above, it is clear that the knowledge-building system of Western science and technology has developed a metaphor of quantification for selecting and organizing particular images of reality. The knowledge system of Aboriginal science in contrast has focused on the interconnectedness of people – their relationship to each other and their environment. Christie has argued that in this instance, Western science has focused on the unifying element of humanity, but has ignored in 'reality that all elements are given meaning by their context, and (similarly, that this) cultivates a metaphor in which they can be manipulated as abstractions without reference to context' (Christie, 1991, p. 27). Aboriginal science has ignored 'the common humanity shared by the 200, and perceives and labels them according to different metaphors appropriate to the context' (Christie, 1991, p. 27).

In the process of building knowledge systems, science utilizes a framework of metaphors for talking and thinking. This knowledge-building process simplifies interactions, events and objects, and establishes boundaries which make it difficult for individuals who have been enculturated into that particular knowledge-building system to think and talk outside of the established boundaries. Christie (1991) has argued that using metaphors in the knowledge-building process immediately acts as a kind of censorship. That is, some things are revealed or highlighted in the process, e.g., interconnectedness, whilst others are obscured. For example, 'The Aboriginal knowledge makers discount quantification as unproductive because it necessitates examining things out of context' (Christie, 1991, p. 27).

Harris (1990, p. 44) contends that the fundamental difference between an Aboriginal world view and a Western world view is 'that Aboriginal world views stem from spiritual and religious beliefs while Westernised cultures have their root in science' (Harris, 1990, cited in Jones et al., 1995).

The world views established in different cultures have added richness to our knowledge web of humanity and scientific and technological enquiry. In postmodernist terms, the differing world views provide for a range of interpretations and ways of coming to know. Yet, Western scientific thinking has generally rejected this post-modernist stance and claims superiority of knowledge and process (scientific enquiry).

Acknowledgement of the two world views has also been detailed by Watson and Chambers (1989). They have shown through *Ganma*, how an Aboriginal Yolngu world view and a Western world view can be brought together. Ganma is a metaphor which illustrates 'the meeting and mixing of two streams which flow – one from the land, the other from the sea – into a mangrove lagoon ... the forces of the stream combine and lead to deeper understanding and truth' (Watson & Chambers, 1989, p. 5).

It is argued by Watson and Chambers (1989, p. 5) that this ancient Yolngu metaphor or ganma theory 'can be applied to the meeting of two cultures – Aboriginal and Western'. The waters of the sea and the waters of the land come together, combining in the lagoon. This is a powerful metaphor for two-way learning:

> The English word 'metaphor' is derived from ancient roots: *meta* meaning change or transformation; *phor* meaning to carry. By carrying meaning into a changed context, we may construct new knowledge, think new thought. (Watson & Chambers, 1989, p. 7)

In order for individuals to begin to appreciate meaning systems and the processes of knowledge construction in another culture, the two cultures must come together and exchange world views. Ganma is a powerful metaphor for realizing this. Science curriculum development in Australia has the potential to provide an avenue for bringing together differing world views in science. However, to what extent are school children exposed to different knowledge systems, particularly in science? What world views do they experience? How differently would science curriculum look if it took into account the differing world views found in multicultural Australia? Is indigenous knowledge in science considered? These are questions researchers, teachers and curriculum developers need to ask themselves and their colleagues.

Little is known about Aboriginal children's thinking in science. Empirical research into Australian Aboriginal children's understandings in science could not be found by searching either IAC for 1980–1995 or ERIC 1985–1995, and hence a fuller discussion is not possible. However, when the literature on an Aboriginal world view is considered, it does tend to suggest that Aboriginal science in traditional communities may include the elements described in Table 1.

Research and Curriculum Development in Science Education: One World View or Many?

Science educators in Australia, New Zealand and to some degree the USA have over the last two decades utilized research which has increasingly been framed from within the tradition of constructivism. This literature has been utilized by practitioners and curricula developers alike, and therefore is strongly influential in shaping children's world view of science whilst at school. As a result, this section will examine the epistemology of constructivism, review studies relating to children's knowledge construction, as are relevant to this paper, and examine the methodological implications. This section seeks to examine how science is being presented to children in schools – how is it being constructed for them? Are there a range of world views acknowledged, valued and considered by teachers?

Constructivism
Central to research activity in science education in Australia is constructivism. This term is defined as the social construction of meaning for the individual. It is based upon two basic principles. First, that knowledge is not passively received. The learners must build or construct knowledge for themselves. Second, learners do not discover truth but rather 'construct viable explanations of ... experiences' (Wheatley, 1991, p. 10).

According to Matthews (1994), constructivism in science education has emerged as two distinct traditions: sociological constructivism and psychological

TABLE 1   Aboriginal science

Holistic versus a reductionist approach	Aboriginal people examine elements of their surroundings in terms of how they relate to each other.	For example, the notion of the seasons (discussed later) only makes sense when considered with the movement of the animals, growth of plants, movement of the water. There is a relationship between each element. An Aboriginal view moves beyond simply examining the wind, clouds and temperature.
Ecologically based approach	People are a part of the environment. Their actions directly impact upon the flora and fauna. People are in and not external to their environment. There is a connectedness with nature and each other rather than the view that nature can be controlled.	The gathering of food or hunting of animals is based on present needs of its people, within the context of ensuring scarce resources will be available in the future. For example, a water hole is important and must be cared for and not depleted.
Inclusive versus the specialization of knowledge	Everyone understands and uses science and technology (but with certain members of the community claiming knowledge of it) as opposed to specialist knowledge held by a limited few.	An understanding of where to find water is knowledge held by all members of traditionally oriented communities. Similarly, the process of hunting for kangaroos (tracking; signing to indicate direction) is known to all, although aspects of this task may be performed by only some.
Knowledge is spiritually framed	Art, dance, music and dreamtime stories link knowledge with the land and its people.	For example, an understanding of day and night may be closely linked with the dreamtime. Stories link people and nature together, and provide a vehicle for passing on cultural knowledge from adults to children.
Contextualized versus decontextualized science	Knowledge is developed and used in context. Scientific enquiry takes place in the everyday situation and not in an environment external to the context in which it will be applied (laboratory).	For example, knowledge of fire lighting is developed as a result of materials available, e.g., rubbing sticks into dried rabbit manure; and using flint stone and gun powder.

constructivism. Sociological constructivism has its roots in the work of Emile Durkheim. This tradition views scientific knowledge as socially constructed and vindicated. It 'ignores individual psychological mechanisms of belief construction' but rather investigates the 'circumstances and dynamics of science's construction' (Matthews, 1994, p. 138). Psychological constructivism (sometimes thought of as personal constructivism) is derived from the work of Jean Piaget. Learning is considered an individual and personal construction as a result of interacting with the physical world.

It is the latter tradition of constructivism which has been so influential in science teaching and learning. This focused attention on children's construction of scientific meaning has led to intense research activity, generating reports, conference papers and articles (e.g., Champagne et al., 1983; White & Tisher 1987; Fensham, 1989), and a number of specialized books in this area (Driver, 1983; Fensham 1988; Osborne & Freyberg, 1985, Pines & West 1985). All major literature reviews and conference programs over the last 10 years have shown the dominance of constructivism (Aikenhead, 1996). For example, Pfundt and Duit (1991), in their review of the literature, have amassed 2500 constructivist-inspired publications since 1980. Matthews (1994, p. 139) has suggested that:

> For many, constructivism has ceased being just a learning theory, or even an educational theory, but rather it constitutes a world view or Weltanschuung ...

Constructivism has become so well accepted in Australia, New Zealand and England, that a critique of this particular world view about science learning is not common. In addition, acceptance of constructivism has meant an unquestioning acceptance of the research that is derived from this paradigm.

Dominant within constructivist-inspired research is the study of children's thinking of scientific phenomena. This literature has identified the range of views held by children about particular scientific concepts and labelled them as misconceptions, alternative frameworks or views, mini-theories, common-sense conceptions, preconceptions and untutored beliefs (Aikenhead, 1996; Driver & Easley, 1978; Driver & Erickson, 1983; Fensham, 1988; Gilbert & Watts, 1983; Gunstone, 1988; Hills, 1989; Pfundt & Duit, 1994). This type of research is so prevalent in the literature it is worthy of note.

Children's Understandings in Science
A meta-analysis of the research literature into children's understandings in science by the Leeds' research team (Leeds, 1992) provides data on the range of views held by children for each of the sciences, as conceptualized within

a Western science framework. The research suggests that children develop understandings about natural phenomena prior to being formally taught science in a school setting. Surveys undertaken in many countries 'have identified common features in children's ideas' (Leeds, 1992, p. 13). An analysis of the research literature also reveals:

> ... that such ideas are to be seen as more than simply pieces of misinformation; children have ways of construing event and phenomena which are coherent and fit with their domains of experiences yet which may differ substantially from the (Western) scientific view. Studies also indicate that these notions may persist into adulthood despite formal teaching. (Leeds, 1992, p. 13)

The research literature falls within a Western science framework, e.g., physics and biology. Specific cultural knowledge and world views were not featured in the studies reviewed. In constructivist-inspired research, Western knowledge construction features. The implication is that differing knowledge constructions in science simply do not exist or are not recognized when expressed. A brief summary of a small portion of the research into one area of children's thinking is discussed below in order to explore these ideas further.

In the area of *Materials*, children think that the term material refers to fabric or building materials, e.g., bricks (Bouma & Brandt, 1990). When materials are cut up, children aged 4–7 years rely upon the perceptual qualities of materials to explain that it is still the same, whilst older children make explicit statements which demonstrate they understand that the material has been affected by cutting (Smith et al., 1984). A mixture of substances causes confusion for children. Mixtures, e.g., air, water, honey or yoghurt are labelled as 'pure' (Bouma & Brandt, 1990; Cosgrove, 1983; Meheut et al., 1985). Similarly, with the change of state of matter, many children think that because powders pour they are not a solid (Jones & Lynch, 1989). Children also believe that liquids (many types) contain water (Leeds, 1992), that air is not a material (Séré, 1985), and confuse concepts e.g., freezing, evaporation and condensing (Leeds, 1992). For example, a four-year-old child stated categorically that you must put chocolate into a fridge to make it melt (Fleer et al., 1995). There is further research into children's understandings of water, rocks, particles and air. Similarly, research has also been conducted into children's understandings of light, electricity, magnetism, sound, heat, energy, forces, gravity and the earth in space. Further, research has also focused on life and living processes (nutrition, growth, microbes, the human body and ecosystems) (Carey, 1985). These studies do not discuss other world views or cultural knowledge construction in science.

Western science is assumed as the norm. Western science is used to position other understandings as alternative. Descriptions of cultural practices provide a way of building a contextual base from which to interpret responses. However, rarely did cultural descriptions feature in the studies reviewed.

Research into children's understandings of the classification of their world provides a useful example of the methodology and research design commonly utilized. It is an area worthy of expansion, since an Aboriginal perspective has been detailed in the literature.

The Organization and Classification of Our World

There is a significant amount of research which has been conducted into children's understandings of living and non-living (Angus, 1981) and plants and animals (Bell, 1981; Bell & Barker, 1982). This research predominantly utilized a technique known as 'interview-about-instance' for the collection of data on children's thinking. Children were asked to classify cards into predetermined categories, e.g., living and non-living, or plant and animal. Children were asked to explain their criterion for classification as each card was organized or as each picture was labelled. Data were then analysed in relation to the Western scientific classification system of the Animal and Plant kingdom. For example, Angus (1981) investigated 6–8-year-old children's conceptions of the living world through showing them cards and asking them to initially identify the picture, then classify them into living or non-living. This was followed by further classification into plant or animal; vertebrates and invertebrates; birds, mammals or other; and finally the bird category was further sorted into those that swim and those that did not. The findings of this study show that children hold alternative views to that of Western science in the classification of animal and plant kingdoms. Bell and Freyberg (1985) found in their study of children's understandings of animals using a similar methodology to Angus (1981) but for children between 5 and 16 years, that the young children were able to classify plants and animals more accurately in terms of Western classification systems than older children. A summary of their findings is shown below in Figure 1.

Meaning Making within a Western Framework

What is interesting to note is that the research into children's understandings of scientific phenomena has been framed from within a Western science perspective. The conceptions being sought are those that relate to Western science. The research identifies children's thinking about Western science only. Those views which do not fit within a Western framework are labelled as alternative. Implicit within this particular term is alternative to Western science. This encapsulates the rather narrow approach taken in the wealth of research conducted. It also

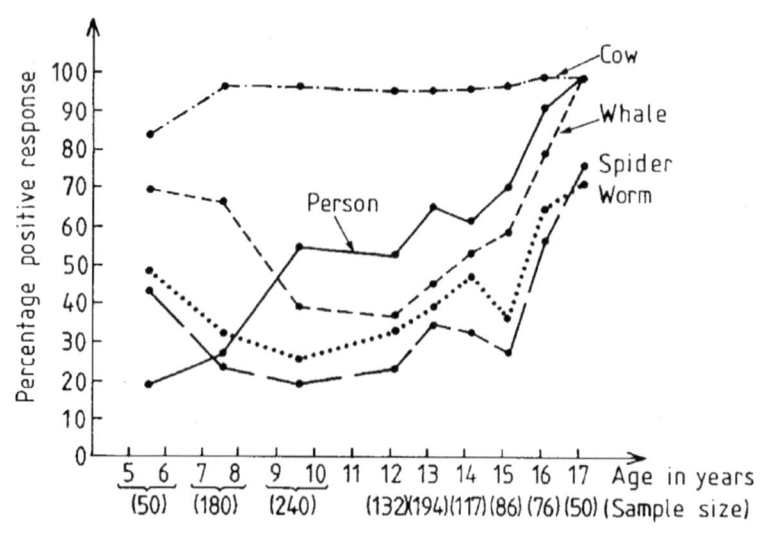

FIGURE 1   Representative sample response to 'is it an animal' (Bell & Freyberg, 1985, p. 31)

highlights an exclusive approach, i.e., it excludes other world views from being considered and positioned in ways which demonstrate that they are equally valued. In each case, the benchmark for analysis of data is how the views being expressed by the children or adults relate to Western science. Similarly, the way the research is framed determines how children will respond. The construction of the 'interview about-instance' research for determining children's understandings of how their world is classified was framed within a Western classification system. The framework used to determine children's classification systems would not easily allow children who have been enculturated into another classification system of their environment, e.g., traditionally oriented Australian Aboriginal children, to express their understandings. The data elicited from such children when interpreted within a Western meaning framework may never reveal knowledge of the classification system or a representation of interrelated features of Aboriginal life and belief, as shown in Figure 2.

The disparity can also be shown in the classification system adopted by Groote Eylandt people. Within a Western framework, it could also be difficult for researchers and teachers to recognize Aboriginal knowledge construction if it were expressed. Harris (1980) provides an example of a Western teacher teaching a science unit on living things:

> She wrote the heading 'birds' on the blackboard and then tried to get the pupils to provide information about birds in general which she recorded on the board with the intention of using the information as the basis of

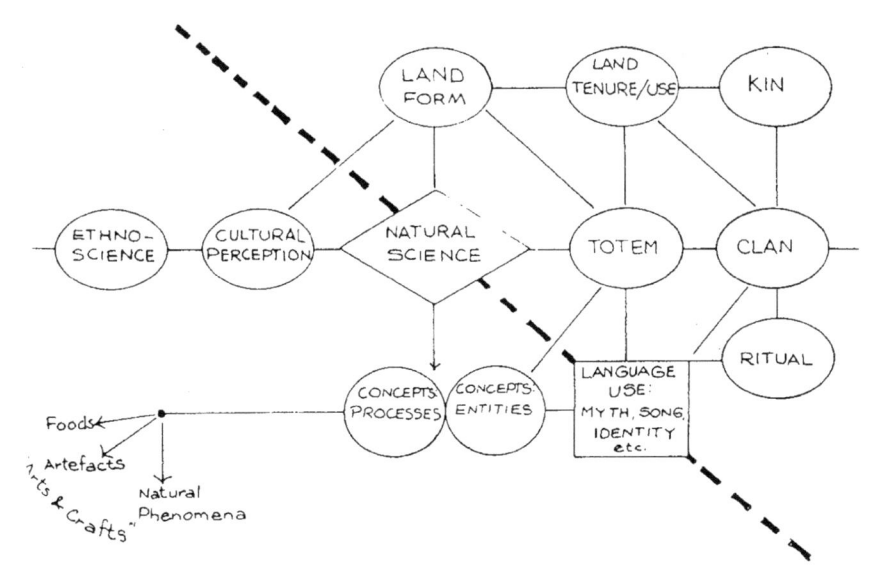

FIGURE 2   Diagrammatic representation of some inter-related features of Aboriginal life and belief (Davis & Morris, 1979, p. 21)

later lessons. She expected – and received – suggestions such as 'flying', 'feathers', 'eggs in nest' etc. However, she was also given suggestions such as 'stings', 'eggs on leaf' and 'buzzing'. The teacher was mystified .... (Harris, 1980, p. 63)

According to Harris (1980), the term 'wurrajija' is often loosely translated into English as 'bird'. However, he suggests that it actually refers to any kind of flying animal. Hence, bat, insect and bird would all be acceptable responses in an Aboriginal context.

These examples from an Australian Aboriginal culture would tend to suggest that the extensive literature on children's understandings in science has been framed from within a Western science perspective, and that we know very little about the meaning systems of non-Western children in science. For example, Loo (1996) has detailed four different Islamic world views in relation to science. Further, Cobert (1996, p. 306) has suggested that research 'must illuminate what it means to understand science from different cultural perspectives', rather than focus on what children know in relation to Western science. These examples highlight the methodological challenges facing researchers. The appropriateness of utilizing measures validated in one culture in research carried out with members of another culture has been the subject of much debate (Triandis, 1974).

Appropriate Methodology for Cross-Cultural Research

Thijs and van den Berg's (1994) extensive review of science education studies conducted in The Netherlands, Indonesia and countries in Africa indicate that, firstly, the same methodological procedures were adopted in each country for studies investigating the same scientific concepts. Secondly, the findings were similar in each country. Their thesis, although concentrating on effective methods for remediation of alternative conceptions, does highlight an interesting point, that consideration should be given to the cultural factors inherent in the teaching–learning process. However, their discussion assumed a Western framework in the analysis of the studies reviewed (Western science perspective) and did not question the methodology employed. Cobern (1996, p. 297) has argued in 'cross-cultural research involving western derived developmental theory and its measures of reasoning ability, for a researcher to assume understanding virtually ensures a negative finding'.

In the Australian context, the question and answer technique so prevalent in science education research, particularly the focus on 'how' and 'why' type questions has been argued by Partington and McCudden (1992) to be inappropriate for some Aboriginal groups. Hamilton (1981) found that Anbarra children from the Northern Territory do not have a single term for the word 'why' in their language. Similarly, the terms 'how' and 'when' are infrequently used, but the word 'where' is common. Partington and McCudden (1992) argue that Aboriginal children know a great deal. However, it is difficult to tap into their understandings because of the Western focus on verbal explanation through the use of 'how' and 'why' questions. This is supported by a recent study into rural Aboriginal children's understandings of night and day (Fleer, in press). When children were asked a series of questions about their understandings of night and day, very little indigenous knowledge was evident. The reliance on a question and answer format, even with the introduction of concrete materials, did not provide explanations of individual children's understandings of night and day.

In addition, the common practice of interviewing children on a one-to-one basis has also been shown to yield very little indigenous data. However, when children are interviewed as a group, children's responses are much richer and more readily given.

What is interesting to note in these studies is the disparity between the methodology employed to find out what children think in a range of cultures and the theory which underpins it – constructivism. If constructivism 'emphasises that science is a creative human endeavour which is historically and culturally conditioned and that its knowledge claims are not absolute' (Matthews, 1994, p. 139), then why is only one cultural construction of science knowledge used as the benchmark for the analysis of children's responses?

Many methodological questions have been raised in this section relating to the plethora of existing research into children's conceptions of scientific phenomena, whether in a cross-cultural context or not. This research has provided the basis for the redevelopment of contemporary science curriculum in schools.

Supporting Curriculum Documentation – Multiple or One View of Science?

In 1994, the Curriculum Corporation of Australia formally released the documents: 'A statement on science for Australian schools' and 'Science – a curriculum profile for Australian schools'. These documents have been incorporated (wholly or partially) into all State and Territory curricula development and implementation programs (except Queensland), (Appleton et al., 1995). Consequently, these documents are powerful influences of what science planning and teaching across Australia should look like. As a result, this section will consider these documents in terms of their acceptance or rejection of multiple world views in relation to science.

In these two seminal documents, it is acknowledged that the knowledge construct *science* in Western societies has been influenced by many cultures. For example: 'The nature and practice of science builds on traditions of inquiry found in many cultures in all parts of the world' (Curriculum Corporation, 1994, p. 3). These documents also specify the influence of Western practices and beliefs on the formation of science: 'Western science has particularly strong links with Greek, Chinese and Arabic cultures' (Curriculum Corporation, 1994, p. 3). Similarly, acknowledgement of views other than Western science are presented:

> Scientific knowledge has been expanded by the cumulative efforts of generations of scientists from all over the world. It has been enriched by the pooling of understanding from different cultures – western, eastern and indigenous cultures including those of Aboriginal peoples and Torres Strait Islanders – and has become a truly international activity. The contributions of women to Australian science are now also being recognised. (Curriculum Corporation, 1994, p. 3)

Although acknowledgement is given to a range of views, there is the implicit assumption that they have come together to support one view, i.e., Western science. In addition, there is no discussion of the imbalance in power between world views, particularly when the valuing of certain ways of thinking and acting scientifically above other practices occurs.

Although the documents were developed by the Curriculum Corporation, they represent the views of the teaching community, parents and the scientific community, and as a result are a collection of compromises (Malcolm, 1993).

The structure of the documents is less like the traditional specializations of biology, chemistry and physics. For example, knowledge is compartmentalized under the strands: Earth and beyond; Energy and change; Life and Living; Natural and processed materials; and Working scientifically. According to Malcolm (1993) this shift away from traditional science knowledge compartmentalization has been met with severe criticism from many within the scientific community.

Within the formation of a collective vision for science education, is clearly the assumption that there is one world view. It can be asked to what degree would groups, e.g., the Aboriginal and Torres Strait Islander people, have been granted the option to develop a document which compartmentalized knowledge from a more holistic Aboriginal perspective? The imbalance of power within the Australian community and within the sciences would certainly have precluded this from occurring. A document which presents science as a knowledge construct which can be re-created in schools from multiple perspectives would be very different to the Science Curriculum Statement and Profile. For example, the model shown in Figure 3 by Davis et al. (1980) demonstrates a very different compartmentalization of scientific knowledge to that of the Curriculum Corporation.

In Figure 3, the months of the year are shown as a comparison (Davis et al., 1980, p. 3). A traditional orientation to knowledge construction in Aboriginal communities is significantly different to the organization of Western science. Davis et al. (1980, p. 2) have argued that:

> ... traditional Aboriginal knowledge of the environment should form the content from which is developed learning skills, scientific process skills, and those appropriate European concepts deemed essential for life in a wider community.

Davis et al. (1980, p. 4) have shown in figure 4 how traditional Aboriginal knowledge and an Aboriginal conceptual and organizational framework can be used in ways which build on Aboriginal thinking and which reflect Western knowledge constructs.

In Figure 4, the key community events and activities are shown as the central framework and 'starting points for leading to development of progressively more complex scientific concepts' (Davis et al., 1980, p. 4). This example illustrates one way of bringing together Western and traditional Aboriginal knowledge. It also serves to demonstrate that both systems of knowledge construction are valid and to be respected. Clearly, two world views become accessible to both Aboriginal children and non-Aboriginal teachers. However, this

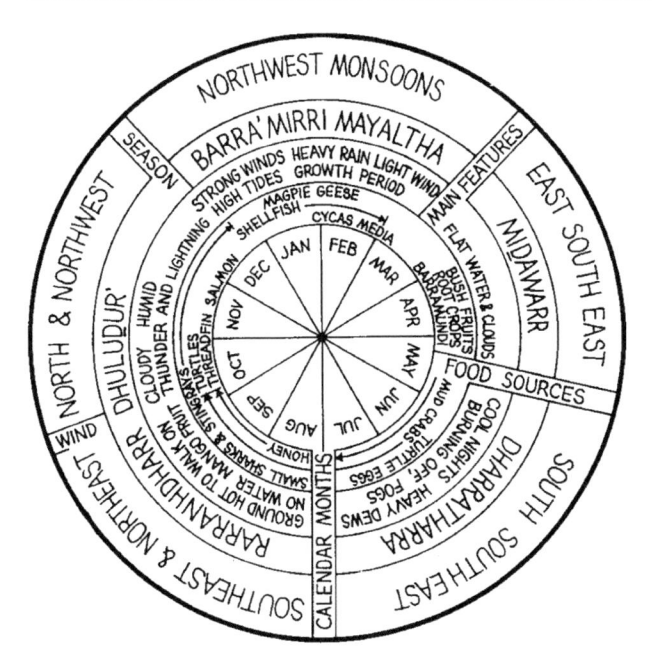

FIGURE 3   Simplified calendar based on Milingimbi data (Davis et al., 1980, p. 3)

example of the development of a shared perspective is atypical. It has not been used by central systems – State and Territory or the National Curriculum Corporation of Australia (although anecdotal evidence suggests that curriculum development in the Northern Territory is working towards two-way learning in science).

Concern for the appropriateness of Western science for indigenous groups and the need to incorporate indigenous science has also been raised elsewhere. For example, in Cobern's (1996) critique of the literature, it is evident that many science programs in Africa only superficially take into account indigenous world views. This is evident in research conducted by Lubben et al. (1996). They have argued that when Western science is contextualized within indigenous cultural practices in Africa (rather than a complete Western framework for learning), learning outcomes were greatly improved. In addition, Africans have seen the establishment of Curriculum Development Centres which have become fully or partially indigenized, so that curriculum materials can be developed appropriately (Ogunniyi, 1996). In New Zealand, curriculum development has also found the task of bringing together different world views as challenging.

In New Zealand, the Maori people were given the opportunity to translate the National Science curriculum into the Maori language. By the very nature of their brief, they were expected to accept one world view of science, i.e., Western science. McKinley and Waiti (1995) write about this experience in terms of

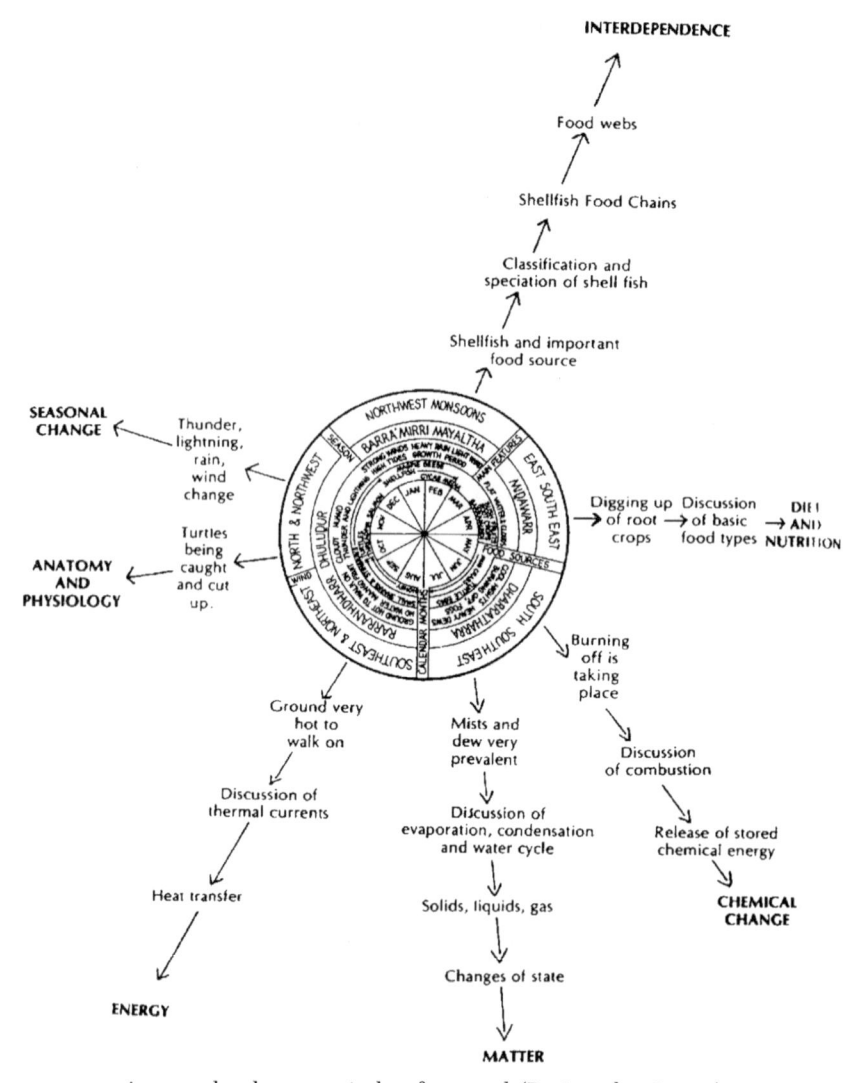

FIGURE 4   A seasonal cycle as a curriculum framework (Davis et al., 1980, p. 4)

how the compartmentalization of scientific knowledge given to them was at odds with Maori beliefs.

Their debates centred on how Maori science may differ from Western science and what that would mean for the development of a national curriculum in science:

> World views and relationships and responsibilities between 'he tangata' and 'te taiao' formed the basis of the initial discussions. (McKinley & Waiti, 1995, p. 85)

McKinley and Waiti (1995) demonstrate explicitly how one world view was assumed in the document through an example of the strand Planet Earth and Beyond:

> What did eventuate was the taking of 'Planet Earth and Beyond' and spreading it across the other three strands of the document. Some people reading this article may see this as a retrograde step as the English versions of the document could be said to represent a breakthrough for Earth Science in that it becomes as important (in terms of the time spent on it) as the more 'traditional' view of science being biology, chemistry and physics. Much of the Planet Earth and Beyond strand, in the Maori versions, has gone into the biological world strand and has been renamed O Mataora. What is important for Maori is that this represents for Maori the joining of Papatuanuk (earth) with the rest of 'living things'. Other than this change, much of the strands are the same. The astronomy objective from Planet Earth and Beyond strand has gone into the Physical World (Ahupungao) strand. (McKinley & Waiiti, 1995, pp. 85–86)

McKinley and Waiti question not only the assumption that Western knowledge should be more highly valued than Maori science knowledge, but ask:

> ... why did Maori have such a low input at the level of the 'content' of the document?' And what stopped the Ministry from doing these documents side by side – to get the groups to *negotiate the criteria for knowledge selection.* (McKinley & Waiti, 1995, p. 92; emphasis added)

At a national level in Australia, these questions not only remain unanswered, but not heard. As in New Zealand, acknowledgement is given to the importance of these groups, or world views (as cited above), but this rhetoric does not translate to the selection of knowledge and knowledge structure found within the Australian curriculum documents. Similarly, supporting documentation for teachers to assist them with the implementation of the science curriculum is overwhelmingly focused on Western science. Some publications do include units on Aboriginal Science (Malcolm, 1995), but significantly more is needed if teachers are to cross over the enculturation boundary. Teachers need to know more about other world views than the one they have been enculturated into, if they are to portray a view that science is socially constructed, and if they are to make sense of the range of children's scientific thinking and ideas that they bring to science lessons. If teachers only have one world view, they will consider the views of children from different cultural groups with different world views as alternative. It has been shown that this is indeed the term given in the science education literature to those views that are not considered by the scientific community (obviously Western) as right. Cobern (1996) contends:

> it is important for science educators to understand the fundamental, culturally based beliefs about the world that students bring to class, and how these beliefs are supported by students' cultures, because science education is successful only to the extent that science can find a niche in the cognitive and socio-cultural milieu of students. (Cobern, 1996, p. 305; original emphasis)

Conclusion

In this paper, the notion of science education as conceptualized in the research literature and within curricula development was explored. It was found that most research was conceptualized within constructivist principles. However, it was also noted that within this view of science and science education, was implicit the assumption of alternative views to Western science. Hence, the focus and attention was directed towards the paradigm and found to be not inclusive of an Australian Aboriginal world view in science.

Curriculum development in Australia, although mindful of Aboriginal science, has been constructed within a Western science framework. In order to facilitate the development of appropriate and more broadly conceived science curricula, more needs to be understood about Aboriginal science. Western science needs to be thought of as one world view among many, and not the main paradigm with Aboriginal science seen as the other. There is an urgent need for more research to occur into Aboriginal science so that curricula development can become the meeting place of differing world views (or the waters), as in ganma theory. In this way, future generations of children, who will be the recipients of this new curricula, will have a broader and more encompassing understanding and knowledge of science.

References

Aikenhead, G. (1996). Cultural assimilation in science classroom: Border crossings and other solutions. *Studies in Science Education, 7*, 1–52.
Angus, J. (1981). Children's conceptions of the living world. *The Australian Science Teachers Journal, 27*, 65–68.

Appleton, K., Crawford, G., Cousins, J., Fleer, M., Jones, B., Kirkwood, V., Palmer, B., Skamp, K., & Tytler, R. (1995). *An Australian curriculum in science? Responses by the states to the statement and profile.* Presented at the Conference for the Australasian Science Education Association, Bendigo, Victoria.

Barnes, B. (1985) *About science.* Basil Blackwell.

Bateson, G. (1979). *Mind and nature: A necessary unity.* E.P. Dutton.

Bell, B. F. (1981). When an animal is not an animal? *Journal of Biological Education, 15,* 213–218.

Bell, B., & Barker, M. (1982). Toward a scientific concept of animal. *Journal of Biological Education, 16,* 197–200.

Bell, B., & Freyberg, P. F. (1985). Language in the science classroom. In R. J. Osborne & P. Freyberg (Eds.), *Learning in science: The implications of children's science.* Heinemann.

Bleier, R. (Ed.). (1986). *Feminist approaches to science.* Pergamon Press.

Bouma, J., & Brandt, L. (1990). A simple method for the teacher to obtain information on pupils preconceptions. *Journal of Chemical Education, 67,* 24–25.

Carey, S. (1985). *Conceptual change in childhood.* MIT Press.

Chalmers, A. F. (1988). *What is this thing called science?* The University of Queensland Press.

Champagne, A. B., Gunstone, R. F., & Klopfer, L. E. (1983). Naive knowledge and science learning. *Research in Science and Technology Education, 1,* 173–183.

Christie, M. J. (1991). Aboriginal science for the ecologically sustainable future. *Australian Science Teachers Journal, 37,* 26–31.

Cobern, W. W. (1996). Constructivism and non-western science education research. *International Journal of Science Education, 19,* 295–310.

Cosgrove, M. (1983). *Mixtures, an introduction to chemistry.* Hamilton Teachers' College.

Curriculum Corporation. (1994). *Technology – A curriculum Profile for Australian schools.* AGPS.

Davis, S., Harris, J., & Traynor, S. (1980). Community based programs for Aboriginal schools. *The Australian Science Teachers' Journal, 7,* 2–10.

Davis, S., & Morris, I. (1979). Natural science: Natural approach and indigenous content in Aboriginal schools. *Developing Education, 7,* 20–24.

Department of Employment, Education and Training. (1991). *Aboriginal student support and parent awareness program. Guidelines.* Australian Government Publishing Service.

Driver, R. (1983) *The pupil as a scientist?* Open University Press.

Driver, R., & Easley, J. (1978). Pupils and paradigms: A review of literature related to concept development in adolescent science students. *Studies in Science Education, 5,* 61–84.

Driver, R., & Erickson, G. (1983). Theories in action: Some theoretical and empirical issues in the study of students' conceptual frameworks in science. *Studies in Science Education, 10*, 37–60.

Eisler, R. (1988). *The Chalice and the Blade*. Harper and Row.

Fensham, P. J. (1988). Familiar but different: Some dilemmas and new directions in science education. In P. Fensham (Ed.), *Development and dilemmas in science education*. The Falmer Press.

Fensham, P. J. (1989). *The place of technology in science education* [Conference session]. Key note address at the CONASTA Conference, Monash University, Melbourne.

Fleer, M. (in press). A cross-cultural study of rural Australian aboriginal children's understandings of night and day. *Research in Science Education*.

Fleer, M., Hardy, T., Baron, K., & Malcolm, C. (1995). *They don't tell the truth about the wind*. Curriculum Corporation.

Gilbert, J. K., & Watts, D. M. (1983). Concepts, misconceptions and alternative conceptions: Changing perspectives in science education. *Studies in Science Education, 10*, 61–98.

Gunstone, R. F. (1988). Learners in science education. In P. Fensham (Ed.), *Development and dilemmas in science education*. The Falmer Press.

Hamilton, A. (1981). *Nature and nurture: Aboriginal child rearing in North-Central Arhhem Land*. Institute of Aboriginal Studies.

Harris, S. (1980). *Culture and learning: Tradition and education in North-East Arnhem Land*. Northern Territory Department of Education.

Harris, S. (1990). *Two way aboriginal schooling*. Aboriginal Studies Press.

Hills, G. (1989). Students 'untutored' beliefs about natural phenomena: Primitive science or commonsense? *Science Education, 73*, 155–186.

Jones, B. L., & Lynch, P. P. (1989). Children's understanding of the notion of solid and liquid in relation to some common substances. *International Journal of Science Education, 11*, 417–427.

Jones, K., Kershaw, L., & Sparrow, L. (1995). *Aboriginal children learning mathematics* Edith Cowan University, Mathematics, Science and Technology Education Centre.

Kuhn, T. (1970). *The structure of scientific revolutions* (2nd ed.). University of Chicago Press.

Leeds. (1992). *Leeds national curriculum science support project: Resources for supporting pupils' learning at Key Stage 3*. Leeds City Council, Department of Education, and the Children's Learning in Science Research Group at the University of Leeds.

Loo, S. P. (1996). The four horsemen of Islamic science: A critical analysis. *International Journal of Science Education, 19*, 285–294.

Lubben, F., Campbell, B., & Dlamini, B. (1996). Contextualizing science teaching in Swaziland: Some student reactions. *International Journal of Science Education, 19*, 311–320.

Malcolm, C. (1993). *Personal communications*. Curriculum Corporation of Australia.

Malcolm, C. (Ed.). (1995). *There's an Emu in the sky*. Curriculum Corporation.

Matthews, M. R. (1994). *Science teaching: The role of history and philosophy of science*. Routledge.

McCarl Nielsen, J. (Ed.). (1989). *Feminist research methods*. Oxford University Press.

McKinley, E., & Waiti, P. (1995). Te Tauaki Marautanga Putaiao: He tauira – the writing of a national science curriculum in Maori. In A. Jones, A. Begg, B. Bell, F. Biddulph, M. Carr, M. Carr, J. McChesney, E. McKineley, & J. Young Loveridge (Eds.), *SAMEpapers 1995* (pp. 75–94). Centre for Science, Mathematics and Technology Education Research.

Meheut, M., Saltiel, E., & Tiberghien, A. (1985). Pupils' (11–12 years old) conceptions of combustion. *European Journal of Science Education, 7*, 83–93.

Ogunniyi, M. B. (1996). Science, technology and mathematics: The problem of developing critical human capital in Africa. *International Journal of Science Education, 19*, 267–284.

Osborne, R., & Freyberg, P. (1985). *Learning in science. The implications of children's science*. Heinemann.

Partinton, G., & McCudden, V. (1992). *Ethnicity and education*. Social Science Press.

Pfundt, H., & Duit, R. (1991). *Bibliography of students' alternative frameworks and science education* (3rd ed.). Institute of Science Education.

Pfundt, H., & Duit, R. (1994). *Students' alternative frameworks and science education* (4th ed.). Institute of Science Education.

Pines, A. L., & West, L. H. T. (Eds.). (1985). *Cognitive structure and conceptual change*. Academic Press.

Séré, M. G. (1985). The gaseous state. In R. Driver, E. Guesne, & A. Tiberghiene (Eds.), *Children's ideas in science* (pp. 105–123). Open University Press.

Smith, C., Carey, S., & Wiser, L. (1984). A case study of the development of size, weight, and density. *Cognition, 21*, 177–237.

Thijs, G., & Van Den Berg, E. (1994). Cultural factors in the origin and remediation of alternative conceptions in physics. *Science and Education, 4*, 1–32.

Triandis, H. C. (1974). Major issues in cross-cultural research. In J. L. M. Dawson & W. J. Lonner (Eds.), *Readings in cross-cultural psychology* (pp. 26–28). University Press.

Wajcman, J. (1991). *Feminism confronts technology*. Alan and Unwin.

Watson, H., & Chambers, D. W. (1989). *Singing the land, signing the land*. Deakin University Press.

Wheatley, G. H. (1991). Constructivist perspectives on science and mathematics learning. *Science Education, 75*, 9–22.

White, R. T., & Tisher, R. P. (1987). *Natural sciences*. Monash University. (Unpublished paper).

Woolgar, S. (1988). *Science the very idea*. Ellis Horwood.

Conceptual Play

New Research Agendas Driven by Policy Changes for Play-Based Settings

Abstract

As with Chapter 1, this second chapter examines the historical context in which early childhood science education was developing. But different to the first chapter, the perspective is on researchers in early childhood education. With the spotlight on how economies can prosper when early childhood education is appropriately resourced, greater societal demands for increasing the cognitive load of children emerged. Known as the academisation of early childhood, new policies changed the research agenda and brought forward a renewed emphasis on researching play, but with a twist. With the introduction of new curricula in many countries, the intentional teaching of concepts emerged in practice. Yet the profession was still within the shadow of Piaget's theory of development where conceptual learning was viewed as coming at a much later stage in the period of a child's educational life. With this dual orientation to play and concept formation, new theoretical tools and different kinds of research were needed. In this chapter this problem is taken up through drawing on cultural-historical theory. Conceptual Play as a construct for naming the play and conceptual learning need, laid an important foundation for the future research of early childhood science education that is showcased in this volume.

Keywords

imagination – theoretical thinking – concepts – conceptual play – cultural-historical – academisation – modelling – rising to the concrete

1   Introduction

Sitting alone in a conference room ready to share my science education research paper was beginning to be the norm. Each year I presented my research at the Australian Research in Early Childhood Education (ARECE) conference to a room filled mostly with air. If I was lucky, a few delegates and some of my undergraduate students would join me. I had thought a paper on "An investigation into children's understandings of their internal body" in 1994 would be of interest. But I soon learned that few were doing or interested in early childhood science education research.

2   National Reviews and Imperatives for Early Childhood Science Education

Why was there so little interest? *A Discipline Review of Teacher Education in Mathematics and Science* (Volumes 1–3; Department of Employment Education and Training, 1989) was undertaken across Australia in 1989 which included early childhood education. The report argued that, "The underrepresentation of early childhood children as subjects of research in mathematics and science education is probably partly due to the low priority hitherto given to both mathematics and science education in early childhood education, and the location of most early childhood programs in institutions where there have not been a strong research emphasis" (pp. 189–190). Were we to blame? Was the academy the problem? Or was this yet again an historical example of a societal undervaluing of early childhood education? The review panel found:

> All of programs acknowledge a presence for mathematics and science and the recent amalgamations have brought early childhood education into the overall field of interest of some universities with the strongest research activity. The Panel believes that the deans of education in these institutions should promote the importance of this field for research in the intra-faculty and inter-faculty debates on research priorities. The young scholars that the Panel found teaching in early childhood programs will need the cooperation and support of more experienced researchers among their new colleagues but the rewards for both will be substantial. (p. 190)

Research in early childhood science education research was in its infancy in Australia. This gave some explanation for the lack of interest in early childhood science education research at ARECE conference. There simply had been no tradition for researching young children's thinking in science within the early childhood education academy. But as was presented in Chapter 1, there was no history of it in the Australian science education community either.

I was sitting in the science lab surrounded by the *Discipline Review* Panel who had come to my university. My workplace had just been re-named. It was no long a College of Advanced Education (CAE) but a university – just as was reported by the Panel in their findings. But unlike the expectation of the panel for fledgling researchers from within early childhood education to be supported by experienced researchers, we did not amalgamate with a university filled with experienced researchers. But I did work with passionate trail blazers in science education. More will be said about this in Chapter 6.

I had just started reading the literature discussed in Chapter 1 and my head was filled with the buzz words of, alternative views, misconceptions ... and of course in responding to questions drew on that body of literature. But I was shocked when the Panel Chair, Peter Fensham questioned these terms. Had I got the literature wrong? Was there disquiet about these terms within the science education research academy? I was unable to reach out to the early childhood education research community for help. All I had experience of was this science education community. But its unofficial leader, Peter Fensham was questioning the status quo that dominated the literature. I later learned that Peter always questioned and always brought forward new ideas – most notably at the conference of the ASERA.

The ASERA conference had no keynote speakers, everyone was equal. The presentations were strictly 20-minutes, followed by 20 minutes of discussion. Often the discussions were better than the papers. This inspired me so much that I initiated the equivalent for researchers in early childhood education. At the time I felt conceptually lonely. I was new to academia and couldn't locate my community of Australian early childhood education researchers – they were spread across disciplines and attending other conferences. I wanted to reach out to them. I wanted to be a part of the early childhood academy and engage with them, learn about what my field was researching, and to contribute to that community. But I could not find them in one place in Australia.

I sent a one-page letter – yes that was how we had to do it then – to every faculty that taught early childhood education degrees in Australia and asked if researchers would come to a conference in Canberra if I hosted it. Putting a perforated line at the end of a single sheet for ease of returning a quick RSVP, I was overwhelmed with positive responses. Closely following ASERA, I called it the *Australian Research in Early Childhood Education* (ARECE) conference. This conference ran successfully for ten years before moving to Monash, where it was eventually internationalised by my colleagues. ARECE became an important space in which experienced and new academics, could test their ideas, network, and mentor/be mentored. But I would have to wait some time before delegates would join my science education presentation and give me feedback.

What were the *big-ticket* items that were consuming the early childhood community? It certainly wasn't children's science, alternative views or misconceptions. Developmentally Appropriate Practice (DAP) was the buzz phrase. DAP was guiding the whole field. It was a form of Piagetian scholarship that had been imported from North America. It was an entrenched theoretical perspective that all new academics were expected to reproduce in their teaching, in their theorising, and ultimately in how they analysed and discussed their research findings. How could there be just one view of children's development, development framed from a particular cultural community, at a particular period in history? Developmental milestones and stages did not speak to the diversity of peoples with different cultural heritages who call Australia their home, especially First Nations peoples.

Early childhood education researchers in Australia at that time had their own wars within the broader academy. As an undervalued profession within the education faculties, courses and research struggled to be resourced. This brought with it an alignment and solidarity around what was unique about young children in the birth to eight period – child development, play, family studies. Core domains of social and emotional development, physical (gross and fine motor) development, language development and cognitive development were the main drivers of curriculum. School discipline subjects like science were usually taught as discovery learning and/or process skills. The courses were staffed by academics from outside of the schools of early childhood education, or were specialist science appointments with either primary or secondary science teaching background. The Discipline Review missed the significance of this context. The report that came from the Discipline Review therefore didn't appear to make a difference. A close study of the content (Fleer, 2001) that was published in the premier journal for early childhood research in Australia confirmed that little research had been done in Australia in early childhood science education to inform these tertiary courses.

– Fleer, M. (2001). Science over 40 years. *Australian Journal of Early Childhood,* 26(1), 39–45. https://doi.org/10.1177/183693910102600108

My theoretical discomfort with the interpretations of Piaget across education (Chapter 1) became an important driver for a step change in my thinking. But it was not easy to go down a different pathway to all of those who were rightly my seniors. The paradigm was set fast in early childhood education. The gate was closed. This was as much about protection of a field constantly under siege, as it was about struggling to engage in a paradigm shift. Years later Professor Bridie Raban from the University of Melbourne, named this condition and struggle as working alongside of "the thought police". Having an entrenched view, such as DAP, meant it was difficult to create a new theoretical path.

Poignantly I recall attending a meeting in Sydney with fellow colleagues in early childhood education, asking if anyone was reading Vygotsky's work. I found someone who was, and this gave me courage to go forward at the next ARECE conference with a one-day symposium to disrupt what I called a DAP-centric view of scholarship in early childhood education (Fleer, 1995b). Evidence centred on cultural diversity and how DAP captured the development of one cultural community and not the diversity of children and families living in Australia. Had we become DAPcentric? Were we not open to other theoretical frames or ways of researching?

My PhD and what I presented prior to 1991 at the ASERA conference and later at the ARECE conference gave me a dual imperative because both fields were still in the shadow of Piaget.

As part of my PhD I took the bold step to jump ship from constructivism and to draw on a different theoretical tradition. A step change in science education research resulted for me when I used cultural-historical theory. I was having my own revolution – just as both Thomas Kuhn (1970) and Lev Vygotsky (1998) theorised.

This is reflected in the naming of my PhD thesis as *scaffolding conceptual change*. This naming is a bit like a culinary fusion where the traditions of cooking and available spices from 2 different cultures create a new dish. That is, *scaffolding* from sociocultural theory, and *conceptual change* from constructivism in the science education research community. But was this early thinking really coherent? Probably not.

The fusion is symbolic of my paradigm shift because it foregrounded the constructivist paradigm of conceptual change theory (Carey, 1985) but did so with new theoretical lenses through introducing the concept of *scaffolding*. Later the tool kit of concepts developed (Chapters 3 and 4) and conceptual change took on a whole new meaning in early childhood science education research for me.

Scaffolding as a term brings forward where Australia was heading in the 1990s. Wood, Bruner, and Ross' (1976) most influential paper set the scene for moving beyond knowing what children think to studying how to change their thinking. We began to see this in the detailed study of Edwards and Mercer (1987) who researched secondary science, where transcripts of teacher and student dialogue were examined. They introduced the concept of common knowledge and this gave a whole new way of thinking about the social construction of knowledge between people. It seemed that even secondary students can change their mind in one lesson (see Chapter 1) when you bring into the data set more than an interview about an incident or a selection of options from a multiple-choice survey.

It was a revolution because unlike many who were trying to marry Piaget with Vygotsky by naming their work as social constructivism, I had eventually come to the conclusion that their works were so conceptually different that they could not even be compared and certainly not joined. This meant treading the theoretical pathway in science education on my own for a while.

Some of the publications that follow are indicative of that fuzzy pre-paradigm period where I brought into my work concepts such as, scaffolding (Fleer, 1990), looked closely at interactions (Fleer, 1995a) and different contexts (Fleer, 1996). These were foundational for my new theoretical thinking in science education research.

– Fleer, M. (1990). Scaffolding conceptual change in early childhood. *Research in Science Education,* 20(1), 114–123. https://doi.org/10.1007/BF02620486
– Fleer, M. (1995a). The importance of conceptually focused teacher – Child interaction in early childhood science learning. *International Journal of Science Education,* 17(3), 325–342. https://doi.org/10.1080/0950069950170305
– Fleer, M. (1996). Fusing the boundaries between home and child care to support children's scientific learning. *Research in Science Education,* 26(2), 143–154. https://doi.org/10.1007/BF02356428

At the time it was not possible in Australia to access the collected works of LS. Vygotsky. The first volume was published in 1987. But knowing about this volume and accessing it was challenging when the internet had not yet been invented. I was an academic in a context where the legacy of a university lecturer having a 'wife at home to look after children' was the norm. A corresponding sabbatical policy stated you had to be out of the country for a full month – who can leave a baby for that long and who can take the family overseas when you have a mortgage? But international travel was the only way to learn about Vygotskian concepts and how others were taking the theory forward. But the resources were not there. My partner once said, "I am sick of us having to subsidise the university so you can do international work".

Vygotsky and the Social Formation of Mind written by Jim Wertsch published in 1985 was a title I found in the library. I took it home and devoured it just like a fiction book. Once I started reading, I couldn't put it down. Where had these ideas been all my academic life I wondered? The term sociocultural theory framed these new concepts I was reading. I later learned from Seth Chaiklin that many who adopted the concepts from Vygotsky did so through their cultural eyes, such as US scholars like Jim Wertsch. Here the concept of the zone of proximal development had become immortalised, despite not having an explicit chapter or section on this concept in the volumes of the Collected works. It was a concept that could support a generation of new ideas to emerge. It was timely in the US because like Vygotsky, scholars were moving beyond behaviourism. The term scaffolding fitted well with ZPD, but there were many other rich concepts from Vygotsky which did not receive the same scholarly attention. It was not surprising that my PhD and the publications around that time, featured the term scaffolding.

But as the collected works were progressively published (Vygotsky, 1987, 1993, 1997a, 1997b, 1998, 1999), the paradigm shift was incremental. It was theoretically significant to bring new tools, theories and thinking into the study of young children engaged in science. Cultural-historical theory broadened the research lens because it brought in:

– studying the processes of conceptual change rather than studying the end result
– holistic conception of the research – how a child enters into, is shaped by, and shapes the learning context
– a revolutionary rather than an evolutionary view of development means very different ways to study what changes

This gave new ways of writing about early childhood science education (Fleer, 2002, 2005, 2006), as well as new ways of writing about early childhood education generally – as the titles in these examples show:

– Fleer, M. (2002). Embedded and disembedded learning in early childhood science contexts. *Delta, Policy and Practice in Education, 54*(2), 120–132. https://research.monash.edu/en/publications/embedded-and-disembedded-learning-in-early-childhood-science-cont
– Fleer, M. (2005). Developmental fossils – Unearthing the artefacts of early childhood education: The reification of 'Child Development'. *Australasian Journal of Early Childhood, 30*(2), 2–7. https://doi.org/10.1177/183693910503000203
– Fleer, M. (2006). Troubling cultural fault lines: Some indigenous Australian families' perspectives on the landscape of early childhood education. *Mind, Culture, and Activity, 13*(3), 191–204. https://doi.org/10.1207/s15327884mca1303_3

Vygotskian concepts for data analysis gave the possibility to look at conceptual change research in a new way. We will return to this in Chapter 3. It was important to bring back these ideas into the science education community to see if the theory was credible and had traction within science education research – some examples of the titles (Fleer, 2008, 2009a, 2009b, 2009c, 2010) that featured in the science journals give an indication of this:

– Fleer, M. (2008). A cultural-historical reading of "culturally sensitive schooling": Thinking beyond a constructivist view of science learning. *Cultural Studies of Science Education, 3*(3), 781–786. https://doi.org/10.1007/s11422-008-9114-0
– Fleer, M. (2009a). A cultural-historical analysis of the place of early childhood science education within ASERA. *Cultural Studies of Science Education, 4*(2), 283–289. https://link.springer.com/journal/11422/volumes-and-issues/4-2
– Fleer, M. (2009b). Understanding the dialectical relations between everyday concepts and scientific concepts within play-based programs. *Research in Science Education, 39*(2), 281–306. https://doi.org/10.1007/s11165-008-9085-x
– Fleer, M. (2009c). Supporting scientific conceptual consciousness or learning in 'a roundabout way' in play-based contexts. *International Journal of Science Education, 31*(8), 1069–1089. https://doi.org/10.1080/09500690801953161
– Fleer, M. (2009d). The re-theorisation of collective pedagogy and emergent curriculum. *Cultural Studies of Science Education, 5*(3), 563–576. https://doi.org/10.1007/s11422-009-9245-y

Incrementally more papers drew upon cultural-historical theory, and exciting new conceptual developments in science education emerged (see Hadzigeorgiou, 2016; Roth, Goulart, & Plakitsi, 2013). These publications laid the foundations for a completely new way of thinking about the problem of early childhood science education research (Fleer & Pramling, 2015).

3 International Imperatives Shaping Early Childhood Education

While the report that resulted from the discipline review of teacher education in mathematics and science did not appear to have traction in the general early childhood education research community, the OECD report on early childhood education and development did.

The OECD (2001) undertook a policy review of early childhood education and development, primarily in European countries. But for some reason, the Australian and New Zealand countries were included. The OECD is the French acronym for The Organisation for Economic Co-operation and Development, and this organisation is highly regarded and recognised by the early childhood community for undertaking robust and significant reviews (OECD, 2001, 2006, 2012, 2017). The accumulated evidence from longitudinal research had put a spotlight on the importance of early childhood education. In what was an international first, policy makers had discovered that a quality early childhood education could transform a generation of children and could make a significant contribution to the economy of a nation.

Policy makers began to invest in early childhood education practice and many organisations espoused the importance of investing early – citing the same research as the OECD. The response from treasury in many different countries was positive. The evidence of investing in early childhood also got the attention of economists. Most notably James Heckman, who was awarded the Nobel prize in economics for the impact of social programs and the methodologies used to measure their effects. The economic modelling of early childhood education and development has had a profound impact on OECD policy development. No equivalent award exists for early childhood education researchers in Australia. Closest is the ARC Laurate Fellowship Scheme. Heckman's papers (Heckman and Masterov, 2007) drew completely on the research of others who showed early on that spending US$1 would yield taxpayer savings of US$7 for interventions over the life course of a child. Similar figures were put forward in Canada. But it was James Heckman who made the strongest economic argument.

Would this policy interest with the accompanying dollars mean that Governments would demand more from the early childhood profession? Yes. Governments began demanding greater cognitive outcomes with country specific evidence of the impact of their investments. The tide had turned, and there was no way to go back, even if we wanted to.

The outcomes of the OECD brought forward not only more policy attention on early childhood education, but generated the need for a national curriculum in Australia. In 2009 the Early Years Learning Framework was released (Australian Government, Department of Education, Employment and Workplace Relations, Commonwealth of Australia, 2009). This was Australia's first national curriculum for the birth to five sector. There was debate surrounding limiting the curriculum content up to five years, and not taking up the international definition of early childhood being from birth to eight years. A federated country like Australia, brought complexity and political wars between states. Early childhood sat across two Australian Commonwealth Government portfolios of education and health. In the end, it was easier to go forward by limiting the reach of the curriculum to five years of age. This meant that the institutional context for the delivery of the Australian curriculum framework for early childhood education in Australia was for play-based settings only.

The curriculum framework introduced into the field of early childhood education the term 'intentional teaching'. Similar concepts appeared elsewhere, such as in the UK with intentionality in play, and in Singapore with purposeful play. In the context of policy demands for greater cognitive outcomes, this new term facilitated a new era of research in Australia, but also internationally.

The curriculum and the new concept of intentional teaching marked a turning point in Australia because it brought with it a new imperative in building research evidence to support early childhood education nationally, and contribute internationally.

One of side effects was a narrowing of what was deemed a quality early childhood experience. Different countries had different imperatives. Rather than recognising that the economic modelling and the positive outcomes of a quality early childhood experience was based on play, some countries chose to change the child's experience completely and formalise the early years. An academisation of early childhood curriculum emerged. This resulted in a schoolification of play-based settings, as shown in a content analysis across many northern hemisphere countries (Fleer & van Oers, 2018).

In contrast, many of the countries in the Asia-Pacific region and some other parts of the world who had formal early childhood programs (i.e., they looked like school classrooms and had formal school content learning) and who did not participate in the OECD review, began to consider how to make their curriculum and programs more playful. This can be seen in legislation in China to introduce play in the early childhood curriculum (Ministry of Education, 2001, 2012), in Hong Kong where the curriculum is named as *Joyful Learning through the Curriculum* (Curriculum Development Council, 2017), and Singapore with the concept of purposeful play (Ministry of Education, 2012). These economies were noticing that creativity and imagination were key for innovation. They wanted innovative thinkers for their workforce. They wanted creative citizens to build new types of economies for unknown futures (Chapter 9).

But this global differentiation didn't become evident until much later (Fleer and van Oers, 2018). The problem was the same – the relationship between play and learning. But the orientation was different. How to make learning more playful or how to bring into play more learning? But this theoretical work demanded time and resources.

4 Concluding Remarks and Future Directions

The paper that is discussed below aligns with the policy review of the OECD in 2001 and the introduction of the term intentional teaching in the new early years learning framework released in 2009. The theoretical focus of Paper 2 is fully embedded within Vygotsky's cultural-historical system of concepts. The theoretical frame of my work no longer straddled the legacy of Piaget and the early popularised Vygotskian concept of scaffolding.

4.1 Paper 2: "Conceptual Play": Foregrounding Imagination and Cognition during Concept Formation in Early Years Education

Although the paper referenced the earlier empirical studies that had come from research into children's play (e.g., Bretherton, 1984), the focus of Paper 2 was theoretically different. In drawing on cultural-historical concepts, examples were presented to theorise how imagination and cognition could work together in play-based programs to support concept formation. The result – Conceptual Play – addressed the problem of how to theorise intentional teaching in play-based settings. It was argued at the time that, "conceptual play will help teachers to work more conceptually with children in their play-based programs" (p. 224).

The theoretical argument to realise Conceptual play brings out six key ideas:

1. *Beyond schoolification:* The international trend to increase the cognitive achievement of early childhood children has generated a need for better understanding how concept formation occurs within play-based programs (p. 224).

Yet play-based programs, and the theories that guide them, were never designed to exclusively deliver academically oriented outcomes. Early childhood institutions were set up specifically to realize play as a child's leading activity, while schools focus on academic learning. With new imperatives from government for greater academic learning in preschools, new concepts were needed to go beyond reproducing school structures and formal learning in early childhood settings.

In trying to solve the problem of how to support concept formation in play-based settings, powerful concepts from cultural-historical theory were used to support new ways of theorising how imagination and cognition could work together in play-based programs.

2. *New conception of play:* Vygotsky (2004, p. 37) argued that imagination plays a dual role, "it can lead a person either toward or away from reality" (p. 228). When imaginative play takes the form of role play, we see a movement towards reality, as children explore the rules of society that govern the roles and activities of its people (Elkonin, 2005) (p. 228). Through the process of foregrounding the duality of reality and imagination it becomes possible to see the unity of imagination with realistic thinking (p. 228).

The dialectical movement towards and away from reality in imaginative play is a contradiction, and therefore is most relevant to early childhood science education. As noted by Vygotsky (1987), "The processes of invention or artistic creativity demand a substantial participation by both realistic thinking and imagination. The two act as a unity" (p. 349).

3. *The unity of imagination and realistic thinking:* Consciousness of ideas in play by the child has its parallels with consciousness of concepts during teaching programs designed to support school learning (p. 229). The imaginary situation is foregrounded, and the rules for how to play are initially less important. However, later, children begin to spend longer debating the rules of play (i.e., making the play rules conscious to all the play partners) than they actually spend participating in the play (p. 229)

To explain this relation between play and concept formation, Davydov's concept of theoretical knowledge and dialectical thinking was needed.

4. *Theoretical thinking as foundational for conceptual thinking in science:* Theoretical knowledge and dialectical thinking support children in building mental models, engaging in thought experiments, and in ascertaining relational connections between many different elements within a system. Davydov (1990, p. 249) argues that "mental experimentation forms the basis of theoretical thought, which operates by *scientific* concept [or academic concept]" (p. 232). Davydov's (2008) theory of developmental teaching involves the idea of core concepts within a whole system, a general-particular dialectic, model building, rising to the concrete, and historical framing of knowledge traditions in order to understand how a particular concept was invented by humans to solve a need (pp. 232–233).

But how to bring theoretical thinking into the pedagogy of teachers in early childhood settings was never theorised by Davydov. His work was centred on secondary students. In the re-published paper that follows the example of a bull ant in the wrong place in the outdoor area of the preschool is used as the science education problem. It is a problem of practice (how to develop theoretical thinking for preschool children), and a theoretical problem about what might be the core concept within this everyday situation that can be understood and pedagogically developed. The paper argues that, rather than the teacher noticing what the child has found, or the children being encouraged to see what else they can find, the teacher considers what might be the core concept that would be necessary for the child to build relational knowledge between what they find, the habitat in which it is found, and the food sources available.

5. *Core concepts:* A core concept that will help the child make meaning of their surroundings. Importantly the teacher must help the child see the inter-dependence between habitat, species and food source (pp. 232–233). ... this rudimentary ecosystem acts as a basic theoretical model that helps children move beyond single and disconnected forays when exploring their environment, to a more systematic conceptual investigation of their natural environment (p. 234). Knowing about the *relational link* between insect and habitat as a rudimentary model for an ecosystem, valued by Western science, is an important concept for children to learn (p. 234).

But how could this be realised in practice for the teachers and the children? Davydov (2008) stated that children need practice at concurrently thinking about the particular (individual organism – e.g., ant), and about the general system of concepts (e.g. insect as a classification system). Rather than the children simply finding insects and sharing their finds with their teacher and each other, the teacher supports the children to think relationally about their finds. This can be achieved by investigating the outdoor area of a preschool plotting finds on a map.

When children are contemplating the problem of the bull ant in the wrong place, they are concurrently dealing with an imaginary (or abstracted) situation of the map and the real situation of the outdoor area. Here they move in and out of the play ('as if' entomologists), and they move in and out of the real world ('as' entomologists with maps). A child who creates an imaginary situation, such as pretending to act like an entomologist, is the same as a child who is thinking as that entomologist mapping their outdoor area. The pre-school child knows that he or she is not a real scientist, but in the process of documenting their finds they are acting scientifically and learning about the rules associated with how a scientist might work. That is, they are moving closer to 'reality' through this activity because they are learning about the rules and roles associated with how to construct empirical evidence and knowl-edge. But because this teacher is working to build relational understanding, between habitat, species, and food source, the children are learning more than empirical knowledge (Davydov, 2008) – they are building relational theoretical knowledge. This is a new way of conceptualising play in early childhood, but also a new way of conceptualising thinking in science that had not yet been brought into the science education community. To catch this way of theorising play, the term *Conceptual Play* had to be invented.

6. *Conceptual Play:* Conceptual play emerged by straddling the research communities of science education and early childhood education.

Paper 2 brings the fields of science education and early childhood education together to conceptualise a new way of thinking about the problem of play and learning. But the big problem of how to systematically bring science concepts into play-based program still needed to be addressed.

References

Australian Government, Department of Education, Employment and Workplace Relations. Commonwealth of Australia. (2009). *Belonging, being and becoming – The early years learning framework for Australia. Canberra: Council of Australian Governments.* http://www.deewr.gov.au/earlychildhood/policy_agenda/quality/pages/earlyyearslearningframework.aspx

Bennett, J., & Tayler, C. (2006). *Starting strong II. Early childhood education and care.* OECD Publishing. https://www.oecd.org/education/school/startingstrongiiearlychildhoodeducationandcare.htm

Bretherton, I. (1984). *Symbolic play: The development of social understanding.* Elsevier Science & Technology.

Carey, S. (1985). *Conceptual change in childhood.* MIT Press.

Curriculum Development Council. (2017). *Kindergarten curriculum guide. Joyful learning through the curriculum.* Education Bureau, Hong Kong. https://www.edb.gov.hk/attachment/en/curriculum-development/major-level-of-edu/preprimary/ENG_KGECG_2017.pdf

Davydov, V. V. (1990). *Types of generalization in instruction: Logial and psychological problems in the structuring of school curricula* (J. Teller, Trans.). National Council of Teachers of Mathematics.

Davydov, V. V., & Davydov, V. V. (2008). *Problems of developmental instruction: A theoretical and experimental psychological study.* Nova Science Publishers.

Department of Employment, Education and Training. (1989). *Discipline review of teacher education in mathematics and science.* Report and Recommendation. Australian Government Publishing Service. https://search.informit.org/doi/abs/10.3316/aeipt.88947

Edwards, D., & Mercer, N. (1987). *Common knowledge. The development of understanding in the classroom.* Methuen.

Elkonin, D. B. (2005). The psychology of play. *Journal of Russian and East European Psychology, 43*(1), 11–21. https://doi.org/10.1080/10610405.2005.11059245

Fleer, M. (1990). Scaffolding conceptual change in early childhood. *Research in Science Education, 20*(1), 114–123. https://doi.org/10.1007/BF02620486

Fleer, M. (1995a). The importance of conceptually focused teacher-child interaction in early childhood science learning. *International Journal of Science Education, 17*(3), 325–342. https://doi.org/10.1080/0950069950170305

Fleer, M. (1995b). *DAPcentrism: Challenging developmentally appropriate practice.* ERIC.

Fleer, M. (1996). Fusing the boundaries between home and child care to support children's scientific learning. *Research in Science Education, 26*(2), 143–154. https://doi.org/10.1007/BF02356428

Fleer, M. (2001). Science education over 40 years. *Australasian Journal of Early Childhood, 26*(1), 39–45. https://doi.org/10.1177/183693910102600108

Fleer, M. (2002). Embedded and disembedded learning in early childhood science contexts. *Delta, Policy and Practice in Education, 54*(2), 120–132. https://research.monash.edu/en/publications/embedded-and-disembedded-learning-in-early-childhood-science-cont

Fleer, M. (2005). Developmental fossils – Unearthing the artefacts of early childhood education: The reification of 'Child Development'. *Australasian Journal of Early Childhood, 30*(2), 2–7. https://doi.org/10.1177/183693910503000203

Fleer, M. (2006). Troubling cultural fault lines: Some indigenous Australian families' perspectives on the landscape of early childhood education. *Mind, Culture, and Activity, 13*(3), 191–204. https://doi.org/10.1207/s15327884mca1303_3

Fleer, M. (2008). A cultural-historical reading of "culturally sensitive schooling": Thinking beyond a constructivist view of science learning. *Cultural Studies of Science Education, 3*(3), 781–786. https://doi.org/10.1007/s11422-008-9114-0

Fleer, M. (2009a). A cultural-historical analysis of the place of early childhood science education within ASERA. *Cultural Studies of Science Education, 4*(2), 283–289. https://link.springer.com/journal/11422/volumes-and-issues/4-2

Fleer, M. (2009b). Understanding the dialectical relations between everyday concepts and scientific concepts within play-based programs. *Research in Science Education, 39*(2), 281–306. https://doi.org/10.1007/s11165-008-9085-x

Fleer, M. (2009c). Supporting scientific conceptual consciousness or learning in 'a roundabout way' in play-based contexts. *International Journal of Science Education, 31*(8), 1069–1089. https://doi.org/10.1080/09500690801953161

Fleer, M. (2009d). The re-theorisation of collective pedagogy and emergent curriculum. *Cultural Studies of Science Education, 5*(3), 563–576. https://doi.org/10.1007/s11422-009-9245-y

Fleer, M. (2015). *A cultural-historical study of children learning science: Foregrounding affective imagination in play-based settings.* Springer.

Fleer, M., & Pramling, N. (2015). A cultural-historical study of children learning science. In K. Tobin, C. Milne, C. Siry, & M. Mueller (Eds.), *A cultural-historical study of children learning science: Foregrounding affective imagination in play-based settings.* Springer.

Fleer, M., & van Oers, B. (2018). International trends in research: Redressing the north-south balance in what matters for early childhood education research. In M. Fleer & B. van Oers (Eds.), *International handbook of early childhood education* (pp. 1–30). Springer.

Hadzigeorgiou, Y. (2016). *Imaginative science education: The central role of imagination in science education*. Springer.

Heckman, J. J., & Masterov, D. V. (2007). The productivity argument for investing in young children. *Applied Economic Perspectives and Policy, 29*(3), 446–493. https://doi.org/10.1111/j.1467-9353.2007.00359.x

Kuhn, T. S. (1970). *The structure of scientific revolutions*. University of Chicago Press.

Ministry of Education. (2012). *Nurturing early learners. A curriculum framework for kindergarten in Singapore*. https://www.nel.moe.edu.sg/teaching-and-learning/iteach-principles/engaging-children-in-learning-through-purposeful-play

Ministry of Education of the People's Republic of China. (2001). *Guidelines for kindergarten education practice – Trial version*. [in Chinese] http://www.gov.cn/gongbao/content/2002/content_61459.htm

Ministry of Education of the People's Republic of China. (2012). *Early learning and development guidelines for children aged 3–6*. [in Chinese] http://www.moe.gov.cn/srcsite/A06/s3327/201210/t20121009_143254.html

OECD. (2001). *Starting strong: Early childhood education and care*. OECD. https://www.oecd.org/education/school/2535215.pdf

OECD. (2012). *Starting strong III, A quality toolbox for early childhood education and care*. Paris, France. https://www.oecd-ilibrary.org/education/starting-strong-iii_9789264123564-en

OECD. (2017). *Starting strong 2017: Key OECD indicators on early childhood education and care*. Starting Strong, OECD Publishing. https://www.oecd.org/education/starting-strong-2017-9789264276116-en.htm

Roth, W.-M., Goulart, M. I. M., & Plakitsi, K. (2013). *Science Education during early childhood: A cultural-historical perspective* (Vol. 6). Springer Science & Business Media.

Vygotsky, L. S. (1987). *The collected works of L. S. Vygotsky: Problems of general psychology* (N. Minick, Trans.; R. W. Rieber & A. S. Carton, Eds., Vol. 1). Plenum Press.

Vygotsky, L. S. (1993). *The collected works of LS Vygotsky: The fundamentals of defectology* (J. E. Knox & C. B. Stevens, Trans.; R. W. Rieber & A. S. Carton, Eds., Vol. 2). Springer Science & Business Media.

Vygotsky, L. S. (1997a). *The collected works of LS Vygotsky: Problems of the theory and history of psychology* (R. Van der Veer, Trans.; R. W. Rieber & J. Wollock, Eds., Vol. 3). Springer Science & Business Media.

Vygotsky, L. S. (1997b). *The collected works of L. S. Vygotsky: The history of the development of higher mental functions* (M. J. Hall, Trans.; R. W. Rieber, Ed., Vol. 4). Plenum Press.

Vygotsky, L. S. (1998). *The collected works of L.S. Vygotsky: Child psychology* (M. J. Hall, Trans.; R. W. Rieber, Ed. Vol., 5). Plenum Press.

Vygotsky, L. S. (1999). *The collected works of L. S. Vygotsky: Scientific legacy* (M. J. Hall, Trans.; R. W. Rieber, Ed., Vol. 6). Springer Science & Business Media.

Vygotsky, L. S. (2004). Imagination and creativity in childhood. *Journal of Russian & East European Psychology, 42*(1), 7–97. https://doi.org/10.1080/10610405.2004.11059210

Wertsch, J. V. (1985). *Vygotsky and the social formation of mind.* Harvard University Press.

Wood, D., Bruner, J. S., & Ross, G. (1976). The role of tutoring in problem solving. *Child Psychology & Psychiatry & Allied Disciplines, 17*(2), 89–100. https://doi.org/10.1111/j.1469-7610.1976.tb00381.x

Paper 2: 'Conceptual Play': Foregrounding Imagination and Cognition during Concept Formation in Early Years Education

This paper originally appeared as Fleer, M. (2011). "Conceptual Play": Foregrounding imagination and cognition during concept formation in early years education. *Contemporary Issues in Early Childhood, 12*(3), 224–240. https://doi.org/10.2304/ciec.2011.12.3.224 Reprinted here with permission from the publisher.

Abstract

The international trend to increase the cognitive achievement of early childhood children has generated a need for better understanding how concept formation occurs within play-based programs. Yet the theories of play for supporting early childhood professionals were originally not conceptualized with this need in mind. In this article, concepts from cultural-historical theory are used to theorise how imagination and cognition can work together in play-based programs to support concept formation. This article theorises at a psychological level how both cognition and imagination work in unity and develop in complexity, with imagination acting as the bridge between play and learning. A dialectical view of imagination and cognition is foregrounded, and through this a new theory of play, named as *conceptual play*, is introduced. It is argued that conceptual play will help teachers to work more conceptually with children in their play-based programs.

•••

In recent years the early childhood education community has witnessed increasing global attention as longstanding research and recent economic analyses (e.g., McCain & Mustard, 1999, 2002; Heckman & Masterov, 2007) have changed policy directions in many countries. Central to these changes has been economic arguments about investing early in childhood education and development (see Heckman & Masterov, 2007). Research from neuroscience has made concrete (e.g., Shore, 1997; National Research Council & Institute of Medicine, 2000) what early childhood educators have known through their own research and practice for some time, that a quality early childhood experience for a child has a profound effect upon the child's schooling outcomes (Belfield et al., 2005; Sylva et al., 2004; Wylie & Thompson, 2003; Wylie et al., 2006) and their later life chances (Mitchell et al., 2008; Schweinhart et al., 1986; Schweinhart & Weikart, 1997, 1998, 1999). In line with these policy developments has also been a greater focus on delivering greater cognitive outcomes in these play-based programs, as increased attention is drawn to young children's literacy and numeracy competence. It is possible that the new international landscape can result in preschool programs becoming more academically oriented at the expense of play. This global change in educational imperatives places pressure upon early childhood professionals to plan and deliver more academically oriented programs in order to meet system targets for higher levels of performance in literacy and numeracy. Yet play-based programs, and the theories that guide them, were never designed to exclusively deliver academically oriented outcomes. The existing theoretical tools used to frame play-based programs within the early childhood sector do not necessarily help professionals to deal with these economic imperatives or the academically oriented system pressures that are directed to early childhood education. New theoretical tools are needed in order to preserve established and well-researched outcomes delivered through play-based programs alongside the need to make visible to those outside of the field how conceptual development for young children occurs within these kinds of programs.

Economic modeling and brain imaging, whilst persuasive to government, do not in their own right show how conceptual development in the early years can be fostered in traditional play-based programs. A deeper theoretical understanding of concept formation within play-based contexts is needed to fully appreciate how the social process of teaching turns everyday practice into the conscious realization of concepts which children use to transform their everyday lives. Yet historically, our profession has been strong on process, and weak on articulating cognitive content (see Hedges & Cullen, 2005; Cullen, 2009). The theoretical problem that has arisen for the field centres on how concept formation can be fostered within play-based programs so that important social outcomes are not lost.

Whilst play is a contested area (see Gaskins et al., 2007; Brooker, 2010), and a range of definitions of play may be found within the literature (see Brock, 2009; Fleer, 2009), it is generally understood that in Western communities play activity can be child directed, adult led, or jointly constructed (see also Department of Education, Employment & Workplace Relations, 2009). Most Western social theories of play tend to focus on stages of play, where children, depending upon the theory used, progress from manipulative play with fingers and toes, and later materials, to solitary play, parallel play, through to role play or fantasy play (see the original studies by Parten, 1932, 1933; Smilansky, 1968. Most contemporary Western publications on play are a slight variation on these). Most of these theories focus on a biological view of play, where play is driven from within the child (e.g., Bretherton, 1984; Brock, 2009), and a maturational view of development, where play stages progress in terms of the child's age. Even cognitive theories of play, such as that of Piaget's (1962), are framed in stages and draw upon a maturational view of play.

A cultural-historical view of play does not focus on stages of development linked with age, but rather draws upon a view of play development related to the kinds of experiences and social interactions that children have which build complexity of play activity (e.g., Bodrova, 2008; Van Oers, 1999, 2008, 2009, 2010; Elkonin, 1999; Ugaste, 2005; Hakkarainen, 2006; Holzman, 2009). Linked to this is a view of child development which concentrates upon the kinds of leading activities that children engage in order to participate within their social and cultural communities (Elkonin, 1993; Fleer, 2010; Hedegaard, 2002, 2008, 2009; Karpov, 2005; Kravtsova, 2005, 2006). For instance, a leading activity is an action-oriented motive that is dominant in a particular cultural community for individuals at a particular point in time. A leading activity is framed in relation to how societies organize the institutions of family, preschool and school. Developmental opportunities are created as children move through the institution of the family, to the preschool, to school and to work (Hedegaard, 2009). In this view of child development, the concept of leading activities is important (Kravtsov, 2009). Within the preschool period play is thought to be the leading activity of children, and as children move to formal schooling contexts, children's leading activity is centred on learning as the central motive for action (Elkonin, 1993; Vygotsky, 1966). In this reading of child development, it does not mean that learning is not occurring within the preschool period, but rather that play is the dominant or leading activity for a child. Early childhood institutions are set up specifically to realize play as a leading activity while schools focus on academic learning. With new imperatives from government for greater academic learning in preschools, these established theories of play (both Western and Russian) are challenged.

As discussed previously, there is a diversity of definitions of play, and some longstanding researchers have even noted that almost every activity a child engages in, has been labeled as play (see Rubin et al., 1983). Traditional approaches to defining play have tended to focus on attributes that distinguish play from other forms of behaviour. Most authors in early childhood education research literature tend to agree that play is an activity that is child centred, free from externally imposed rules, and is usually initiated and driven by the child, often showing some form of pretense. In order to solve the theoretical problem that has emerged from the heightened interest in greater cognitive outcomes in play-based programs, a new way of thinking about play is needed. However, this definition attributes play activity and motive solely within the child and deemphasises the role of adults in the cultural development of children's play.

In this article, Vygotsky's (1966) original writings on play and his 2004 theory of imagination are used to show how play-based programs build children's conceptual thinking in play. In this article I also draw upon Davydov's (2008) writings on theoretical knowledge and dialectical thinking in order to show how play-based programs can build children's theoretical thinking in play, where imagination acts as the bridge between play as a leading activity and learning as a leading activity. Here conceptual play is more evident when the perspective of the child is considered in relation to the perspective of the teacher. Through this it is possible to realize a pedagogy for building concepts in play.

The concepts that I draw upon in this article come from important cultural-historical works not widely used within the field of early childhood education. Yet they hold great potential for better understanding concept formation within play-based programs. This article begins with an overview of Vygotsky's (2004) theory of imagination, followed by a discussion of Davydov's (2008) work on theoretical knowledge and dialectical thinking in relation to the pedagogical practices that support early childhood play-based programs. Within the confines of the word limit for this article, only some of the key cultural-historical concepts are discussed. Other concepts central to concept formation, such as everyday and scientific concepts (Vygotsky, 1987), can be found discussed in Fleer (2010) in relation to early childhood education. Further, it is recognized that some translations, such as Vygotsky's (1978), are problematic, and that seminal works, such as in Vygotsky (1966), have used English terms (e.g., stages) or words (e.g., 'age' instead of 'periodisation') which make it difficult to gain a full reading or understanding of Vygotsky's theory. More problematic still, is the over-reliance by researchers of secondary sources, without ever reading or drawing upon the Collected Works (6 volumes). These problems can only be signposted here.

Taken together, the theoretical perspectives introduced in this article seek to make visible and to theorise how conceptual development occurs within existing play-based programs. This article seeks to add to educators' toolkit an additional theory of play designed specifically for working more academically with children in play-based programs. The article does not seek to replace other theories of play outlined above, only to provide a theory of play that is useful for supporting early childhood professionals in solving the new imperatives of increased academic performance from play-based programs. Cultural-historical writings provide a powerful theory for undertaking this important work and for going one step further by expanding upon the existing cultural-historical reading of play. What follows is an articulation of this new theory of play which I have named *conceptual play*.

Imagination and Play

Imagination has traditionally been viewed as an individual activity, disassociated from reality. Imagination is something thought to be 'contained within the individual', as something an individual constructs for themselves (Gajdamaschko, 2005; Vygotsky, 2004). This perspective makes it very difficult for early childhood professionals working within play-based programs to take an active pedagogical role in developing children's imagination (Ferholt, 2010; Holzman, 2010). It is also difficult to theorise imagination in relation to concept formation. However, when we draw upon a cultural-historical view of imagination we move from the traditional belief of an internal, subconscious and biological process to a conscious and social act, where mediation becomes important (see also Egan, 2005; Egan & Madoc-Jones, 2005; John-Steiner et al., 2010).

Vygotsky (2004) argued that 'imagination is not just an idle mental amusement, not merely an activity without consequences in reality, but rather a function essential to life' (p. 13). Imagination becomes the means for broadening a person's experience. Vygotsky (2004) suggests that humans imagine what they cannot see, conceptualise what they hear from others, and think about what they have not yet experienced. That is, a person, 'is not limited to the narrow circle and narrow boundaries of his [sic] own experience but can venture far beyond these boundaries, assimilating, with the help of his imagination someone else's historical or social experience' (Vygotsky, 2004, p. 17). In this theoretical reading of imagination, the social relations that a child is a part of, must be foregrounded and not viewed as separate from the child's imaginative activity. Contemporary research by Egan and Madei (2010) and Connery et al. (2010) have shown through educational theatre, creative arts and play-worlds (Ferholt, 2010) how imagination, cognition and emotional experience (*perezhivanie*) must be conceptualized in unity.

Imagination can also be conceptualized historically. Vygotsky (2004, p. 25) stated that 'Every act of imagination has a very long history'. The creation of new ideas and inventions requires a particular form of imagination that is culturally and socially located. Vygotsky (2004, p. 30) argued that 'Creation is a historical, cumulative process where every succeeding manifestation was determined by the preceding one'. These imaginings of inventors or 'even a genius, is also a product of his [sic] time and his environment. His creations arise from needs that were created before him and rest on capacities that also exist outside of him' (2004, p. 30). Importantly, imaginative creations arise when the material and psychological conditions that are necessary for its formation are available. In this sense, we note that imagination is a collective historical experience that even very young children can be lifted into with more experienced play partners or through the social actions of adults who plan and implement play-based programs. In these kinds of cultural-historical programs, the relations between imagination and the material world become conscious to the child. A cultural-historical view of imagination foregrounds the importance of rethinking the concept of play as it has currently been researched and theorized within Western communities. In the following three sections, a cultural-historical reading of imagination is used to theorise the bridge between play as a leading activity and learning as a leading activity in programs which seek to support concept formation.

Consciousness of Object-Meaning Relations

Imagination is fore and foremost a conscious act (Bodrova, 2008). For instance, when children are in an imaginary situation playing, they participate in two kinds of actions simultaneously – internal and external. That is, children direct their attention to the external material world (reality), whilst at the same time thinking about the meanings associated with their external engagement. For instance, a child can imbue objects with meaning, but at the same time change

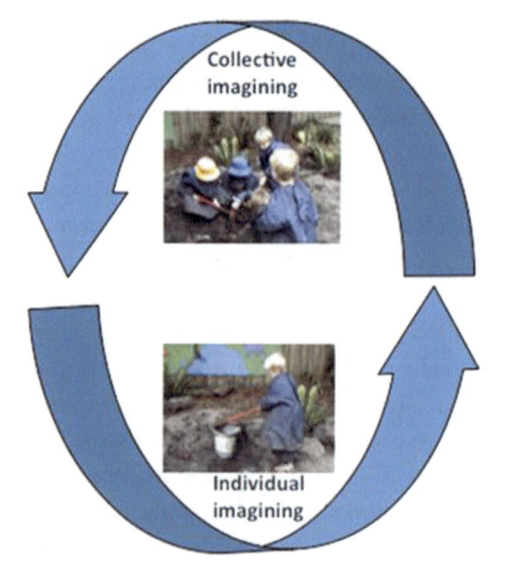

FIGURE 1
Object–meaning relations in play

the meaning of an object through imagination. Vygotsky (1966) cites the example of a stick becoming a horse for the child to illustrate how the child inverts the fraction object/meaning to meaning/object (see Figure 1). The external and visible object of the stick, is no longer seen in the external world (reality) as a stick, but rather through the internal process of imagination, the stick becomes a horse, and the child becomes a rider. However, in this fraction, reality and imagination cannot be separated, they give meaning to each other through their obvious contradiction. That is, they are dialectically related to each other.

The child gives new meaning to an object through the process of imagination. The child's focus of attention is no longer on the object, but rather the meaning that the child has given to the object. The *object–meaning relations*, as shown in Figure 1 are an important dimension of the development of imagination as experienced through play-based programs in early childhood. Through the object-meaning inversion, imagination becomes a conscious act by the child. A child can move from the objective field (external material world) to the sense field (internal) in an imaginary situation (Kravtsova, 2008). The parallels can be drawn between the real concrete world presented to children in early years programs, and the abstractions that are demanded during the process of concept formation. The simultaneous movement between external and internal, as shown in play, is also noted between concrete and abstract, within learning programs. That is, the *concrete-abstract relations* needed for concept formation are possible through imagination, where concept formation becomes a conscious act by the child. The child gives new meaning to the particular teaching situation. Imagination becomes the bridge between both the *object-meaning relations* in play, and the *concrete-abstract relations* foregrounded in schools. Vygotsky (1987) argues that a:

> more profound penetration of reality demands that consciousness attains a freer relationship to the elements of that reality, that consciousness departs from the external and apparent aspects of reality that is given directly in perception. The result is that the processes through which the cognition of reality is achieved become more complex and richer. (1987, p. 349)

Vygotsky (2004, p. 37) argued that imagination plays a dual role, 'it can lead a person either toward or away from reality'. When children imbue objects with new meanings, and change their sense, we see that children move away from reality. The object can initially act as a placeholder for meaning. It becomes a symbol in play for the meaning that is created by the child – i.e. the stick acting as a symbol for the horse in the horse-riding game that is being enacted. Vygotsky (1966) suggests that the child uses the stick as a pivot in play. Once again, it is possible to see the parallels in the concrete-abstract relations found in schools where symbols are introduced to children as pivots to support concept formation as children simultaneously participate in concrete and abstract experiences in learning programs.

The Dialectical Relations between Imagination and Reality

When imaginative play takes the form of role play, we see a movement towards reality, as children explore the rules of society that govern the roles and activities of its people (Elkonin, 2005). Children test out these rules within the imaginary situation they create with their play partners. When children give new meanings to objects in their play they move away from reality, but when they test out the rules of society through role play, they move towards reality. Here the dialectical nature of imagination is most evident because we see the dual role imagination plays in moving towards and away from reality. As Vygotsky (1987, p. 349) noted, 'Imagination is a necessary, integral aspect of realistic thinking'.

Vygotsky (1966) showed the dialectical relations between reality and imagination as a fraction. In Figure 2 the fraction, *role/imaginary situation*, is shown with the role initially being foregrounded because the child examines the real

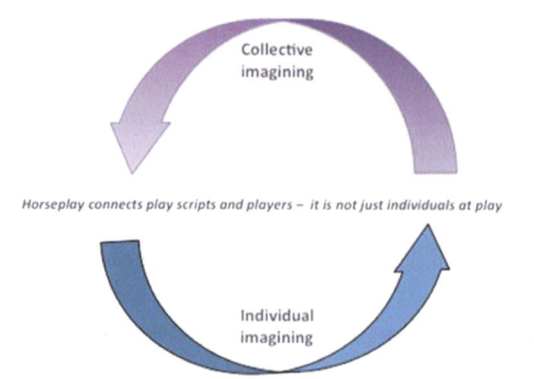

Horseplay connects play scripts and players – it is not just individuals at play

FIGURE 2
The dialectical relationship between
reality and imagination

world for rules associated with a particular role, such as 'being a mum' or 'being a firefighter'. In the first instance, the child explores the rules and expectations associated with the role in society. Initially, children concentrate upon playing out the role. Development in play can be expressed through the fraction becoming inverted to *imaginary situation/role*, as shown in Figure 2. Here the focus moves from imitating a role found in everyday life (reality) to play that is focused on the imaginary situation. The system of relations between roles, and the variety of possibilities that may be expressed, now dominates. In research on play development by Bodrova and Leong (2001), children are deliberately exposed to different community workers in order to develop their role play skills. Children not only visit real contexts, such as the hospital, but their attention is drawn to the variety of roles played out in the context, such as the receptionist, the ambulance driver, the cleaner, the radiographer, rather than the most obvious roles of the doctor, nurse and patient. Bodrova (2008) argues that this active support is necessary for play development to progress.

Through the process of foregrounding the duality of reality and imagination it becomes possible to see the unity of imagination with realistic thinking. Significantly, educators interested in developing imagination must work with imagination in unity with thinking, whilst at the same time recognizing the child's activity as a dual and dynamic process that moves to, from and between reality and imagination. The complexity of this unity is highlighted in the writings of Vygotsky (1987) where he notes a contradiction:

> There is a contradiction inherent in the problem as it actually exists. No accurate cognition of reality is possible without a certain element of imagination, a certain flight from the immediate, concrete, solitary impression in which the reality is presented in the elementary acts of consciousness. The processes of invention or artistic creativity demand a

> substantial participation by both realistic thinking and imagination. The two act as a unity. (1987, p. 349)

In order to engage in higher forms of cognition and imagination 'consciousness departs from the external and apparent aspects of reality that is given directly in perception'. The cognition of reality and the development of imagination become richer and more complex. In Vygotsky's theorization of imagination and reality, we note that imagination moves a child away from reality to give higher forms of cognition. Higher forms of cognition are expressed through volition or consciousness on the part of the child. Consciousness of ideas in play by the child has its parallels with consciousness of concepts during teaching programs designed to support school learning. It is well understood that children who think consciously about concepts are able to use them to interact in new ways in their everyday world (Fleer, 2010). Consequently, imagination and consciousness must be viewed as significantly important components of a child's learning and development, and therefore playbased programs which support imagination will make a difference to children's capacity in existing and future cognitive tasks, including priority areas such as literacy and numeracy.

It is possible to see in Vygotsky's (1966) writings on play, how higher forms of consciousness occur as play complexity develops. Vygotsky (1966) gives the example of two sisters who pretend to be sisters in their play. In playing sisters, the children follow the rules of what governs sisterhood– how to be a sister in play, and what sisters might do in this imaginary situation. Earlier forms of play may focus on the role of being a sister, with latter forms of play concentrating more on the imaginary adventures they may have together. As play complexity develops, the play partners spend longer imagining their adventures and the rules associated with what might be possible in their play, than they do playing out the role of sisterhood. This change in focus to the imaginary situation is represented by Vygotsky (1966) as a fraction of *imaginary situation/ rules* (see Figure 3). The imaginary situation is foregrounded, and the rules for how to play are initially less important. However, later, children begin to spend longer debating the rules of play (i.e., making the play rules conscious to all the play partners) than they actually spend participating in the play. The fraction inverts to *rules/imaginary situation* as shown in Figure 3. For example, when focusing on the possible adventures between play partners, one sister may regularly stop the play and correct the other play partner, with the consequence of spending more time outside of the play focusing on the rules which govern the play, than actually inside of the play, playing out the imaginary situation.

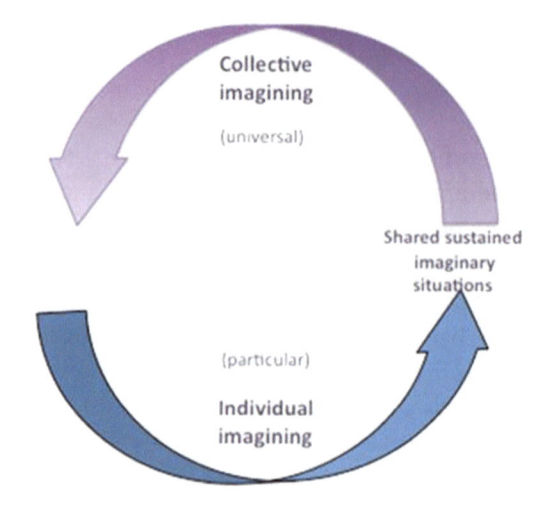

FIGURE 3
Imaginary situation–rules
dialectic

Games with rules also fall into this category. The rules of the game dominate, with the imaginarysituation backgrounded. The children's focus of attention is on the rules, making sure everyone understands and uses the agreed
rules. What is significant here for children's psychological development is their
capacity to easily move from 'inside the play' to 'outside of the play'.

Consciously Moving inside and outside of Play

Kravtsova (2008) draws attention to the idea of children being inside of the
play, such as when they take on a particular role within an imaginary situation.
For example, a child is inside the play when they put a pillow on their back
and play at being a turtle. Kravtsova (2008) contrasts this with how children
can be outside of the play. For example, a child can take a matchbox car, and
direct the car to perform in a particular game. Here the child is outside of the
play directing it. Longstanding research by Bretherton (1984), has shown that
when groups of children play together, they use language and actions inside of
the play to keep the play moving, such as saying 'rock, rock, rock' to underscore
the importance of rocking a baby in a game of home play. Or they may move
outside of the play and signal that a particular aspect of the play is not allowed
when another play partner suggests this. She calls this being *inside of the frame*
and *being outside of the frame*. At higher forms of play, Kravtsova (2008) notes
that children also act either 'inside' or 'outside' of the play. For instance, in
school theatre, older students take on the role of being the actors and can also
take on the role of being the director of the school play. The director can be
watching or directing outside of the play, but the director can also be inside the

play when demonstrating how a particular playscript scene should be acted out. Students will also be in role, such as when they are acting out the play during a dress rehearsal, and then out of role, when taking a break from the play.

These examples illustrate the significance of *moving in and out of reality*, and also in *moving in and out of an imaginary situation*. Kravtsova (2008) suggests that it is important for children to experience being 'in' and 'out' of the play and both need to develop simultaneously. In her theory of play she shows how play complexity develops in relation to how children position themselves in play. In earlier forms of director play, children direct the objects in play (pushing a matchbox car), and in later forms of director play, students direct people, such as when they are the producer or the director of a play-script in theatre. The psychological significance of being inside or outside of play/reality cannot be underestimated for concept formation, as will be shown in this section.

Related to the idea of being in and out of play, is the notion of building a common understanding of the imaginary situation amongst all the play partners. When children create scenarios of play (scenario play) they work towards a shared understanding of the imaginary situation. In the example that follows, Rowan and Sophie (aged 3½) formulate the play 'outside of the play scenario' when they state:

Sophie: Pretend I was a doctor and I [meaning the other child] was a doctor too.
Rowan: 'tend I was a nurse, 'tend I was a nurse.

The children maintain and develop the play through stating the storyline to each other (see below). The sing-song cadence in their play narrative signals to all the players inside of the play, how the play should progress (sing-song with high pitched sound at the end of each statement):

Rowan: ... and it was time for all those to go home.
Sophie: What do you need?
Rowan: Good night.
Sophie: Let's ...
Rowan: And the nurse got some long medicine.
Sophie: And the baby was sick and she had to go to bed. And I put her bed socks off.

In this example, the children stay within the play scenario through verbalizing their imaginings and creating and sustaining their shared imaginary situation. However, children do also step out of the lay, when there is a disagreement or an uncertainty about the development of the play narrative within the imaginary situation. For example:

Rowan: And the other babies had to get medicine. There, all the ones in this pile are better.
Sophie: No, this one is really sick! [*Tone changes from sing-song to commanding*]

Play complexity develops in tandem with play competence by the play partners. Stepping out and into the play is an important dimension of the play. Children achieve play complexity by stepping out of the play to make clear to the other play partners how the play narrative is evolving or how the storyline should be enacted through the imaginary situation. Complexity forms because children have a shared understanding of the imaginary situation. Stepping inside and outside of the imaginary situation is important for developing not only the play, but the play partners' competence. Children practice at being in and out of an imaginary situation through play. At the same time, they practice moving in and out of reality. This conceptualization of play is shown in Figure 4.

Play-based programs which develop imagination through play exemplify the dialectical relations between reality and imagination discussed previously. That is, children practice through their play the movement of stepping in and out of reality. Through making conscious the distinction between imagination and reality in play, children are conceptually primed to work with real objects and imagined (or abstract) ideas which represent reality. Thus allowing for a profound penetration of reality whilst at the same time becoming liberated from earlier and more primitive forms of cognition. This kind of contradiction between imagination and reality creates the dynamic force which allows for theoretical knowledge to be contemplated by young children. This dynamic tension is inherent in concept formation and is shown in Figure 5.

Figure 5 foregrounds how imagination becomes the bridge between *play as a leading activity in preschool to learning as the leading activity in school* (see also Kravtsov, 2009). In this conceptualization of play, children give new meaning to objects, thus providing children with valuable experience in consciously considering their concrete world. With this background play experience, children can engage with the concrete materials deliberately introduced to them as representations of ideas that teachers wish children to examine – such as when a one-centimeter block is used to represent a rudimentary measurement tool in mathematics. Giving new meaning to a block (i.e., a measurement device) is not such a huge conceptual leap for children when they have

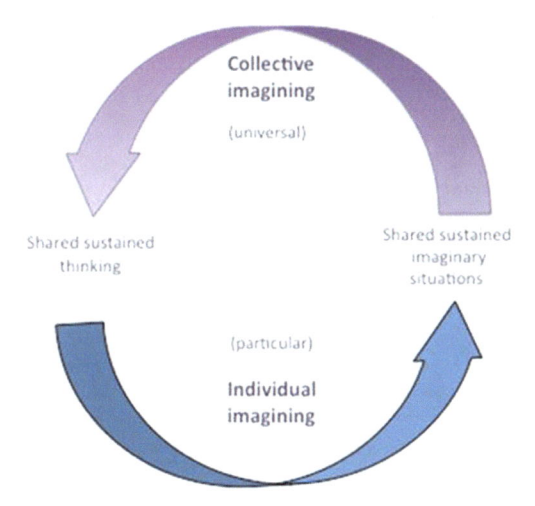

Collective
imagining

(universal)

Shared sustained
thinking

Shared sustained
imaginary
situations

(particular)

Individual
imagining

FIGURE 4
Stepping inside and stepping outside of the imaginary situation

had experiences in imaginary situations giving new meanings to objects in play. Working together with their teacher to create a new learning situation (as an imaginary situation) which involves measurement is also possible because children can move in and out of reality, and in and out of the imagined situation that the teacher creates in the classroom – such as when measurement is used for creating a fairy house. Finally, when children have had experience in play of dealing with roles and rules, making explicit how the play should progress, this means that these children can also think consciously about the concepts that are introduced to them in the learning programs introduced by teachers. Thinking consciously about concepts is not so far removed from children discussing the rules of play.

Play-based programs which afford the kind of development of imagination as that shown in Figure 5, position children to more easily deal with the social process of working with abstract symbols, content knowledge and thinking that pre-literacy and pre-numeracy demand. When the relations between imagination and reality are conceptualized together with Vygotsky's (2004) work on the imaginary situation in play (including when objects are given new meaning and roles make conscious the rules about how society works), then a way of thinking about concept formation in early childhood education becomes possible. This perspective on a child's psychological development can be theorized as conceptual play. Conceptual play is a way of thinking about how conceptual development occurs in Western play-based programs (rather than seeing young children only engaged in pseudo concepts – see Vygotsky, 1987) where a need has arisen to focus on academic concepts. It gives insights into what can happen conceptually for children in playbased programs, and is

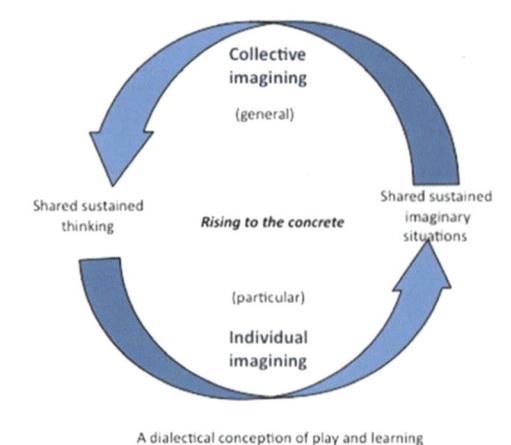

Collective
imagining

(general)

Shared sustained
thinking   *Rising to the concrete*   Shared sustained
imaginary
situations

(particular)

Individual
imagining

A dialectical conception of play and learning

FIGURE 5
Imagination as the bridge between play
and learning

much more productive for teachers and those outside of the field, than saying that 'children learn through play' or 'children learn number concepts in play'. From the psychological perspective, conceptual play gives a more detailed explanation of how play-based programs turn everyday social practices of children into the conscious realization of concepts.

Naming this as conceptual play makes visible important psychological processes in early childhood play-based programs.

We now turn to a theoretical discussion of how to realize conceptual play within early childhood education programs. Through this, important pedagogical practices are foregrounded, and the existing umbrella situation of undifferentiated 'play-based programs' is made problematic.

A Pedagogy for Realizing Conceptual Play

The concepts that early childhood children develop through giving new meaning to objects, through moving in and out of reality, and through playing with roles to understand societal rules, means that it is easier for children to engage with academic concepts when they start school. Engaging with the knowledge domain and tradition of mathematics, science or literacy also involves the child moving into an imaginary situation of a mathematics knowledge tradition, and giving new mathematical meanings to objects, such as when the wiping of a table is turned into conscious thought about the existence of a surface with a boundary, and later surface area that can be measured. Davydov (2008) researched and theorised how teachers should work with school-aged children to build theoretical knowledge and dialectical thinking when working with academic concepts. His ideas are useful for examining how a pedagogy for conceptual play may be possible within the early childhood period.

As discussed previously, imagination when used consciously by children helps them to rise above reality, to descend to reality, to document reality, and to play with reality. Davydov (1984, 1990, 2008) also refers to this, conceptualizing it as building theoretical knowledge through the process of *rising to the concrete*. Theoretical knowledge and dialectical thinking support children in building mental models, engaging in thought experiments, and in ascertaining relational connections between many different elements within a system. Davydov (1990, p. 249) argues that 'mental experimentation forms the basis of theoretical thought, which operates by *scientific* concept [or academic concept]'. These complex and rich ideas bring together understandings of concept formation in children, but also the pedagogical practices which support conceptual development. Davydov's (2008) theory of developmental teaching involves the idea of core concepts within a whole system, a general-particular dialectic, model building, rising to the concrete, and historical framing of knowledge traditions in order to understand how a particular concept was invented by humans to solve a need. These are discussed briefly below with an example to show the ideas in practice for preschool teachers. The examples have been kept deliberately simple and illustrative of the types of practices that already exist within preschools, so that the new *relational* concepts can be more easily discussed.

According to Davydov (2008) a concept can both *represent* a material object and be used to reflect on the material object. The concept allows for a particular mental action to occur. To do this, a child must first be aware of the material object, as a conscious mental representation. Giving a new sense to a material object, as occurs in play, helps children to think consciously about the material object. It is well understood that much of a young child's world is experienced without conscious awareness. For example, young children will interact with their natural environment, such as their outdoor preschool area, without conscious realization that they are a part of an ecosystem. That is, they will pick up leaves and bark whilst walking around and in this process they may find insects. The children will notice the insects, but it is less likely that they will think about the insects' habitat. Rather a more tacit form of understanding may emerge through regularly finding insects when in the outdoor area.

In Figure 6 an example is shown, where a child identifies that a bull ant is in the 'wrong place', thus affording a teaching opportunity to develop theoretical knowledge in children. That is, to build a theoretical model of an ecosystem.

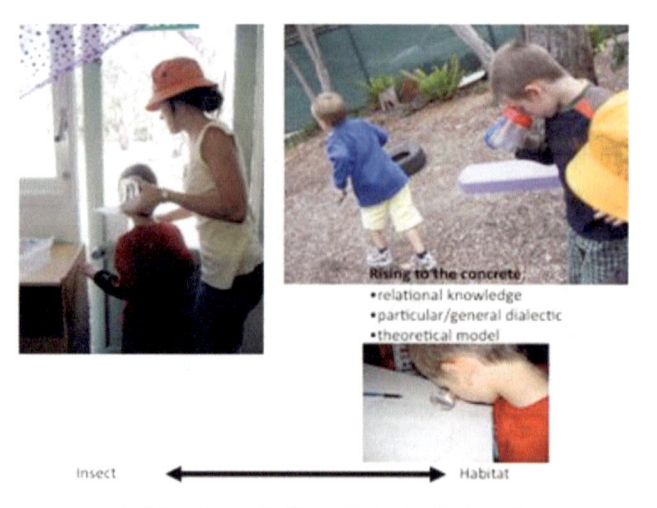

FIGURE 6   Building theoretical knowledge in play-based programs

Rather than the teacher noticing what the child has found, or the children being encouraged to see what else they can find, the teacher considers what might be the core concept that would be necessary for the child to build relational knowledge between what they find, the habitat in which it is found, and the food sources available. That is, the teacher reduces the complexity of the material world to the essence of a core concept. A core concept that will help the child make meaning of their surroundings. Importantly the teacher must help the child see the interdependence between habitat, species and food source. It is an understanding of the relations between these that creates theoretical thinking for the young child. When children have established a concept of habitat, a concept of species, and food source, as totally interdependent relations, then the child has built a theoretical model that can be transported to other environmental contexts or be considered abstractly. Initially, this rudimentary ecosystem acts as a basic theoretical model that helps children move beyond single and disconnected forays when exploring their environment, to a more systematic conceptual investigation of their natural environment.

Children's investigations begin as 'flashing impressions', where elements of significance are singled out or are conceptualized as the 'essence of the thing' being observed. That is, children may notice that a specific insect can be found in specific locations within the preschool, such as a woodlouse under rotting wooden logs, or ants coming out of ant holes. Knowing about the *relational link* between insect and habitat as a rudimentary model for an ecosystem, valued by Western science, is an important concept for children to learn. In play-based programs opportunities are afforded to visit and revisit experiences, and with teacher support, establish relational links and build theoretical knowledge. Davydov (1990), in drawing upon Davydova, has argued that theoretical knowledge 'always pertains to a *system of interaction*, the realm of successively connected phenomena that, in their totality, make up an organized whole' (Davydov, 1990, p. 254). Children considering the idea of an 'insect' (as apposed to the specific insect, such as the woodlouse) can only think about this as a concept if they understand a system of relational concepts which together make up the universal concept of 'an ecosystem' and 'classification system of living things', as is detailed in many science curriculum documents.

In this particular example of the bull ant in the wrong place, the teacher systematized the children's explorations into a series of investigations, where detailed mapping of finds was encouraged. That is, the teacher gave the children blank pieces of paper that they used to reproduce both the insects they found and the details of their habitats. This allowed for an in situ examination and discussion of the insect, the habitat and the food sources available. Here the children were working directly in the material world, mapping what they could see, but as a relational image. Further to this, the children took their finds out of the habitat for closer study and used a range of resources provided by the teacher to better understand the form and structure of the particular insects they were finding. This helped them later to classify their insects into a broader schema. This then allowed the children to begin to notice the kinds of classification systems and criteria that are used by Western scientists to categorise their world. Davydov (2008) stated that children need practice at concurrently thinking about the particular (individual organism – e.g., ant), and about the general system of concepts (e.g., insect as a classification system). Investigating an outdoor area of a preschool, organized as a map, allowed children to move from the general to the particular, and from the particular to the general – as a dialectical process.

When the children are contemplating the problem of the bull ant in the wrong place, they are concurrently dealing with an imaginary (or abstracted) situation of the map and the real situation of the outdoor area. As discussed in the previous section, movement between reality and imagination occurs when children play. They move in and out of the play, and they move in and out of the real world. A child who creates an imaginary situation, such as pretending to be a jockey riding a horse in play, is the same as a child who acts as a scientist mapping their outdoor area. This is conceptually congruent. The preschool child knows that he or she is not a real scientist, but in the process of documenting their finds they are acting scientifically and learning about the rules associated with how a scientist might work. That is, they are moving closer to 'reality' through this activity because they are learning about the rules and roles associated with how to construct empirical evidence and knowledge. But because this teacher is working to build relational understanding, between habitat, species, and food source, the children are learning more than empirical knowledge and paradigmatic thinking (Davydov, 2008) – they are building relational theoretical knowledge.

What is important here for building children's theoretical knowledge and thinking is how the child's relationship to the material world changes. That is, the environment in the centre has not changed – the outdoor area is still the same – but the child's thinking about this environment has changed because the child has developed a theoretical model of an ecosystem. We see this also in other forms of knowledge valued in society and part of the curriculum – such as mathematics. For example, young children who accompany their family on shopping trips, helping to find groceries, will develop everyday understandings about a shopping centre, knowing that if asked to find a toothbrush, that this item will be found somewhere along one of the aisles. They are likely to run up and down the aisles until they find it. However, if a child has a concept of a shopping centre being a classification system, then their actions are likely to be very different – that is, they are likely to find the toiletries section first, and then locate the toothbrush. This is a more direct and theoretically informed approach. Having a concept of a classification system as a theoretical model is a highly imaginative activity, allowing for a transformation of how children think and act in the material world.

Davydov (2008) has argued that to establish the essence of the concept (e.g., ecosystem in their outdoor area), children need to reproduce the concrete into some form of abstraction, such as a model (Aidarova, 1982). Representing thinking as a model is possible within play-based programs because resources and time are readily available for engaging in drawing, painting, collage and box construction. In the example of the bull ant in the wrong place, the teacher invited the children to represent their understandings as action drawings, paintings and collage. In addition, the mapping activity built the basis for the children's modeling. For example, taking a blank piece of paper into the outdoor area, with the view to mapping finds and their habitat, is an example of a model closely connected to the material world – that is, a model that is created in the specific context under investigation. To turn a piece of paper into a map required imaginative thinking on the part of the children. To develop the modeling process further, the teacher provided rich resources, including a range of actual maps, classification charts of insects, and the opportunity for the children to photocopy relevant pictorial information so that further study of the insects and their habitat was possible. The latter materials tended to be used away from the context of the outdoor area. That is, more imagination was required to work with these materials as they were more decontextualized. The net result was that the children took their individualised photocopied resources with them as they explored the outdoor area, as they painted, worked with playdough, and as they read books and used the play boxes (e.g., small space with natural materials, picture books, and plastic models of insects) in their preschool. Their booklet of resources provided a further opportunity to inform their activity across a range of experiences available within the centre.

Modeling helps children to *rise to the concrete*. Rising to the concrete encompasses the pedagogical principle of initially examining a holistic system and mentally ascending to this system in order to determine its specific nature. Through establishing the individual relations it is possible to observe its universal character. Through this kind of contemplation, children learn a general law. For example, a bull ant can be found in relation to its habitat. In this relational model the child sees the specific individual form of a bull ant and an ant hole, in its universal form it is an organism and habitat. The relations between habitat and organism represents knowledge generation that was created historically, as a form of classifying and organizing the world, as a scientific knowledge tradition. This knowledge was represented through the insect charts and maps. Consequently, a concept must reflect the process of its historical and scientific development. That is, the child must also have the opportunity to investigate its environment and notice the bull ant and ant hole are always linked (specific) with the experience of generating a scientific model of organism and habitat (general). This historical and scientific development can be reflected through the knowledge base of the teacher, as the teacher directs the children's attention to specific features of the ecosystem, or through the strategic use of books and charts which in themselves contain the history of knowledge of Western science. Whilst children are not working independently to rediscover bodies of established knowledge, they do engage in an investigative process guided by their teacher, which allows them to build theoretical knowledge and use dialectical thinking for establishing the relational knowledge (in the form of a model) that underpins the historical and scientific journey undertaken initially in revealing the discovery and building the knowledge system. In this process, 'Theoretical thinking sets itself the goal of reproducing the essence of the object of study' (Davydov, 2008, p. 107). Ascent is the leading and primary thinking activity. It is through these forms of thinking and knowledge-generation processes that social consciousness arises and historically formed universals become available for individuals to use within society. To successfully undertake both the specific investigations and build universal understandings requires that children can move into reality (the ant's habitat) and out of reality (the modeling and building of universal understandings). As such, it is possible to see how play-based programs where the teacher takes an active conceptual role, provide important conceptual development in play, but also in academic concepts. *Conceptual play* is helpful for making this visible to early childhood teachers and to those outside of the field.

Conceptual play illustrates the dialectical nature of imagination and cognition (doubled experience), and shows that they must act in unity. The generation of an *imaginary situation* by the teacher or the child is an important conscious act where children can rise above reality, descend to reality, connect with reality and play with reality. Through the unity of imagination and cognition, the bridge between play as the leading activity is extended to learning as the leading activity for the child. It is not the environment that has changed for the child, but rather, it is the child's relation to the material and social world that has changed. The child has a new self-awareness of the environment. If conceptual development has occurred, then the child now sees an ecosystem within the outdoor area of the preschool rather than a space where it is possible to find bugs. The teacher's deliberate framing of play for the children to work conceptually, draws upon Vygotsky's (1966, 2004) theorization of both imagination and play and Davydov's (2008) theory of developmental teaching. Taken together, these works are useful for both a theory of conceptual play and a pedagogical approach for realizing conceptual play.

Conclusion

The unity of imagination and cognition helps solve the pressing need early childhood teachers have – how to focus more explicitly on cognition within a play-based program. It has been argued in this article that conceptual play as a theoretical framework can support teachers in bringing together imagination and cognition in their play-based programs. This framing gives permission to teachers to take a more active role in leading conceptual development in play, but in ways which take into account the child's perspective. Imagination becomes an important bridge between play as a leading activity and learning as a leading activity.

The theoretical discussion in this article has foregrounded the importance of actively developing imagination as a psychological resource for improved cognitive outcomes for children, not just within the preschool years, but as the foundation for the school years. Some evidence for this claim can be found in research undertaken in the US (e.g., Bodrova, 2008; Diamond et al., 2007). It is through the unity of cognition and imagination that young children have the psychological resources they need to engage in the conscious movement between reality and abstract representations (ideal). The assumption that is made in this article is that, without these psychological resources, children will find it difficult to engage in the literacy and numeracy programs that governments are advocating. Indeed longitudinal research in the United Kingdom (Siraj-Blatchford, 2007, 2009) has shown that early childhood programs which have a major impact upon children's achievement in later school learning have had interactions between children and teachers where 'shared sustained thinking' occurs within play-based programs. Conceptual play provides a way of theorising how concept formation can occur within play-based programs without losing sight of the child. The unity of conceptual play and conceptual pedagogy are introduced as another tool for teachers when explicitly dealing with greater academic outcomes within the early childhood period. Conceptual play signals to all the importance of imagination for building concepts within the early childhood period and beyond.

Acknowledgement

The conceptual work in this article has been developed from the findings of an Australian Research Council Discovery grant. Avis Ridgway acted as the research assistant in this project. Special acknowledgment of the staff and children who participated in the study is also made. Valuable feedback from the reviewers and the chief editor was gained, which allowed for a clearer final work to be developed.

References

Aidarova, L. (1982). *Child development and education*. Progress Publishers.

Belfield, C., Nores, M., Barnett, W. S., & Schweinhart, L. (2005). Updating the benefit-cost analysis of the High/Scope Perry preschool program through age 40. *Educational Evaluation and Policy Analysis, 27*(3), 245–263.

Bodrova, E. (2008). Make-believe play versus academic skills: A Vygotskian approach to today's dilemma of early childhood education. *European Early Childhood Education Research Journal, 16*(3), 357–369. http://dx.doi.org/10.1080/13502930802291777

Bodrova, E., & Leong, D. J. (2001). *Tools of the mind: A case study of implementing the Vygotskian approach in American early childhood and primary classrooms*. Innodata Monographs – 7. UNESCO, International Bureau of Education.

Bretherton, I. (1984). *Symbolic play: The development of social understanding*. Academic Press.

Brock, A. (2009) Curriculum and pedagogy of play: A multitude of perspectives? In A. Brock, S. Dodds, P. Jarvis, & Y. Ousoga (Eds.), *Perspectives on play: Learning for life* (pp. 67–93). Pearson Longman.

Brooker, L. (2010). Learning to play, or playing to learn? Children's participation in the cultures of homes and settings. In L. Brooker & S. Edwards (Eds.), *Engaging play* (pp. 39–53). Open University Press.

Connery, M. C., John-Steiner, V. P., & Marjanovic-Shane, A. (Eds.). (2010). *Vygotsky and creativity: A cultural historical approach to play, meaning making and the arts*. Peter Lang.

Cullen, J. (2009). Co-constructing professional knowledge. In A. Anning, J. Cullen, & M. Fleer (Eds.), *Early childhood education: Society and culture* (pp. 80–90). Sage.

Davydov, V. V. (1984). Substantial generalization and the dialectical-materialistic theory of thinking. In M. Hedegaard, P. Hakkarainen, & Y. Engestrom (Eds.), *Learning and teaching on a scientific basis: Methodological and epistemological aspects of the activity theory of learning and teaching* (pp. 11–32). Psychology Institute, Aarhus University.

Davydov, V. V. (1972–1990). Types of generalization in instruction: Logical and psychological problems in the structuring of school curricula. *Soviet Studies in Mathematics Education, 2* (J. Teller, Trans.). National Council of Teachers of Mathematics.

Davydov, V. V. (2008). *Problems of developmental instruction: A theoretical and experimental psychological study*. Nova Science Publishers.

Department of Education, Employment and Workplace Relations. (2009). *Belonging, being and becoming: The early years learning framework for Australia*. Commonwealth of Australia.

Diamond, A., Barnett, W. S., Thomas, J., & Munro, S. (2007). Preschool program improves. *Cognitive Control, Science, 318*, 1387–1388.

Egan, K. (2005). *An imaginative approach to teaching*. Jossey-Bass.

Egan, K., & Madei, K. (Eds.). (2010). *Engaging imaginations and developing creativity in education*. Cambridge Scholars Press.

Egan, K., & Madoc-Jones, G. (2005). Editorial. *Education and Imagination, Teaching Education, 16*(1), 1–2. http://dx.doi.org/10.1080/1047621052000341563

Elkonin, D. B. (1993). The crisis of childhood and foundations for designing forms of child development. *Journal of Russian and East European Psychology, 31*(3), 56–71. http://dx.doi.org/10.2753/RPO1061-0405310356

Elkonin, D. B. (1999). The development of play in preschoolers. *Journal of Russian and East European Psychology, 37*(6), 31–70.

Elkonin, D. B. (2005). The psychology of play. *Journal of Russian and East European Psychology, 43*(1), 11–21.

Ferholt, B. (2010). A synthetic-analytic method for the study of perezhivanie: Vygotsky's literary analysis applied to playworlds. In M. C. Connery, V. P. John-Steiner, & A. Marjanovic-Shane (Eds.), *Vygotsky and creativity: A cultural-historical approach to play, meaning making and the arts* (pp. 163–180). Peter Lang.

Fleer, M. (2009). A cultural-historical perspective on play: Play as a lading activity across cultural communities. In I. Pramling-Samuelsson & M. Fleer (Eds.), *Play and learning in early childhood settings: International perspectives* (pp. 1–18). Springer.

Fleer, M. (2010). *Early learning and development: Cultural-historical concepts in play.* Cambridge University Press.

Gajdamaschko. (2005). Vygotsky on imagination: Why an understanding of the imagination is an important issue for schoolteachers. *Teaching Education, 16*(1), 13–22.

Gaskins, S., Haight, W., & Lancy, D. F. (2007). The cultural construction of play. In A. Goncu & S. Gaskins (Eds.), *Play and development: Evolutionary, sociocultural, and functional perspectives* (pp. 179–202). Lawrence Erlbaum.

Hakkarainen, P. (2006). Learning and development in olay. In J. Einarsdottir & J. T. Wagner (Eds.), *Nordic childhoods and early education: Philosophy, research, policy, and practice in Denmark, Finland, Iceland, Norway and Sweden* (pp. 183–222). Information Age Publishing.

Heckman, J. J., & Masterov, D. V. (2007). *The productivity argument for investing in young children.* Discussion Paper 2725. Institute for Labour Study.

Hedegaard, M. (2002). *Learning and child development: A cultural-historical study.* Aarhus University Press.

Hedegaard, M. (2008). A cultural-historical theory of children's development. In M. Hedegaard & M. Fleer (Eds.), *Studying children: A cultural-historical approach* (pp. 10–29). Open University Press.

Hedegaard, M. (2009). Children's development from a cultural-historical approach: Children's activity in everyday local settings as foundation for their development. *Mind, Culture and Activity, 16*, 64–81. http://dx.doi.org/10.1080/10749030802477374

Hedges, M., & Cullen, J. (2005). Subject knowledge in early childhood curriculum and pedagogy: Beliefs and practices. *Contemporary Issues in Early Childhood, 6*(1), 66–79. http://dx.doi.org/10.2304/ciec.2005.6.1.10

Holzman, L. (2009). *Vygotsky at work and play.* Routledge.

Holzman, L. (2010). Without creating ZPDs there is no creativity. In M. C. Connery, V. P. John-Steiner, & A. Marjanovic-Shane (Eds.), *Vygotsky and creativity: A cultural-historical approach to play, meaning making and the arts* (pp. 27–40). Peter Lang.

John-Steiner, V. P., Connery, M. C., & Marjanovic-Shane, A. (2010). Dancing with the muses: A cultural-historical approach to play, meaning making and creativity. In M. C. Connery, V. P. John-Steiner, & A. Marjanovic-Shane (Eds.), *Vygotsky and creativity: A cultural-historical approach to play, meaning making and the arts* (pp. 3–16). Peter Lang.

Karpov, Y. V. (2005). *The neo-vygotskian approach to child development.* Cambridge University Press.

Kravtsov, G. G. (2009). *Periods of psychic development* [Conference session]. Paper presented at the Golden Key Summer School Program. Belay Kylavita, Russia, 26 June.

Kravtsov, G. G., & Kravtsova, E. E. (2009). Cultural-historical psychology in the practice of education. In M. Fleer, M. Hedegaard, & T. Jonathan (Eds.), *Childhood studies and the impact of globalization: Policies and practices at global and local levels: World yearbook of education* (pp. 202–212). Routledge.

Kravtsova, E. E. (2006). The concept of age-specific new psychological formations in contemporary developmental psychology. *Journal of Russian and East European Psychology, 44*(6), 6–18. http://dx.doi.org/10.2753/RPO1061-0405440601

Kravtsova, E. E. (2008). *Using play for teaching and learning.* Monash University, Peninsula Campus, 15 December 2008.

Kravtsova, Y. Y. (2005). The concept of age: Novel formation in modern developmental psychology. *Cultural Historical Psychology, 1*(2), 23–24.

McCain, M., & Mustard, F. (1999). *Early years study final report: Reversing the real brain drain.* Founders Network.

McCain, M., & Mustard, F. (2002). *Early years study three years later.* Founders Network.

Mitchell, L., Wylie, C., & Carr, M. (2008). *Outcomes of early childhood education: Literature review: Report to the ministry of education.* Ministry of Education.

National Research Council & Institute of Medicine. (2000). From neurons to neighborhoods: The science of early childhood development. Committee on integrating the science of early childhood development. In J. P. Shonkoff & D. A Phillips (Eds.), *Board on children, youth, and families, commission on behavioral and social sciences and education.* National Academy Press.

Piaget, J. (1962). *Play, dreams, and imitation in childhood.* W.W. Norton.

Parten, M. (1932). Social participation among preschool children. *Journal of Abnormal and Social Psychology, 27,* 243–269. http://dx.doi.org/10.1037/h0074524

Parten, M. (1933). Social play among preschool children. *Journal of Abnormal and Social Psychology, 28,* 136–147. http://dx.doi.org/10.1037/h0073939

Rubin, K. H., Fein, G. G., & Vandenberg, B. (1983). Play. In P. H. Mussen (Ed.), *Handbook on child psychology* (4th ed., vol. 4, pp. 693–774). John Wiley.

Schweinhart, L. J., & Weikart, D. P. (1997). The high/scope perry preschool curriculum comparison study through age 23. *Early Childhood Research Quarterly, 12,* 117–143. http://dx.doi.org/10.1016/S0885-2006(97)90009-0

Schweinhart, L. J., & Weikart, D. P. (1998). Why curriculum matters in early childhood education. *Educational Leadership, 55*(6), 57–60.

Schweinhart, L. J., & Weikart, D. P. (1999). The advantages of high/scope: Helping children lead successful lives. *Educational Leadership, 57*(1), 76–78.

Schweinhart, L. J., Weikart, D. P., & Larner, M. B. (1986). Consequences of three preschool curriculum models through age 15. *Early Childhood Research Quarterly, 1*(1), 15–46. http://dx.doi.org/10.1016/0885-2006(86)90005-0

Shore, R. (1997). *Rethinking the brain: New insights into early development.* Families & Work Institute.

Siraj-Blatchford, I. (2007). Creativity, communication and collaboration: The identification of pedagogic progression in sustained shared thinking. *Asia Pacific Journal of Research in Early Childhood Education, 1*(2), 3–23.

Siraj-Blatchford, I. (2009). Quality teaching in the early years. In A. Anning, J. Cullen, & M. Fleer (Eds.), *Early childhood education: Society and culture* (pp. 137–148). Sage.

Smilansky, S. (1968). *The effects of socio-dramatic play on disadvantaged pre-school children.* Wiley.

Sylva, K., Mehuish, E., Sammons, P., Siraj-Blatchford, I., & Taggart, B. (2004). *The final report: Effective preschool education*, Technical Paper 12. Institute of Education, University of London.

Ugaste, A. (2005). The child's play world at home and the mother's role in the play, Jyvaskyla studies in education. *Psychology and Social Research, 259*, University of Jyvaskyla.

Van Oers, B. (1999). Teaching opportunities in play. In M. Hedegaard & J. Lompscher (Eds.), *Learning, activity and development* (pp. 268–289). Aarhus University Press.

Van Oers, B. (2008). Inscripting predicates: Dealing with meanings in play. In B. Van Oers, W. Wardekker, E. Elbers, & R. Van der Veer (Eds.), *The transformation of learning: Advances in cultural-historical activity theory* (pp. 370–379). Cambridge University Press. http://dx.doi.org/10.1017/CBO9780511499937.023

Van Oers, B. (2009). Developmental education: Improving participation in cultural practices. In M. Fleer, M. Hedegaard, & J. Tudge (Eds.), *Childhood studies and the impact of globalization: Policies and practices at global and local levels: World yearbook of education* (pp. 213–229). Routledge.

Van Oers, B. (2010). Children's enculturation through play. In L. Brooker & S. Edwards (Eds.), *Engaging play* (pp. 195–209). Open University Press.

Vygotsky, L. S. (1966). Play and its role in the mental development of the child. *Voprosy Psikhologii, 12*(6), 62–76.

Vygotsky, L. S. (1978). *Mind in society.* Harvard University Press.

Vygotsky, L. S. (1987). Imagination and its development in childhood. In R. W. Rieber & A. S. Carton (Eds.), *The collected works of L.S. Vygotsky. Vol. 1, Problems of General Psychology* (N. Minick, Trans.). (pp. 339–350). Plenum Press.

Vygotsky, L. S. (2004). Imagination and creativity in childhood. *Journal of Russian and East European Psychology, 42*(1), 7–97.

Wylie, C., Hodgen, E., Ferral, H., & Thompson, J. (2006). *Contributions of early childhood education to age-14 performance.* New Zealand Council for Educational Research.

Wylie, C., & Thompson, J. (2003). The long-term contribution of early childhood education to children's performance: Evidence from New Zealand. *International Journal of Early Years Education, 11*(1), 69–78.

Building an Evidence-Based Model for Early Childhood Science Education

The Place of Emotions in Science, Motivating Learning into Play, and the Teacher in Play Relations

Abstract

The trajectory of empirical and theoretical movement towards understanding imagination in play and imagination in STEM has its inception within this chapter. It is through the suite of 3 papers (Papers 3–5) that foundational evidence is built for developing an evidence-based model for the intentional teaching of science in play-based programs. Paper 3 brings new thinking from cultural-historical theory forward through affective imagining, where cognition and imagination are studied as drama. The dramatic moments create a tension that is motivating for children. But Paper 3 does not solve the problem of a child's motives for learning science, or the motivating conditions needed for learning in play-based settings. It is in Paper 4 that the different leading activity of two children (one to play and one to learning) in a play-based setting are identified. Studying how children with a different leading activity interact during free choice time brings out an important dynamic tension that has so far been unrecognised in play-based programs. Paper 5 takes this further by studying the role of the teacher in imaginary play, and identifying a typology that has implications for capturing, maintaining and amplifying the learning of science concepts in play-based settings.

Keywords

motives – demands – pedagogical positioning – affective imagination – digital – leading activity – pair pedagogy – discovery learning – process skills – social situation of development – drama – emotions

•••

I am walking down the dark and rather unattractive corridor of what is now the old education building at Monash University. The Dean at that time hears me talking with colleagues as I am walking. She rushes from her office and intercepts me with shouts of congratulations on winning an ARC Discovery grant with Richard Gunstone.

It was my first ARC grant, and I was emotionally charged with excitement. I had not expected this good news, even though I had impeccable mentoring from Richard – who kept asking me questions about things I wrote about early childhood that were not obvious to someone from outside of the field. My responses to his questions with new text in the application was critical for the success of the application. At the time, all the assessors were from outside of early childhood education.

The title of the ARC discovery grant was aligned with the problem I had identified previously, of how to bring into play-based settings the learning of science concepts: *The sociocultural construction of early childhood science learning: Learning of scientific concepts within situated playful encounters in early childhood contexts.*

I was finally not alone in my quest to better understand science learning in play-based settings. How this developed as a result of this prestigious resourcing, and what was learned about early childhood science education, is presented in this chapter across a set of three papers – which together paved the way for building an evidence-based model of early childhood science education (Chapter 4).

1 Big Research Problems Need a Suite of ARC Discovery Grants

Sitting in my office at my previous university, The Vice Chancellor Don Aikin, popped his head into my office and said, "You should come up to the Chancellery for a chat about your future". I of course assumed he was just being nice and encouraging. I didn't for one moment expect he really meant it, or would have time to simply chat with me about my career. So, I did not follow up. A month later, the Deputy VC was at a meeting I was at. He sat next to me and whilst we waited for the meeting to start, he asked, "Are you busy after this meeting?". I said if the meeting does not run over, then yes, I am free. At the conclusion of the meeting, he walked with me to the Chancellery mentioning that I should be applying for a personal chair, and as we neared his door he turned to me and said, "Now that you are this far, go in that door and make an appointment with the VC's PA. He is expecting you".

One of the things I learned from the VC was that a professor has to have a scholarly vision. He asked me, "What do you stand for? What is your vision? What do you profess?".

My ARC with Richard was the first step in realising my vision. The theoretical problem demanded more than one ARC grant as Figure 3.1 shows.

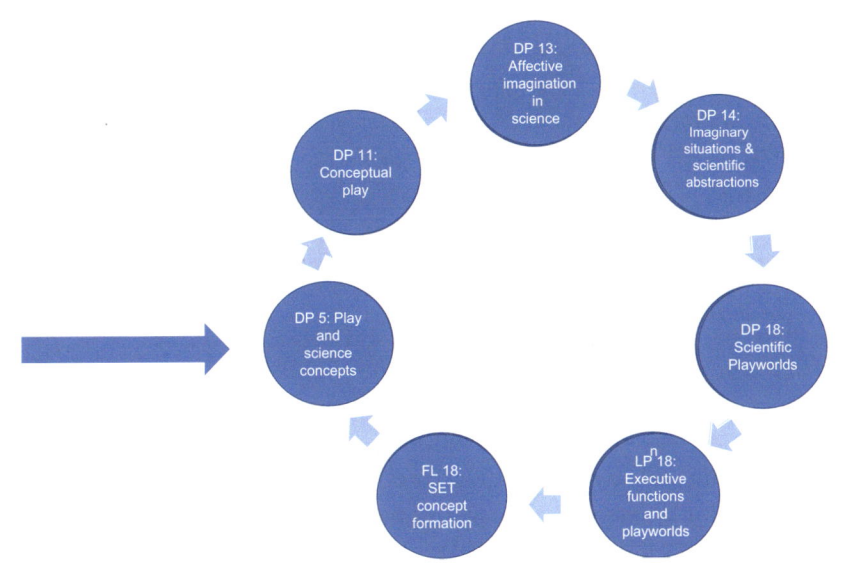

FIGURE 3.1   Australian Research Council grants between 2005–2018

Big research problems need a suite of research grants. The ARC grants (DP5-DP18) incrementally resourced the theoretical problem of how to bring STEM concepts into a play-based program.

In 2005 when Richard Gunstone and I were awarded our ARC Discovery grant we wanted to study the organization of early childhood children's participation in everyday routines in the home and across cultural communities in order to better understand how scientific learning in everyday practice takes place. The study was framed from a cultural-historical perspective – although at the time of writing the ARC application, I was still using the term sociocultural theory.

We had huge aims for the research.

Aim 1: How, in playful contexts such as early childhood settings and home settings, do scientific ideas:
– move and change with individuals?
– are appropriated across groups of children and adults?
– move and change as a result of the topics and the respective concepts being investigated?
– are constructed differently as a result of the family and cultural belief?
– move and change as a result of the play-based pedagogy found in early childhood education?

This conceptualisation was directly tied to cultural-historical theory (Chapter 2). But importantly, the results would set the stage for the second aim which was oriented to beginning the important work of building a model of science teaching that would be suitable for supporting teachers who worked in early childhood education and other play-based environments. However, it was not until much later that the model was developed (see Chapter 4) and researched (Chapter 5).

Aim 2: Use these results to begin the process of building models of science teaching suitable for supporting teachers who work in early childhood and other play-based settings

I had been most ambitious in what we had expected to achieve.

In line with Chapter 1, my rationale was not to blame the victim who had limited access to science education because of the low expectations for girls and women in those fields. I had in mind what Margaret Carr called a 'credit model'. A positive view of early childhood teachers' capacity could perhaps reveal something different. We wrote the abstract in a way that positioned the problem not as one of teachers' lack of competence, but rather as teachers not yet having the right model of practice – after all, it was well established at this point that no such model had been built on research for play-based settings (Chapter 1). We expressed it like this in the application:

> Gaining a better understanding about how scientific learning can be organized within playful early childhood contexts would lead to more appropriate models of science teaching for Australian early childhood teachers, more science being taught, and a more scientific literate population.

What I did not know then, was that Richard and I could not achieve the second aim because there was just so much to learn about the nature of children's play and how this had to be conceptualised and studied differently if we were to work out how to bring in the learning of science concepts. As reported in Chapter 2, we began to capture this dynamic complexity between play and science learning as *Conceptual Play*.

Building on this first ARC study, the second ARC Discovery application was also funded, and that went further by actually researching *Conceptual Play* – But did so with a renewed emphasis on imagination and cognition – two concurrent problems of bringing concepts into children's play, and using children's imagination to think abstractly about the science they cannot actually see. The title of the grant was:

> Conceptual play: Foregrounding imagination and cognition during concept formation in early years science education

The international trend to increase the cognitive achievement of early childhood children was now a central focus of governments in Australia (Chapter 2). This goal had generated a need for better understanding how concept formation occurs within play-based programs. Yet none of the theories of play were originally conceptualized with this need in mind.

Therefore, the second ARC investigated how cognition and imagination worked together to support conceptual development in science for preschool aged children. At the time it was argued that these data were urgently needed for the creation of a new theory of learning through play which could lead to concept formation within the early childhood years.

The research question was theoretical: How do preschool aged children give scientific meaning (sense field) to the objects in their world (objective field) as they move in and out of an imaginary situation?

Solving this theoretical problem was important for better understanding the nature of children's play, the psychological function of imagination, and how this changed over the cultural age periods. This was only one small theoretical part of building a new model of science teaching – but this time the proposal to the ARC was not so ambitious with its aim of solving the latter problem.

These two ARC grants were just the beginning. Whilst we could begin to establish a theoretical relationship between play and learning science concepts, this alone could not deal with the problem of how to build learning over time for such young children in play settings. This too was both a theoretical problem and a problem of practice – how to tie learnings from one science lesson/experience to another science lesson/experience on another day. It is a challenge of practice because young children experience the world *in the moment*. A model of teaching science in play settings would need to deal with this aspect of a child's psychological functioning. As was discussed in Chapter 1, young children changed their thinking from moment to moment.

Discovery learning and process approaches as models of practice gave some direction (Fleer & Pramling, 2015). As did an interactive approach to teaching science (Biddulph & Osborne, 1984), where a question drove the inquiry and answering it over days and weeks worked for older children. This important work was coming from New Zealand and guiding teachers who wanted to engage with alternative views held by children. But this model did not work for preschool aged children (Fleer, 1992).

The research on interactive teaching in preschool settings flushed out the problem that children just didn't ask scientific questions when in preschool, let alone investigable questions (Fleer, 1996). Stimulating the question asking of children through discovery activities, as was suggested in Biddulph and

Osborne's (1984) interactive teaching model, didn't solve the problem of how to turn a question into an inquiry for children in the birth to five sector.

What could drive children to want to keep going from day to day on a single problem? My PhD data with gasps from my supervisor, had already established it was challenging. How could you propel or motivate preschool children into wanting to solve a problem they had encountered when playing with resources?

2   Bringing in Emotions and Drama into Science

In 2013 another ARC discovery application was submitted with this problem in mind. Although the title might not appear at first glance to reflect this research question:

> Affective imagination in science education: Exploring the emotional nature of scientific and technological learning and engaging children and teachers

The successful ARC Discovery application was framed around two key research questions:
1.   What are the relations between affect and intellect in group settings where fairy tales act as a cultural device for framing scientific and technological learning?
2.   What is the emotional nature of the scientific and technological learning and how do teachers engage in and mediate this through fairy tales?

The science education research community had entered into a new era in research where emotions were allowed. Objective truth devoid of humans had long since passed. Many were making inroad into this important area – with some studying feelings and emotions related to the learning of science concepts. The important research of Alberto Bellocchi continues until today. In 2013 though, the research looked very different for preschool children.

The research was elaborated as:

> The emotional nature of scientific and technological enquiry of young children is investigated in order to find out how to motivate and increase concept formation in science teaching in preschools. The research will make visible the relations between affect and cognition in group settings where fairy tales act as a cultural device for framing scientific learning, and where children use emotional imagination to work scientifically.

The study will yield foundational knowledge about how affect interacts with concept formation, as well as, generate new early childhood science teaching methodologies that engage early childhood teachers to teach more science.

Could creating emotionally charged situations in a narrative context of a fairy tale be the driving force for linking science learning from day to day in play-based settings? Could this solve the problem of how to bring into play a scientific inquiry for children under five years? Paper 3 speaks to these problems.

2.1 Paper 3: Affective Imagination in Science Education: Determining the Emotional Nature of Scientific and Technological Learning of Young Children

Paper 3 brings out seven key ideas about children and teachers co-experiencing an emotionally charged narrative of a fairy tale of Goldilocks and the 3 Bears to support science learning.

1. *Distributed nature of science learning in early childhood settings*: The collective sense of investigating was always present. In the paper an example of the children investigating a rainbow whist setting up the 3 bear's house is presented. The children and teacher collectively studied the spectrum of light in a rainbow by looking through coloured lenses at a rainbow that was projected on the wall

2. *Need for a collective scientific narrative to join up experiences*: The idea of inventing a porridge-cooling machine had arisen when the children were discussing the porridge across both the everyday context of cooking porridge and also the imaginary context where they sought to help the bears by inventing a cooling down machine for the porridge (pp. 2026–2027). The central idea of cooling and heating as a process of energy transfer as a result of a temperature difference is something that is not only of personal interest to children (e.g., so they do not burn their tongues when eating porridge) but, as explained in the re-published paper that follows, it is also within children's grasp when a narrative is developed collectively to support scientific thinking.

3. *Affective scientific imagination*: The anticipation of "hot porridge" and the need for "cooling the porridge" created an emotional tension in the story which built an affective scientific imaginary situation.

4. *Flickering between real and imaginative scientific worlds*: Through flickering between the real and imaginary worlds, a new scientific self-awareness and scientific perspective were developing for the children. Science becomes a valuable tool for early childhood children for helping them

solve the problems inherent in the fairy tale, such as designing a porridge-cooling machine.

5. *Taking a scientific perspective*: Everyday understandings of "hot porridge" and "cold porridge" lay important foundations for understanding the scientific concept of "heating and cooling". A cultural– historical theorization would suggest that conductivity, convection and radiation could only be understood through the everyday experiences and discussions of "hot" and "cold" (p. 2102).
6. *Emotional filtering*: The teacher emotionally charges events: The teacher knowingly created situations that helped the children to pay attention to scientifically noteworthy situations and through this gave the possibility for scientific discussions and learning (p. 2103).
7. *A scientific gaze*: When children consciously experience things, they are more likely to not only pay "scientific" attention, but are positioned positively to make scientific meaning of their everyday lives (p. 2103).

The emotional nature of science learning brings out drama not as a pedagogy in the traditional sense of the practice, but as a theoretical concept for solving the problem of how to create the motivating conditions for children and teachers to engage in science concepts – from day to day (see below, Fleer, 2012a, 2012b, 2016a; Fleer et al., 2014, 2019; Fleer & Hammer, 2013).

A series of publications emerged where affective imagination as a concept from cultural-historical theory brought with it children and teachers co-experiencing science learning through the narrative of a fairy tale and family folktales important for different cultural communities, such as Dinka families living in Australia (Fleer, Adams, Gunstone & Hao, 2016).

– Fleer, M. (2012). Imagination, emotions and scientific thinking: What matters in the being and becoming of a teacher of elementary science? *Cultural Studies of Science Education, 7*(1), 31–39. https://doi.org/10.1007/s11422-011-9365-z
– Fleer, M., & Hammer, M. (2013). 'Perezhivanie' in group settings: A cultural-historical reading of emotion regulation. *Australasian Journal of Early Childhood, 38*(3), 127–134. https://doi.org/10.1177/183693911303800316
– Fleer, M., Hammer, M., & March, S. (2014). A cultural-historical reading of the emotional development of young children. *Asia-Pacific Journal of Research in Early Childhood Education, 8*(2), 47–67. http://www.pecerajournal.com/detail/62138
– Fleer, M., Adams, M., Gunstone, R., & Hao, Y. (2016). Studying the landscape of families and children's emotional engagement in science across cultural

contexts. *International Research in Early Childhood Education, 7*(1), 122–141. https://eric.ed.gov/?id=EJ1138874

– Fleer, M. (2016). An everyday and theoretical reading of "Perezhivanie" for informing research in early childhood education. *International Research in Early Childhood Education, 7*(1), 34–49. https://doi.org/https://eric.ed.gov/?id=EJ1138756

– Fleer, M., Adams, M., & Gunstone, R. (2019). Transformative pedagogy: Dinka playgroups as spaces for cultural knowledge productions of Western science. *Cultural Studies of Science Education, 14*(4), 1045–1069. https://doi.org/10.1007/s11422-018-9908-7

But the research into affective imagination did not fill the gap in understanding the emotional nature of science learning in a fast-paced technological world. In 2014 a further ARC Discovery grant sought to investigate the relations between imaginary situations and scientific abstractions in preschool digital play:

> Imaginative play is the leading activity of preschoolers. But imagination is also important in scientific work – see work of Niels Bohr, Barbara McClintock. Aided through digital tablet technology to create animations of scientific learning, this study examines how imaginative play helps children to imagine scientific explanations not visibly supported in real life, such as the Earth circling the Sun, or science concepts not directly observable, such as, how sugar dissolves faster in hot water. Studying imagination in play and imagination in science will contribute to new understandings about the nature of science teaching in preschools.

Something new was being proposed by bringing imagination and abstract thinking together in a context of how thought leaders in science conceptualised their work. The rationale was centred on the idea that if eminent scientists used imagination (Barbara McClintock: see Fox Keller, 1983) and theoretical thinking (Bohr, 1950) when acting scientifically, so too could young children.

Barbara McClintock was famous for working differently in science. She imagined herself going down the microscope and into the petri dish to study genes, whilst she was recalling the corn fields she tended as part of her science laboratory. By doing this, she revolutionised the course of genetics because she conceptualised a new paradigm in research with her concept of the jumping gene.

But how did her way of working scientifically inspire the research into children imagining science concepts they could not see?

The virtual platform gave a new theoretical space to interrogate because it was both in a child's physical reality, and their virtual experience. This contradiction of physical and virtual was rich with possibilities for deepening research because it needed very different kinds of research questions:

1. How do digital tablet technologies and virtual play by children help them to make visible abstract science concepts?
2. What is the nature of the relationship between imagination in play and imagination in science for preschool aged children?

This grant generated new thinking and publications about the virtual scientific learning lives of children. But this research was only a stepping stone to thinking differently about the core problem that began in Chapter 1.

The published work that came from the results of this particular ARC research focused on something very different. Each paper unpacked one dimension – such as how a child with visual impairment positively engaged in their world through the magnification power of an iPad (Fleer & March, 2015), how digital tools align and amplify children's imaginary play (Fleer, 2016b), and how digital tools change the developmental trajectories of children because digital tools capture and make conscious the scientific concepts they are using in their role play (Fleer, 1917, 2020):

- Fleer, M., & March, S. (2015). Conceptualizing science learning as a collective social practice: Changing the social pedagogical compass for a child with visual impairment. *Cultural Studies of Science Education, 10*(3), 803–831. https://doi.org/10.1007/s11422-014-9616-x
- Fleer, M. (2016). Theorising digital play: A cultural-historical conceptualisation of children's engagement in imaginary digital situations. *International Research in Early Childhood Education, 7*(2), 75–90. https://eric.ed.gov/?id=EJ1138705
- Fleer, M. (2017). Digital role-play: The changing conditions of children's play in preschool settings. *Mind, Culture, and Activity, 24*(1), 3–17. https://doi.org/https://doi.org/10.1080/10749039.2016.1247456
- Fleer, M. (2020). Examining the psychological content of digital play through Hedegaard's model of child development. *Learning, Culture and Social Interaction, 26*, 100227. https://doi.org/10.1016/j.lcsi.2018.04.006

This research set the stage for a closer alignment between children's motives and the motivating conditions created in preschools to learn science. But a further paradigm shift was needed to propel this research agenda forward. But to understand this shift, we need an interlude into a theoretical journey that was necessary for re-analysing the ARC data so that the core problem of imagination in play and imagination in STEM could move forward.

3 Motives and Motivating Conditions

The ground is covered in snow. Freezing conditions are forecast for all those assembled at the Vygotsky Institute, Russian State University for the Humanities. Professor Elena Kravstova is the conference president. She is L.S. Vygotsky's granddaughter. I am sitting in the conference room totally overdressed in what feels like a sauna. No one told me that European temperature settings were so high. I had no sleep. Time difference between Australia and Moscow did not help.

Elena stands proud and tall and through a translator announces that the medal for outstanding contributions to cultural-historical theory is to go to the new ISCAR president, Professor Marilyn Fleer. I am shocked. I did not know there was such a medal. I felt like a rabbit stunned by head lights from a car. I am asked to receive the award and to make a speech. I stand. But have no idea what to say. Seth Chaiklin, the previous ISCAR president looks to me as I start walking to the podium. I say to him as I walk, "What do I say?". He supportively says, "Just be presidential". Sage advice.

I stand tall and take on a presidential pose. The fear leaves me, and I speak with confidence about the importance of cultural-historical theory, and the significant role of the Vygotsky Institute and its champion Professor Elena Kravstova. She both validated and brought forward to the international community the Collected Works of L.S Vygotsky. Dorothy Robbins a friend of Elena's later said to me that my points about cultural-historical theory, rather than sociocultural theory, as the terminology of choice for me now, was controversial and brave, but important for recognising the origins of this body of work.

ISCAR is the acronym for the International Society for Cultural-historical Activity Research. It is the premier society that brings together scholars interested in the study of the human condition. Importantly, the Society draws on the foundational concepts of L.S. Vygotsky and his collaborators and followers over generations.

I didn't know about the Society and the Congress that it hosts each three years until I emailed Barbara Rogoff and asked her advice on which conferences to go to. Her reply was swift, "ISCAR is one of the best". But what is ISCAR? I had never heard of this acronym. In her next email she wrote it out in full and then I recalled Bert van Oers encouraging me to go to this conference after I had presented a paper at an early childhood conference – European Early

Childhood Education Research Association. At the end of the presentation, he came up to me, and said pointing to my overhead transparency (yes that was the technology of choice then), "Do you see all those names – Elkonin, Davydov, Leontiev – the Congress that discusses their ideas is ISCAR. You should go".

Two of my theoretical ideals had recommended the same Congress. Jumping on to the website I saw that the date for submitting a paper had passed. But there was hope. The Congress chair was Bert van Oers! I emailed him and asked if I could still sign up to attend, and could I still present a paper? "Of course" came the immediate reply. That proved to be an important turn of events for me and my research.

At the Congress I found on display publications from Arhus University. I bought every single title I could find on cultural-historical theory – no matter how hard it was going to be to bring them home to Australia in my luggage.

At the Congress I learned about a section called CHACDOC – Mariane Hedegaard was its founder and champion – and still is.

CHACDOC is the acronym that describes those researchers interested in Cultural-Historical Approaches to Children's Development and Childhood.

On the website it says, "The purpose of this section is to create a forum for researchers who are interested in developmental psychology and childhood, with a special focus on using activity theory and the cultural-historical research approach as a way to unite these two opposing approaches to the study of children. Developmental psychology has often been characterised historically as the study of 'the general child', with a focus on developing a model that can be used to evaluate individual children and their changing relation to society as they grow up. Childhood studies have focused on the study of children anchored in historical time and settings; such approaches are more commonly found within anthropological and sociological traditions, especially those that focus on situated and localised practice with children. Cultural-historical approaches seek to unite the general principles in relation to historical time and place".[1]

Mariane's thesis is that demands afford new possibilities for children's development (Hedegaard, 2009). Central to the child's transition from one institutional practice to another is how demands in the new practice are successfully negotiated. This began a new chapter in my journey in solving the problem of how to bring concepts into play through the lens of Davydov's work on theoretical thinking and significantly for my thinking on the place of core concepts, as discussed by Mariane and Seth in relation to a germ cell (Hedegaard & Chaiklin, 2005) – something that Conceptual Play was seeking to achieve.

Mariane Hedegaard became the single most important person in my academic journey.

4   **Leaping Forward …**

I am sitting at Mariane's desk in her light and airy apartment in Copenhagen. We discuss many concepts in a context of a joint study we had conceptualised and independently gathered data for across countries. This research was realised as a book published with Cambridge University Press (Hedegaard & Fleer, 2013).

The conceptual journey began as we studied how everyday life for children from different families across Australia and Copenhagen created drama. The drama we found in everyday life, such as, when being asked to go to bed, or leaving the house to arrive on time at school. These moments of drama were important for children's development. Drama gave developmental possibilities when successfully resolved. Analysing the family data was almost like doing my PhD all over again, but this time having a colleague who knew the central concepts established by Vygotsky well, and me having the collected works to delve into as I struggled with the theoretical problem we had pioneered.

Someone once asked me what I would take from my house if a bush fire was approaching – I would take the baby photos, and then the Collected Works of L.S. Vygotsky (1987, 1993, 1997a, 1997b, 1998, 1999), with all of my annotated comments and highlights. I had read and re-read each volume many times. Every challenge I faced was met with another dive into the Collected Works.

Moving from Mariane's desk to a café in the afternoon was our routine. My sabbatical was enriched by the café experience of discussing our joint research. This book and the many papers published as forerunners to it, had developed my mind and now I was ready to go back to the central problem that is the focus of this book – the relations between play and science learning? It had sat dormant in my mind whilst I was conceptually and theoretically enriched by the work of Mariane Hedegaard and our joint project.

5   **Going Back …**

Funded by the ARC, I had decided to go deeper into the theoretically complex question of digital play. By moving into a green field of children creating animations of their science and play experiences – Goldilocks and the 3 bears – this offered children the possibility to study heat as a core science concept.

Mariane had said that the "child's motives are related to what is meaningful and important for them" and that "A child's motive is related to the child's intentions in specific situations, but a person's motives surpass the specific situation and can be seen as the dynamic that characteristics specific activities across different situations" (Hedegaard, 2012, p. 134).

Consequently, an activity is only motivating for a child if the activity setting is linked with the child's already developed motives. Therefore, the problem of cooling down the porridge before Goldilocks visits, seemed a motivating condition for children to learn science concepts, because it was personally meaningful and aligned with the leading activity of play.

Putting props out on a table to role-play the fairy tale gave opportunities to explore the narrative of the story, but also to use the photographic function on the digital device to capture images of the story being retold. When photographic images are put together, they create a movie of the story and the experience of cooking the porridge in the microwave. I went back to the data armed with new concepts to understand the new demands that are placed on children and teachers alike during free choice time in a preschool when a digital device is introduced for making an animation. This time I drew on the dialectical concepts of the social situation of development and the social situation (Vygotsky, 1994) and examined the children's play in a context of the leading activity for play. Paper 4 is the result of this analysis.

5.1 *Paper 4: The Demands and Motives Afforded through Digital Play in Early Childhood Activity Settings*

Two children's experiences were studied – Owen and Ginger. Initially, I was interested to know, "How children moved between imagination and reality within the concrete activity setting of free play where digital tablets were made available?". But as I analysed the data, I could see that it was not enough to look at the new demands of the digital device and make an animation, I had to also look at each child's social situation of development – was it for play or was it for learning?

In the study it was found that Owen's motive orientation was towards play, and he was not interested to learn how to use the slowmation app and to make an animation (for the children this was a movie)—other than pressing the camera button.

However, for Ginger, she found the activity motivating because she was interested to learn how to make a movie and represent the story in a new way. She was not oriented to playing with the objects but rather she was motivated towards using the objects to achieve the goals of the activity setting.

Mariane (Hedegaard, 2012) had advised that in educational settings it is important to be aware of the "child's motive orientation as well as directing the introduced activities towards supporting new motives" (p. 135).

It was determined through the study that Owen did not take up the learning goals of an activity setting when his leading activity was to play. Whilst Ginger's leading activity was to learn. An analysis of the new demands created through the introduction of digital tablets in the play-based setting gave the possibilities for understanding this new dimension of learning in play not previously discussed in the literature. This gave new insights that I could take forward in subsequent research. Moving sideways and armed with new concepts (Fleer, 2018b, 2019), had paid off.

Two additional papers were published which brought a step change in solving the theoretical problem from looking concepts in play, to the question of the relations between imagination and science concepts.

- Fleer, M. (2018). Digital animation: New conditions for children's development in play-based setting. *British Journal of Educational Technology, 49*(5), 943–958. https://doi.org/10.1111/bjet.12637
- Fleer, M. (2019). Digitally amplified practices: Beyond binaries and towards a profile of multiple digital coadjuvants. *Mind, Culture, and Activity, 26*(3), 207–220. https://doi.org/10.1080/10749039.2019.1646289

Whilst the focus of the research that Mariane and I did was anchored in the conceptual work she had developed, the orientation was primarily to children and not teachers. I was still thinking about the second aim in my first ARC discovery grant, and how Richard I also wanted to build a model of teaching for early childhood educators. I was now interested to look more closely at the teachers and the motivating conditions they created in relation to children's play. But there were some obstacles to realising this research agenda.

Teachers inside of children's play was a 'no go zone'. I had been to many conferences and read many books where the focus was on play. Play had always been core to the work of early childhood teachers and is a key pedagogical tool, whilst also being the source of preschool children's development. The message in the literature was clear. It cannot be play if adults are involved. Another Piagetian shadow to contend with as research moves forward in early childhood science education. Could another theoretical perspective on play change how the role of the teacher could be conceptualised? Vygotsky's granddaughter had been researching play for some time and had further developed Vygotsky's cultural-historical conception of play.

6   Thinking Differently about the Problem: Teachers inside of
        Children's Play

Great excitement abounds as Professor Elena Kravtsova comes to Monash University. Elena was another one of our visiting scholars. We felt privileged that she had accepted our invitation to come. But she was on a mission. She work-shopped concepts with us for 8 hours each day for 4 weeks, even though we had tried to take her to see the sights of Melbourne. She was determined she would not return to Moscow until she felt confident that we fully understood the key cultural-historical concepts pertinent to play as a source of development for young children. She brought to Monash University two key ideas. One was the pedagogy of the Golden Key Schools, and the second was the active role of the teacher.

The key idea that was of greatest interest to our research group was how Elena Kravtsova (Kravtsov & Kravtsova, 2010) described the role of the adult. It was not just a child/ren interacting with a teacher, but rather she conceptualised 3 important aspects of interactions in classrooms:

1. multi-age group settings
2. different pedagogical positions – primordial we, equal, above, below and independent.
3. teachers working into pairs – pair pedagogues

First, she said that in extended families, rather than nuclear families, we find that adults – and there are many – and children all relate to each other in unique ways. She said that in extended families expertise is distributed across the whole family. For instance, if grandma is the expert in a particular method of planting, she will teach the grandchildren how to produce the best harvest. If a child is good at using the mobile phone, then the child teaches grandma to download an app for ordering their meal, or to use a QR code when checking into a restaurant. Grandma and the grandchildren are living in a multi-age group and are not in a learning context as we see in classrooms and centres, where same age cohorts are all together. The latter positions the teacher as primarily having all of the expertise.

The second related idea is the 'positioning' of the teacher. Returning to the idea of the extended family and the different roles members of the family have with each other, it becomes possible to see how Grandma was above the grandchildren in her expertise of gardening, but in relation to using the mobile phone it was the children who were in the above position. An interactive moment between the teacher and children can be categorised in many ways, and Elena's research into the Golden Key Schools identified five roles: as 'above the child', 'equal with the child', 'below the child', 'child as independent of the teacher' and in the 'primordial we' position. The equal position means that children and the teacher are working side by side with equal expertise. The primordial we position fuses the adult and child as one working unit – as though an umbilical cord is connecting them. Elena Kravstova showed this is classrooms when an adult puts their hand over the child's hand and supports them with letter writing or cutting and tearing paper. However, this can also be conceptual, as we might see when a child and adult count together with an adult supporting one-to-one correspondence and numeral naming as a child and adult go up and down a step – sometimes in the arms of the adult, feeling the count; and other times walking each step together. The independent position is where the adult and child are together, but the child is leading whilst also socially referencing back to the adult to ensure they are still there as they take risks. The adult gives more space for agency and risk taking conceptually and physically. The emotional or conceptual tether is long but is still in existence and wanted by the child despite saying they can do something on their own.

The third related idea is to have more than one teacher in a classroom or centre. Elena captured this practice as pair pedagogues. In most early childhood centres, it is the norm to have more than one teacher. But is not the norm to plan how the two teachers will relate to each other. That is, planning their pedagogical positioning with each other – above, below, equal, primordial we, independent – and with the children. Elena argued that when there are pair pedagogues then one teacher can be in one position (e.g., above) and the other teacher can be in another position (e.g., below). In this scenario, the teacher in the below position can ask questions of the teacher in the above position – How can we do that? What does this do? Where can we go next? The teacher is modelling quality question asking in this example. By having pair pedagogues in classrooms, it becomes possible to bring into play and into exploration many different approaches which enhance children's development. Teachers plan their role in relation to the children and in relation to each other.

But what did this all mean for early childhood play and science learning? Elena's research gave new possibilities in analysis for research directed to understanding how teachers enter into children's play. Paper 5 is the result of this analysis.

6.1   *Paper 5: Pedagogical Positioning in Play – Teachers Being Inside and Outside of Children's Imaginary Play*

Paper 5 presents the findings of a study into the role of adults in children's play within play-based settings. Specifically, the research question asked was, "What role do teachers take when inside the imaginary play situation in play-based settings?". All of the comparable data from the studies across the ARC funded research were brought together and analysed, as Table 3.1 shows.

At this time few researchers had examined the role of the adult in children's play primarily because most conceptualised play as something only for

TABLE 3.1   Overview of sample and date generated

Centre	Number of teachers	Number of children	Age range	Observation period	Data generated
Centre A	3	53	3.3–4.4 Years; mean age of 3.8 years	8 weeks	242 h
Centre B	1	20	4.6–5.7 Years; mean age of 5.0 years	5 weeks	55 h
Centre C	1	30	3.3–5.3 Years; mean age of 4.2 years	3 weeks	74 h
Centre D	2	24	4.0–5.2 Years; mean age of 4.5 years	4 weeks	20 h
Centre E	2	24	4.4–5.5 Years; mean age of 4.11 years	3 weeks	8 h

children. But some cultural-historical researchers had theorised the important role adults had in children's play. For example, Singer et al. (2014) have shown teachers physically positioning themselves in close or distant proximity to toddlers in their research in Dutch childcare centres, noting the close relationships between teacher proximity and a positive level of play engagement in two- and three-year-old children.

In my analysis of ARC data sets, the typology of play pedagogy that emerged from the analysis of data across sites showed that the teachers acted in five different ways in relation to the imaginary play situation.

1.   Teacher proximity to children's play
2.   Teacher intent is in parallel with the children's play intent
3.   Teacher is following the children's play
4.   Teacher is engaged in sustained collective play with groups of children
5.   Teacher is inside the children's imaginary play

Significantly, the findings showed that teachers do not routinely become a part of children's play (inside their imaginary play). So how is it possible to take forward an agenda where concepts are introduced into children's play? There was some hope. I had found the research of Pentti Hakkarainen and Milda Bredikyte.

Hakkarainen and Bredikyte (2014) have shown in storyworlds how the "joint play of adults and children creates collective higher mental functions" (p. 249) because play complexity is actively built, the ideal forms of play interactions found in the fairy tales and narratives available to children, form the basis of the collective joint play that teachers introduce. Additionally, the plot is shared through the story with all the children and becomes a common plot to be played out and elaborated.

Relevant to my research in science education is that the problem formulations are introduced through the stories, which set up tension that the characters of the play must solve. Role play gives children opportunities to see and experience living adult models, as adults too are part of the imaginary play, acting as a character in the improvised and extended stories – thus modelling complex forms of play. Hakkarainen and Bredikyte (2014) argued that "Play offers an opportunity, or invitation, to experiment with transforming ideal into real forms of behaviour without overwhelming responsibility (play is just play)" (p. 248), where children "decide whether to accept the invitation or not" (p. 248).

This research gave insights into why teachers became involved in children's play. When the teacher is part of the imaginary play, she/he has an opportunity from inside of the imaginary play, to develop the play further, introducing complexity and genuinely using learning goals detailed in curriculum to help solve the tensions in the imaginary situations. Rather than smuggling in content (see Hedges, 2014), or bolting onto an existing play event a learning goal (Pramling Samuelsson and Asplund Carlsson, 2008), when the teacher is inside of the imaginary play with the children, she/he is more in tune with the storyline evolving or being acted out, and can better establish intersubjectivity inside of the imaginary play (Fleer, 2015). But the teacher being involved in children's play remains controversial.

It is possible that in the push to make play more academic (Chapter 2) that the diversity of play–pedagogy had narrowed, leaving teachers firmly outside of children's play?

7 Concluding Remarks: Building an Evidence Model

The ARC research grants (DP5-DP18) resourced the studies that make up the suite of 3 papers that follow. The outcomes of the research (Figure 3.2) gave new ways of bringing emotions and science concepts together into children's play (Paper 3), an understanding of the new demands made (or not) on children in play-based settings when in a digital learning activity (Paper 4), and new ways of positioning the teacher in relation to children's play (Paper 3). But also, the theoretical concepts I was working with brought forward new ways of researching and writing about early childhood science education.

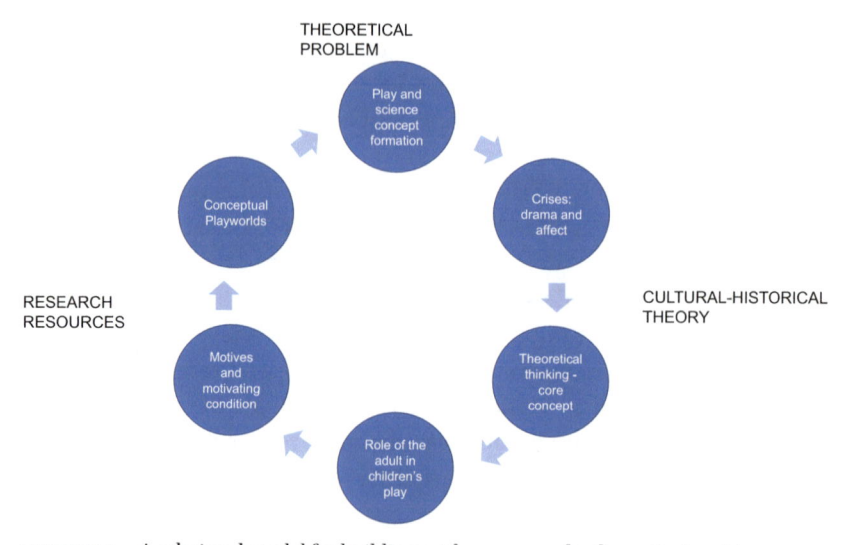

FIGURE 3.2   A relational model for building evidence around a theoretical problem

The findings of the respective studies pointed to a new way of thinking about the theoretical problem of learning concepts in play-based settings. The role of the adult and the social situation of development of children to play in play-based settings flushed out what was key for solving the theoretical problem. The cultural-historical literature into play gave new directions. The research of Pentti and Milda offered a unique pedagogy that gave a more active role for the teacher in children's play – a role that was mostly absent in preschools. The narrative of the story with its drama, created motivating conditions in which children explored scientific concepts. Anchored in affective imagination, children's science learning was being amplified by teachers in their play. But affective imagination, the many different roles of the teacher, the pedagogy of a playworld with a dramatic narrative, and the contradiction of teachers introducing concepts to children when their leading activity is to play, needed more research and theorisation.

Note

1 https://www.iscar.org/organisation/sections/thematic-sections/

References

Biddulph, F., & Osborne, R. (1984). *Making sense of our world: An interactive teaching approach*. Science Education Research Unit, University of Waikato.

Bohr, N. (1950). On the notions of causality and complementarity. *Science, 111*(2873), 51–54. https://doi.org/10.1126/science.111.2873.51

Fleer, M. (1992). The suitability of an interactive approach to teaching science in early childhood. *Australian Journal of Early Childhood, 17*(4), 12–23. https://search.informit.org/doi/abs/10.3316/aeipt.58802

Fleer, M. (1996). Fusing the boundaries between home and child care to support children's scientific learning. *Research in Science Education, 26*(2), 143–154. https://doi.org/10.1007/BF02356428

Fleer, M. (2012). Imagination, emotions and scientific thinking: what matters in the being and becoming of a teacher of elementary science? *Cultural Studies of Science Education, 7*(1), 31–39. https://doi.org/10.1007/s11422-011-9365-z

Fleer, M. (2015). Pedagogical positioning in play – Teachers being inside and outside of children's imaginary play. *Early Child Development and Care, 185*(11–12), 1801–1814. https://doi.org/10.1080/03004430.2015.1028393

Fleer, M. (2016a). An everyday and theoretical reading of "Perezhivanie" for informing research in early childhood education. *International Research in Early Childhood Education, 7*(1), 34–49. https://eric.ed.gov/?id=EJ1138756

Fleer, M. (2016b). Theorising digital play: A cultural-historical conceptualisation of children's engagement in imaginary digital situations. *International Research in Early Childhood Education, 7*(2), 75–90. https://eric.ed.gov/?id=EJ1138705

Fleer, M. (2017). Digital role-play: The changing conditions of children's play in pre-school settings. *Mind, Culture, and Activity, 24*(1), 3–17. https://doi.org/10.1080/10749039.2016.1247456

Fleer, M. (2018). Digital animation: New conditions for children's development in play-based setting. *British Journal of Educational Technology, 49*(5), 943–958. https://doi.org/10.1111/bjet.12637

Fleer, M. (2019). Digitally amplified practices: Beyond binaries and towards a profile of multiple digital coadjuvants. *Mind, Culture, and Activity, 26*(3), 207–220. https://doi.org/10.1080/10749039.2019.1646289

Fleer, M. (2020). Examining the psychological content of digital play through Hedegaard's model of child development. *Learning, Culture and Social Interaction, 26*, 100227. https://doi.org/10.1016/j.lcsi.2018.04.006

Fleer, M., Adams, M., & Gunstone, R. (2019). Transformative pedagogy: Dinka playgroups as spaces for cultural knowledge productions of Western science. *Cultural Studies of Science Education, 14*(4), 1045–1069. https://doi.org/10.1007/s11422-018-9908-7

Fleer, M., Adams, M., Gunstone, R., & Hao, Y. (2016). Studying the landscape of families and children's emotional engagement in science across cultural contexts. *International Research in Early Childhood Education, 7*(1), 122–141. https://eric.ed.gov/?id=EJ1138874

Fleer, M., & Hammer, M. (2013). 'Perezhivanie'in group settings: A cultural-historical reading of emotion regulation. *Australasian Journal of Early Childhood, 38*(3), 127–134. https://doi.org/10.1177/183693911303800316

Fleer, M., Hammer, M., & March, S. (2014). A cultural-historical reading of the emotional development of young children. *Asia-Pacific Journal of Research in Early Childhood Education, 8*(2), 47–67. http://www.pecerajournal.com/detail/62138

Fleer, M., & March, S. (2015). Conceptualizing science learning as a collective social practice: Changing the social pedagogical compass for a child with visual impairment. *Cultural Studies of Science Education, 10*(3), 803–831. https://doi.org/10.1007/s11422-014-9616-x

Fleer, M., & Pramling, M. (2015). *A cultural-historical study of children learning science. Foregrounding affective imagination in play-based settings.* Springer.

Fox Keller, E. (1983). *A feeling for the organism, 10th aniversary edition: The life and work of Barbara McClintock.* Macmillan.

Hakkarainen, P., & Bredikyte, M. (2014). Understanding narrative as a key aspect of play. In E. Brooker, L. Brooker, M. Blaise, & S. Edwards (Eds.), *The Sage handbook of play and learning in early childhood* (pp. 240–251). Sage Publications.

Hedegaard, M. (2009). Children's development from a cultural-historical approach: Children's activity in everyday local settings as foundation for their development. *Mind, Culture, and Activity, 16*(1), 64–82. https://doi.org/10.1080/10749030802477374

Hedegaard, M. (2012). Analyzing children's learning and development in everyday settings from a cultural-historical wholeness approach. *Mind, Culture, and Activity, 19*(2), 127–138. https://doi.org/10.1080/10749039.2012.665560

Hedegaard, M., & Chaiklin, S. (2005). *Radical-local teaching and learning.* Aarhus University Press

Hedegaard, M., & Fleer, M. (2013). *Play, leaning and children's development: Everyday life in families and transition to school.* Cambridge University Press

Hedges, H. (2014). Children's content learning in play provision: Competing tensions and future possibilities. In E. Brooker, L. Brooker, M. Blaise, & S. Edwards (Eds.), *The Sage handbook of play and learning in early childhood* (pp. 192–203). Sage Publications.

Kravtsov, G. G., & Kravtsova, E. E. (2010). Play in LS Vygotsky's nonclassical psychology. *Journal of Russian & East European Psychology, 48*(4), 25–41. https://doi.org/10.2753/RPO1061-0405480403

Samuelsson, I. P., & Carlsson, M. A. (2008). The playing learning child: Towards a pedagogy of early childhood. *Scandinavian Journal of Educational Research, 52*(6), 623–641. https://doi.org/10.1080/00313830802497265

Singer, E., Nederend, M., Penninx, L., Tajik, M., & Boom, J. (2014). The teacher's role in supporting young children's level of play engagement. *Early Child Development and Care, 184*(8), 1233–1249. https://doi.org/10.1080/03004430.2013.862530

Vygotsky, L. S. (1987). *The collected works of L. S. Vygotsky: Problems of general psychology* (N. Minick, Trans.; R. W. Rieber & A. S. Carton, Eds., Vol. 1). Plenum Press.

Vygotsky, L. S. (1993). *The collected works of LS Vygotsky: The fundamentals of defectology* (J. E. Knox & C. B. Stevens, Trans.; R. W. Rieber & A. S. Carton, Eds., Vol. 2). Springer Science & Business Media.

Vygotsky, L. S. (1997a). *The collected works of LS Vygotsky: Problems of the theory and history of psychology* (R. Van der Veer, Trans.; R. W. Rieber & J. Wollock, Eds., Vol. 3). Springer Science & Business Media.

Vygotsky, L. S. (1997b). *The collected works of L. S. Vygotsky: The history of the development of higher mental functions* (M. J. Hall, Trans.; R. W. Rieber, Ed., Vol. 4). Plenum Press.

Vygotsky, L. S. (1998). *The collected works of L.S. Vygotsky: Child psychology* (M. J. Hall, Trans.; R. W. Rieber, Ed., Vol. 5). Plenum Press.

Vygotsky, L. S. (1999). *The collected works of L. S. Vygotsky: Scientific legacy* (M. J. Hall, Trans.; R. W. Rieber, Ed., Vol. 6). Springer Science & Business Media.

Paper 3: Affective Imagination in Science Education: Determining the Emotional Nature of Scientific and Technological Learning of Young Children

Marilyn Fleer

This paper originally appeared as Fleer, M. (2013). Affective imagination in science education: Determining the emotional nature of scientific and technological learning of young children. *Research in Science Education, 43*(5), 2085–2106. https://doi.org/10.1007/s11165-012-9344-8 Reprinted here with permission from the publisher.

Abstract

Vygotsky (1986) draws attention to the interrelationship between thought and language and other aspects of mind. Although not widely acknowledged, Vygotsky (1999) also drew attention to the search for the relations between cognition and emotions. This paper discusses the findings of a study which examined imaginary scientific situations within the early years. The central research questions examined: What is the emotional nature of scientific learning? and How does *affective imagination* support early childhood science learning? Video observations were made of the teaching of science from one site in a south-eastern community in Australia (232 h of video observations). The teachers used fairy tales and Slowmation as cultural devices to support the concept formation of 3- and 4-yearold children (n = 53; range of 3.3 to 4.4; mean of 3.8 years). The findings of this underresearched area (e.g. Roth, *Mind, Culture, and Activity* 15:2–7, 2008) make a contribution to understanding how affective imagination can work in science education in the early years.

Keywords

cultural–historical – sociocultural – early childhood – fairy tales – emotions imagination – creativity science – technology – early years

Introduction

The situations that children meet in collective environments, such as early childhood settings, create multiple possibilities for developing new understandings of the material and social environment (Bozhovich, 2009). These early childhood settings also provide opportunities for developing young children's scientific self-awareness and, through this, knowledge of what it means to act scientifically (Saracho & Spodek, 2008). Working scientifically brings not only conceptual understandings but also the possibilities for emotional engagement and commitment. Roth (2008) has eloquently argued that "Consciousness in activity [concepts]... is inherently shaped by current emotional states and oriented towards higher emotional valence, both at the collective level (motive and society) and at the individual level (goal)" (p. 6). Vygotsky (1999) drew attention to the search for the relations between concepts and emotions. He suggested that their "separation as subjects of study is a major weakness of traditional psychology" (Vygotsky, 1986, p. 10). A cultural–historical perspective seeks to examine scientific learning in relation to how everyday situations create scientific encounters that are emotionally charged and socially mediated in actions and activities within pre-school settings.

Understanding about the collective, rather than just the individual relations between emotions and cognition, is an important line of enquiry in group settings where teachers can emotionally frame scientific learning. In this paper, it is asked specifically, how do children *collectively* co-construct scientific learning in imaginary and real situations in early childhood settings, and what emotions and motives frame children's scientific interactions? Surprisingly, these questions have not been asked within early childhood science education research.

In order to foreground the emotional dimensions and to give a focus to scientific learning, the research reported in this paper specifically brings together imagination and science through the use of a traditional cultural device of fairy tales (El'Koninova, 2002) and a contemporary cultural device of Slowmation (Hoban, 2007). Slowmation is a software program (abbreviated from "Slow Animation") that generates a simple stop-motion animation played slowly at two frames per second. Children photograph objects, creating a sequence of photographic images, which they put together as a video clip, with self-generated narration to explain the science concepts or story being created (see also Hoban & Neilson, 2010; Hoban et al., 2011). Previous research suggests that Slowmation (Fleer et al., 2012) helps children to more consciously consider concepts, and fairy tales offer a context for making visible emotions and cognition (Zaporozhets, 2002), which post Vygotskian researchers suggest still require more theorization (Gonzalez Rey, 2012) and research. In addition, the study of emotions and cognition as cultural–historical concepts has not yet been applied to early childhood science education research, and this conceptualisation offers new directions for supporting science learning and teaching. The paper begins with a brief theoretical overview of cultural–historical theory, followed by a more focused discussion of the conceptual framework. This is followed by the details of the study design and the findings. The paper concludes with a psychological discussion of early childhood science learning where emotions and cognition are brought together during science learning.

Theory Informing the Study

The research reported in this paper draws upon cultural–historical theory to theorise fairy tales in scientific educational programmes because this theory offers a *cultural device for making conscious to children* the dynamic relationship between emotions and the scientific development of concepts. Emotions are connected to the development of scientific and technological concepts when children discuss and develop security systems for keeping Goldilocks out of the three bears' house or invent ways of insulating mother bear's porridge bowl so its content does not get cold. It will be argued that a dynamic unit of scientific consciousness will be realised in these kinds of emotionally charged situations. It is suggested that fairy tales (El'Koninova, 2002) can *collectively* develop a consciousness of scientific and technological concepts and emotionality.

Collective communities that form in early childhood settings offer a dynamic social situation (Bozhovich, 2009) for children's scientific development that needs to be better understood. Similarly, early childhood settings also play an important role in the development of scientific concepts and, as such, are significant for a child's scientific and technological development. Investigating teaching practices which use fairy tales and Slowmation as cultural devices offers the possibility for mapping how children's scientific understandings develop and change as a result of the scientific narrative that forms through the use of fairy tales.

In both fairy tales and scientific encounters, it is possible to apply Vygotsky's (1994) concept of perezhavnie[1] to understand the dynamic unit of human consciousness. Veresov (2013) explains that Vygotsky's concept of *perezhavnie* has been inaccurately translated, stating that the concept can be understood as:

> According to the general generic law of cultural development, every higher mental function appears twice—first it appears as social relations in a form of emotionally experienced dramatical collision (category) and then within an individual as emotionally experienced internal dramatic collision. Therefore perezhivanie is not only a kind of prism which refracts the interaction of the ideal and real form. [but also] The concept of perezhivanie determines the very essence of such an interaction. Perezhivanie is the personal way of experiencing of a dramatical event— the category. It is a form in which this dramatical event is reflected and experienced by an individual. (p. 10)

What is significant here for the study reported in this paper is the suggestion that emotionally charged events are enacted through the drama of the fairy tales, and through this drama, pertinent concepts become consciously realised by the children. This theorization can be applied to science learning in pre-school settings. In Table 1, the link between science and the conceptual literature on fairy tales is shown, in order to show the possibilities for pursuing this line of enquiry. Column one summarises the conceptual points, which are discussed in more detail in the next section ("Conceptual Framework"), and column 2 draws on the literature on emotions that result through studying fairy tales. Column 3 theorises how science too can be an emotionally charged event for children, linking it directly to the literature in column 2.

This paper brings together the conceptual relations between established cultural–historical understandings of the psychological value of fairy tales and the learning of scientific concepts in early childhood. These are presented

---

1   The Russian term *perezhivanie* is used here because the term is difficult to translate into English.

TABLE 1   Concepts informing collectively constructed imaginary scientific situations

Concept	Emotionality in fairy tales	Emotionality in scientific and technological learning
Collective investigations and narratives	Children *want* to identify with the hero of the story, wishing to assist the hero, and through this, they *together re-enact the ideal moral response to the given situation, along with all of the associated risks, in reaching the final victory.*	
	Children imagine the feeling state of the fairy tale characters, and empathise and want to help the characters to solve the collective problem.	*Children collectively* develop a consciousness of scientific and technological *concepts and emotionality* by working together with other children to solve the problem.
		In a *scientific narrative*, children empathise and want to help the characters to solve the collective scientific and technological problem.
Affective imagination or emotional imagination	Through the re-enactment of fairy tales, children gain a sense of the main character's actions in role play, whilst clarifying their own feeling state because the story plot is mirrored in the acted-out actions of the children.	Through role play of scientific narratives and learning, the children collectively begin to anticipate the results of each others' actions in the play, begin to anticipate their own actions, including image-bearing dramatisation, verbal descriptions, prop use and transformation, and importantly, the scientific solutions created through the support of the teacher.
Zaporozhets (2002) shows that through emotional and cognitive participation in fairy tales that children reach "the ideal plane of *emotional imagination*" (p. 58).	Children are not "*enacting the story, but really living in it*" (El'Koninova, 2002, p. 45).	

(*cont.*)

TABLE 1   Concepts informing collectively constructed imaginary scientific situations (*cont.*)

Concept	Emotionality in fairy tales	Emotionality in scientific and technological learning
Flickering Children *flicker* between real and imaginary worlds.	In fairy tales, children begin to separate out the imaginary world from the real world and find themselves in the borderline between these worlds.	It is the border of the imaginary world and the real world that creates a dialectical relation and emotional tension that promotes scientific conceptual development, which helps children imagine scientific explanations not easily observable.
Imagination, thinking and emotions in play	Children give new meanings to objects and actions in play, such as, when a stick becomes a hobbyhorse and the child a rider—creating a new sense of the situation.	Children give new meanings to objects and actions to everyday situations when learning science—creating a new scientific sense of the situation.
Dual role of emotions in thinking	Children must be inside of the plot living the story, and outside of the plot as a real person. El'Koninova (2002) argues that a child must "gropingly look for a "territory" where this is possible" (p. 41). Feeling happy in role play, but also feeling frightened when pretending to be Goldilocks seeing the 3 bears.	Children feeling happy enacting or exploring a science narrative with others, but also feeling excited or curious by learning new things and solving scientific and technological problems in order to scientifically help the characters in the narrative.
Emotional anticipation Fairy tales provide children with the possibilities for emotional tension, engagement and selfawareness	In fairy tales, the emotional anticipation of what is to unfold develops. Children begin to think consciously about the present and future situation and build emotional anticipation.	In scientific investigations, children's feeling state becomes connected with the learning as they anticipate *finding a solution*. Through consciously considering feeling states in science, emotions become intellectualized, generalized and anticipatory, while cognitive processes acquire an affective dimension, performing a special role in meaning discrimination and meaning formation (e.g. gut feeling this is going to work).

(*cont.*)

TABLE 1   Concepts informing collectively constructed imaginary scientific situations (*cont.*)

Concept	Emotionality in fairy tales	Emotionality in scientific and technological learning
Emotional filtering Emotional filtering is "where kindergarten teachers attribute emotional significance to events" (Iakovela, 2003, p. 93)	Teachers emotionally charge events, actions and objects which focus the children's attention, thinking and feeling state.	Teachers help children in knowing what is noteworthy to pay attention to in science learning. What should they notice or look for? The gesturing of teachers is usually accompanied by expressive sounds and surprised or interested facial expressions.

together in order to show the possibilities for drawing upon cultural–historical concepts on emotionality for informing science learning of very young children. It is through examining the dynamic unit of human consciousness enacted through the fairy tales and scientific enquiry that it is possible to better understand how children emotionally experience scientific learning. It is this conceptual framework that has informed the study design that is reported in this paper.

Central to what is presented in Table 1 are the relations between emotions and cognition. Here, Vygotsky's theoretical stance of interpsychological and intrapsychological functioning is used to explain this relation. First, the concept is explained; then, it is used to explain the relation between cognition and emotion generally, and then finally, it is linked to science learning.

Vygotsky argued that it is through the dynamic interactions between people and things (interspychological functioning) that children learn about what matters in their particular community, what is valued, and what one pays attention to in everyday life. Initially, children, with the support of others, engage and participate in higher levels of cognition and action than they would do independently. Through social participation and through what they bring to the dynamics of everyday interactions in preschools, teachers help children conceptualise their experiences by naming or attributing social significance to particular experiences. Zinchenko (2007), in drawing attention to the conclusion of Vygotsky's final work before he died, stated that he concluded with this statement "The *word* full of sense is a microcosm of human consciousness" (p. 229; my emphasis). In a theoretical sense, the *word* captures the experiences, but also the *word* gives meaning to a set of experiences. There is a dialectical relation, and through this, a consciousness of what is being experienced emerges for the child. Zinchenko (2007) highlights that "the transition from thought to language is a very complicated process of dismemberment of a thought and its recreation in a word" (Vygotsky, 1987, p. 357), but importantly, "thought is not expressed by language but takes place in it" (Vygotsky, 1982–1984, v. 2, p. 356) (p. 216). New experiences (interpsychological) are captured through the introduction of new words, creating concepts. These concepts name the experiences as part of the child's cultural development, and when understood (interpsychological level), children can use these words independently of those experiences. That is:

> the child's higher psychological functions, his [sic] higher attributes which are specific to humans, originally manifest themselves as forms of the child's collective behaviour, as a form of co-operation with other people, and it is only afterwards that they become the internal individual functions of the child himself. (Vygotsky, 1994, p. 349)

Children's experiences of their social and material environment as a form of interpsychological and intrapsychological functioning are also refracted through their emotions. Vygotsky (1994) argued that the "emotional experiences [perezhivanie] arising from any situation or from any aspect of his [sic] environment, determines what kind of influence this situation or this environment will have on the child" (p. 339). Zaporozhets (2002) argued that "emotion is not itself an activation process, but a *special form of refection of reality* used for the mental control of activation" (p. 53; my emphasis). Emotions as a reflection of reality are evident when consideration is given to "how a child becomes aware of, interprets, [and] emotionally relates to certain events[s]" (Vygotsky, 1994, p. 341). Emotions not only act as the prism through which the environment is experienced, but the experiences are emotionally charged. This emotionality is carried with experience to the intrapsychological level, where the concept or word acquires an emotional residue, which in turn speaks back to the environment and determines the relationship the child has to a given situation. Emotions therefore also act as a prism through which interpsychological and intrapsychological functioning occurs. Holodynski and Friedlmeier (2006) in their expansive work suggest that a consciousness of one's emotional state, as a form of emotion regulation, is acquired through the movement from interpsychological to intrapsychological functioning. In drawing together these complementary theoretical concepts and applying these to science education, it is thought that the relations between emotions and cognition in science learning in preschools, as a form of interpsychological and intrapsychological functioning, is a fruitful line of enquiry that will yield insights into affective imagination in science education.

Conceptual Framework

Fairy tales are told, role played and read in early childhood centres. Dramatisation of fairy tales is commonplace in many early childhood programmes. Vygotsky (1999) stated that in drama, the feeling of "we" rather than "I" is created as a *form of social consciousness*. The actor creates on the stage infinite sensations, feelings or emotions that become the emotions of the whole theatrical audience. *Collective scientific investigations* (see Table 1) are also a form of social consciousness, particularly when the problem formulation is embedded in an engaging and imaginative context when a problem situation presents itself. Vygotsky put forward the concept of *affective imagination*, where the child imagines the feeling state of the characters, and as Zaporozhets (2002) shows in his research, children empathise and want to help the characters to solve the collective problem that forms in the fairy tale or scientific encounter.

Zaporozhets (2002) showed how fairy tales provided children with the possibilities for emotional tension, engagement and self-awareness (i.e., the collision that Veresov discusses). He was able to show that "Vygotsky's assumption about the higher, specifically human 'intelligent' emotions being cortical was confirmed" (p. 33). That is, his research showed the "existence of tightly-knit and sequentially evolving relations between the intellectual and the motivational–emotional aspect of child personality" (p. 33). In the re-telling or performing of fairy tale stories, children have the opportunity to experience and act out the central characters and the plot, which Zaporozhets (2002) and his colleagues have shown to bring together intellectual and motivational–emotional aspects of children's development. It is thought that science learning for very young children can also be an emotional experience for children, when they use science to help re-create the narrative of the fairy tale and together engage in scientific experiences to support the story plot. As with fairy tale narratives, a *scientific narrative gives purpose and develops a motive* for engagement in thinking and acting scientifically.

Through the re-enactment of fairy tales, over and over again, children test out "the sense of the main character's actions but also clarified their own internal world of feeling" and distinguishing a real action "from its function in a role" (El'Koninova, 2002, p. 47). Through the repetition of telling, re-telling and re-enacting fairy tales, children come to understand differences between real actions and role actions. "A child seeks, clarifies, and comprehends sense in the process of repetitions" (p. 48). El'Koninova (2002) argues that the story plot is mirrored in the acted-out actions of the children. Children are not "*enacting the story, but really living in it*" (El'Koninova, 2002, p. 45; original emphasis). As with Zaporozhets's (2002) research, El'Koninova (2002) argues that children want to identify with the hero of the story, wishing to assist the hero, and through this, they *together re-enact the ideal moral response to the given situation, along with all of the associated risks, in reaching the final victory*, as is the common ending for fairy tales. It is thought that the children's wish to assist the main character can provide a *motivating and emotionally charged context* within which children can scientifically and technologically support the story plot.

Research into the everyday scientific encounters of 5- and 6-year-old children by Siry and Kremer (2011) has shown that everyday life is full of abstract but tantalising events that children wish to imaginatively develop or scientifically understand. For instance, in their study of how children encountered and understood rainbows, they noted that "Although rainbows are an abstract, complex phenomena to try to reproduce in the classroom, the children demonstrated their often sophisticated understandings of natural science, as well as their creative 'magical thinking' as related to rainbows" (p. 654). These magical moments often present themselves through the illusive question of finding the end of the rainbow.

Children aged 3 to 6 years regularly feature real and imaginary situations in their discourse and play. El'Koninova (2002) suggests that when children begin to separate out the imaginary world from the real world, they "find themselves on the borderline between them" (p. 47). The child is at the boundary line between a real and an imaginary world. Children *flicker* between real and imaginary worlds (see Table 1). It is thought that flickering between real and imaginary situations can also support children to think in situated and imaginary ways that together support children's ability to imagine scientific explanations often not visibly supported in real life, such as the Earth circling the Sun, or as discussed in Hadzigeorgiou (2001) the "idea that sugar dissolves faster in hot water is not something that children can directly observe!" (p. 68).

El'Koninova (2002) showed in her research that when children are listening to a fairy tale (from beginning to end), they must hold on to two things simultaneously—the children must be inside of the plot living the story and outside of the plot as a real person. El'Koninova (2002) argues that a child must "gropingly look for a "territory" where this is possible" (p. 41). It is the border of the imaginary world and the real world that creates this dialectical relation (Fleer, 2010) and emotional tension that is worthy of further investigation in relation to scientific conceptual development.

Study Design

"Finding a method is one of the most important tasks of the researcher" (Vygotsky, 1997, p. 27). Although this statement was made more than 80 years ago, it is as pertinent now as it was then. Vygotsky argued that traditional approaches to research represents a post mortem approach to research, when what is needed is to investigate the unfolding development of the child within his or her social and historical context. Digital video observations (see Hedegaard & Fleer, 2008) bring together the dynamics of the whole in motion in ways that demand analysis in layers and as action movements (non-linear and not static). Such analysis seeks to find the *relational dimensions* between emotions and cognition. This is particularly important in early childhood research because young children are still developing language, cannot yet "read surveys", do not necessarily present the same or logically coherent "interview data" when interviewed or feel the need to follow established research protocols about performing in an experimental situation. Their verbal language and gross bodily movements need to be viewed in relation to their social relations and material interactions as presented in the moment, as well as recast from the past. The dynamics and motion of "scientific conceptual development" as it occurs in progress can easily be captured with digital video observations, and keeping these data "together" during the analysis adds to the rigour of the research. The research reported in this paper seeks to use digital video tools to capture the wholeness of the researched situation (Hedegaard & Fleer, 2008).

Research Questions

What are the relations between emotions and cognition in group settings where fairy tales and Slowmation act as cultural devices for framing scientific learning? What is the emotional nature of the scientific learning of early childhood children?

Participants

Three staff and a total of 53 children aged 3 to 4 years (range of 3.3 to 4.4; mean of 3.8 years as at the start of the study) agreed to participate in the study. The centre the children attend is located in a middle class community, approximately 75 km south of a major capital city in Australia.

Procedure

1. Staff participated in an in-service in the use of Slowmation for supporting science learning and were supported in the development of a unit of science drawing upon the fairy tale of Goldilocks and the three bears.
2. Unit of work was implemented over 8 weeks.
3. Storytelling, re-telling, dramatisation and role play were used alongside of a problem formulation investigated by the children. The scientific challenge that emerged was: How do we cool porridge down? The technological challenge was "Can we design a porridge-cooling machine?"

4. Digital video observations using two and sometimes three cameras captured children's and teachers' investigations and play over an 8-week period, generating 232 h of data.

5. Two focus children were digitally video observed at home, involved in a science walk, and doing everyday activities at home, including leisure activities and family jobs where everyday scientific interactions may feature (total of two visits per family, 5 h of video observations). (These data are not discussed in this paper.)

Digital Video Observations

Digital technologies allow the researchers to simultaneously consider all the data sets because these are visible at all points in the analysis. Video analysis allows the researcher to hold constant many different dimensions of an event, activity or social exchange. It allows the researcher to go back and forth between data sets to find possibilities that contributed to an emotional exchange from previous exchanges. The researcher codes this and tries to make meaning from everyday interactions that have "somehow" emotionally charged activities in ways that are not always visible to the observer on first viewing, and which would have been missed had traditional paper and pencil observations been made. To achieve this, a system for the organisation of the data, conceptual themes and three layers of analysis were undertaken.

Organisation of Data

1. Digital video was downloaded into iMovie (standard with Macs) as a "raw folder" and time sequence logged.

2. Video clips, photographs and field notes were linked through a word document protocol for each hour of video data gathered. Folders for each file (video clips, photographs, video log of video content) were created.

Analysis—Conceptual Themes

3. After a general everyday interpretation of data sets (see below) to identify themes, data were organised in iMovie in order to show the relational dimensions between emotions and cognition. An analysis protocol was created to support this "unity of analysis". This protocol was amended as new categories emerged from the data, resulting in Table 2 below (situated level analysis—see below).

4. Data were kept intact through the raw file, but copies were created as video clips, representing instances of where emotions and cognition were in unity. Specific analysis of scientific interactions by children and staff was copied as "events" into video clips. Capturing the dynamics

TABLE 2   Concepts that were coded

Concept	Theoretical explanation	Activity example
Collective scientific investigations	A scientific narrative forms as children collectively work together to solve scientific and technological problems.	Images of rainbows in children's artwork Objects in room which show light and the refraction of light Teacher and/or groups of children discuss rainbows and work with light in some way.
Emotional imagination	Children are not "enacting the story but *really living it*"	Role play of children where engagement of children is evident (i.e. dramatical expressions) Teacher and children together re-telling and dramatising a story
Flickering	Children flicker between real and imaginary worlds	Children move into an imaginary situation in role play, such as when they announce they are being the little bear in the re-telling of the story for their Slowmation, they move out of the imaginary situation to move an object for their Slowmation creation
Imagination, thinking and emotions in play	Creating a scientific sense of the situation	Children explicitly discussing light and making imaginative comments; children explicitly discussing hot and cold and making imaginative comments or actions
Dual role of emotions in thinking	Children must be inside of the plot living the story, and outside of the plot as a real person	Discussing a dream in relation to real world events Being the bear in play cooking, and also being a child asking about hot and cold
Emotional anticipation	In scientific investigations, children's feeling state becomes connected with learning as they anticipate finding a solution.	Children anticipate in the story of Goldilocks and the 3 bears that the porridge needs to be cooled, and they show emotional anticipation for the arrival of Goldilocks through squealing.
Emotional filtering	Teachers attribute emotional significance to events.	When a teacher shows exaggerated response to something that can lead to scientific understandings, such as finding a rainbow projected on the wall

and motion as "scientific development in progress" was done digitally because keeping these data "together" during the analysis was important. This allowed for a thematic analysis in order to build confidence in the representations of data emerging (see below).

Three Levels of Analysis (Hedegaard & Fleer, 2008)

5. Level 1 of the analysis involved a common sense approach to generating interpretations of the data. That is, all of the video observation data were viewed in relation to the science learning that was occurring.
6. The second level of analysis involved examining the clips created from the common sense interpretation for situated practices around the key concepts in Table 2 and specific forms of intentional teaching associated with fairy tales and science.
7. The third level of analysis involved a thematic approach, which sought to examine interpretations across data sets for multiple evidence of specific concepts/activity. This is where data were rigorously examined for common themes across contexts.

The levels of analysis allowed for a comprehensive synthesis, which in turn provided the framework for determining the relations between emotions and cognition.

Findings

An exploration of the conceptual value and pedagogical nature of scientific learning for 3-and 4-year-old children has been undertaken before (e.g. Cowie & Otrel-Cass, 2011). However, what is new here is an investigation of how children flicker in and out of real and imaginary situations when learning science and how teachers show scientific significance to events or objects that they encourage children to pay attention to. Although "play is the leading activity" of pre-school-aged children (Elkonin, 2005) and it is well recognized that children psychologically and socially explore the relations between "real and imaginary" situations generally (Wellman et al., 2001), few have studied this borderline in order to better understand science learning of children at such a young age as 3 years.

The study sought to understand the psychological development of pre-school-aged children learning science, whilst at the same time also examining what kind of pedagogy was needed for realising science concept formation of 3-year-old children. The former is taken up explicitly in this paper. The latter is discussed in Fleer et al. (2012).

The relations between *emotions and cognition* were examined closely during the teaching of a unit of science and technology that used fairy tales and Slowmation as cultural devices for learning. The findings revealed five elements which are discussed in turn: *Distributed nature of science learning* in early childhood settings, need for a collective scientific narrative to join up experiences, *affective scientific imagination*, flickering between *real and imaginative scientific worlds*, and *taking a scientific perspective*. Together, these draw attention to the relations between emotions and cognition in science learning.

Distributed Nature of Science Learning in Early Childhood Settings

Traditional views on the nature of how children learn generally have tended to map concept formation in relation to particular ages and stages of children's overall development. That is, children will learn specific concepts as detailed in the scope and sequence of curricula. This approach is suggestive of age being an important criterion for both presenting when something should be taught, but also when something should be assessed. Individual progression and assessment of the individual's learning follow from this basic view of child development. Constructivist views have also focused on the individual and how the individual constructs scientific learning (see Carter, 2007; Leach & Scott, 2003; Osborne, 1996; Pressick-Kilborn et al., 2005). Unfortunately, the foundational view of child development that has dominated early childhood education in the past has focused researchers' attention on the individual and their expected scientific development in relation to age (Fleer, 2010, 2011a, 2011b, 2011c). In this study, what was overwhelmingly evident was the collective nature of science learning that was supported so cleverly by the early childhood teacher throughout the 8 weeks of investigating science learning. Whilst children clearly responded through an individual voice, their responses were generally within the context of a scientific narrative that was evolving and deepening over the 8 weeks across the whole group. A distributed form of scientific learning was evident within the early childhood centre. This is in line with Rogoff's (1990) definition of distributed learning, where concepts and ideas are not held within the individual mind but are distributed across people and time to collectively build a cultural practice.

Two concepts were featured in the centre; one was in relation to the ongoing exploration of "light", and the other was in relation to the concept of "heat" that the research team had suggested might arise from the storytelling of Goldilocks and the three bears. This conceptual focus contrasts with earlier studies which suggest that early childhood teachers do not engage with scientific concepts (see Hedges & Cullen, 2005, 2011). The example of "light" follows.

Distributed Concept Formation—"Light"

Eight children are jumping around the early childhood centre, calling out to each other that they have seen a rainbow on the wall and roof of the centre. The children are calling out "rainbow", "sun", "light". The teacher J moves across to the window where a prism sits permanently on the window ledge. She stands under the prism facing into the room and looking at the children, and raises her arm so it points towards the prism and says "Sun shining through the ... (pausing)?" The children are looking to her and saying "sunlight, glass", then looking towards the rainbow on the wall. The teacher continues "... the glass prism". The children move about the area between the teacher and the wall as she says "It bends the sunlight and makes a rainbow". As she speaks the children go up to the wall and put their hands on the rainbow which is at head height to the children. They walk back to the teacher smiling. J says "Is it on your hand Harris?". Harris smiles and nods and then removes his hand and cradles his hand whilst walking towards J, saying "I can't feel it". Four children go back to the rainbow on the wall and each put their hands on the rainbow observing the light on their hands. Mark says "Which way does it go?". The children look around the room. Harris says "I think that way", pointing upwards.

Although the teacher does not discuss the refraction of the light as the cause of the appearance of the rainbow, the young children do respond positively and in an excited way to the appearance of the rainbow on the wall and the ceiling. The children collectively appear to make the link between the prism and the rainbow, as evident through their body positioning, their exploration of the rainbow on their hands and through their mentioning of the sun in response to the appearance of the rainbow. The reactions are collectively created, and their explorations are collectively driven. The collective sense of investigating was always present, for example, the children followed up their observations of the rainbow in the room by collectively investigating the rainbow with coloured blocks as lenses for looking at the rainbow on the wall:

> Some of the children rush over to the overhead projector and take coloured blocks (which are framed by a wooden structure) and put it to their eyes as they walk towards the rainbow on the wall. The teacher moves closer to the children and kneels. Four children have different coloured blocks. The teacher helps Mandy hold the block to her eyes and says "Look, all the blue's gone". Mandy nods positively and then takes the

block away from her eyes and looks at the rainbow again. Melanie holds her block to the rainbow and the teacher asks "Melanie what colour disappears when you put the red one on?". Jennifer says "It's up there too" (pointing the rainbow on the ceiling".The children continue to try different coloured blocks and the teacher continues to ask them about what they are noticing.

The investigations were initiated by the children as they used the available materials to explore the refracted light. Later, when the teacher went on a "science walk" with the research team, she stated that "It's because we are so into rainbows that I just try to get things that reflect that theme, which the children, as you saw, notice, comment on, talk about…". Siry and Kremer (2011) suggest that focusing on children's interest helps "build upon the theories they have already generated about science phenomena" (p. 643; original emphasis). A distributed view of science learning takes into account the "complexities of young children's emergent ideas in science" (Siry & Kremer, 2011, p. 645), where "children learn *from*, and *with*, each other" (p. 647; original emphasis). In their research, they noted that:

> Conversations between her [researcher] and the children about rainbows shed light on children's prior knowledge, and served as a resource as she engaged children in activities that explored the spectral colours to address some of the questions they had raised (p. 647).

This was also evident in this study, as children brought to their collective investigations their prior knowledge, but with the teacher guiding what they paid attention to, allowing for new investigative possibilities emerge.

Need for a *Collective Scientific Narrative* to Join up Experiences

Not only were the exploration of concepts distributed across the centre through the children and their collective investigations, but the teacher supported the growing scientific narratives that were forming through continually picking up on their conversations in situ, as shown above, but also through explicitly planned experiences. In the following example, the teacher seeks to explore the concept of heat by discussing the idea of cooling down the porridge that the children had made previously many times. The idea of inventing a porridge-cooling machine had arisen when the children were discussing the porridge across both the everyday context of cooking porridge and also the imaginary context where they sought to help the bears by inventing a cooling down machine for the porridge.

> Four children are sitting or standing around a table which has a large pile of Lego pieces in the centre. The teacher is seated at the table. She begins a discussion about porridge making so that she can discuss the idea of designing some sort of device for cooling down the porridge:

Teacher:	Remember what the 3 bears cooked and ate for breakfast?
Child 1:	Porridge.
Teacher:	Yum. Do you remember how to make porridge?
Child 2:	Yeah (other children nod in agreement).
Teacher:	How did we make it?
Child 1:	With some milk.
Teacher:	Milk. Yes. And?
Child 3:	Then you put it into the microwave.
Teacher:	And what did the microwave do to make porridge?
Child 2:	Warm it up.
Child 3:	Make porridge.
Teacher:	Warmed it up, or cooked it?
Child 2:	Cooked it.
Teacher:	What was it like when it came out of the microwave?
Child 3:	Hot.
Child 2:	Hot.
Teacher:	A little bit hot, or very, very, very, very, very, very, very, very, very, very, hot.
Child 3:	Very hot.
Child 2:	Very hot.
Teacher:	It was nearly boiling.
Child 3:	It was.
Teacher:	Why did it nearly have to be boiling?
Child 3:	Because it was in there for a long time.
Teacher:	So we have got boiling hot porridge. So can we eat it when it's boiling hot?
Child 3:	No (all children shake their heads). My grandmother only eats porridge when its cold.
Teacher:	Does she wait until its got cold before she eats it?
Child 3:	Yeah and puts yoghurt in it.

The teacher re-visits the children's experiences of porridge before she embarks upon supporting the children to design and create their "porridge-cooling down machine". In her discussions with the children, she helps the children to consider the idea of cooling by discussing the temperature in relation to their everyday experiences of cooking porridge in the centre, but she also accepts their home experiences. It is noted in particular that child 3 discusses her grandmother's preferences for eating porridge. Embedding scientific learning within children's real-world experiences created in the centre or at home allows for a deeper engagement and exploration of what matters scientifically to children. However, in this study, children also brought to these learning contexts imaginative aspects that were quite unexpected. For example, the discussion that emerged between the teacher and child 3 revealed a very interesting porridge-cooling machine, which she later went on to make in the outdoor area, drawing upon the resources available (e.g. sand and plant matter, stripped from the garden):

> Child 3: We could make a fridge to cool down the porridge.
> Teacher: Alison how can we make a fridge?
> Child 3: By putting some dog hair on it, and putting some dog hair and some cement, and mixing the cement with the dog hair up, and putting it straight into the oven, and then put it on an ice block and then hammer it, and then it will turn into red.

As suggested by Siry and Kremer (2011) when investigating rainbows, children frame their ideas as magical moments in both their questions (e.g., Can we catch a rainbow, stand on a rainbow or hold a rainbow?) and their explanations. These examples illustrate the movement between children's imaginary world and real world, as introduced in Table 1 previously. This idea will be taken up further later in this paper.

The collective narrative that formed through the teacher's intentionality in exploring the concept of heating and cooling was orchestrated by the use of "and", "do you remember" and use of specific questioning. Exploring children's thinking in science is supported through the development of a narrative connected to past experiences and tied to the specific scientific concepts under investigation, such as "cooling" and "heating". The literature on children's alternative views has suggested that "Children think of cold or coldness as a substance. They often view cold as the 'opposite' of heat: they do not think of hot and cold as part of the same continuum" (Leeds National Curriculum Science Support Project, 1992). The particulars of the transfer of energy associated with heating (conduction, convection and radiation) are clearly outside of the psychological scope of 3-year-old children. However, the central idea of cooling and heating as a process of energy transfer as a result of a temperature difference is something that is not only of personal interest to children (e.g. so they do not burn their tongues when eating porridge) but, as this study has shown, is also within their grasp when a narrative is developed collectively to support scientific thinking.

Because children hear the words "hot" and "cold" all the time in everyday situations, and often in the context of waiting for food to cool, then tackling the concept of heating or cooling as a process within the same continuum makes personal sense to them. Drawing upon the personal narrative to deliberately co-create the narrative of the scientific concepts that have been explored through cooking and eating porridge provides an important vehicle for re-visiting experiences and applying or discussing scientific concepts to give new scientific meaning to past events and activities in the early childhood centre. Specifically, the distribution and re-distribution of energy during the cooling process were something that the children explored when they discussed how to cool down the porridge across a range of contexts, including when making a "cooling machine" for the porridge, and in free play within the centre, as the following example shows. Here, Jason was exploring some of the concepts associated with heating, as he shakes the small pieces of drinking straw he has taken to the imagination table (which had props for role playing three bears) from the collage area, simulating the distribution of heat whilst mentioning how hot the porridge becomes when cooked in the microwave.

> Jason is at the 3 bears table. He has taken to the table a bowl of small cut straws and is pouring these into the 2 equal sized bowls that are at the table. One larger bowl also stands on the table. Jason pours the straw pieces back into the basket, and then turns to the research assistant Shukla and asks:
>
> What can I get for you today? Shukla says she would like something.
> Jason: Porridge?
> Shukla: Yes. I'd like porridge.
> Jason: Porridge.
>   Jason takes the small basket of sticks, shakes them around as he says:
> Jason: But, I'm going to put it into the microwave, because it gets very hot.
> Shukla: OK. Is it too hot?
> Jason: Yes (shaking the basket of cut drinking straws). When I put it in this bowl (about to pour the cut straws into the bowl). Do you want it in this middle sized bowl or the big one, 'cause we don't do middle sized ones (shaking his head). Do you want a little one (correcting himself) or a big one, 'cause we don't do middle sized ones?

The collective scientific narrative arises incidentally and formally with the teacher within the centre for both the ongoing concept of "light" that the teacher had planned and the introduced concept of "heating" and "cooling" as part of the expansive scientific exploration of Goldilocks and the three bears.

Affective Scientific Imagination

According to Vygotsky's (1966) theory, pre-school children's leading activity is play. In play, children create an imaginary situation, where they change the meaning of objects, such as when cut straw becomes porridge in a bowl for the three bears or sand in a container in the sandpit becomes porridge to be cooked. Children change the meaning of the object from what they see to what they imagine it represents in their play. The objects act as pivots in children's play, and groups of children must negotiate the meaning of these objects in their collective imaginary situations (see Table 1) that they create in order to maintain and progress their play. That is, all the children need to imagine the objects in the same way where they all give the object the same meaning in their play. In imaginary situations, objects take on a new sense, and children act in accordance with the new imaginary situation. That is, they are no longer children, but they are bears cooking porridge. In this study, the children regularly engaged in imaginative play, reproducing the story of Goldilocks and the three bears. The imagination table (see Figure 1 below) which held many props to support imaginary play, was a space where a social expectation for play was created and where an emotional anticipation and enactment of the storyline was built. Added to this was the facility to create a Slowmation animation, where the iPad was positioned so that the children could photograph the play to build a sequenced storyline and activity (see Figure 1 below), including the cooking processes for making porridge, where the anticipation of the "hot" porridge featured. The emotional anticipation of actions, as images of expected parts of the story, was represented through imagination. The imaginary situation is created, and the imagined events to come are anticipated, as a form of affective imagination. Slowmation helps make this process concrete through capturing as images the story in action and consciously reproducing it. The use of props provides the pivots for supporting the children as they recreate the story and anticipated problem of the bears leaving the house whilst they wait for the porridge to cool.

In the dramatised verbal descriptions and expressive vivid depictions that were built through the teacher telling, re-telling and role playing Goldilocks and the three bears, the emotional anticipation of the "hot porridge" was created, and it was this that played out in the children's play, as was shown in the

FIGURE 1   Children consciously capture through Slowmation the anticipated scientific problem

example above of Jason inviting Shukla to share porridge with him, but cooling
it down for her. In this example, the cut-up straws were used to represent porridge, but at other times, children also used Lego bricks to represent porridge
when playing. Sand and playdough were also used for pretend cooking of porridge. These free play events were featured regularly during the 8 weeks. In these
imaginary situations, the children draw upon the science concept of "cooling"
at an everyday level. The anticipation of "hot porridge" and the need for "cooling
the porridge" created an emotional tension in the story which built an affective scientific imaginary situation. Imagination supports scientific thinking in
play, because in play, the process of the distribution of heat through the cooling
process is played out when the small cut-up straws and Lego pieces are used
to represent porridge. Imagining these scientific processes are easier for young
children in playful events that they can come back to again and again in their
play. The imagination table with props for role playing the three bears gives this
space and opportunity for imagination where scientific concepts can be played
out as a form of affective scientific imagination at the everyday level. Changing
the meaning of objects in play is important for being able to imagine new possibilities, ones that are not physically present or directly observable. As pointed
out by Hadzigeorgiou (2001), "many scientific concepts are imaginary constructions rather than the consequences of any direct observation" (p. 68). Anticipat-
ing these scientific features in their imaginary play is an outcome of this study

and is in line with emotional imagination introduced in Table 1. In the context of science education, this can be considered as affective *scientific* imagination.

Flickering between Real and Imaginative Scientific Worlds

Postitivist views in science have generally discounted the emotionality of learning and examined children's scientific conceptions as a result of science-related activities organised by teachers (Aikenhead & Michell, 2011). Yet in this research, when emotionality was examined, it was found that the children were drawing upon emotionality all the time. It was noted not only in their pleasure at engaging in science experiences, but also as they moved between real situations and imaginative situations. In the following example, it is possible to see that Matthew discusses his dream with his teacher. The intentional teaching of light in the centre had clearly found its way into Matthew's dreams.

Matthew:	I saw a rainbow.
Teacher:	When did you see a rainbow Matthew?
Matthew:	In a dream.
Teacher:	In a dream, what a lovely thing.
Matthew:	And I, and it hasn't got any bad things, bad dreams. You were in there, and kids.
Teacher:	So I was there, kids and a rainbow in your dream.
Matthew:	And I had another dream about coming here. Last time it was. But it wasn't that one (pointing to the rainbow on the ceiling).
Teacher:	Which one was it? Is it the one that shines through our prism in the afternoon.
Matthew:	Yeah.
Teacher:	You know the one that shines on the floor and the wall?
Matthew:	No, outside (points out of the window).
Teacher:	Outside. An outside rainbow.
Matthew:	It was it.
Teacher:	Was it in the sky or our wind (moves fingers gesturing windmill action)?
Matthew:	The window was blowing the rainbow away (gesturing with hands).
Teacher:	Was it?
Matthew:	And I had to go on it (gesturing with hands)
Teacher:	What a beautiful dream.

In this example, Matthew was simultaneously discussing his lived experiences of rainbows in the centre and the imaginative dimensions of rainbows, as something to "go on". Cultural–historical approaches to research do not separate out concepts from the lived lives of children, but rather seek to examine concept formation more broadly, as noted by Wardekker (1998) in his discussions of scientific concepts and reflection, van Oers's (1998) critique of the fallacy of decontextualisation, suggesting that abstract thinking is never disassociated from practice, and Hedegaard's (1998) view that thinking and concept formation are related to children's everyday life. A cultural–historical perspective allows researchers to examine the flickering between children's lived experiences of concepts and the experiences that teachers create to build concept formation. Matthew was flickering between the real world of rainbows and the fantasies commonly associated with rainbows. His depiction of the dream not only represented this but was the vehicle through which the teacher and he could discuss his imagined rainbow in relation to the rainbow made in the centre by a prism, or the "outdoor rainbow" that was regularly featured in the children's environment. This example is illustrative of flickering discussed in Table 1. Siry and Kremer (2011) argue that "Rainbows are quite common occurrences, and a likely phenomenon that the children have had direct experiences with in their own neighbourhoods. ... and rainbows are often depicted in children's books and cartoons." But as Siry and Kremer (2011) point out, "they are quite abstract as science concepts" (p. 646). The imaginary situation of the dream, and the real world of the centre and outdoor area where "real" rainbows feature, provide a useful movement or flickering between "real" and "imaginary" situations that help children work with difficult scientific concepts, such as the prism refracting light and creating a rainbow, or the child dreaming about the rainbow in the sky and not the one created with the prism in the centre. In the study reported in this paper, children flickered between the real world and the imagined world continually. As shown in Figure 2 below, it is noted that children continually changed the meaning of objects in their play to reflect the kinds of science experiences that were occurring in the centre, but clearly also in their everyday lives—such as when the cooking porridge experience that was organised by the teacher, is played out in the sandpit with other children. As discussed in Table 1 and in the previous section, when children see an object (e.g. sand) and change its meaning (e.g. porridge), they move from the real world of the tangible object of sand to an imaginary world where the sand has a new sense and takes on the meaning of porridge. In this imaginary world, a child can be a bear cooking porridge and can pretend to have hot porridge and to discuss with her other bear players the need to cool the porridge. The heating–cooling continuum can be imagined through imaginary play, thus paving the way for

FIGURE 2   Scientific flickering

more easily understanding difficult concepts such as convection or conduction later on. In this study, the flickering between real and imaginary was a positive movement that is thought to help children to imagine difficult concepts.

Taking a Scientific Perspective—Scientific Noticing

Vygotsky (1987) argued that in everyday situations, children build everyday concepts, such as paying attention to the dark (lack of light) rather than focusing on the sunlight within which they are bathed. It is the adult that draws children's attention to light sources, that helps them notice that light travels in straight lines, that it can be reflected, absorbed or refracted—with the latter needing more imagination and concrete experience to come to these understandings—that stopping the light creates a shadow, that darkness is the absence of light and that the eyes receive light rather than transmit it. Whilst children can observe many of these concepts themselves, it is through the interactions with others that children become consciously aware of the scientific concepts which explain how their world works. Vygotsky (2004) suggested that these everyday experiences and understandings pave the way for building scientific understandings. That is, his theory would suggest that the alternative views that may form do not necessarily get in the way of scientific concept formation but rather that these everyday concepts are needed for building scientific understandings about light. Children need to experience a range of temperatures before they can come to an understanding of the heating and cooling process, where hot and cold are on a continuum. Everyday understandings of "hot porridge" and "cold porridge" lay important foundations for understanding the scientific concept of "heating and cooling". A cultural–historical theorization would suggest that conductivity, convection and radiation could only be understood through the everyday experiences and discussions of "hot" and "cold".

Noticing and therefore having access to scientific concepts as a result of the teaching experience in preschools means that children can think about their everyday world in new ways. That is, their thinking and acting in everyday situations is transformed because they now know that by putting a metal spoon in the hot porridge, that heat will be conducted more quickly through the metal than the ceramic bowl, that they can stir the porridge to spread out the concentration of the energy, releasing it more quickly because of the greater surface area. That is, the children's environment has not changed, but the way young children relate to it has, because they are using concepts for interacting in their everyday lives in new and different ways, consciously using concepts. The children develop a scientific perspective of their environment. Aspects of this deliberate conceptual movement were noted in the comments made by the teacher when discussing the "light" area that she had set up in the centre to support children's conceptual development of light:

> The children are progressing through the stacking of the blocks on the overhead projector, to now, you saw that Jarrad gets that you lay them flat. There are some that are still going between that stacking and looking at them themselves, moving to the projection, and *us doing the three bears actually helped them to shift from the focusing on the projector table to looking at the wall*. So now, there is more of that looking at the wall, creating patterns that are on the wall starting to happen. So that conversation will now, like we had with Jarrad, we start with looking at what colours, what will happen if you put that colour on that colour. So that is a progression.

Although the light table with the coloured blocks and overhead projector were organised separately from the unit of work which drew upon fairy tales and Slowmation, the teacher had noted how Slowmation helped the children think more consciously about how light travels, even though their understandings were clearly still developing. The change in perspective and re-orientation of how to use the projector and the iPad were important developments in children's psychological functioning.

In this study, it was also noted that the teacher helped the children pay attention to specific scientifically important events in the centre, as shown in the example under the heading: "Distributed Concept Formation—Light" where the children were observing the rainbow on the wall created by the glass prism on the window ledge. The teacher used gestures (i.e. pointing to the prism) to help the 3-year-old children know where to look for the source of light refraction; she asked specific questions to draw attention to things that were noteworthy to look at, such as "Is it on your hand, Harris?" But importantly, she put a prism on the window ledge deliberately so that she can simulate what the children experienced regularly—rainbows—as a way of drawing attention to scientifically significant concepts which she knew were also of interest to the children. In Table 1. emotional filtering was discussed. Emotional filtering is where the teacher emotionally charges events. In this study, the teacher knowingly created situations that helped the children to pay attention to scientifically noteworthy situations and through this gave the possibility for scientific discussions and learning.

Vygotsky uses the example of the pointing gesture to illustrate the cultural construction of signs and symbols by discussing the idea that infants have to learn that the pointing gesture means you look in the direction in which the finger is positioned and follow that line of sight into the distance—rather than just looking at the finger. In many respects, the teacher in this study was building the same kind of cultural knowledge; she was constructing *a scientific gaze* or a *scientific noticing* for the children through supporting them to notice everyday things in their environment, but in scientific ways. Helping children to notice things makes these events and experiences not only obvious but conscious to children. When children consciously experience things, they are more likely to not only pay "scientific" attention, but are positioned positively to make scientific meaning of their everyday lives.

Conclusion

A cultural–historical perspective is recognized as useful for describing and understanding children's scientific learning because this theorisation goes beyond looking at science content in relation to age as the central criterion for determining what young children should learn. In this study, it was found that children gave a new scientific sense to their everyday life, that they engaged in collective scientific conversations which were shared by the children and the teacher. The *children collectively* changed the meaning of objects in their environment as they explored the storytelling, role play and Slowmation creation of Goldilocks and the three bears. That is, the children and the teacher collectively gave scientific meaning to their activities (see Table 1).

The argument put forward by Zaporozhets (2002) and shown in Table 1 in relation to science education shows that in emotional and cognitive participation in fairy tales that children reach "the ideal plane of *emotional imagination*" (p. 58). Through the role play of fairy tales, the children collectively begin to anticipate the results of each others' actions in the play, begin to anticipate their own actions, including image-bearing dramatisation, verbal descriptions, prop use and transformation, and importantly, the scientific solutions created through the support of the teacher. In this study, it was possible to document and analyse affective imagination in science. Through children's scientific engagement with their teacher, through the creation of scientific tensions and curiosities, and through the use of Slowmation to re-create the learning journey, children developed a sense of acting, feeling and thinking scientifically. In response to these experiences, the children flickered between the real world and the imaginary situations that were collectively created in the centre. The children developed a scientific gaze as the teacher helped them to pay attention to aspects of their everyday life as a form of *scientific noticing*. These findings have pedagogical significance for an early childhood profession who has traditionally been less engaged in science than in other areas of the curriculum.

It is argued that affective imagination supported the realisation of role play, the use of Slowmation and, though this, an engagement in non-directly observable scientific concepts. Affective imagination also named the way in which the children went beyond the immediately obvious and began to contemplate the way light was being refracted through the prism. Through the flickering between the real and imaginary worlds, a new scientific self-awareness and scientific perspective were developing for the children. It is through this emotional–cognitive activity that children can position themselves in specific ways in relation to the fairy tale plot or the scientific encounter. The child is able to participate in imaginary actions and accomplishments, acting out the ideal, and experiencing the meaning of a given situation, including the potential consequences for themselves and others within the role play of the fairy tale. Here, science becomes a valuable tool for early childhood children for helping them solve the problems inherent in the fairy tale, such as designing a porridge-cooling machine. As such, the study went beyond emotional imagination (see Table 1) and realised a form of *scientific affective imagination* for the children in this centre.

Taken together, it is suggested that there is pedagogical worth in using fairy tales to support scientific learning, and as was shown in Table 1, children collectively develop a form of scientific consciousness as they help the bears invent a cooling down machine, they create scientific narratives about hot and cold when they cook and role play the cooking process, they flicker between the borders of the imaginary world and the real world when they discuss their dreams about rainbows, they use imaginative thinking and emotionality as they give new meaning to the pieces of cut straw and act in new ways as they shake the straws to simulate the cooling of porridge and they anticipate the storylines of Goldilocks and the three bears, where the cooling of porridge has scientific significance.

As a result of this study, it is argued that fairy tales and Slowmation can both act as useful cultural devices for examining the emotional nature of young children's scientific learning in pre-school. Insights into understanding the dynamic unit of human consciousness during scientific learning became possible in this study because the teacher successfully brought together science and fairy tales into a form of scientific drama that children examined in reality and in play.

Acknowledgments

Funds from the Australian Research Council Discovery Grant provided the resources for enabling the study to be undertaken. Research assistance from Sue March (Field leader) and a volunteer student research team include Feiyan Chen, Judith Gome, Shukla Sikder, and Devi Sukmawati. Marie Hammer supported the professional development programme. Finally, the Staff, children and families from the early childhood centre gave generously of their time to participate in the study. An earlier version of this paper was presented at the 43rd annual Australasian Science Education Research Association Conference, 27th-30th June 2012, University of the Sunshine Coast, Australia.

References

Aikenhead, G., & Michell, H. (2011). *Bridging cultures: Indigenous and scientific ways of knowing nature*. Pearson.

Bozhovich, L. I. (2009). The social situation of child development. *Journal of Russian and East European Psychology, 47*(4), 59–86.

Carter, L. (2007). *Sociocultural influences on science education: Innovation for contemporary times*. Wiley InterScience. https://www.interscinece.wiley.com

Cowie, B., & Otrel-Cass, K. (2011). Exploring the value of 'horizontal' learning in early years science classrooms. *Early Years: An International Journal of Research and Development, 31*(3), 285–295.

Elkonin, D. B. (2005). The subject of our research: The developed form of play. *Journal of Russian and East European Psychology, 43*(1), 22–48.

El'Koninova, L. I. (2002). The object orientation of children's play in the context of understanding imaginary space—time in play and in stories. *Journal of Russian and East European Psychology, 39*(2), 30–51.

Fleer, M. (2010). *Early learning and development. Cultural–historical concepts in play*. Cambridge University Press.

Fleer, M. (2011a). Conceptual play: Foregrounding imagination and cognition during concept formation in early years education. *Contemporary Issues in Early Childhood, 12*(3), 224–240.

Fleer, M. (2011b). Kindergartens in cognitive times: Imagination as a dialectical relation between play and learning. *International Journal of Early Childhood, 43*(3), 245–259. Invited article for special themed issue.

Fleer, M. (2011c). Shared sustained imaginary conversations: Teachers and children consciously engaging in concepts during play. In S. Sheridan & P. Williams (Eds.), *livslångt lärande* (pp. 134–148). Liber.

Fleer, M., Gomes, J., & March, S. (2012, June 27–30). *A cultural-historical reading of scientific concept formation: Affordances for science learning in preschools* [Conference session]. Paper presented at the 43rd annual Australasian Science Education Research Association Conference, 2012, University of the Sunshine Coast, Australia.

Gonzalez Rey, F. (2012). Advancing on the concept of sense: Subjective sense and subjective configurations in human development. In M. Hedegaard, A. Edwards, & M. Fleer (Eds.), *Motives in children's development. Cultural–historical approaches* (pp. 45–62). Cambridge University Press.

Hadzigeorgiou, Y. (2001). The role of wonder and 'romance' in early childhood science education. *International Journal of Early Years Education, 9*(1), 63–69.

Hedegaard, M. (1998). Situated learning and cognition: Theoretical learning and cognition, scientific concepts and reflection. *Mind, Culture, and Activity, 5*(2), 114–126.

Hedegaard, M., & Fleer, M. (2008). *Studying children: A cultural–historical approach*. Open University Press.

Hedges, H., & Cullen, J. (2005). Subject knowledge in early childhood curriculum and pedagogy: Beliefs and practices. *Contemporary Issues in Early Childhood, 6*(1), 66–79.

Hedges, H., & Cullen, J. (2011). Participatory learning theories: A framework for early childhood pedagogy. *Early Child Development and Care*, 921–940. doi:10.1080/03004430.2011.597504

Hoban, G. (2007). Using slowmation for engaging pre-service elementary teachers in understanding science content knowledge. *Contemporary Issues in Technology and Teacher Education, 7*(2), 1–9.

Hoban, G., Loughran, J., & Nielsen, W. (2011). Slowmation: Engaging preservice elementary teachers with science knowledge through creating digital animations. *Journal of Research in Science Teaching, 48*, 985–1009.

Hoban, G., & Nielsen, W. (2010). The 5 Rs: A new teaching approach to encourage slow-mations (student generated animations) of science concepts. *Teaching Science, 56*(3), 33–37. Learning Science through Creating Animations 25.

Holodynski, M., & Friedlmeier, W. (2006). *Development of emotions and emotion regulation: Kluwer international series of outreach scholarship.* Springer Science+Business Media.

Iakovela, E. L. (2003). Emotional mechanisms underlying personal and creative development, *Journal of Russian and East European Psychology, 41*(6), 92–100.

Leach, J., & Scott, P. (2003). Individual and sociocultural views of learning in science education. *Science Education, 12*, 91–123.

Leeds National Curriculum Science Support Project. (1992). *Resources for supporting pupils' learning at key stage 3. Part 4, heating.* Leeds City Council, Department of Education, and the Children's Learning in science Research Group at the University of Leeds.

Osborne, J. F. (1996). Beyond constructivism. *Science Education, 80*(1), 53–82.

Pressick-Kilborn, K., Sainsbury, E., & Walker, R. (2005). Making sense of theoretical frameworks and methodological approaches: Exploring conceptual change and interest in learning from a sociocultural perspective. *The Australian Educational Researcher, 32*(2), 25–47.

Rogoff, B. (1990). *Apprenticeship in thinking: Cognitive development in social context.* Oxford University Press.

Roth, W.-M. (2008). Editorial. Knowing, participative thinking, emoting. *Mind, Culture, and Activity, 15*, 2–7.

Saracho, O. N., & Spodek, B. (2008). *Contemporary perspectives on science and technology in early childhood education.* Information Age Publishing.

Siry, C., & Kremer, I. (2011). Children explain the rainbow: Using young children's ideas to guide science curricula. *Journal of Science Education and Technology, 20*, 643–655.

van Oers, B. (1998). The fallacy of decontextualization, scientific concepts and reflection. *Mind, Culture, and Activity, 5*(2), 135–142.

Veresov, N. (2013). *Perezhivanie and cultural development: A key which opens the door?* Unpublished paper presented at Monash University, Peninsula Campus.

Vygotsky, L. S. (1966). Play and its role in the mental development of the child. *Voprosy Psikhologii, 12*, 62–76.

Vygotsky, L. S. (1982–1984). *Sobranie sochinenii v 6 tomakh* [*Collected works in 6 volumes*]. Pedagogika.

Vygotsky, L. S. (1986). *Thought and language* (A. Kozulin, Trans.). MIT Press. Original work published in 1934.

Vygotsky, L. S. (1987). In R. W. Rieber & A. S. Carton (Eds.), *The collected works of L.S. Vygotsky, vol. 1, problems of general psychology* (N. Minick, trans.). Plenum Press.

Vygotsky, L. S. (1994). The problem of the environment. In J. Valsiner & R. van der Veer (Eds.), *The Vygotsky reader* (pp. 347–348). Blackwell.

Vygotsky, L. S. (1997). In R. W. Rieber (Ed.), *The history of the development of higher mental functions. The collected works of L.S. Vygotsky* (M. H. Hall, trans.), vol. 4. Plenum Press.

Vygotsky, L. S. (1999). The teaching about emotions: Historical–psychological studies. In R. W. Rieber (Ed.), *The collected works of L.S. Vygotsky* (vol. 6, pp. 69–235). Plenum Press.

Vygotsky, L. S. (2004). Imagination and creativity in childhood. *Journal of Russian and East European Psychology, 42*(1), 7–97.

Wardekker, W. L. (1998). Scientific concepts and reflection. *Mind, Culture, and Activity, 5*(2), 143–153.

Wellman, H. M., Cross, F., & Watson, J. (2001). Meta-analysis of theory-of-mind development: The truth about false belief. *Child Development, 72*(3), 655–685.

Zaporozhets, A. V. (2002). Toward the question of the genesis, function, and structure of emotional processes in the child. *Journal of Russian and East European Psychology, 40*(2), 45–66.

Zinchenko, V. P. (2007). Thought and word: The approaches of L.S. Vygotsky and G.G. Shpet. In H. Daniels, M. Cole, & J. V. Wertsch (Eds.), *The Cambridge companion to Vygotsky* (pp. 212–256). Cambridge University Press.

Paper 4: The Demands and Motives Afforded through Digital Play in Early Childhood Activity Settings

This paper originally appeared as Fleer, M. (2014). The demands and motives afforded through digital play in early childhood activity settings. *Learning, Culture and Social Interaction, 3*(3), 202–209. https://doi.org/10.1016/j.lcsi.2014.02.012 Reprinted here with permission from the publisher.

Abstract

In drawing upon cultural–historical concepts this paper examines the demands that children meet when digital tablet technology is introduced during free play in early childhood settings. In particular, this paper reveals how an iPad and movie making program create new demands on children that afford a new relation between play and learning. Through analyses of video observations of children in one child care center in Australia it was found that how children respond to the new demands depends upon their motive orientation as they engage with tablet technology. The concept of *flickering* is introduced to capture how the microgenetic movement between collective and individual imagining in an activity occurs, between being in and out of an imaginary situation, and between concrete objects and virtual representations.

Keywords

early childhood education – cultural–historical – play – digital

Introduction

Play in the early years has generally been conceptualized in relation to its value as a pedagogical tool for supporting the development of children's learning; and much of this research has theorized play from a maturational point of view (e.g., Roopnarine, 2011). Longstanding theories of play within this framework have shown how it follows predetermined stages, such as solitary, parallel, and cooperative play (e.g., Smilansky, 1968), where the age of the child determines what kind of play might be expected. These developmental theories of play conceptualize play as universal and intrinsic to the child, unfolding in predictable ways along a common life span.

Yet recent case study research has shown that imaginary play is learned in families (Gaskins, Haight, & Lancy, 2007; Hedegaard & Fleer, 2013; Ugaste, 2005), and laboratory based studies have found that some parents signal and teach pretense in play to their infants (e.g., Lillard, 2007). Evidence also shows cultural variations in play across communities, disrupting the common belief that all children naturally play in exactly the same way (Goncu, Jain, & Tuerer, 2007; Pellegrini, 2011; Roopnarine, 2011). Here, the development of play is thought to be culturally constructed and not simply signaled by a child's movement from one age to the next.

Theories of play that are framed as universal and naturally unfolding are not helpful for understanding, for example, how new settings such as digitally interactive virtual conditions afford new ways of playing and learning. The argument in this article is that we need new ways of thinking about play that takes us beyond *a biologically oriented theoretical gaze* in order to recognize new possibilities in new settings. Virtual imaginative play for preschoolers appears to invite a new kind of play (Marsh, 2010; Singer & Singer, 2005), creating new demands and motives that are needed to be better understood.

   This article draws upon the cultural–historical concepts of demands and motives as conceptualized by Hedegaard (2012), in order to examine the *nature* of digital tablet technologies and what this affords for children's learning and development. The analyses focus on the transitions between activities within a free play activity setting in order to offer a better understanding of children's play and learning with digital technologies. The discussion is premised on the view that transition *between activities* is a central concept for understanding children's learning and development. This paper goes one step further than Hedegaard's analyses of transitions between activity settings (see Hedegaard, 2008) and examines microgenetic movements *within* a concrete activity setting where an iPad and movie making software program are introduced.

   This paper acknowledges recent theorizations about the nature of play and learning in relation to development (Hennig Rossen, 2013; Van Oers, 2013), the conceptualization of the play–learning child (Sommer, Pramling Samuelsson, & Hundeide, 2010), the microgenetic analysis of narratives for affording play development (Hakkarainen, 2010), and the nature of digital play in early years settings (e.g., Marsh, 2010). However, what is missing is how digital tablets create different demands on children's play and learning as understood through a child's social situation of development (Bozhovich, 2009). To capture demands and motives for play and learning in these simultaneously virtual and concrete settings, we draw upon Schousboe's (2013) spheres of play/reality and previous theorizations of collective and individual imagining (Fleer, 2010) in order to make visible how children *flicker* between the concrete activity and imagination. In this literature, it has been shown that children flicker between the concrete objects and the imaginary situation (Fleer, 2010) or move across the *porous sphere* of an imaginary situation collectively created, to staging new events, whilst always being cognizant of reality, as is evident when play fighting. These microgenetic movements in play provide a conceptualizations for thinking about the nature of digital play in free play settings where there are elements of learning in play that are needed by children for successfully playing in virtual and concrete situations.

   We begin this paper with a discussion of the key cultural-historical concepts of development, learning and play, in the context of demands, motives and transitions. This is followed by an analysis of the demands that digital tablet technology makes on children within a concrete activity setting. The analysis is based on a case study of three year old children creating a slowmation[2] of *Goldilocks and the three bears*. The paper concludes with a discussion of the

---

2 A simplified form of stop-motion digital animation which plays at 2 frames per second enabling children to narrate their creation (see examples on www.slowmation.com).

idea of *flickering between play and learning* within concrete activity settings where play is the leading activity. Here new insights are offered about how digital tablets in free play settings can lead to a change in the relationship between play and learning.

A Cultural–Historical Conception of Play, Learning and Development

Anchored in the works of Vygotsky (1998), Elkonin (1999) and Hedegaard (2012) put forward a conception of learning and development which argues for recognizing an analytic unity which includes the perspectives of the society, the institution, and the child (see also Hedegaard, 2008). One consequence of the centrality of the institution in this unity is that children's transition between different institutional practices, such as from home to school, presents them with new demands. Hedegaard's thesis is that these demands afford new possibilities for children's development (Hedegaard, 2009). In brief, central to the child's transition from one institutional practice to another is how demands in the new practice are successfully negotiated: how for example, a child learns that persistence is highly valued in a school practice where days are organized into blocks of time.

Hedegaard (2012) argues that the "dialectic between the child's orientation within an activity setting and the demands from the setting and other persons influence the child's activities within the child's zone of proximal development" (Hedegaard, 2012, p. 127). That is, development occurs when the demands and support within the concrete situation, and demands and actions from the child her/himself, lead to a new motive orientation for the child. In the context of early childhood, we see a development when the child's motive for play makes the transition into a learning motive so that learning in school becomes the child's new leading activity within the school setting. In concrete terms, when children start school they must deal with the new demands of reading, writing and mathematics. The practices that constitute schooling require them to move on from the leading activity of play, creating new demands and also possibilities for children to move on from a motive orientation of play to one of learning.

Based on our research in family and school settings (Hedegaard & Fleer, 2008, 2013) we have previously argued that the new demands children meet in both school and family life create new possibilities for both learning and development. In taking the child's perspective when analysing children's development in specific institutions, such as preschools, the concept of *motives* must also be foregrounded. Motives are not internally developed but are culturally shaped as a result of a child's participation in everyday life. Hedegaard (2002) argues that we know very little about how institutional goals become children's personal motives. As children enter an institution, such as a pre-school centre, often "the motive that lies behind the school activity is hidden from the child" (p. 61). The motive a teacher has for the particular activities s/he creates and that the child may participate in, may be very different to the motive the child has for entering into that particular activity. That is, play may be the dominating motive when children begin school. For the teacher to support the transition from a play to a learning motive as part of the child's development, s/he must not only be aware of the child's actual motive, but must keep in mind the ideal motive that "should develop through the school activity" (Hedegaard, 2002, p. 66). To determine a child's actual motive is challenging. Leontiev (1983), cited in Hedegaard (2002, p. 61) argues that "The true motive can only be explained objectively, "from the side", for example by studying the child's "playing school", because the personal "meaning" of playing can easily be brought to light through role play, and this, is its motive" (p. 212).

In the context of a childcare centre, it is the creation of the activity settings that orients the child towards either a play or a learning motive. In childcare centres in Australia the dominant practice tradition is play because play is promoted as the leading activity of children who attend these centres. In these institutions teachers are charged with the responsibility to create activity settings and offer activities within them that support children's play.

In this paper the relation between motives and demands within a specific activity setting of free play are used to analyse how new cultural devices – digital technologies – may lead to children's learning and their development. The concept of transition between activities within a free play setting is employed to capture how the change in relations between motives and demands took place during children's encounters with digital technologies in a childcare setting in a South-Eastern community within Australia. Here transition is not defined as a movement between institutions, or activity settings, but as a transition between activities during the activity setting of free play.

A cultural–historical definition of play assumes that a child creates an imaginary situation within an activity, where s/he changes the meaning of objects and actions as s/he enacts different roles and situations. Objects often support meaning-making in play but over time children no longer use objects to represent meaning, replacing them with ideas and actions in the imaginary situations they create. In preschool settings, teachers provide objects, space and time for play that allows children to create their own imaginary situations; whilst they support children in developing complexity in their play. New tools, such as digital tablets, have the potential to enrich the complexity of play, creating new conditions within an activity in free play. How digital tablet technology creates new demands and develops new motive orientation as children engage with it within a free play activity setting is investigated.

Study Overview

The 29 place childcare centre is located in an urban middle class community in Southern Australia. All the families are of British and European heritage background. Approximately 25 children (n = 53; range of 3.3 to 4.4; mean of 3.8 years) attend each session and most children come on two days per week. Staff included a degree qualified teacher, a two year trained technically qualified teacher and a volunteer. Data were gathered over eight weeks.

The children had available to them in their childcare centre a table which offered a series of props to support their play, as shown in Figure 1 below. The children experienced the telling and re-telling, dramatization and role-playing of the story of *Goldilocks and the three bears*. In addition to the regular preschool program, the children made porridge, investigated how porridge was cooked and cooled, and set up and investigated a porridge cooling machine. These experiences were repeated many times, and later the children, with support from the adults, also created a slowmation of the fairytale, which included the cooking experience as part of the storytelling. An iPad was placed on the three bears table, as is also shown in Figure 1. A software slowmation program (Hoban, 2007) was used on the iPad to help make this process concrete (e.g., children needed to photograph the story in action, consciously reproducing the sequence as a series of stills, which together formed their movie). This is shown in Figure 2.

Data Gathering and Analysis

All the children's play associated with the resources was video recorded, resulting in 232 h of observational data. Two and sometimes three cameras documented the everyday activities of children in the centre. A camera on a tripod captured the general activities in the centre. Another camera followed a focus child as they participated in the activity settings. Sometimes a third camera was used to capture more detail from the particular activity setting (i.e. two angles on the same activity). During whole group time, only one camera was used. These data were segmented into play episodes (e.g., when children were role-playing the fairytale or creating other imaginary situations, where children changed the meaning of objects and actions) and learning episodes (e.g., when

FIGURE 1   The imaginary table—Goldilocks and the 3 bears

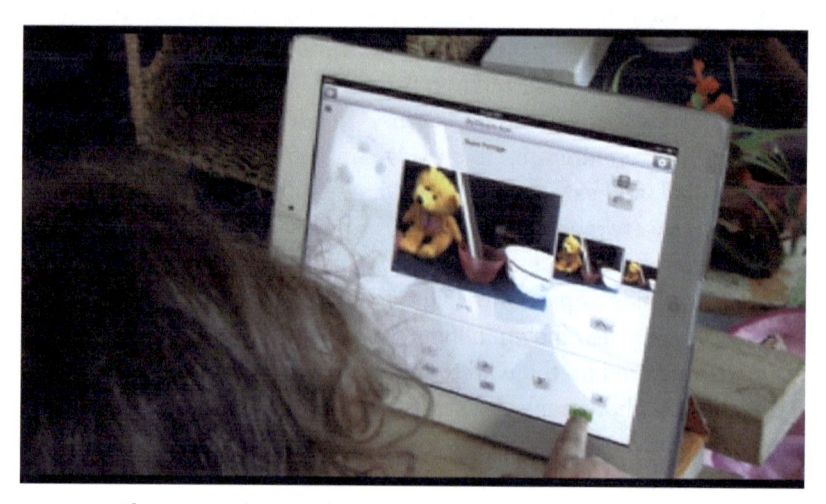

FIGURE 2   Slowmation photographic representation

children were learning how to use the software, or discussing the sequence of story content, or cooking, making or setting up props) and analysed in relation to the demands and motives within and across activity settings where a common sense, situated and thematic analysis was applied (see Hedegaard & Fleer, 2008). In particular, analyses focused on:

- how did the child relate to other children in play during free play when given a digital tablet?
- what activities did the children create when given a digital tablet?
- what motive orientations were evident when using the digital tablet?
- how children moved between imagination and reality within the concrete activity setting of free play where digital tablets were made available?

To give focus to the discussion in this paper, the transitions, demands and motives evident within one concrete activity settings were analysed from data gathered over three days (21/5 10 am–1.30 pm; 28/5 10–5.30 pm; 31/5 9–11.30 am). These data represent a total of 39 h of video observations.

The Differences in Demands within One Concrete Activity Setting

As has been noted by Bozhovich (2009), different children within the same activity setting will experience an activity differently because of what they bring to the activity setting. In this study it was found that the children brought different motives and competencies to the activity of creating a slowmation or movie of *Goldilocks and the three bears*. This could be understood by examining the different demands that the slowmation put upon the children in relation to what they brought to the activity. In the following extract from the data, Ginger (3.9 years) has an orientation to learning how to create a slowmation of the story, whilst Owen (3.9 years) has a motive orientation towards play. The demand made upon Ginger was in relation to how to introduce the objects so they could be photographed and used for making the movie. For Owen, the objects afforded opportunities for the role-play of the story; whilst the slowmation made few demands upon him when compared with Ginger. The notes that follow are a written description of the video recording.

> Five children are either standing or seated at the table where Sue (the research assistant) is actively supporting Ginger and Owen to make a movie of Goldilocks and the three bears. An iPad is positioned in front of an upturned box which acts as a stage for the 3 soft toys (3 bears) and 3 bowls (2 small and 1 large) [see Figure 1 for image of space]. The space between the stage and the iPad is used to bring into view each of the objects for telling the story and for photographing the objects as part of making the movie. Sue says as she moves a small bowl into the space "We put baby bear's bowl into the picture ...". Ginger moves her head to follow the placement of the bowl and to look at the iPad to see if the object is in the field of view. Ginger then moves the soft toy bear towards Sue's hand and Sue takes the soft toy bear and moves it into the space saying "and mummy bear comes in". Ginger then takes over, and moves the bear around in the space, checking her hand movements in relation to the iPad screen. Sue says "Do you want to take the picture?". Owen is looking on. As Sue asks this question Owen moves his hand towards the iPad and takes the picture. Sue then says "Move mummy bear along, and take the picture". Owen points to the bigger bear and says "He looks grumpy,

doesn't he?". He then looks to the other bears, appearing to check out their expressions, whilst making growling noises and scrunching up his face to simulate looking grumpy. He turns back to the iPad and presses the camera button.

As Sue discusses the need for considering the process of showing the making of the porridge by the bears, Owen focuses only on the objects. In response to Sue's comments, Owen says "Here's some oats" as he picks up the Goldilocks doll and shakes her above the bowl, pretending that oats have fallen into the bowl. As he makes the shaking movements, he also makes 'sh sh sh' sounds. Owen then takes a metal stick and begins to stir the imaginary oats (Lego bricks) in the bowl. He focuses on the objects only, moving them about and saying "That's Goldilock's clothes". He then unsuccessfully tries to dress Goldilocks and returns to stirring the porridge. Sue and Ginger move the iPad so that they can photograph the stirring action. But Owen is oblivious to this. Ginger continues to look to the objects in the context of capturing a photograph of them on the iPad. Eventually Owen finishes stirring the porridge and focuses on what is showing on the iPad.

Whilst Owen was oriented towards the iPad as a new object to explore, his focus of attention was on playing with story objects rather than trying to photograph them for the making of a movie. For Owen, play was the leading motive which shaped how he interacted with the objects and people in the activity setting. As such, the slowmation made few demands upon Owen. However, the iPad made huge demands upon Ginger, who continued to try and place objects in and out of the field of vision in relation to the story sequence. Owen's play with the objects made it difficult for her to photograph the story sequence, placing additional demands upon her. When Owen left to go to another concrete activity in the centre, Ginger continued to interact closely with Sue to realize the goal of photographing the story sequence to make a movie.

When the *child's* perspective as an analytical device is used to examine the concrete activity setting, it is possible to determine that Owen's motive orientation was not in relation to the goal of making a movie. His focus of attention was on reproducing the story, by role-playing *Goldilocks and the three bears* with the objects in the concrete activity setting. The objects provided the structure for re-telling the story, including giving him opportunities to add to the story by introducing to the storyline porridge making (e.g., by putting oats into the bowls). But his attention was not on how to accurately photograph and re-present the story in digital form. Owen's motive orientation reflected his actual intentions for play, and not the goals of the concrete activity setting as planned by the educational program. Owen brought to the concrete activity setting his own social situation of development, where play was the leading activity, and where the objects were used as pivots for his role-play. In contrast, Ginger brought a very different social situation of development to this same concrete activity setting. In following Ginger's intentions further within the concrete activity setting it is possible to determine that many demands were being made upon her because she was interested to learn how to use the slow-mation program to make a movie. This can be seen in the following extract taken from the video recordings.

> Ginger is standing in front of the iPad. Sue (research assistant) is to her right. Ginger takes the big bear and places it into view ready for photo-graphing. But the bear flops. Sue says "Do you want a rock to lean the bear on?". Ginger says "Yes. She is only 1, 2, 3, 4" as she moves the bear up and down to steady it into a sitting position. Sue asks "Is she in the picture?" to which Ginger replies "Yes" as she looks to the screen of the iPad. As Sue says "Is she in the right spot or do you want to move her a bit?" Ginger moves the bear backwards. Both Sue and Ginger move the bear until they are happy with its position. They then have a similar discussion about the placement of the bear's bowl, with Ginger saying "Maybe move this one [metal block], out of the way. Yes". Sue moves the bowl and the bear backwards so that the objects are shown as a smaller image on the iPad. As she does this, Ginger says "That's better". Ginger picks up the metal block which she uses as a spoon, and begins to stir inside of the bowl. Ginger tries to press the button of the camera program to take a photo-graph, and Sue noticing her difficulty says "It's tricky to stir and take the pictures at the same time isn't it?" to which Ginger responds "Yes". Ginger continues to work towards this goal and with Sue supporting the process, she successfully takes photographs of the stirring process (see Figure 2 for example of the photo sequence).

We can see that children from the same childcare centre have very differ-ent social situations because the same activity setting is understood differently as a result of the motive orientation of the children and their own particular social situation of development. As a result of Ginger's orientation and inten-tions in the concrete activity setting, she experienced many demands. She had to work out how to position the objects in the field of vision so that they could be photographed, she needed to remember not only to move the object just slightly, but also to press the camera button so that it would be visually recorded, and she needed to learn how to use equipment accurately and with new techniques, such as 'pinching the screen' to minimize images, to 'flick' the fingers to move across photographs to simulate the movie, and later to work with sound.

Motives and Competencies

Hedegaard (2012) has argued that a "child's motives are related to what is meaningful and important for them" and that "A child's motive is related to the child's intentions in specific situations, but a person's motives surpass the specific situation and can be seen as the dynamic that characteristics specific activities across different situations" (p. 134). Consequently, an activity is only motivating for a child if the activity setting is linked with the child's already developed motives. In the case of Owen, his motive orientation was towards play, and he was not interested to learn how to use the slowmation—although he liked pressing the camera button. For Ginger, she found the activity motivating because she was interested to learn how to make a movie and represent the story in a new way. She was not oriented to playing with the objects but rather she was motivated towards using the objects to achieve the goals of the activity setting. Hedegaard (2012) has argued that in educational settings it is important to be aware of the "child's motive orientation as well as directing the introduced activities towards supporting new motives" (p. 135). We see the motive orientation of the children through the intentions of both Yoka (3.5 years) and Megan (4.1 years) in the following example in the same concrete activity setting, where Megan is shown how to use the software by Yoka.

> Yoka and Megan are standing in front of the iPad. Megan is controlling the iPad whilst Yoka looks on. Megan has open a selection of photographs. She moves back and forth between the full screen image and the collection of photographs which Yoka observes. Megan then moves from the menu of programs and into camera mode. She takes a photograph, and then returns to the display of photographs she has just taken. Yoka says "Can I do it?". Megan points to the correct button on the screen and says "Here you are". Yoka immediately presses the button. Megan instructs Yoka: "You have to go here" to which Yoka responds: "Let me just try that" ... (children's interactions continue).
>
> Yoka is now on her own at the iPad. She flicks through the photographs and then walks around the iPad and towards the objects. She adjusts the bears and as she does this she uses self-talk to discuss her actions: "There you are. You over here. And this one [big bear], goes here." She picks up

the small bear and places it on the small chair saying "Baby bear sits there". She then places the big bear behind the small bear and returns to the iPad. She says as she presses the button on the frame of the iPad "You got to press it here". She then returns to the menu of programs and selects the camera button saying "Press that". She then moves her finger to the camera button on the screen and presses the button to take a photograph saying "Right". She then flicks through the photographs—going backwards and forward from the photo she has taken earlier, making a 'swish, swish' sound as she flicks.

It is through iteratively participating in the concrete activity settings over time that we see within the one institution new forms of competencies emerge. These competencies emerge as a result of the new demands that are placed on children who have a learning motive within the play based setting in which they attend each day. It is through the continual demands and the small crises they meet, that the development of small competencies become evident. As Hedegaard (2012) reminds us, "Learning occurs when there is a qualitative shift in the child's participation in an activity setting and thereby in his or her relations to other persons" (p. 136). This could be seen when Megan showed Yoka how to work with the iPad and slowmation program and where Yoka later worked with the iPad and slowmation program independently.

Different Kinds of Flickering

The range of demands noted during play and learning when using digital tablets, can be thought about as small back and forth movements or flickering. These *microgenetic movements* can be conceptualized as flickering in and out of imaginary situations, flickering between individual and collective activity, and flickering between concrete objects and virtual representations.

Flickering in and out of imaginary situations was noted in the first example of Owen and Ginger where Owen continued to move back and forth between the real situation of the concrete activity setting and the imaginary situation of the story. Owen spent most of his time in the imaginary situation, but as has been shown by Schousboe (2013), children, even when in imaginary situations, continue to stay connected with reality, and that the boundaries between real and pretend are rather porous. El'koninova (2002) introduced the idea of children flickering between the concrete and the imaginary world. Flickering as a form of transition best represents how Owen moved between pretense and reality within the same concrete activity setting. Owen spent most of his time in the imaginary situation, even though he moved back to the concrete activity setting regularly. The flickering was directly under his control. He was not required to stay focused on the goals of the concrete activity setting. But Sue's continual suggestions, such as 'Who wants to take this photograph?' or 'Shall we move the bear?' or 'Is the bowl in the right position?' were prompts for Owen to return to the goals of the activity setting.

Flickering between individual and collective activity is also another form of movement that was noted in this study. A sense of the collective was established through the role of the adult where the narrative inherent in both the fairytale and in the continual narration of the story by Sue meant that the children were united in their activity towards the common goal. This allowed for children to not only flicker in and out of the imaginary situation, but to pursue their own goals whilst working collectively with other children and adults. The activity was held together through the narrative of the adult, and the children contributed more or less towards the goals of the concrete activity setting. For instance, Owen flickers from the imaginary situation of stirring the porridge and dressing Goldilocks to the concrete situation of pressing the camera button on the iPad as a result of Sue saying 'Who would like to press the button?' This was also seen when Megan and Yoka collectively created a movie on the iPad and when Yoka later used self-talk to create the movie, acting as though Megan was there instructing her.

As with the concept of children creating an imaginary situation that is commonly shared and negotiated, the collective concrete activity setting, even with the diversity of what individual children bring in terms of motives and competences, was an important condition for supporting the *microgenetic movements* between lower and higher forms of competence, an observation which is in line with Vygotsky's (1966) view that competencies are social before they become individual. Concepts and actions appear between people as part of their social relations, usually mediated by a more expert other. That is, "first between people as an intermental category (social), then within the child as an intramental category (psychological collision)." (Vygotsky, 1997, p. 106).

Flickering between concrete objects and virtual representation on tablets was also noted. It was found that children tended to flicker between the concrete objects on the table and the representations of the same objects on the iPad. Digital tablet technology allows for the dual process of being both in the play on the stage (using concrete objects) and in front of the stage as the audience (looking at the photographic images on the iPad as a digital placeholder). This creates new demands in play and affords new insights into the imaginary situation for very young children. Children had to distinguish between the concrete objects and the photographic representation because the iPad likeness was so sharp.

Children can see their play objects as photographed images representing a re-enactment of the fairytale play. In re-creating their play into a movie, and in viewing the images, the children must act more consciously when placing objects to be photographed. But this also sets up a demand of being able to distinguish between the concrete scene and the photographed scene. The child must move beyond objects and action in their play, and to work with meaning at a new level. The point here is to recognize what these new demands mean for the children's development, and how the flickering between play and learning is heightened through the new technologies. This requires further study to fully appreciate what kinds of *microgenetic movements* that might be observed in digital play.

Conclusion

The findings of this study point to the need for better understanding the relations between motive orientations and demands in free play activity settings where teachers are seeking to introduce specific learning outcomes. This study has attempted to fill this gap by introducing the idea of *microgenetic movements* within one concrete activity setting where the leading activity is play. The *microgenetic movements* between the story activity and the iPad activity that were noted have been described here as a flickering between collective and individual activity, between being in and out of an imaginary situation, and between play and learning.

The movement from the story to iPad activity and back again can be conceptualized not as a movement at one point in time and in one direction, but as small, consistent and iterative *microgenetic movements* within a concrete activity setting. As this study has shown, these *microgenetic movements* occur during the play of Goldilocks and the 3 bears as well as when learning how to use the new digital tools for the first time, but also when exploring how to represent play virtually on the digital tablets.

The findings have also shown that even in play based settings which afford dimensions of learning, how children take up learning is dependent upon the child's social situation of development. Children do not take up the learning goals of an activity setting when their leading activity is play. Analysing the new demands created through the introduction of digital tablets in the play-based setting gave the possibilities for understanding this new dimension of learning in play not previously discussed in the literature.

Taking the child's perspective has allowed us to see how the child moves between play and learning with the help of tools which require the child to reflect on her/his actions. It can be argued that the introduction of digital tablets create new demands in play-based settings affording new possibilities for both play and learning, and the identified microgenetic movements show a new kind of relations between play and learning.

Acknowledgment

Funds from the Australian Research Council Discovery Grant provided the resources for enabling the study to be undertaken, including allowing for research assistance from Sue March (field leader), Feiyan Chen, Judith Gomes, Shukla Sikder, and Devi Sukmawati. Feedback on earlier versions of the paper by members of team, colleagues (Liang Li and Denise Chapman) and the special issue editors (Mariane Hedegaard and Anne Edwards) was very much appreciated.

References

Bozhovich, L. I. (2009). The social situation of child development. *Journal of Russian and East European Psychology, 47*, 59–86.

Elkonin, D. B. (1999). Toward the problem of stages in the mental development of children. *Journal of Russian and East European Psychology, 37*(6), 11–30.

El'koninova, L. I. (2002, March–April). The object orientation of children's play in the context of understanding imaginary space: Time in play and in stories. *Journal of Russian and East European Psychology, 39*(2), 30–51.

Fleer, M. (2010). *Early learning and development: Cultural-historical concepts in play.* Cambridge University Press.

Gaskins, S., Haight, W., & Lancy, D. F. (2007). The cultural construction of play. In A. Goncu & S. Gaskins (Eds.), *Play and development: Evolutionary, sociocultural, and functional perspectives* (pp. 179–202). Lawrence Erlbaum.

Goncu, A., Jain, J., & Tuerer, U. (2007). Children's play as cultural interpretation. In A. Goncu & S. Gaskins (Eds.), *Play and development: Evolutionary, sociocultural, and functional perspectives* (pp. 155–178). Lawrence Erlbaum.

Hakkarainen, P. (2010). Cultural-historical methodology of the study of human development in transitions. *Cultural-Historical Psychology, 4*, 75–81.

Hedegaard, M. (2002). *Learning and child development: A cultural–historical study.* Aarhus University Press.

Hedegaard, M. (2008). A cultural–historical theory of children's development. In M. Hedegaard & M. Fleer (Eds.), *Studying children: A cultural–historical approach* (pp. 10–29). Open University Press.

Hedegaard, M. (2009). Children's development from a cultural–historical approach: Children's activity in everyday local settings as foundation for their development. *Mind, Culture, and Activity, 16,* 64–81.

Hedegaard, M. (2012). Analyzing children's learning and development in everyday settings from a cultural–historical wholeness approach. *Mind, Culture, and Activity, 19,* 127–138.

Hedegaard, M., & Fleer, M. (2008). *Studying children: A cultural–historical approach.* Open University Press.

Hedegaard, M., & Fleer, M. (2013). *Play, leaning and children's development: Everyday life in families and transition to school.* Cambridge University Press.

Hennig Rossen, L. (2013). Play to learn, learn to play: Boundary crossing within zones of proximal development. In I. Schousboe & D. Winther-Lindqvist (Eds.), *Play and playfulness: Cultural-historical perspectives* (pp. 141–164). Springer.

Hoban, G. (2007). Using Slowmation for engaging preservice elementary teachers in understanding science content knowledge. *Contemporary Issues in Technology and Teacher Education, 7*(2), 1–9.

Leontiev, A. N. (1983). *Virksomhed, bevidsthed og personlighed.* Sputnik (Org. Activity, consciousness and personality). Prentice Hall.

Lillard, A. (2007). Guided participation: How mothers structure and children understand pretend play. In A. Goncu & S. Gaskins (Eds.), *Play and development: Evolutionary, sociocultural, and functional perspectives* (pp. 131–153). Lawrence Erlbaum.

Marsh, J. (2010). Young children's play in online virtual worlds. *Journal of Early Childhood Research, 8*(10), 23–39.

Pellegrini, A. D. (Ed.). (2011). *The Oxford handbook of the development of play.* Oxford University Press.

Roopnarine, J. L. (2011). Cultural variations in belief about play, parent–child play, and children's play: Meaning for childhood development. In A. D. Pellegrini (Ed.), *The Oxford handbook of the development of play* (pp. 19–37). Oxford University Press.

Schousboe, I. (2013). The structure of fantasy play and its implications for good and evil games. In I. Schousboe & D. Winther-Lindqvist (Eds.), *Play and playfulness: Cultural-historical perspectives* (pp. 13–27). Springer.

Singer, D. G., & Singer, J. L. (2005). *Imagination and play in the electronic age.* Harvard University Press.

Smilansky, S. (1968). *The effects of sociodramatic play on disadvantaged pre-school children.* Wiley.

Sommer, D., Pramling Samuelsson, I., & Hundeide, K. (2010). *Child perspectives and children's perspectives in theory and practice.* Springer.

Ugaste, A. (2005). *The child's play world at home and the mother's role in the play* [Dissertation]. Faculty of Education, University of Jyvaskyla.

Van Oers, B. (2013). An activity theory view on the development of playing. In I. Schousboe & D. Winther-Lindqvist (Eds.), *Play and playfulness: Cultural-historical perspectives* (pp. 231–250). Springer.

Vygotsky, L. S. (1966). Play and its role in the mental development of the child. *Voprosy Psikhologii, 12*(6), 62–76.

Vygotsky, L. S. (1997). The history of the development of higher mental functions (M. J. Hall, Trans.). In R. W. Rieber (Ed.), *The collected works of L. S. Vygotsky* (Vol. 4). Plenum Press.

Vygotsky, L. S. (1998). Child psychology (M. J. Hall, Trans.). In R. W. Rieber (Ed.), *The collected works of L. S. Vygotsky* (Vol. 5). Kluwer Academic and Plenum Publishers.

Paper 5: Pedagogical Positioning in Play – Teachers Being inside and outside of Children's Imaginary Play

Marilyn Fleer

This paper originally appeared as Fleer, M. (2015). Pedagogical positioning in play – teachers being inside and outside of children's imaginary play. *Early Child Development and Care, 185*(11–12), 1801–1814. https://doi.org/10.1080/03004430.2015.1028393 Reprinted here with permission from the publisher.

Abstract

Although there is a long tradition of play pedagogy in early childhood education, teachers have mostly taken a passive role in children's play. There are relatively few studies of the pedagogical roles adults take from inside of children's imaginary play. This paper seeks to fill this gap through presenting the findings of a study where the play pedagogy of five Australian childcare centres was analysed. Video observations of nine teachers interacting with children (3.3–5.5 years) during free play time (399 h of video observations) were analysed using the concept of subject positioning. It was found most teachers positioning themselves outside of children's play. A typology of play is presented which includes teacher proximity to children's play; teacher intent is in parallel with children's intent; teacher is following the children's play; teacher is engaged in sustained collective play; and teacher is inside the children's imaginary play.

Keywords

early childhood pedagogy – play – cultural–historical theory – sociocultural – playworlds

Introduction

Although a huge volume of the literature on children's play in early childhood education exists, very little of this research systematically examines the role of the teacher in children's play (Singer, Nederend, Penninx, Tajik, & Boom, 2014). Mostly, there is a belief that for something to count as play, then adults should not be involved (see Pellegrini, 2011). However, some studies have questioned this maturational assumption (van Oers, 2013) and have argued that adults can enrich and develop children's play when they act as play partners (e.g., Hakkarainen, 2010), that children need adult support in their play (e.g., Singer et al., 2014), because they no longer know how to play in some communities (e.g., Bodrova, 2008), and that in social contexts, adults do actually teach children how to play (e.g., Ugaste, 2005), suggesting that play is a learned cultural practice (see Goncu & Gaskins, 2007). These cultural–historical studies support the perspective that play should not be viewed as the private business of children.

The majority of research assumes a universal conception of play pedagogy (Fleer, 2014), and does not analyse the pedagogical role of adults when inside of children's imaginary play. To fill this gap, this paper presents the findings of a study that sought to analyse the pedagogical practices of teachers in play-based settings in order to give a more nuanced understanding of play pedagogy. This paper goes beyond conceptualising the role of adults in play as a simple binary of the adult being or not being involved in children's play. Rather, the theoretical framing of this paper draws upon cultural–historical theory (Vygotsky, 1966) where play is defined as the creation of an imaginary situation, in which children and adults change the meaning of objects and actions, giving them a new sense within the imaginary play situations (Vygotsky, 1966, 2005). Kravtsova (2014) has stated that in addition to imagination being a central criterion of a cultural–historical definition of play, that 'in play a child is at the same time inside it (i.e., crying like a patient) and outside it (i.e., rejoicing as a player)' (p. 22) highlighting the double subjectivity of players. This premise has been adopted as the central dimension of play pedagogy.

This paper begins with a theoretical discussion of the central cultural–historical concepts that informed this study, followed by the study design and the findings, and concludes with a typology of play pedagogy for better understanding the diversity of roles adults take in play-based settings. The paper goes beyond a universal understanding of play pedagogy, and a binary conceptualisation of the role of adults, and examines the everyday pedagogical practices of teachers in play-based settings.

A Cultural–Historical Conceptualisation of the Role of the Adult in Children's Play

Like the long-standing research of Bretherton (1984) into children being in or out of the play frame, Kravtsov and Kravtsova (2010) have drawn attention to the concept of being inside (pretending to be cooking) or outside (gathering materials to support the play) of an imaginary play situation. This important psychological concept (Bredikyte, 2010) draws attention to the imaginary situation in play and the valued place of the players (pretending to be chiefs) in reading the play situation. The perspective taken in the long-standing (e.g., Garvey, 1977) and contemporary cultural–historical research (e.g., Schousboe & Winther-Lindqvist, 2013) has always been in relation to the child and the imaginary situation that she/he creates. Little attention has been directed to the teacher being inside of the imaginary situation together with the children. Paying attention to what the teacher does in the context of the imaginary situation as a unit of analysis for better understanding pedagogical practices in play has generally not been undertaken, and as a result, the pedagogical role of the adult inside the imaginary situation is not well understood.

What is known is that teachers do have an important role in developing children's play (Hakkarainen & Bredikyte, 2010). For instance, Hakkarainen, Bredikyte, Jakkula, and Munter (2013) have examined how teachers in play-worlds collectively create imaginary situations with children. Playworlds were first introduced into the literature through the research of Lindqvist (1995) in Sweden. The focus of playworlds is the teacher and the children collectively role-playing together complex themes with problem situations from stories, fairy tales, and other narratives. Hakkarainen et al. (2013) have identified seven characteristics for supporting the development of play in playworlds, which centre mostly on the conditions for play (e.g., fascinating play script, dramatic tension in the play script, and motivating shared theme). However, they also state that adults must be emotionally involved in the play, elaborate critical turns in the play, such as anticipation, introducing new characters and events, or introduce critical incident so that the play continues to develop. Importantly, they recommend that adults take a role in the imaginary play, such as a character in the storyline. In particular, they suggest that 'We believe that professionals working with young children not only have to support the development of ongoing play, but also have to present and model higher forms of play' (Hakkarainen et al., 2013, p. 216). This is consistent with research in New Zealand where it is argued that 'it is vital to have teachers who position themselves within play-based teaching and learning interactions' (Hedges, 2014, p. 198). This is a very different perspective to not interfering in children's play as has been observed as key to defining what constitutes play (see McInnes, Howard, Crowley, & Miles, 2013).

There is a growing body of research that positions the adult inside of children's play. Beginning with the seminal work of Lindqvist (1995) into playworlds, scholars in the USA (Ferholt, 2010), Finland (Bredikyte, 2011), and Australia (Fleer, 2013a) have introduced play pedagogy that positions the adult as taking an active role inside of children's play, rather than what constitutes the norm of acting as an observer or supporter from outside of children's play. Although the playworlds research has not been conceptualised distinctly from other play research as the 'adult being inside of the play', this is clearly an important difference between playworlds and many other forms of pretend play that feature generally in free play-based settings in many early childhood centres in European and European heritage contexts.

Hakkarainen (2010) has examined the specific pedagogical characteristics in playworlds for building a narrative methodology for developing children's play. The pedagogy is illustrative of how playworlds work and the active role the adult assumes inside of children's play. According to Hakkarainen (2006), the pedagogy of playworlds is framed through the telling or reading of a story and the children and the teacher work together to create the play. However, the play evolves through the introduction of new elements where the teacher and children elaborate the basic theme or plot, constructing scenes and enacting specific roles where they 'agree jointly to imagined particular settings and props' (p. 210). Hakkarainen (2010) has recommended the following pedagogical principles that are reproduced here in order to show the active positioning of the adult inside of children's play:

1. 'Children are invited to enter jointly created imaginary situations based on tales, stories and children's fiction (ideal cultural forms) which serve as the basis of adult-child joint playworlds and child-initiated pretend play.

2. Themes are carefully selected to reflect basic human values and dichotomies as well as coincide with educational needs of the classroom and individual children.

3. The theme is brought alive with adults' participation and emotional involvement (in roles, dramatizations, story telling etc.). Sense and significance of events and relations between characters has to be emphasized and made as clear as possible (without directly telling everything!).

4. Dramatic collisions of tales and stories raise children's questions and are starting points of joint reflection (Why Kai became mean after getting a piece of mirror in his eye [Snow Queen]). Changing or adding dramatic events from other stories causes more collisions and helps in inventing dilemmas, which have to be solved realistically before the story an continue (Shipwreck stopped captain Hook's voyage and children are asked to help him building (planning) a new ship).

5. Creating environments and reserving time for child-initiated play is essential in the development of children's reflection on playworld events. Observation of child-initiated play reflecting playworld events offers valuable hints about new turns or further elaboration of joint playworld themes' (p. 79).

Singer et al. (2014) have shown the importance of how the teacher physically positions him or herself in close or distant proximity to the infants and toddlers that they research in Dutch childcare centres, noting the close relationships between teacher proximity and a positive level of play engagement in two- and three-year-old children. Singer et al. (2014) found that teachers mostly spent their time walking around and focused on the individual needs of infants, rather than being sensitive to the collective group play being enacted by the infants and toddlers. Through the individualised approach of care by teachers in the Dutch childcare centres, it would seem that the possibilities for being inside of group play were seriously reduced. This is consistent with research by Goncu (1998) who noted the importance of intersubjectivity or shared understanding between children and adults in social pretend play. His review found that 'intersubjectivity changes from one point to another as a result of continuous knowledge exchange and negotiation between partners' (p. 120) and in pretend play, this means that, 'children take for granted that their partners share their knowledge, leaving implicit some of their meaning. Doing so obliges children to make and test assumptions about what their partners mean, thus creating intersubjectivity' (p. 121). In the context of research into mothers and their infants, the communication of shared meaning when signalling something as pretence (see Lillard, 2007) features exaggeration of gesture, sound and physical movements, as is observed between children when using meta-communicative language (originally in Bateson, 1955) to establish intersubjectivity in pretend play as noted by Goncu (1998). Intersubjectivity in group settings for establishing social pretend play between children and teachers has not been the focus of research attention and little is known about the pedagogical role of teachers in such contexts.

These studies suggest that a greater understanding of the role of the teacher is needed, particularly in relation to what role the teacher takes (or not), within the children's imaginary play situations.

Study Design

Research Question

This study sought to understand the role adults take in children's play within play-based settings, such as childcare, preschool, and kindergarten. Specifically, it asked, 'What role do teachers take when inside the imaginary play situation in play-based settings?' Previous research in this area has been in the context of playworlds, which is limited in number and across countries. This study focuses only on the general pedagogical practices of teachers found in five Australian contexts where playworlds was not a part of teachers' day-to-day play practices.

Sample and Scope of Data Gathering

In order to answer the research question, video observations were made of nine teachers interacting with children during free play time and group time. Teachers, families, and children were invited into the study, and informed consent was gained through informal gatherings with families and teachers about the intent of the research. Distribution of letters and consent forms took place at this time. Children were asked if they wished to participate on an ongoing basis, and the digital video camera marked the field of the data gathering process for the children. Children actively engaged in looking through the view finder in order to gain insights into the video documentation process of themselves and their friends. Only consenting families and children were filmed. A summary of the sample and data gathered is shown in Table 1.

All the teachers in the study are credentialed with an early childhood qualification, and have a minimum of 10 years of teaching experience. Eight of the nine teachers were of European heritage background, and one was of Asian descent.

Three of the five centres are located in urban regions, one in a capital city, and one in a rural context in Australia. Teachers use the national curriculum framework that advocates for both free play and intentional teaching (Australian Government, 2009). Collectively, the children were drawn from families of European heritage, Asian heritage, and African heritage backgrounds. This range is typical for the regions in which the centres are located. In all centres,

TABLE 1   Overview of sample and data generated

Centre	Number of teachers	Number of children	Age range	Observation period	Data generated
Centre A	3	53	3.3–4.4 years; mean age of 3.8 years	8 weeks	242 h
Centre B	1	20	4.6–5.7 years; mean age of 5.0 years	5 weeks	55 h
Centre C	1	20	3.3–5.3 years; mean age of 4.2 years	3 weeks	74 h
Centre D	2	24	4.0–5.2 years; mean age of 4.5 years	4 weeks	20 h
Centre E	2	24	4.4–5.5 years; mean age of 4.11 years	3 weeks	8 h

teachers introduced concepts into the play-based settings to support children's play and learning.

Video observations were made using at least one camera and sometimes three. One camera (and sometime a second camera) followed the children during free play time for detailed close up filming of playful activities. Another camera on a tripod captured a long view of the centre during free play time. Usually, only one camera filmed whole group time, which took place twice per day during the observation period in each of the centres. A total of 399 h of video data were generated.

Teachers were also informally interviewed about their role in the play and learning planned in the centre. These informal interviews were undertaken in situ or at the end of a day of filming, in order to gain greater insights into teacher thinking and planning about play and learning. In addition, teachers were involved in professional learning activities associated with the cultural–historical concepts of play, learning and development, in the context of play and learning science concepts in early childhood. These sessions were video recorded and constituted approximately 2–5 h of video data per centre from the overall data set detailed above.

Analysis

Video observations were analysed using the analytical concept of subject positioning (Kravtsov & Kravtsova, 2010) to examine the roles the teachers and the children took during the free play sessions. Kravtsov and Kravtsova (2010) in their pedagogical research have conceptualised teachers into pairs (i.e. pair pedagogues) where 'positioning' is always a relation to the other teacher or a child(ren). An interactive moment can be categorised as 'above the child', 'equal with the child', 'below the child', 'child is independent of the teacher' and in the 'primordial we' position. This is shown in Figure 1.

Adult and child positioning in play can mean many different things in the analysis frame. For instance, when a teacher leads children, then the teacher is 'above the children', as we might see when a teacher makes suggestions in playful settings. Play positioning can also include an interaction where a teacher takes the lead from the child. According to Kravtsov and Kravtsova (2010), the teacher is then in the 'below position'. When the teacher takes an 'equal position', then the child and the teacher are contributing equally to the play moments and interactions. In the 'primordial we position', the teacher actively models to the child playful interactions, where the child is swept along with the play, being a part of it, but not necessarily understanding or demonstrating agency in that context. This can be seen in children's play when older children lead the play, but allow younger children to enter the play and to be a part of the storyline, even if they do not necessarily understand the storyline or the imaginary situation being generated. For example, an older child or a teacher might take the hand of a younger child and help them to 'mix a cake' in pretence. The younger child may be making mixing actions, but does not necessarily follow the intricacies of the imaginary cooking experience being developed by the older child or teacher. In the independent position, the child is acting without the teacher, but she/he does engage in social referencing from a distance. For example in play, a child will play independently of the teacher, but will regularly look back to the adult for confirmation or to see if they are physically present or observing them.

In Kravtsov and Kravtsova's (2010) research, they have used subject positioning in pair pedagogy contexts, showing how one teacher can be in one position, such as 'above the child' while the other teacher can be 'equal with the children'. In the Australian context, this theoretical positioning of pair pedagogy is unfamiliar to teachers and could not be used as part of the unit of analysis. As such, the concepts of subject positioning were used in the context of adult–child interactions, rather than pair pedagogy (i.e. adult–adult–child) interactions, as was originally conceptualised by Kravtsov and Kravtsova (2010). Furthermore, the study also drew upon Vygotsky's (2004) concept of

TEACHER					CHILD
Above					Below
Below					Above
Equal					Equal
Primordial we (above)					Primordial we (below)
Independent					Independent

FIGURE 1   Adult and child positioning in play pedagogy

imagination and creativity and his theory of play (Vygotsky, 1966) as discussed above, in order to analyse the teachers' positioning in the context of being inside or outside of the imaginary situation that the children were playing within. This latter analysis has not yet been explicitly undertaken in subject positioning, and offers a new way of framing the analysis of the teachers' role in play-based settings.

Limitations

Although nine teachers across five centres could never seek to be representative of early childhood teachers in Australia or elsewhere, the detailed analysis of video observations of playful interactions in these settings does give some insights into a range of pedagogical possibilities in play-based settings. A broader sample would and should reveal other possible adult–child interactions during free play time, and potentially illuminating further pedagogical positioning in play. As such, the findings reported in the next section, should be viewed with this limitation of sample size in mind.

Findings and Discussion

As might be expected, the findings show that a diversity of teacher pedagogical positioning in play was evident across and within the centres. However, what was new was how teachers demonstrated pedagogical positioning in the context of being in or out of the imaginary situation. It is this particular finding that is elaborated in this paper. The typology of play pedagogy that emerged from this research shows that the teachers acted in five different ways in relation to the imaginary situation.

1.   Teacher proximity to children's play
2.   Teacher intent is in parallel with the children's play intent
3.   Teacher is following the children's play

4.   Teacher is engaged in sustained collective play with groups of children
5.   Teacher is inside the children's imaginary play

These five categories within the play-based settings were determined in relation to whether or not the teachers were acting inside of children's imaginary play. The categories are discussed in the context of an example that is illustrative of the full data set.

Teacher Proximity to Children's Play

Consistent with the research of Singer et al. (2014), the physical positioning of the teacher mattered. When the teacher was sitting close by the children who were at play during free play time, the teacher had the opportunity to enter into the children's play, and to sensitively support them, as we see in the example below of two- and three-year-old children.

> The teacher is seated low on a child's chair next to a light table and projector. She is next to Harry and Warren who are role-playing Goldilocks and the three bears. The children have placed on to the light table a series of blocks and transparencies of characters from the fairy tale they have drawn. The children are moving the objects and observing the images that are projected onto a wall, but become distracted by the projector light and the shadow their hands are making. The teacher points to one of the children's transparencies they have drawn and says, 'Baby bear, and the...' (pausing for a response). Warren instantly says 'Papa bear'. The teacher continues and says '...and the (pausing). Harry responds by saying 'Mumma bear'. The children continue their roleplay, being supported through prompting by the teacher.

Because the teacher knew the storyline that the children were attempting to role-play, she was able to prompt the children, and therefore able to help them play together to recreate the fairy tale of Goldilocks and the three bears. Being in close proximity meant she could analyse their efforts and determine when to enter into the imaginary situation. Interestingly, the teacher supported the children from inside the imaginary situation as a narrator rather than an actor in the children's play, as we might see in the pedagogical practices of teachers drawing upon a storyworlds approach.

Teacher Intent Is in Parallel with the Children's Play Intent

In line with previous research (Fleer, 2010; Goncu, 1998) which has shown that when the level of intersubjectivity between teachers and children is not closely aligned, both children and teachers find themselves in completely different imaginary situations. In this study, there were many examples of rich imaginary situations which were completely missed or misinterpreted by the teachers, often because they were not proximally close (Singer et al., 2014). However, the most common misalignment was due to the educative agenda that was being overlaid on particular imaginary situations by the teacher. It is not surprising that teachers would focus on learning outcomes. Hedges' (2014) refers to this pedagogical practice as smuggling content knowledge into play. For example, a small group of three children are seated around a tub of water, and are actively involved in role-playing pirates. The teacher introduces into the play a block of ice:

> The teacher invites the children to consider how to melt a block of ice that she has placed into a tub of water. The tub contains a boat with oars, and two small clear plastic containers. Sam is holding a plastic Lego pirate, and says in response to the invitation made by the teacher, 'The pirate's hat is too big.' The teacher smiles at Sam, and then returns to the block of ice, touching it and saying, 'Is it melting?'. Corey says 'No.' The teacher says, 'Shall we leave it in there for a while?' to which Corey says, 'To make it melt'. The teacher and Corey discuss several ideas about the melting ice. Eventually the teacher is called away to deal with a distressed child, and Sam says, "The pirate's hat is too big' returning to the original storyline he put forward previously.

As might be expected, many instances of misalignment were due to the nature of large group settings, where many imaginary situations are taking place simultaneously, making it difficult for a teacher to closely align or follow all of the play themes running in the centre. In the example of the pirate boat (child's perspective) and the block of ice (teacher's perspective), the children and the teachers were working in parallel worlds. The children were already in an imaginary situation. The teacher had an educational agenda of introducing science concepts into the play materials she had provided for supporting their play activity. The teacher was smuggling into the play-based setting a science education agenda. That is, she provided materials to support the development of a range of imaginary play to emerge. But she also wanted to use the same play infrastructure for science learning outcomes. Consequently, the children drew upon the materials for imaginary play, play that was being established, but which did not link at all with the introduction of the science education agenda. In contrast, the playworlds literature shows pedagogical practices that involve all the children in one imaginary situation, rather than having a range of self-initiated play themes simultaneously occurring. The agenda in playworlds is to develop an imaginary situation with all the children, and to use props to enrich the imaginary play. This is different from the example above, because in playworlds, problems are initiated and solved in the context of the plot or storyline. The example of the block of ice melting in the context of the broader literature suggests that a continuum of how problems can be introduced into children's play may exist.

Teacher Is Following the Children's Play

The predominant mode of interaction and the time spent interacting in the play-based settings across the teachers was to monitor or supervise children's play. As might be expected in early childhood contexts, teachers were skilled at setting up and resourcing children's play. Their role was predominantly to observe rather than to enter the play. Many of the teachers spent their time outside of children's play resourcing the emerging and developing play themes. For example,

> Alicia is drawing a design, which captures the ideas she has put forward about making a fridge to cool down things in the centre. She takes the drawing over to the teacher who is helping children at the painting easel. Alicia holds up her drawing to show her. The teacher says, 'Can you put it on the table and show me all the different parts?' Alicia takes the drawing back to the table and says as she points to different parts of her drawing, 'That's the part over there with the cement, and that's the dog hair.' The teacher follows her, but stands and says 'I just love the idea of the dog hair mixed with the cement.'. Alicia smiles and murmurs. 'Ummm'. The teacher asks, 'Can you tell me what the dog hair does to the cement?' Alicia responds by saying, 'Makes it softer.' The teacher repeats this and asks, 'Will the cement still set with the dog hair in it? What will it look like do you think?' Alicia says, 'Black cement'. The teacher adds, 'Cement with bits of dog hair through it.'
>
> Do you use a little bit of dog hair or a lot of dog hair?'. Alicia says, 'A little bit'. The teacher asks, 'That much (showing with hands) or that much (moves hands further out)?' Alicia responds by saying, 'That much (showing hands cupped together).' The discussion continues, and then Alicia goes outside and takes a wheelbarrow and begins to collect all the ingredients by picking leaves and sticks from the garden. She adds sand to the wheelbarrow, and then places the organic objects into the sand, mixing as she goes. She verbalizes to herself the cement 'ingredients', taking with her the drawing (which she names as 'instructions'). The teacher stays inside and continues to help children at the painting easel.

This example explicitly shows teacher interest in Alicia's play. However, the teacher stays outside of her play. She does not follow up or become part of her imaginary play. Rather, she quizzes her about the content of the play, inviting Alicia to elaborate and verbalise her thinking. This example was the most common form of teacher–child interaction in play found across all of the teachers in the study.

Teacher Is Engaged in Sustained Collective Play with Groups of Children

There is a body of research in the UK that shows the importance of sustained and shared conversations with children for supporting children's learning (Siraj-Blatchford, 2007) and for supporting the development of their play (Hakkarainen (2010)). Consistent with this research, this study also found that teachers engaged in shared sustained conversations related to imaginary play (Fleer, 2013b). However, sustained collective imaginary situations were noted rarely, suggesting that this mode of teacher interaction is less common in play-based settings. In contrast, the playworlds literature focuses completely on building sustained and shared imaginary play with a whole group of children.

Teacher Is inside the Children's Imaginary Play

The teachers were predominantly outside of children's play, only acting as visitors to their play for short periods, or interacting in parallel with their play. Most teachers did not go inside of the children's play. As might be expected, evidence of initiating and leading children's play from within the imaginary situation was rare. Although teachers actively set up imaginary play situations by providing materials or reading/telling stories, they did not take an active role in the play, as has been suggested by Hakkarainen (2010) as important for developing children's play.

Although all the teachers were predominantly outside of the imaginary play situation, in the context of reading a story or telling a fairy tale story, the teachers did enter into the imaginary situation created through the story being told/read. But, the teachers did not take on a character from the story or fairy tale when transforming the telling/reading of the story into a role play, as suggested by Lindqvist (1995) and Hakkarainen (2010). Rather the teachers acted as coordinators and resources for the role play. However, on some occasions, the teachers did take on a role in the play, but it was restricted. For example,

It is group time and the children and the teacher are gathered together. Four children volunteer to be characters in the fairy tale of Goldilocks and the three bears. The teacher asks the children to decide which bear they would like to be, but for expediency, she gives each child a soft toy of the character that they will role-play. The teacher acts as a narrator to the story and counts off each character to begin the story, 'We've got, 1, 2, 3 bears'. She then asks, 'Have we got three chairs?'. The children look around, and together decide they have 3 chairs. The teacher then asks, 'Do we have three bowls...to tell our story?'. Three bowls are found and placed with the other props. The teacher asks Goldilocks to 'Go and hide'. The story begins by the teacher saying, 'Once upon a time in the'. The teacher pauses and asks, 'Where did they live?'. The children together with the teacher tell the story of Goldilocks and the three bears, using the props. The children move the props as the story is narrated by the teacher. The children 'speak in character' as the storyline progresses. However, when they arrive at the scene of needing to cook the porridge the children ask, 'Where is the microwave oven?'. The teacher responds by saying, 'Here. I am the microwave' as she postures into a square shape, receiving each bowl of porridge to be cooked. The story continues to be narrated, and the children roleplay each scene.

In this example, the teacher is narrating the story and therefore actively positioning herself outside of the imaginary situation. She keeps the storyline moving. But as was shown in this example, she also entered into the imaginary situation, acting as the microwave oven. She did this so as not to interrupt the role play being enacted by the children. Once she had finished being the microwave oven, she returned to acting as the narrator.

Overall, the teachers were mostly outside of children's play. Teachers did enter into play as the example shows, but not as actively as is suggested by Hakkarainen and Bredikyte (2014). Collectively, the teachers' relationship with the imaginary situation can be symbolised as shown in Figure 2. In this figure, the teacher is conceptualised as being inside of the play or outside of play across a range of play-based settings.

Taken together, what was new in this study from previous research into play was whether or not the teacher was inside of the imaginary play with the children in traditional (not playworld settings) play-based settings. The practice of being inside of the imaginary play with the children in play-based settings was not common in this study of the nine teachers. Apart from the emerging playworlds literature across a number of countries, having an adult inside of children's play does not appear to be a standard conceptualisation of the role of teacher in the pedagogical practice of supporting children's play.

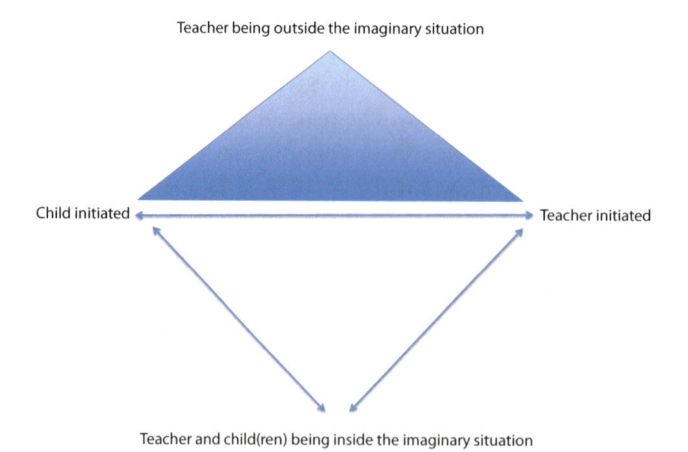

FIGURE 2   Pedagogical positioning inside and outside of children's play

Conclusion

Overall, the findings identified a diversity of pedagogical play practices that featured the teacher mostly outside of children's play. Specifically, the pedagogical positioning of the teacher included being in parallel with the child, as a narrator or prompter of the imaginary play, being in close proximally when supporting children's play, but generally not engaged in sustained collective play inside of the imaginary situation. As might be expected, teachers did not act as a play partner when engaged in children's play, but did focus on learning outcomes in the context of their play. Play–pedagogy of this kind with its focus on 'smuggling in content knowledge' (Hedges, 2014), rather than focusing on developing children's play complexity (Bredikyte, 2011; Kravtsova, 2014), is consistent with the work of Wood (2014) who has examined the play–pedagogy interface in the context of contemporary international debates about play. She has found that there are three modes of play–pedagogy evident – child-initiated, adult-guided and technicist-/policy-driven – where the latter is gaining more international ground. She suggests that the global push to position play in relation to curriculum goals for academic learning emerged as a strong policy force in many countries. She names Hong Kong, the UK, and the USA as recent examples, stating that 'Policy constructions of play as pedagogy are instrumental: the focus is on planned and purposeful play, and the forms of learning that are privileged reflect developmental levels and learning goals' (p. 152). Hakkarainen and Bredikyte (2014) have also noted the international trend to make play more academic, stating that:

> Different play forms are combined with a variety of learning objectives, producing the concept of 'playful learning'...Often 'playful' means the addition of elements of play (game, toys, singing, role characters, etc.) to school lessons.... The partial use of play elements indicates that 'playful learning' is dominated by learning objectives.... (p. 249)

Wood (2014) puts forward in the adult-guided categorisation an alternative perspective which has synergy with the research of Hakkarainen and Bredikyte (2014), suggesting that '*children need more challenging forms of play* that support progression towards social and symbolic complexity' (p. 153; my emphasis). In the research of Hakkarainen and Bredikyte (2014), they have shown in storyworlds how the 'joint play of adults and children creates collective higher mental functions' (p. 249) where play complexity is actively built, because the ideal forms of play interactions found in the fairy tales and narratives, that form the basis of the collective joint play that teachers introduce, are shared with all the children and become a common plot to be played out and elaborated. The problem formulations introduced through the stories, set up tensions that the characters of the play must solve. Role play gives children opportunities to see and experience living adult models, as adults too are part of the imaginary play, acting as a character in the improvised and extended stories – thus modelling complex forms of play. Hakkarainen and Bredikyte (2014) argue that, 'Play offers an opportunity, or invitation, to experiment with transforming ideal into real forms of behaviour without overwhelming responsibility (play is just play)' (p. 248), where children 'decide whether to accept the invitation or not' (p. 248). What is unique about playworlds is that the adult is part of the imaginary situation, taking on a character, or having a clear play partner role. When the teacher is part of the imaginary play, she/he has an opportunity from inside of the play, to develop the play further, introducing complexity and I would suggest genuinely using learning goals that are detailed in curriculum to help solve the tensions in the imaginary situations. Rather than smuggling in content, or bolting onto an existing play event a learning goal, as was shown in this study, when the teacher is inside of the play, she/he is more in tune with the storyline evolving or being acted out, and can better establish intersubjectivity inside of the imaginary play. It is possible that in the push to make play more academic that the diversity of play–pedagogy has narrowed, leaving teachers firmly outside of children's play. The findings of this study suggest that teachers do not routinely become a part of children's play. But this finding must be considered in the context of the limitations of the sample size.

Wood (2014) has stated that, 'The challenge for the early childhood community is to maintain an expansive understanding of play and pedagogy, and to hold that space against reductionist policy discourses' (p. 155). The diversity of play–pedagogy noted in this Australian study, contributes to beginning to address this challenge. However, a more theorised view of play pedagogy is urgently needed if important elements of play pedagogy are to be intentionally used (see Ryan & Northey-Berg, 2014) for supporting the development of play, as well as for providing a broader range of play practices for meeting the country specific learning outcomes of early childhood education that have become increasingly political imperatives. More needs to be understood about the pedagogical practice of adults inside of children's imaginary play, so that a more nuanced understanding of play pedagogy from inside of children's play can be developed.

Acknowledgements

Special acknowledgement of the teachers is made. Their generosity in participating in the study was important for building new understandings about the pedagogy of play. Full ethics approval was granted for the project by Monash University Ethics Committee.

Disclosure Statement

No potential conflict of interest was reported by the author.

Funding

Funds from the Australian Research Council *Discovery Grant* provided the resources for enabling the study to be undertaken, including allowing for research assistance from Avis Ridgway and Sue March (field leader for team that follows), Megan Adams, Feiyan Chen, Rowan Fleer-Stout, Judith Gomes, Yijun Hao, Madeleine Holland, Hasnat Jahan, Shuhuan Pang, Shukla Sikder, Devi Sukmawati, and Pui Ling Wong.

References

Australian Government, Department of Education, Employment and Workplace
    Relations. Commonwealth of Australia. (2009). *Belonging, being and becoming – The*

early years learning framework for Australia. Council of Australian Governments. Retrieved December 20, 2014, from http://www.deewr.gov.au/earlychildhood/policy_agenda/quality/pages/earlyyearslearningframework.aspx

Bateson, G. (1955). A theory of play and fantasy. *Psychiatric Research Reports, 2*, 39–51.

Bodrova, E. (2008). Make-believe play versus academic skills: A Vygotskian approach to today's dilemma of early childhood education. *European Early Childhood Education Research Journal, 16*(3), 357–369.

Bredikyte, M. (2010). Psychological tools and the development of play. *Cultural-Historical Psychology, 4*, 11–18.

Bredikyte, M. (2011). The zones of proximal development in children's play [PhD thesis]. University of Oulu, Faculty of Education, Finland.

Bretherton, I. (1984). Representing the social world in symbolic play: Reality and fantasy. In I. Bretherton (Ed.), *Symbolic play: The development of social understanding* (pp. 3–41). Academic Press.

Ferholt, B. (2010). A synthetic-analytic method for the study of perezhivanie: Vygotsky's literary analysis applied to Playworlds. In M. C. Connery, V. P. John-Steiner, & A. Marjanovic-Shane (Eds.), *Vygotsky and creativity: A cultural-historical approach to play, meaning making, and the arts* (pp. 163–179). Peter Lang.

Fleer, M. (2010). *Early learning and development: Cultural-historical concepts in play*. Cambridge University Press.

Fleer, M. (2013a). Affective imagination in science education: Determining the emotional nature of scientific and technological learning of young children. *Research in Science Education, 43*(5). doi:10.1007/s11165-012-9344-8

Fleer, M. (2013b). Collective imagining in play. In I. Schousboe & D. Winther-Lindqvist (Eds.), *Children's play and development: Cultural-historical perspectives* (pp. 73–88). Springer.

Fleer, M. (2014). *Theorising play in the early years*. Cambridge University Press.

Garvey, C. (1977). *Play*. Harvard University Press.

Goncu, A. (1998). Development of intersubjectivity in social pretend play. In M. Woodhead, D. Raulkner, & K. Littleton (Eds.), *Cultural worlds of early childhood* (pp. 117–132). Routledge.

Goncu, A., & Gaskins, S. (Eds.). (2007). Play and development: Evolutionary, sociocultural, and functional perspective. Lawrence Erlbaum Associates.

Hakkarainen, P. (2006). Learning and development in play. In J. Einarsdottir & J. T. Wagner (Eds.), *Nordic childhoods and early education: Philosophy, research, policy, and practice in Denmark, Finland, Iceland, Norway and Sweden* (pp. 183–222). Information Age Publishing.

Hakkarainen, P. (2010). Cultural-historical methodology of the study of human development in transitions. *Cultural-Historical Psychology, 4*, 75–89.

Hakkarainen, P., & Bredikyte, M. (2010). Strong foundation through play-based learning. *Psychological Science and Education, 3*, 58–64.

Hakkarainen, P., & Bredikyte, M. (2014). Understanding narrative as a key aspect of play. In L. Brooker, M. Blaise, & S. Edwards (Eds.), *The Sage handbook of play and learning in early childhood* (pp. 240–251). Sage.

Hakkarainen, P., Bredikyte, M., Jakkula, K., & Munter, H. (2013). Adult play guidance and children's play development in a narrative play-world. *European Early Childhood Education Research Journal, 21*(2), 213–225.

Hedges, H. (2014). Children's content learning in play provision: Competing tensions and future possibilities. In L. Brooker, M. Blaise, & S. Edwards (Eds.), *The Sage handbook of play and learning in early childhood* (pp. 192–203). Sage.

Kravtsova, E. E. (2014). Play in the non-classical psychology of L. S. Vygotsky. In L. Brooker, M. Blaise, & S. Edwards (Eds.), *The Sage handbook of play and learning in early childhood* (pp. 21–42). Sage.

Kravtsov, G. G., & Kravtsova, E. E. (2010). Play in L. S. Vygotsky's nonclassical psychology. *Journal of Russian and Easter European Psychology, 48*(4), 25–41.

Lillard, A. (2007). Guided participation: How mothers structure and children understand pretend play. In A. Goncu & S. Gaskins (Eds.), *Play and development: Evolutionary, sociocultural, and functional perspectives* (pp. 131–153). Lawrence Erlbaum.

Lindqvist, G. (1995). The aesthetics of play: A didactic study of play and culture in preschools. *Uppsala Studies in Education, 62*.

McInnes, K., Howard, J., Crowley, K., & Miles, G. (2013). The nature of adult-child interaction in the early years classroom: Implications for children's perceptions of play and subsequent learning behavior. *European Early Childhood Education Research Journal, 21*(1), 268–282.

van Oers, B. (2013). Is it play? Towards a reconceptualisation of role play from an activity. *European Early Childhood Education Research Journal, 21*(2), 185–198.

Pellegrini, A. D. (Ed.). (2011). *The Oxford handbook of the development of play*. Oxford University Press.

Ryan, S., & Northey-Berg, K. (2014). Professional preparation for a pedagogy of play. In L. Brooker, M. Blaise, & S. Edwards (Eds.), *The Sage handbook of play and learning in early childhood* (pp. 204–215). Sage.

Schousboe, I., & Winther-Lindqvist, D. (Eds.). (2013). *Children's play and development: Cultural-historical perspectives*. Springer.

Singer, E., Nederend, M., Penninx, L., Tajik, M., & Boom, J. (2014). The teacher's role in supporting young children's level of play engagement. *Early Child Development and Care, 184*(8), 1233–1249.

Siraj-Blatchford, I. (2007). Creativity, communication and collaboration: The identification of pedagogic progression in sustained shared thinking. *Asia-Pacific Journal of Research in Early Childhood Education, 1*(2), 3–23.

Ugaste, A. (2005). A child's play world at home and the mother's role in the play [Unpublished doctoral dissertation]. University of Jyvaskyla.

Ugaste, A., Tuul, M., Niglas, K., & Neudorf, E. (2014). Estonian preschool teachers' views on learning in preschool. *Early Child Development and Care, 134*(3), 370–385.

Vygotsky, L. S. (1966). Play and its role in the mental development of the child. *Voprosy Psikhologii, 12*(6), 62–76.

Vygotsky, L. S. (2004). Imagination and creativity in childhood. *Journal of Russian and East European Psychology, 42*(1), 7–97.

Vygotsky, L. S. (2005). Appendix. From the notes of L. S. Vygotsky for lectures on the psychology of preschool children. *Journal of Russian and East European Psychology, 43*(1), 90–97.

Wood, E. (2014). The play-pedagogy interface in contemporary debates. In L. Brooker, M. Blaise, & S. Edwards (Eds.), *The Sage handbook of play and learning in early childhood* (pp. 145–156). Sage.

Conceptual PlayWorlds

New Model of Practice for Supporting Early Childhood Teachers in the Intentional Teaching of STEM

Abstract

The deficit positioning of early childhood teachers as not being competent and confident in STEM has a long history. The argument in this chapter is that these teachers have not had the right tools. It is suggested that limited research has been directed to play-based settings, and models of STEM teaching available have tended to be designed on research from contexts that are more formal. The assumption underpinning this chapter is a credit model of early childhood teachers – teachers who are experts in play, have deep knowledge of child development, and demonstrate an extraordinary capacity in observing and planning for young learners. The theory and the research method that underpin *Conceptual PlayWorlds* as a model of STEM teaching is the focus of this chapter.

Keywords

cultural-historical – ideal and real form – teacher confidence – teacher competence – conceptual PlayWorld – educational experiment – methodology – method – digital – app

∙ ∙ ∙

The tutorial room at the University of Copenhagen is filled with scholars from Brazil, Moscow, Australia, the Netherlands and more. I am listening to Milda Bredekyte and Pentti Hakkarainen as they talk about their research in Finland on playworlds with preservice teachers. The passion for the new practice and the theoretical concepts they introduce, made me excited.

I watch the video of the preservice teachers creating playworlds with children. Milda and Pentti had designed an afterschool program for children from 3 to 10 years where preservice teachers could take an active and responsive role in children's play. Their research resulted in a series of outstanding journal papers and book chapters (Hakkarainen, 2010; Hakkarainen & Bredikyte, 2015, 2019; Hakkarainen, Bredikyte, Jakkula, & Munter, 2013) that foregrounded children's narratives and teachers' participation as play-partners to mature children's play.

Their presentation and the papers I subsequently read and re-read, gave me greater confidence to move forward with solving the pressing theoretical problem we had in Australia (Chapter 2) of how to bring concepts into children's play, and how to deal with play as a 'no go zone' for teachers. I had been inspired by Gunilla Lindqvist's PhD thesis on the aesthetics of play, a didactic study of play and culture in preschools, and saw for the first time in the videos presented by Milda and Pentti, a playworld in action.

Like Lindqvist (1995), who had originally theorised playworlds, Pentti and Milda's research operationalised in practice Vygotsky's (1966) conception of play as both a pedagogy and as a source of development. They brought forward the theoretical idea that play itself can develop, but to achieve this they argued, adults need to support this development. This meant helping preservice teachers to know how to play with children. The controversies I was meeting in Australia and in the literature about play (Chapter 2) were absent in the discussions in Copenhagen as we viewed the video data and heard the analysis. A new kind of theorisation of practice was being showcased and a new way of dealing with the problem of how to bring adults into children's play was being realised.

Their research had immediate synergy for me and spoke directly to the problem in Australia of teachers not wishing to interrupt children's play by becoming involved in their play narratives. But taking forward research where teachers in Australia needed to become play partners and be inside imaginary play situations with children, co-experiencing the drama of the story, was not something that could happen overnight or by chance. This would need teachers and researchers to work together.

But *first* I had to know more about playworlds with the problem of bringing concepts into children's play in mind. So, I analysed Lindqvist's (1995) original theoretical writing and her drama model of "an aesthetic pedagogy of play in preschools" (p. 19) to better understand the assumptions underpinning her work. Four key insights immediately relevant to the problem of play being a 'no go zone' for teachers were noted.

1. *Children's play is not a scripted plot. But playworld is different to free play because it has a plot and dramatic narrative that all the children participate in.* Lindqvist (1995) said, "In role-play, everyone is free to make their own interpretations, whereas in drama, everyone has to be part of a common fiction" (p. 37).

2. *Adult involvement in play.* Gunilla said, "Play is regarded as an activity free of adult influence, an activity which expresses the child's natural

development" (Lindqvist, 1995, p. 16). Moreover, "pedagogues are unsure of whether they should influence the children's play or not" (p. 19). Significantly she determined that, "these theories reflect a biological approach to knowledge, with an emphasis on nature instead of culture" (Lindqvist, 1995, p. 19).

A key phrase in Lindqvist's (1995) work gave further confidence that a play-world model could become an important part of the research for dealing with the problem of how teachers could become involved in children's play. She said, "the pedagogue needs to inspire the child to play, in order to develop the dramatic nature of the play" (p. 35). Lindqvist (1995) suggested that it is through the interplay between emotions and intellect that imagination in play arises. In Chapter 3 the drama of the play and affective imagination had become important for science learning. But there was other evidence too. Rainio (2008) studied a child who was considered to be unmotivated and problematic and found that the playworld changed the interaction conditions between adults and children. The teachers' role changed, and it was found when in role-play teachers listened more attentively and engaged in new ways with the focus child. Ferholt and Nilsson (2017) had also noted this, stating "the playworld deepened the teachers' listening to the children" (p. 67). Research had also shown that narrative length, coherence, and comprehension developed in the playworlds of 5–7-year-olds (Baumer, Ferholt, & Lecusay, 2005), and adults in playworlds "promotes narrative competence" (Nilsson & Ferholt, 2014, p. 942).

But could adults comfortably become involved in children's play when there was no tradition for this in Australia?

Second, Lindqvist's original research has shown how important playworlds were for changing the roles of adults and children in day-care settings, giving rise to new pedagogical practices of the teachers. Lindqvist (1995) argued that "the theories of drama pedagogy show how children and adults can serve to develop a dynamic relationship to reality, and such a working method can provide new angles of approach to preschool pedagogy" (p. 38).

3.   *Cultural development reveals itself in children's play action, it acts as a window into children's imagining, and gives insights into how a child become conscious of their world.*

4.   Children do not just reproduce the world in which they live, but rather they produce the reality they experience. They produce their own play scripts and in so doing, make conscious the roles and rules of the society in which they live. By this Lindqvist (1995) meant that "consciousness is the key concept ... and to children play is the activity through which they become conscious of the world" (p. 4; original emphasis).

Third, when we take the first two points and consider Lindqvist's (1995) research into the aesthetics of play, this work collectively revealed:
- Drama is a dynamic force for play development
- Teacher has an active role in children's play
- Play is the activity through which children consciously consider and make meaning about their world
- The practice of creating a shared fiction is foundational for a playworld
- The unity of emotions and cognition exists through imagination
- A contradiction exists between the world of the child and the world of the adult, and this can act as a productive force in development

Subsequent research into playworlds (e.g., Baumer & Radsliff, 2010; Ferholt, 2009, 2010, 2015; Ferholt & Nilsson, 2016, 2017; Ferholt, Lecusay, & Nilsson, 2019; Ferholt & Rainio, 2016; Ishiguro, 2017; Rainio & Hilppö, 2017; Talamo, Pozzi, & Mellini, 2010) has shown that in keeping with the original model, a playworld includes:
- a focus on children's literature,
- teachers were inside the imaginary play with the children,
- drama or problem situations are introduced and children solve or co-create solutions with adults

Although the research of Lindqvist (1995) and those that followed, solved the problem of how to bring the adult into children's play, they did not explore the question of: How to bring STEM concepts into children's play?

In examining the assumptions underpinning Lindqvist's original research, I concluded that playworlds was indeed a productive way forward. But this analysis of assumptions (Fleer, 2019) – took nearly 2 years before it was published. The reviewers of my paper were most discerning and wanted evidence for each of the claims I had made. The result was a publication that was rich with complexity and full of quotations to support the essence of my synthesis of the literature.

- Fleer, M. (2019). A tapestry of playworlds: A study into the reach of Lindqvist's legacy in testing times. *Mind, Culture, and Activity, 27*(1), 36–49. https://doi.org/10.1080/10749039.2019.1663215

Playworlds could give a planning structure. It was theoretically consistent with all the reading, thinking and researching I had been doing. Even though learning was not the focus of those who followed Lindqvist, what I had determined was that each researcher drew on the model in relation to the country specific problem they were seeking to solve. Therefore, it was not unusual then for me to take this model forward into by research – even though it was not framed to deal with the central problem I was investigating: The relations between play and science learning. Therefore, it was important to study how this might or could happen. This meant re-framing the research question as "What is the relations between imagination in play and imagination in learning?" (Paper 6). Then to use the results to see how this could be applied directly for the teaching of science concepts – thereby going back into the science education research community (Paper 7). The model that emerged from this process – a Conceptual PlayWorld – resolved how to bring play and the learning of science concept together (Paper 8) and set the stage for further research into imagination in play and imagination of learning (Chapters 5 and 6).

– *Paper 6: Conceptual Playworlds: The role of imagination in play and learning;*
– *Paper 7: Fleer, M. (2019). Scientific Playworlds: a model of teaching science in play-based settings;*
– *Paper 8: Fleer, M. (2019). Conceptual PlayWorlds as a pedagogical intervention: Supporting the learning and development of the preschool child in play-based setting*

These papers and others written, provide the evidence around the new model called a Conceptual PlayWorld – where the focus is primarily on how to bring concepts into children's play.

But what kind of method was developed that would allow for this kind of research and these kinds of outcomes detailed in Papers 6–8? What was the methodology that was theorised to capture the new approach to studying children, teachers and researchers?

Lindqvist (1995) mentioned in her thesis that Mariane Hedegaard was using an educational experiment in Denmark to collaborate with teachers in order to create new practices. Could this offer a way forward in solving the theoretical problem of how to bring concepts into children's play? But Lindqvist's educational experiment was not oriented to concepts. Rather, the method was oriented to capturing and analysing data in relation to how playworlds mature children's play through the drama of stories. Similarly, the early research of Milda and Pentti was also not centred on how to bring the learning of concepts into a playworld. And Mariane was not researching play at that moment. But she had conceptualised an educational experiment which looked promising.

1 An Educational Experiment and a Conceptual PlayWorld as an Intervention

It was 2007 and Mariane had just invited me into a book on Studying Children to be published by Open University Press. We had both been approached to publish with them. Mariane had published in Danish a really important book on how to undertake research that involved young children and she suggested this could form the basis of methodology book on studying children. As Mariane and I had worked collaboratively on our family research (Chapter 3), we already had a common frame for studying children in homes, schools and childcare centres. But we had no book in English to capture how we researched.

At Monash University, we had received many student visitors and academics interested in learning how to undertake research using digital tools. I also had a growing number of PhD students who needed a methodology book to support their research endeavours. However, no such book existed.

It was through this common need, that Mariane and I worked together on writing the many pages of the book we called, Studying Children. Our family project shared with Jytte Bang and Pernille Hviid gave the opportunity to show across countries, methods, and research questions, how cultural-historical concepts could be used to conceptualise a cultural-historical approach to studying children. But it was the chapter by Mariane Hedegaard on an educational experiment that set my mind on fire.

Mariane had brought together the contradictory paradigmatic practices of a traditional experiment with action research – however, she theorised it very differently. She said, "The educational experiment contains element of the paradigms of both the traditional experiment and of the action research, but there are significant differences between the methodology" of both (Hedegaard, 2008, p. 185).

In complex traditional experiments variables are not only relationally considered but are organised in ways that allow in the analysis to control for particular variables, so that the effect of the independent variable on the dependent variable can be investigated. Hypotheses are tested in relation to the connections noted between the variables. However, Mariane (Hedegaard, 2008) also argued that in "the traditional experiment, in which all conditions are controlled and only one factor varies, cannot be used when trying to understand the development of the child within the complexities of normal life pattern" (p. 185). Although not stated, but implied by Mariane, the educational experiment draws from the traditional experiment the idea of looking relationally at the variables, but does so under different kinds of research conditions. Rather than controlled conditions, the educational experiment studies the naturalistic conditions of everyday life in which a child is engaged – this can be the home, the community and the school or preschool setting – as the institutions in which the child is naturally participating and developing over their life course.

Action research is oriented to the study of a practice problem, whereby the researcher and the participants work collaboratively to realise the research. Often the researcher is also the teacher who is studying a problem of practice to effect practice change for better pedagogical outcomes or learning outcomes for children – depending on the focus of the research question. The study design is iterative, cycles, and draws heavily on reflection when resolving the practice problem. But as Mariane (Hedegaard, 2008) has said, "The difference between action research and the educational experiment is that the intervention is planned in relation to a theoretical system and not simply from agendas of practice" (p. 186). What is the same, is that in action research and in an educational experiment, a researchers and the teachers cooperate and plan the research. In the case of the educational experiment, the teachers and researchers seek to solve the theoretical problem. The research that is the focus of this book was connected to a theoretical problem of how to bring concepts into a play-based program? But also, the idea of an educational experiment of a play-worlds as the primary intervention for solving this theoretical problem was a most attractive option for realising a step change in my research.

On page 185 of her chapter, Mariane says: "The educational experiment is a multi-faceted planned preparation of teaching which has, as its goal, the creation of optimal conditions for learning and development of the participating children". In reading the goal of this method, there was hope now for finding a way to study with teachers the theoretical connection between play and learning, and how to bring concepts into play-based settings.

Grounded historically in Davydov's (1990) educational teaching experiment in secondary schools, the educational experiment that Mariane (2008) had theorised for primary schools offered a way forward. But at this time, she had not undertaken an educational experiment in a play-based settings. But Gunilla Lindqvist (1995) had.

Gunilla Lindqvist (1995) said,

> The educational experiment has become well-developed method within the cultural historical school of thought – a further development of Vygotsky's methodology. The educational experiment can be said to represent a form of action or intervention research, where everyday situations are systematically intervened, and an educational perspective is combined with a research perspective. (p. 67)

Different to other forms of research, Gunilla Lindqvist (1995) went on to state that, "In short, new methods of education are being tried within the frame of a pedagogic research program" (p. 67).

So how do we realise the educational experiment as a collaboration with teachers to solve the theoretical problem of how to bring concepts into children's play? Mariane (Hedegaard, 2008) said that "The researcher can then observe whether such an intervention results in changes in the complexity of the child's normal life activities by monitoring and studying these activities over a protracted period" (p. 185).

Our intervention was the Conceptual PlayWorld for the intentional teaching of STEM (Fleer, 2018). A proforma was developed to support teachers in planning for their own Conceptual PlayWorld (Table 4.1). This planning proforma summarises the model reported in Papers 6–8 that follow this chapter.

2   The Five Characteristics of *Conceptual Playworlds* [1]

The method was the educational experiment. The papers that were the result of these educational experiments were centred on Australia but also, I worked closely with my colleague Liang Li as she undertook an educational experiment in China (Fleer & Li, 2020). The latter problem was to support formal preschool learning to become more oriented to play. Our PhD students also began to use the methodology and intervention for solving the latter problem but in the contexts of Indonesia (Utam, Fleer, & Li, 2020) and orphanages in China (Meng, Fleer, Li, & Hammer, 2022).

– Fleer, M. (2019b). Conceptual PlayWorlds as a pedagogical intervention: Supporting the learning and development of the preschool child in play-based setting. *Obutchénie: Revista De Didática E Psicologia Pedagógica, 3*(3), 1–22. https://doi.org/10.14393/OBv3n3.a2019-51704
– Fleer, M. (2019c). The 5 characteristics of a Conceptual Playworld: New approaches to supporting play and learning in kindergarten. *Journal of Studies in Early Childhood Education, 11.* [in Chinese] http://rdbk1.ynlib.cn:6251/qw/Paper/725355
– Fleer, M., & Li, L. (2020). Curriculum reforms as a productive force for the development of new play practices in rural Chinese kindergartens. *International Journal of Early Years Education,* 1–16. https://doi.org/10.1080/09669760.2020.1778447
– Utami, A. D., Fleer, M., & Li, L. (2020). Shift in teachers' pedagogical practices in play-based programme in Indonesia. *International Journal of Early Years Education, 28*(4), 397–412. https://doi.org/10.1080/09669760.2020.1777846

The papers that are at the end of this chapter emerged from this foundational research. But it was the most recent ARC discovery project in 2018 (see Chapter 3) that put centre stage the educational experiment in the context of digital technologies – something that had not previously been presented in the literature. The funds allowed for the conceptualisation and development of an app

TABLE 4.1   A Conceptual PlayWorld as an intervention: planning proforma provided to all
             teachers

Pedagogical characteristics	Pedagogical practices that are planned
Selecting a story for the *Conceptual Playworld*	– Working with understandings of the context of children's development and their interests – Selecting a story that is enjoyable to children and adults – Building empathy for the characters in the story – A plot that lends itself to introducing a problem situation to the children – Being clear about the concept and its relation to the story and play plot to be developed
Designing a *Conceptual Playworld* space	– Creating different spaces that give opportunities for exploring both concepts (e.g., anatomy of the spider) and social and emotional development (e.g., empathy with Fern in the story of Charlotte's Web) – Designing different opportunities for child-initiated play in ways that develop the play plot further or explore concepts and make them more personally meaningful – Planning different opportunities for representing children's ideas and expressing their understandings
Entering and exiting the *Conceptual Playworld* space	– Whole group enters the *Conceptual Playworld* – All the children are in the same imaginary situation – Children choose characters as they enter into the imaginary situation – Teacher is always a character in the story or acting as a human prop (e.g., such as a tree or the Sun)
Planning the play inquiry or problem scenario	– Children have enough knowledge to be able to solve the problem – introduced inside or out of the imaginary situation – The problem scenario is dramatic and engaging – Problem scenario is not scripted, but a general idea of the problem is planned – Being clear about the concepts that will be learned from solving the problem situation – Concepts are in service of the play
Planning teacher interactions to build conceptual learning in role	– Teachers working in interactional pairs: Teachers are not always the same character. Roles are not scripted – There are different roles teachers can take: Teachers plan their role for the playworld to be equally present with the children, or to model practices in role, or to be needing help from the children. Their role can also be physically and intellectually together with the child (primordial we), where they literally cradle the child or hold their hand and together act out the role or solution – Conceptual intentions are planned: Planning of who will have more knowledge and who will be present with the children to model solving the problem

that could showcase an ideal form (Vygotsky, 1994) of a Conceptual PlayWorld as a tool for supporting an educational experiment with teachers interested in the problem of using a Conceptual PlayWorld in their centre to meaningfully bring STEM concepts into children play.

The idea of this digital Conceptual PlayWorld app (see Figure 4.1) was to put into teachers' and researchers' hands a tool to support their collaborations on the theoretical problem of, "how to bring concepts into children's play?". This aligned with how Mariane (Hedegaard, 2008) had discussed the theoretical principles of an educational experiment as "the teacher's concrete implementation of teaching practice, the children's activities and how these contribute to the children's motive development, and the appropriation of knowledge and thinking strategies" (p. 186). The digital app could capture these kinds of relational data dynamically and in the process of developing. But the digital app gave other possibilities.

First, the digital Conceptual PlayWorld app mirrors the professional development that teachers undertook as part of the educational experiment. The intervention of a Conceptual PlayWorld that was introduced to teachers as part of their professional development was presented initially through videos of the new practices and then workshopped using the Conceptual PlayWorld proforma (Table 4.1).

The Conceptual PlayWorld app (Figure 4.1) allows teachers to select from the menu each of the characteristics of the Conceptual PlayWorld and view videos in relation to each characteristic. A further feature of the app is that teachers

FIGURE 4.1   Conceptual PlayWorld app: Videos of the characteristics of a Conceptual
             PlayWorld in action

can download videos of a Conceptual PlayWorld specific to the cultural age period they are working in – such as infants and toddlers, pre-schoolers, and school settings.

The intervention that is the basis of the educational experiment should be available from the very beginning in its final or ideal form. This is in keeping with Vygotsky's (1994) conception of the relations between the ideal and real form for children's development: "that which it is possible to achieve at the end and as a result of the developmental process, is already available in the environment from the very beginning" (pp. 347–348). A Conceptual PlayWorld intervention is present on the app in video form and is immediately accessible.

Theoretically, the design feature of having digital video to view follows the conception of Vygotsky (1994) who argued that *"the environment should not be regarded as a condition of development ... but one should always approach environment from the point of view of the relationship which exists between the child and its environment at a given stage of his* [sic] *development"* (p. 338; original emphasis). The app was conceptualised as a tool to support the educational experiment, by creating a virtual environment, from the point of view of the relationship which exists between the teachers and researchers.

Teachers are also in the process of developing their practices, and in the context of an educational experiment are oriented towards solving a theoretical problem. In the professional development, teachers use a planning tool (Table 4.1) and are supported by the researchers to plan their own Conceptual PlayWorld. Teachers also share their planning in the context of, "how to bring concepts into children's play" so that the concepts are personally meaningful to children (Hedegaard & Chaiklin, 2005). Their planned practices and theoretical solutions are shared with each other and the researchers, and this acts as a dynamic force for teacher development of their practices (Fleer, Fragkiadaki, & Rai, 2021). Vygotsky (1994) drew attention to this dynamic force for children's development, when he said, "And it is not simply present in the environment from the very start, *but it exerts an influence* on the very first steps in the child's development" (p. 348; emphasis added).

Second, as a methodological tool the app was theorised to also support the cultural development of teachers in developing their practice as part of the educational experiment. The screen shown in Figure 4.2 showcases the digital recording feature, where teachers in the educational experiment document their practices during a Conceptual PlayWorld. The idea is that teachers can record practices and capture the process of development, rather than the end product (Vygotsky, 1987), so that over time qualitative developmental changes in the context of practices can be determined.

FIGURE 4.2   Conceptual PlayWorld app: Tool to video record Conceptual PlayWorld in action

The characteristics of the Conceptual PlayWorld is representative of a systematic intervention that is brought into the everyday practices of the preschool. In an educational experiment the teachers and researchers are interested to deliberately study the intervention in the process of its development.

Third, the app has also been conceptualised to support teachers and researchers to become consciously aware of the relations between the planned activities and the children's actual realities. In Figure 4.3 teachers record and store their video clips captured during the process of the play developing in a Conceptual PlayWorld intervention. Teachers can mark their clips for discussion as part of the collaboration between researchers and teachers as they examine the theoretical problem of "how to bring concepts into children's play?".

The app supports the process of tagging video clips with content. Specifically, teachers can tag videos they wish to discuss with text about what happened before and what happened after the video was created (Figure 4.4).

Teachers can also categorise video clips in relation to the characteristic of a Conceptual PlayWorld as shown in Figure 4.5.

This content allows teachers in collaboration with researchers to discuss specific practices, qualitative changes in children's play, and conceptual development that is in the process developing through the intervention of a Conceptual PlayWorld (see Figure 4.6).

The app as a tool to support the educational experiment brings out the relationship between the ideal form in the context of the real form of teacher development. Vygotsky (1994) stated that, "ideal in the sense that it acts as a model for that which should be achieved at the end of the developmental

FIGURE 4.3   Conceptual PlayWorld app: Tool to gather examples of recurrent practices from within the activity setting of a Conceptual PlayWorld

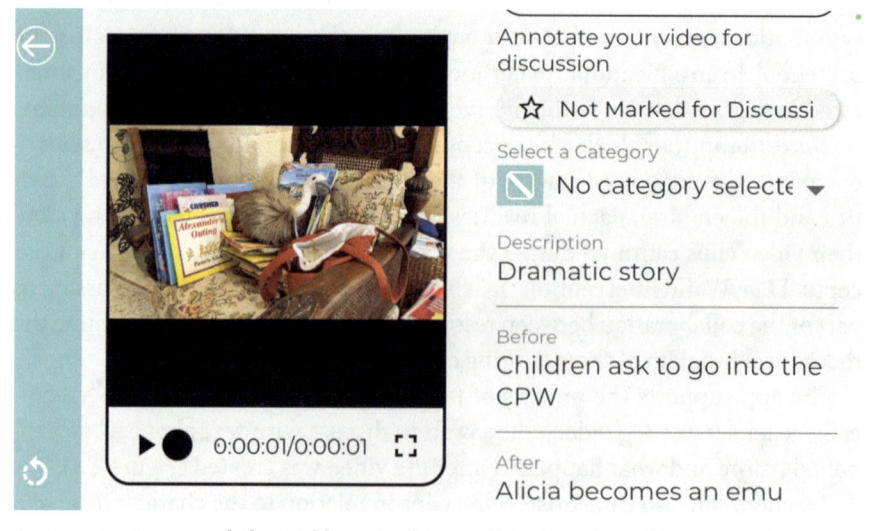

FIGURE 4.4   Conceptual PlayWorld app: Tool to annotate video clips with contextual statements for a more holistic data set

period; and final in the sense that it represents what the child [teacher] is supposed to attain at the end of his [sic] development" (p. 348). The real form of the development of the teacher is conceptualised through the educational experiment as "a continuous interaction process with the ideal form" (p. 350). The app with the videos means that the ideal form is always present and accessible to the teachers. The digital videos that teachers gather, creates a context

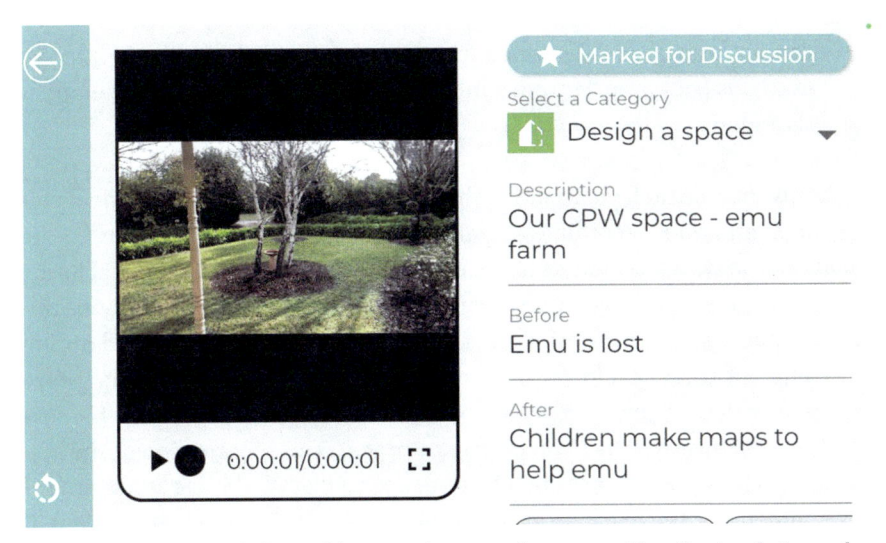

FIGURE 4.5   Conceptual PlayWorld app: Tool to tag and annotate video clips in relation to the
characteristics of a Conceptual PlayWorld

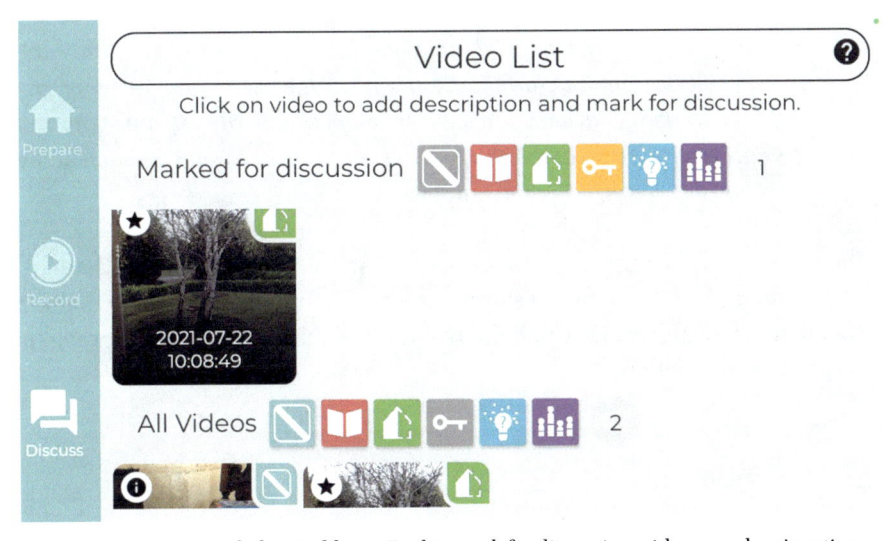

FIGURE 4.6   Conceptual PlayWorld app: Tool to mark for discussion with researchers' particular video clips from the suite of videos recorded

for the relation between the ideal and real form supported through how the
researchers collaborate with the teachers. In the context of children's development, Vygotsky said,

> An ideal or final form is present in the environment and it interacts with
> the rudimentary form found in children [teachers], and what results is a

certain form of activity which then becomes a *child's [teacher's] internal asset*, his [sic] property and a function of his personality. (p. 353; emphasis added)

With this theoretical logic in mind, the app was designed with both ideal videos and digital video recordings, tagging and categorising of clips as part of the collaboration with researchers in the educational experiment. The ideal forms of a Conceptual PlayWorld influences teachers "from their very early beginnings as part of the process of mastering of the rudimentary form. And during the course of their development", teachers acquire, "as their personal property, that which originally represented only a form of their external interaction with the" researchers (Vygotsky, 1994, p. 352). This theorisation of the app aligns with how the intervention of a Conceptual PlayWorld acts as a source of development for the teachers as they seek to solve the theoretical problem of the educational experiment with the researchers as a collaboration. Vygotsky (1994) argued that

> the child's higher psychological functions, his [sic] higher attributes which are specific to humans, originally manifest themselves as forms of the child's collective behaviour, as a form of co-operation with other people, and it is only afterwards that they become the internal individual function of the child himself. (p. 353; original emphasis).

The features of the app (Figures 4.3–4.6) illustrate the processes of that collaboration and subsequent development, with Figure 4.2 specifically making available the ideal form in which the real form of the teacher's development is in constant interaction.

3   Conclusion

The research problem of how to bring science concepts into children's play generated a Conceptual PlayWorld model for the intentional teaching of STEM (Papers 6–8). An educational experiment supported with different teachers across time and centres, and the Conceptual PlayWorld as an evidenced based model, were foundational for the Laureate Fellowship application (as was introducing in Chapter 1) (Figure 4.7), where a Conceptual PlayWorld model was to be rolled out across Australia to build capacity in STEM.

But how could a Conceptual PlayWorld intervention reach teachers across Australia? Recruitment through social media was the answer.

Impact research -
Baseline and impact
study of STEM
Playworlds for
increased STEM
learning

*Pioneering
methodological
innovations -* for
researching concept
formation, including a
digital imagination in
STEM scale

New knowledge -
understandings about infants,
toddlers and preschool concept
formation of STEM in homes
and play-based settings

FIGURE 4.7   Capacity building – a new generation of early childhood education researchers as world leaders for early childhood STEM research

Note

1   https://www.monash.edu/education/research/projects/conceptual-playlab/publications

References

Baumer, S., Ferholt, B., & Lecusay, R. (2005). Promoting narrative competence through adult–child joint pretense: Lessons from the Scandinavian educational practice of playworld. *Cognitive Development, 20*(4), 576–590. https://doi.org/10.1016/j.cogdev.2005.08.003

Baumer, S., & Radsliff, K. (2009). Playworlds of children and adults: Cultural perspectives on play pedagogy. *Mind, Culture, and Activity, 17*(1), 11–13. https://doi.org/10.1080/10749030903348755

Davydov, V. V. (1990). *Types of generalization in instruction: Logial and psychological problems in the structuring of school curricula* (J. Teller, Trans.). National Council of Teachers of Mathematics.

Ferholt, B. (2009). *The development of cognition, emotion, imagination and creativity as made visible through adult -child joint play: Perezhivanie through playworlds* [Doctoral dissertation]. University of California. https://escholarship.org/uc/item/0w22g2jd

Ferholt, B. (2015). Perezhivanie in researching playworlds: Applying the concept of perezhivanie in the study of play. In A. Marjanovic-Shane, B. Ferholt, H. G. Clemson, S.-M. Jansson, & S. Davis (Eds.), *Dramatic interactions in education* (pp. 57–75). Bloomsbury Publishing.

Ferholt, B. (2018). A synthetic-analytic method for the study of Perezhivanie. In A. Marjanovic-Shane, M. C. Connery, & V. John-Steiner (Eds.), *Vygotsky and creativity* (pp. 163–179). Peter Lang.

Ferholt, B., Lecusay, R., & Nilsson, M. (2018). Adult and child learning in playworlds. In J. Kroeker (Ed.), *The Cambridge handbook of play* (pp. 511–527). Cambridge University Press. https://doi.org/10.1017/9781108131384.028

Ferholt, B., & Nilsson, M. (2016). Perezhivaniya as a means of creating the aesthetic form of consciousness. *Mind, Culture, and Activity, 23*(4), 294–304. https://doi.org/10.1080/10749039.2016.1186195

Ferholt, B., & Rainio, A. P. (2016). Teacher support of student engagement in early childhood: Embracing ambivalence through playworlds. *Early Years, 36*(4), 413–425. https://doi.org/10.1080/09575146.2016.1141395

Ferholt, B., & Nilsson, M. (2017). Playworlds and the pedagogy of listening. In T. Bruce, M. Bredikyte, & P. Hakkarainen (Eds.), *The Routledge international handbook of early childhood play* (pp. 261–273). Routledge.

Fleer, M. (2018). *Conceptual playworlds: Foregrounding imagination and creativity as foundational for children's learning.* Monash University Working Paper. https://www.monash.edu/education/research/projects/conceptual-playlab/publications

Fleer, M. (2019a). A tapestry of playworlds: A study into the reach of Lindqvist's legacy in testing times. *Mind, Culture, and Activity, 27*(1), 36–49. https://doi.org/10.1080/10749039.2019.1663215

Fleer, M. (2019b). Conceptual Playworlds as a pedagogical intervention: Supporting the learning and development of the preschool child in play-based setting. *Obutchénie: Revista De Didática E Psicologia Pedagógica, 3*(3), 1–22. https://doi.org/10.14393/OBv3n3.a2019-51704

Fleer, M. (2019c). The 5 characteristics of a Conceptual Playworld: New approaches to supporting play and learning in kindergarten. *Journal of Studies in Early Childhood Education, 11.* [in Chinese] http://rdbki.ynlib.cn:6251/qw/Paper/725355

Fleer, M., Fragkiadaki, G., & Rai, P. (2021). Collective imagination as a source of professional practice change: A cultural-historical study of early childhood teacher professional development in the motivated conditions of a Conceptual Playworld. *Teaching and Teacher Education, 106,* 103455. https://doi.org/https://doi.org/10.1016/j.tate.2021.103455

Fleer, M., & Li, L. (2020). Curriculum reforms as a productive force for the development of new play practices in rural Chinese kindergartens. *International Journal of Early Years Education,* 1–16. https://doi.org/10.1080/09669760.2020.1778447

Hakkarainen, P. (2010). Culturalhistorical methodology of the study of human development in transitions. *Cultural-Historical Psychology, 4*, 75–82. https://psyjournals.ru/en/kip/2010/n4/Hakkarainen.shtml

Hakkarainen, P., & Bredikyte, M. (2015). How play creates the zone of proximal development. In S. Robson & S. F. Quinn (Eds.), *The Routledge international handbook of young children's thinking and understanding* (pp. 31–42). Routledge.

Hakkarainen, P., & Bredikyte, M. (2019). The adult as mediator of development in children's play. In P. K. S. J. L. Roopnarine (Ed.), *The Cambridge handbook of play. Developmental and disciplinary perspectives* (pp. 457–474). Cambridge University Press.

Hakkarainen, P., Brėdikytė, M., Jakkula, K., & Munter, H. (2013). Adult play guidance and children's play development in a narrative play-world. *European Early Childhood Education Research Journal, 21*(2), 213–225. https://doi.org/10.1080/1350293x.2013.789189

Hedegaard, M. (2008). The educational experiment. In M. Hedegaard, M. Fleer, J. Bang, & P. Hviid (Eds.), *Studying children: A cultural-historical approach* (pp. 181–201). Open University Press.

Hedegaard, M., & Chaiklin, S. (2005). *Radical-local teaching and learning.* Aarhus University Press

Ishiguro, H. (2017). Collaborative play with dramatization: An afterschool programme of "Playshop" in a Japanese early childhood setting. In T. Bruce, P. Hakkarainen, & M. Bredikyte (Eds.), *The Routledge international handbook of early childhood play* (pp. 274–288). Routledge. https://doi.org/10.4324/9781315735290-26

Lindqvist, G. (1995). *The aesthetics of play: A didactic study of play and culture in preschools* [Doctoral thesis, Uppsala University]. Almqvist & Wiksell International.

Meng, X., Fleer, M., Li, L., & Hammer, M. (2022). A cultural-historical study of the development of emotion regulation through collective play in an institutional care setting in China. *Learning, Culture and Social Interaction, 32*, 100590. https://doi.org/10.1016/j.lcsi.2021.100590

Nilsson, M., & Ferholt, B. (2014). Vygotsky's theories of play, imagination and creativity in current practice: Gunilla Lindqvist's "creative pedagogy of play" in US kindergartens and Swedish Reggio-Emilia inspired preschools. *Perspectiva, 32*(3), 919–950. https://doi.org/10.5007/2175-795X.2014v32n3p919

Rainio, A. P. (2008). From resistance to involvement: Examining agency and control in a playworld activity. *Mind, Culture, and Activity, 15*(2), 115–140. https://doi.org/10.1080/10749030801970494

Rainio, A. P., & Hilppö, J. (2017). The dialectics of agency in educational ethnography. *Ethnography and Education, 12*(1), 78–94. https://doi.org/10.1080/17457823.2016.1159971

Talamo, A., Pozzi, S., & Mellini, B. (2009). Uniqueness of experience and virtual playworlds: Playing is not just for fun. *Mind, Culture, and Activity, 17*(1), 23–41. https://doi.org/10.1080/10749030903342220

Utami, A. D., Fleer, M., & Li, L. (2020). Shift in teachers' pedagogical practices in play-based programme in Indonesia. *International Journal of Early Years Education,* *28*(4), 397–412. https://doi.org/10.1080/09669760.2020.1777846

Vygotsky, L. S. (1966). Play and its role in the mental development of the child. *Voprosy* *Psikhologii,* *12*(6), 62–76. https://doi.org/https://doi.org/10.2753/RPO1061-040505036

Vygotsky, L. S. (1987). *The collected works of L. S. Vygotsky: Problems of general psychol-ogy* (N. Minick, Trans.; R. W. Rieber & A. S. Carton, Eds., Vol. 1). Plenum Press.

Vygotsky, L. S. (1994). The problem of the environment (T. Prout, Trans.). In R. van der Veer & J. Valsiner (Eds.), *The Vygotsky reader* (pp. 338–354). Blackwell.

Paper 6: Conceptual Playworlds: The Role of Imagination in Play and Learning

This paper originally appeared as Fleer, M. (2018). Conceptual Playworlds: The role of imagination in play and learning. *Early Years,* 1–12. https://doi.org/ 10.1080/09575146.2018.1549024 Reprinted here with permission from the publisher.

Abstract

Increasingly concerns are expressed about the formalisation of early childhood edu-cation and the loss of opportunities for children's play in a range of European and European heritage countries. This paper takes up this challenge by discussing, from a cultural-historical perspective, the relations between play and learning in pre-school settings. A theoretical discussion of practices and affordances of a Conceptual Play-world, grounded in a cultural historical conception of play, is presented. New concepts are needed for understanding the relations between play and learning in pre-school settings, where the focus has traditionally been on play as the leading activity. Theo-rised are four key characteristics that emerge from the practice of a Conceptual Play-world illustrated through a practice example of Charlotte's Web. In this context, it is argued that imagination in play is foundational for imagination in conceptual learn-ing, and therefore play-based programs make a key contribution to the development and learning of the young child.

Keywords

cultural-historical – play – Playworlds – imagination – schoolification – leading activity

Introduction

The aim of this paper is to speak back into those communities that increasingly foreground formal learning in early childhood education by presenting a contemporary theoretical rationale for why imagination in play is foundational for imagination in conceptual learning. Learning is usually conceptualised as involving a cognitive change of some kind for the learner, such as gaining knowledge of school discipline subjects such as science or literacy. To achieve the aim of this paper, we begin by discussing play as the leading activity of pre-school children, followed by a brief review of what is known about Playworlds research. A theoretical discussion of how imagination in play and imagination in learning intertwine is presented through a discussion of children's participation in a Conceptual Playworld. Examples of curriculum practice from a Conceptual Playworld based on Charlotte's Web (by White, 1952) are presented. It will be argued that without opportunities for imaginative play, children may find it difficult to imagine and use abstract concepts for learning later in school. This paper gives a rationale in support of the importance of maintaining play-based programs in pre-school settings.

Play as a Leading Activity of Young Children

Leading activity is a concept that comes from cultural-historical theory (Vygotsky, 1966). It is a useful theoretical construct because in child development terms, it can capture the dynamic nature of the relations between play and learning found in early childhood settings. At a time when Governments in many northern hemisphere countries are demanding greater cognitive outcomes for pre-school children (Fleer & van Oers, 2018), it has become important to have terms and concepts to analyse the new practices that are emerging and increasingly expected of play-based settings.[1] In the context of increasing demands to formally teach school subject discipline knowledge in pre-school settings, there appears to be a need to reclaim the place of imagination in play.

Leading activity is a concept that was first mentioned by Vygotsky in a lecture on play. The stenographic account of this presentation was subsequently published as a representation of Vygotsky's later theoretical work and thinking on play (Vygotsky, 1966). In order to understand this concept, leading activity must be discussed in relation to Vygotsky's (1998) theory of child development. Four key theoretical points are presented in order to show the reach of this

---

1   van Oers (2013) has queried this positioning of constructs as potentially being interpreted as a dichotomy and thereby problematic.

concept, and thereby lay the theoretical foundation for discussing the relations between play and learning in the section that follows.[2]

First, although not well recognised, leading activity was introduced by Vygotsky (1966) to explain the predominant activity of the pre-school child. Subsequently, Elkonin (2005) and Leontiev (1978) drew upon leading activity to build
a picture of the culturally developing child. They argued that a child is primarily
orientated to play in the pre-school years, and to learning in the early years of
school (Elkonin, 1971, p. 1). However, Leontiev (1978) argued that the leading
activity is not the only activity of the young child, but it is the predominant activity during each period of development. It is important for understanding the
relations between play and children's development to note Kravtsova's (2010)
argument that, 'Our analysis shows that Vygotsky used the concept of leading
activity only in regard to play' (p. 11), leaving it to others to take this concept
forward into other periods of development, such as learning as a leading activity of the school child. In line with this argument, how play as a leading activity
becomes learning as a leading activity is still to be fully understood (Kravstova,
2010). *Consequently, the concept of leading activity opens up an important discussion on what is the force for a change in development from play as the leading
activity to learning as the leading activity of the pre-school child.*

Second, moving on from the original theoretical contributions of Vygotsky
(1966), Kravtsova (2010) argued that the relationship between a child's leading
activity and Vygotsky's conception of child development, is that the child is in a
contradictory situation due to being simultaneously in the earlier developmental period (with play as the leading activity) and the period which they are entering (with learning as leading activity). In Vygotsky's (1998) original revolutionary
view of child development, we find a possible theoretical construct to solve this
contradictory situation. Vygotsky introduced the concept of drama or dramatic
situation as a force for projecting forward from one developmental period to
another. He also discussed drama as a dramatic process in his thesis in the Psychology of Art (1971). He said, 'The substance of a drama is a struggle ...' (p. 227)'
and the drama '... combines two conflicting affects, that of the norm and that
of its violation; this is why we perceive ... [this process] dynamically, not as an
object, but as a process' (p. 231). *Consequently, drama becomes an important concept for considering a possible change from play as a leading activity to learning.*

Third, how these moments of drama are experienced in play-based programs can be better understood in the context of contemporary research that

---

2 Conceptual Playworld project of Charlotte's Web can be found in the App Store as a free
   app (simply search for Fleer's Conceptual Playworld or find it on https://www.monash.edu/
   conceptual-playworld).

examines how play acts as a source of development. Kravtsova (2010) showed, in her theory of play, that when a child has gained the ability to be both inside the imaginary play situation and outside of the play, acting as a director, the child can control the play activity and develop the plot. She argued, 'if children are able to break free and look at their imagination and play "from the side"' (Kravtsova, 2010, p. 14) then this play activity acts as a positive source of development. The child is able to be above their play and consciously looking at the content and the evolving plot and thereby able to control it at will. Vygotsky's (1966) original assertion was that the child at play is 'a head taller than himself [sic]' (pp. 11–12). To understand this proximal development, Vygotsky (1987) introduced the scientific concept of imitation. Imitation is not the simple copying of an action, but rather acting with understanding, and this appears as a sign that the child's maturing functions are developing within their zone of proximal development. In this scientific reading, imitation is a convenient concept for noticing development (Vygotsky, 1998) and for determining how the play actions of children act as a potential source of development.

Finally, for play to act as a source of development, play itself must develop. Mature forms of play are evident when children create imaginary situations where they change the meaning of actions and objects and give them a new sense inside the imaginary situation (Vygotsky, 1966). The content of the play is everyday life. In line with Vygotsky's reading of imitation in play, this activity is not a copy of reality, but rather it is the reworking of everyday life events known to the child (Lindqvist, 1995). In this theoretical reading of play, a tension exists been the reproduction of reality and the production of something new that is imagined and created in play. Contemporary researchers have sought to capture this dynamic relation as a sign of the development of play (Lindqvist, 1995). Significant for the focus of this paper is that reproduction is associated with memory, whilst production is tied to creativity and imagination (Vygotsky, 2004). Children have the possibility to become conceptually conscious of everyday practices as a theatrical production in which the child is an active agent (playfulness), rather than as a passive photographic reproduction of their world (memorising facts). According to Linqvist (1995), the dynamic between the reproductive and productive nature of play activity acts as a positive force in the development of play.

Taken together, there appear to be four assumptions about play: play is a leading activity, play is dramatic, play is a source of child development and play matures through the dynamic between the reproductive and productive natures of play activity. These four theoretical assumptions about play can be seen in the contemporary model of practice known as Playworlds.

What Is Known about Playworlds

The original research of Gunilla Lindqvist is important for the focus of this paper. She developed an aesthetic play pedagogy to capture the dynamic relation between the productive and reproductive nature of children's play in order to study how play acts as a source of children's development. Lindqvist (1995) and a drama pedagogue worked with pre-school teachers over 12 months to develop an aesthetic play pedagogy that she named as Playworlds. Her specific focus was aesthetics and development of children's play in pre-school children (6 years) and, later, toddlers. Playworlds is a model of practice where the teacher takes a play role with the children and together all of the children enter into an imaginary physical Playworld space, such as a hot air balloon. The teacher reads and also role-plays stories taken from children's literature, folk tales and fairy tales in order to help the children to re-live and develop the dramatic moments through play. Adults act as play partners with the children, going on adventures (e.g., visiting other lands with the hot air balloon), co-developing the play scripts and dramatising the fiction and play plots over extended periods of time.

Inspired by Lindqvist's cultural-historical study, researchers from many countries have sought to implement and study Playworlds. For example, Playworld research can be found in Australia (Fleer, 2017), China (Fleer, Li, & Yan, 2018), Finland (Hakkarainen, 2010), Italy (Talamo, Pozzi, & Mellini, 2010), Japan (Marjanovic-Shane et al., 2011), Lithuania (Hakkarainen et al., 2013), Serbia (Marjanovic-Shane et al., 2011), Sweden (Nilsson, Ferholt, & Lecusay, 2017) and the US (Ferholt & Lecusay, 2010). The focus of each Playworld study is slightly different. Some have studied the development of the teacher (Ferholt & Lecusay, 2010), others have investigated on-line contexts (Talamo, Pozzi, & Mellini, 2010). Some have explored child agency (Rainio, 2008), and a growing number have examined how to develop the children's narrative (Hakarrainen & Bredikyte, 2008) and communication competence (Baumer, Ferholt, & Lecusay, 2005). The focus of this paper is how researchers of Playworlds have created the dramatic conditions for children's development in a context of pressure to increase cognitive outcomes.

When the Playworlds found in the literature are reviewed in relation to play and learning, it is evident that only a few have focused on how imagination in play and imagination in learning are developed through the Playworlds. What is known has come from studies of creativity and education where Playworlds and exploratory learning are featured. Ferholt et al. (2015) analysed teachers' pedagogical documentation, an animated film project and a Playworld and learned that 'imagination is tightly connected to realistic thinking, and important in exploratory learning' (Ferholt et al., 2015, p. 280). This in turn is supportive of developing hypotheses about natural phenomena, such as light, sound and time. Exploratory learning was also tightly connected to aesthetic-semiotic activity, play and Playworlds in animated film making. But creative imagining through play also mattered in the role-playing of children's stories. This study found that there is a dialectical relationship between play and exploration (Ferholt et al., 2015). In a scientific Playworld (Fleer, 2017) there is also a unique relation between imagination in play and the learning of concepts. In this study, it was found that the process of transforming imaginary situations of the Playworld into a collective scientific narrative required building discourses of wondering, creating imaginary scientific situations and introducing cultural devices that mirror science experiences. The development of narrative competence has also been foregrounded in the Playworld studies of Baumer, Ferholt, and Lecusay (2005) and Hakkarainen (2008), among others.

These findings speak to the current schoolification context, because they show how researchers can reclaim the importance of play as the leading activity of pre-school children. But at the same time, they show how, in Playworlds, teachers do already create the conditions to support children's development from play to learning as the leading activity. Learning concepts is not a simple reproduction tied to memory but, as discussed previously, a productive and imaginative and creative act (Vygotsky, 2004). However, more needs to be known about how Playworlds create motivating conditions for children's learning during the process of navigating between play as a leading activity and learning as a leading activity in pre-school settings. In the section that follows, this is taken up through an example from practice, to illustrate how teachers can push against the pressure to formalise learning and foreground imagination in support of concept development in early childhood settings.

Developing a Conceptual Playworld (2)

The curriculum project of Charlotte's Web is introduced as an example from practice that shows how a Conceptual Playworld was planned, implemented, and reviewed in relation to how imagination in play and imagination in learning were intertwined. The two teachers had co-taught two cohorts of pre-school children (4 years) once each week over 2 years using the Playworld model of practice. A total of six Playworlds were implemented. In this paper only examples from one Playworld are featured, and only as practice examples (rather than data from research).

Both teachers had extensive teaching experience, and both were familiar with the literature on Playworlds. The teachers had participated in professional learning on play as a leading activity, on the role of drama to create emotionally engaging play plots from the literature, to support imagination in play and imagination in learning, and on how to create motivating conditions for the productive development of play that would lead to conceptual learning of scientific and engineering concepts. The story of how the teachers created the dramatic conditions for children's development in a context of increased cognitive outcomes is illustrated. The pathway taken is theorised in relation to what caused the move from reproduction associated with memory to production tied to creativity and imagination (Vygotsky, 2004).

The Dynamic Relations between Imagination in Play and Imagination in Learning

In the story of Charlotte's Web farm life is dramatised through the pages of a chapter book and through the Playworld of Farmer Zuckerman's farm introduced by the teachers. That is, the Playworld creates an imaginary play situation through the fiction of a story. The fiction builds the drama of the runt of the pig litter being potentially culled. This is realised by the readers, but not the main character of Wilbur the pig—who only gradually becomes aware of this. Through the literary device of a young child called Fern, the children co-experience the drama of keeping Wilbur alive. The conversation between Fern and the father sets up the dynamic emotional tension of life on the farm, which is about producing animals for food, and Fern believing it is unfair to kill a runt just because it is small. *Here the fiction of the story acts as the content of the Playworld, where the rules of daily farm life and the subsequent dramatic adventures build through the course of the chapters in the book.* Similarly, there is a tension in the story between Charlotte the spider, and children's feelings about spiders in general—often perceived as frightening. This contradiction is featured in the rationale for why the teachers selected the story of Charlotte's Web.

> Well, when we were selecting the story, we were responding to some of the children's reactions in the room. So, some of them were frightened of spiders, or were horrified at the thought of spiders. And we really felt like we needed to do something, be proactive about it and think of perhaps stories we could choose that would help them to have some empathy ... for the spider. And to really make a strong connection with the spider, and how it has an important part to play in our eco-system. We felt Charlotte's Web was the perfect one for that. I think, emotional investment to the story was very important. (Oriana)

> [The children went from] originally not liking spiders, to by the end being so fond of Charlotte, the main character, and to think that she was beautiful and wise. (Rebecca)

As is noted above, spiders are frightening for some of the children, yet Charlotte the spider is portrayed in the fiction as kind and wise. The emotional response to spiders and learning about spiders are brought together in the Playworld—fictional characters and imagined spiders. In this story context, imagination in play and imagination in learning are intermingled. This foregrounds in the Playworld a conceptual space for imagining in play (Charlotte) and imagining in learning (spiders) which together create the dynamic force or motive for learning.

We also know from the Playworld literature that teachers set up physical spaces to build the Playworld, but how this supports learning had to be carefully considered by the teachers. For instance, the teachers discussed this need, but only after implementing more than one Playworld:

> When planning the physical play space, it took a little bit of practice for us to realize that you do actually need a designated area where you can go and be play partners with the children, and that can be quite open-ended. (Rebecca)

In these designated spaces, the relationship between the real world of the kindergarten and the imaginary play situation of the Playworld is made explicit to the children. Interestingly, although the space is physical the imagining is more psychological and, according to the literature, the teacher has an important role in creating this group imagining: 'Themeaning- [s] of things and actions do not depend on the real perception of the child, but on the intent that is initially proposed by an adult, which the child subsequently carries out independently' (Kravtsov & Kravtsova, 2010, p. 31). For instance, because the teachers designed a Playworld of the imaginary situation of Charlotte's Web, designated spaces in the indoor and the outdoor areas changed their meaning from a physical outdoor/indoor play space into an imaginary situation of the Zuckerman's farm where Fern lived and where the pigs' barn could be found. This was noted by the teachers,

> We had a soft toy pig in the home corner, and they really enjoyed feeding, pretending to be Fern and feeding Wilbur. And that nurturing side of the play. (Rebecca)

Not only were the teachers changing the optical field (home area became a barn) but, as this example shows, children independently changed the optical field for themselves. For a child to realise that s/he can change the optical field through imagination, giving it a new sense, is illustrative of how the child can consciously work with imagination (Kravtsov & Kravtsova, 2010) in a Playworld. But the teachers became increasingly aware of how the Playworld focused more on imagining of concepts:

> But then we also had a lot of books with facts. We had some children who had just started the anatomy of the spider. So, it provided a lot of opportunities. (Rebecca)

In this example, the children are not just supported with building their imagination through fiction, but they are also supported to consider the science associated with spiders and farm life. Imagination in play and imagining of the science of spiders were intermingled in this Conceptual Playworld of Charlotte's Web. The real and the imaginary work together in practice. But this needs to be supported by the teachers, as noted:

> ... it's kind of like there's switching in and out of the play, so they know that this is what we are doing. We are entering into this [imaginary] space with our teachers and with the other children. (Oriana)

> When we returned [from the imaginary space], we would go back to being children and teachers ready to enter back into the kindergarten. We close the gate of the farm, and back in we go. And so that helps, I think, the children to know when they're exploring those particular concepts and then when they are going back, although it's very fluid because we will continue to chat throughout the day about various characters from the story. (Oriana)

As the comments show, the Playworld foregrounds and actively works with imagination. Specifically, the teachers found that the entering and exiting of the Playworld space felt like crossing a border (El'koninova, 2002) and they needed to help children with this border crossing. For example, the teachers helped children to select a play role from the story before entering the Playworld:

> So, in this situation that was Charlotte's Web, it was Zuckerman's farm, it was the barn. So, we would line up on the log, and the children would choose their characters, and sometimes you know two people want to be Wilbur, that's fine. Some days, everyone is a spider. Some days ... its real

> ... really doesn't matter, as long as we get into that space as a collective. (Rebecca)

The teacher illustrates how children collectively change from their real relations with each other in the pre-school to forming play relations inside the imaginary play situation. Changing from the real relations to play relations is cognitively challenging. However, in a Playworld teachers actively work with children to support the positions the children take. The Playworld created opportunities for children to be different characters and therefore have different positions—real position as a person, and an imaginary position as a character. To support this, the teachers gave 'lots of opportunities for them to explore the play with the characters or the concepts' (Rebecca). Kravtsov and Kravtsova (2010) suggest that 'To understand and create this space, a player must be simultaneously inside and outside of the play. ... play through the simultaneous stance of taking two positions' (p. 29). In the imaginary play situation of Charlotte's Web, the children take on a role in the play inside the imaginary situation, but children on subsequent days can be different characters entering the Conceptual Playworld. This means children have, 'The opportunity to change different roles during the play process [and this] helps a player to consider different situations from different positions' (Kravtsov & Kravtsova, 2010, p. 39). Experiencing the difference between play relationships and real relationships is most pronounced in their relations with their teachers. As the teachers also noted:

> And as the teacher, I would always choose a character. So, depending on what we had planned for that day's experience, so brings up with if we were introducing a new character, I might be the rat that day, or I might be part of the ecosystem. So, I might be the sunshine that day. So, it was a good way to get the children in to the right headspace where we are all imagining similar things. (Rebecca)

As this example shows, the teachers become a character in the story, and this means the children relate to their teachers in play relations rather than real relations of being a child and a teacher. But the action and narrative that builds is not random, but is in keeping with the imaginary fiction from the story and the planned inquiries that unfold. That is, '... *play relations* that are associated with the logic of a play's plot and real relations, which have been formed in the process of a person's real life activity' (Kravtsov & Kravtsova, 2010, p. 29; original emphasis) emerge in the Conceptual Playworld. Theoretically, the differences between real relations and play relations support the children to think more consciously about the characters in the story. In Playworlds children appear to imagine their own role and the role of others more explicitly. The collective imaginary situation of Charlotte's Web keeps a common fiction alive, supports the development of the common narrative, and appears to create the need for learning more about spiders, pigs and farm life. That is, the Playworld also foregrounds a conceptual orientation.

As was discussed previously, the Playworlds literature notes how Playworlds feature a problem situation that the children and teachers must solve. In the Playworld of Charlotte's Web, the teachers found that there is a need to be clear about the concepts that are to be learned from solving the problem situation. For example,

> Being really clear about the concepts that you are teaching, and how and trying to draw those concepts with the stories, being able to tie them in together was really important for us, so that we were always clear about why we were creating a particular play scenario. And why we were wanting to develop a specific message or idea with the children. I think that was very important for us. (Oriana)

The teachers noted that in the planning of a play inquiry, they introduced learning of concepts in support of the children's play. The teachers found that this created the play conditions in which conceptual learning becomes more personally meaningful to children— but also an engaging approach for the teachers. For instance, the teachers noted how the problem scenarios in the Playworld worked for them and for the children:

> I think we had a lot of fun, working this way, and teaching this way [It was powerful], using the drama. So, the day you present the problem to the children is always a very exciting day for the teachers as well. I think it's really important for us to know that we have prepared the children enough in terms of developing that conceptual knowledge because we are discussing conceptual Playworlds. So, we need to know that we have supported them and created the conditions that they have enough knowledge and understanding that they will be able to, with our support, and with their more knowledgeable peers, to solve the problems together through play. So, it's something that we do when we feel confident that the group, the whole group, will ... something we'll be able to solve together. So that's quite satisfying. (Rebecca)

The importance of also have a conceptual orientation in the Playworld emerged for the teachers. But in order for the children to imagine the solutions to the problem situations in the Playworld, careful planning was needed, as is illustrated by the teachers:

> It was always a lot of fun thinking about the problem and how we were about to go about it. So, when we were thinking of the story of Charlotte's Web, and the particular problem that took a while to think really carefully of how again when we thinking about the playworlds approach and how emotionally invested the children were. … it was, you know we wanted that important hook. So, we thought long and hard about this, but again, coming in as a character, as farmer Zuckerman, we were able … I was able to just completely think of this, this problem with the children. And the beauty of that is that the children were able to completely connect with that character. And then we knew and we could take them on board, in terms of being able to develop that … that concept. (Oriana)

> So being able to be really clear again about that concept and then help us to plan very carefully about how that actual problem would be presented through the character with the children, so that we could immerse them in it with us together, and really hear the child's voice in that … in that problem. (Oriana)

As this example shows, the teachers had to think carefully about the concepts—how to embed them into the Playworld of Charlotte's Web. But also, how they could act in the service of the children's play. Similarly, by solving the problem together in the Playworld, the teachers position themselves as active agents in the play and the learning. Being together with children in the imaginary play is often viewed as problematic. van Oers (2013) says, 'The problem is closely related to the role of the adult and the question whether she or he can "employ" play for deliberately promoting specific learning processes' (p. 189). This is a philosophical problem as the teachers also noted.

Rebecca: And I think obviously there is always a debate about how much to interfere with children's play, but in terms of …

Oriana: … This approach gave us a lot of confidence.

Rebecca: … to jump in when they get stuck because we saw how … how much more complex the play can be. So rather than being repetitive or them exploring, a particular angle we felt that we could really add layers by just a suggestion here and a suggestion there.

Oriana: Well children embrace it. They completely embrace …

Rebecca: … and it was incredible how far they took it. By the end of our Charlotte's Web project, we were talking about photosynthesis. And

this was coming from obviously some of the children who were
really ready to be extended. But just layer upon layer upon layer ...

Oriana: That's right.

Rebecca: ... which I felt by us being able to enter the play, and particularly
role playing the scientific concepts.

Much of the early childhood literature is oriented towards adults not being
involved in children's play because this is the domain of the child. Children are
expected to create their own developmental conditions through child-initiated
play, where children are free to act as they wish. However, in the Playworlds
literature the adult has a central role and children are supported by the play
role of the teachers to imagine the fiction and problem scenario as the play
narrative develops. In this way children imagine in play and imagine the concepts that are supporting their play. This relationship is captured as learning
of curriculum concepts in the service of children's play through a Conceptual
Playworld. The practices described by the teacher and theorised in this paper
expand on the original research of Lindqvist (1995) and those that have used
her work in different countries.

Conclusion

Play is the leading activity of the pre-school child, and pre-school settings
are organised to support children's play. But at a time when Governments are
expecting children to learn concepts at an increasingly early age, teachers need
new practice models that recognise play as the leading activity of the child but
in ways that orient children to learning. Like van Oers (2013), this paper gives
insights into the 'perplexing question for play researchers or practitioners following a play-based educational philosophy ... [to determine an] explanation
of learning in the context of play' (van Oers, 2013, p. 188).

   A theoretical analysis of the practice example of the Playworld of Charlotte's Web revealed that imagination in play and imagination in the learning
appear to be in relationship with each other.

   The relationship between play and learning exemplified through the fiction
of the story of Charlotte's Web illustrates how play-based programs can support
learning. What is new in this theoretical paper, is the focus on how a Conceptual
Playworld creates the pedagogical conditions to productively build a dynamic
relation between play and learning, which the profession currently needs for
maintaining play as the leading activity in preschool settings. It is argued that
without opportunities for imaginative play, children may find it difficult to

imagine and use abstract concepts for learning later in school. This paper seeks to support the importance of maintaining play-based programs in pre-school settings. Conceptual Playworlds offer a possible model of practice that appears to foreground imagination in play for usefully pushing against the promotion of formal learning. In so doing, a Conceptual Playworld is helpful in reclaiming the importance of play as the predominant activity of the pre-school child, play as the source of the child's development, and the role of play in developing imagination and the learning of school curriculum concepts. But what is different, is that a Conceptual Playworld would appear to do this in ways that are productive for the child's creativity and imagination rather than reproductive of content that is focused primarily on the development of memory.

Disclosure Statement

No potential conflict of interest was reported by the author.

Funding

This work was supported by the Australian Research Council [DP180101030].

References

Baumer, S., Ferholt, B., & Lecusay, R. (2005). Promoting narrative competence through adult-child joint pretense: Lessons from the Scandinavian educational practice of Playworld. *Cognitive Development, 20,* 576–590. doi:10.1016/j.cogdev.2005.08.003

El'koninova, L. I. (2002). The object orientation of children's play in the context of understanding imaginary space-time in play and in stories. *Journal of Russian and Eastern European Psychology, 39*(2), 30–51. doi:10.2753/RPO1061-0405390230

Elkonin, B. D. (2005). On the historical origin of role play. *Journal of Russian and East European Psychology, 42*(1), 49–89. doi:10.1080/10610405.2005.11059243

Elkonin, D. B. (1971). Towards the problem of stages in the mental development of the child. *Voprosy Psikhologii, 4,* 538–563.

Ferholt, B., & Lecusay, R. (2010). Adult and child development in the zone of proximal development: Socratic dialogue in a Playworld. *Mind, Culture and Activity, 17*(1), 59–83. doi:10.1080/10749030903342246

Ferholt, B., Nilsson, M., Jansson, A., & Anervik, K. (2015). Creativity in education: Play and exploratory learning. In T. Hansson (Ed.), *Contemporary approaches to activity theory* (pp. 264–284). IGI Global.

Fleer, M. (2017). Scientific Playworlds: A model of teaching science in play based settings. *Research in Science Education.* doi:10.1007/s11165017-9653-z

Fleer, M., Li, L., & Yan, Z. (2018). Problematising pedagogical imports and creating new conditions for children's development: A case from China. In M. Fleer, F. G. Rey, & P. P. E. Jones (Eds.), *Cultural-historical and critical psychology: Common ground, divergences and future pathways.* Springer.

Fleer, M., & van Oers, B. (2018). International trends in research: Redressing the North-South balance in what matters for early childhood education research. In M. Fleer & B. van Oers (Eds.), *International handbook on early childhood education* (pp. 1–30). Springer.

Hakkarainen, P. (2008). The challenges and possibilities of a narrative learning approach in the finish early childhood education system. *International Journal of Educational Research, 47*, 292–300. doi:10.1016/j.ijer.2008.12.008

Hakkarainen, P. (2010). Cultural-historical methodology of the study of human development in transitions. *Cultural-Historical Psychology, 4*, 75–89.

Hakkarainen, P., & Bredikyte, M. (2008). The zone of proximal development in play and learning. *Cultural-Historical Psychology, 4*, 2–11.

Hakkarainen, P., Bredikyte, M., Jakkula, K., & Munter, H. (2013). Adult play guidance and children's play development in a narrative play-world. *European Early Child Education Research Journal, 21*(2), 213–225. doi:10.1080/1350293X.2013.789189

Kravtsov, G. G., & Kravtsova, E. E. (2010). Play in L. S. Vygotsky's non-classical psychology. *Journal of Russian and Eastern European Psychology, 48*(4), 25–41. doi:10.2753/RPO1061-0405480403

Kravtsova, E. E. (2010). The cultural-historical foundations of the zone of proximal development. *Journal of Russian and Eastern European Psychology, 47*(6), 3–18.

Leontiev, A. N. (1978). *Activity, consciousness, and personality.* Prentice-Hall.

Lindqvist, G. (1995). *The aesthetics of play: A didactic study of play and culture in preschools.* Gotab.

Marjanovic-Shane, A., Ferholt, B., Miyazaki, K., Nilsson, M., Rainio, A. P., Hakkarainen, P., Pesic, M., & Beljanski-Ristic, L. (2011). Playworlds-an art of development. In C. Lobman & B. E. O'Neill (Eds.), *Play and performance: Play and culture studies* (pp. 3–32). University Press of America.

Nilsson, M., Ferholt, B., & Lecusay, R. (2017). The playing-exploring child: Reconceptualizing the relationship between play and learning in early childhood education. *Contemporary Issues in Early Childhood, 1*(15), 1–15. doi:10.1177/1463949117710800

Rainio, A. P. (2008). From resistance to involvement: Examining agency and control in a Playworld activity. *Mind, Culture, and Activity, 15*(2), 115–140. doi:10.1080/10749030801970494

Talamo, A., Pozzi, S., & Mellini, B. (2010). Uniqueness of experience and virtual Playworlds: Playing is not just for fun. *Mind Culture and Activity, 17*(1), 23–41. doi:10.1080/10749030903342220

van Oers, B. (2013). Is it play? Towards a conceptualization of role play from an activity theory perspective. *European Early Childhood Education Research Journal, 21*(2), 185–198. doi:10.1080/1350293X.2013.789199

Vygotsky, L. S. (1966). Play and its role in the mental development of the child. *Voprosy Psikhologii, 12*(6), 62–76.

Vygotsky, L. S. (1987). Problems of general psychology (N. Minick, Trans.). In R. W. Rieber (Ed.), *The collected works of L.S. Vygotsky* (Vol. 1). Kluwer Academic and Plenum Publishers.

Vygotsky, L. S. (1998). The collected works of L. S. Vygotsky (R. W. Rieber, Trans.). In M. J. Hill (Ed.), *Child psychology* (Vol. 5). Plenum Press.

Vygotsky, L. S. (2004). Imagination and creativity in childhood. *Journal of Russian and East European Psychology, 42*(1), 7–97. doi:10.1080/10610405.2004.11059210

Vygotsky, L. V. (1971). *The psychology of art*. MIT Press.

White, E. B. (1952). *Charlotte's web*. Harper & Row Publishers. https://en.wikipedia.org/wiki/Charlotte%27s_Web

Paper 7: *Scientific Playworlds*: A Model of Teaching Science in Play-Based Settings

Marilyn Fleer

This paper originally appeared as Fleer, M. (2019). Scientific Playworlds: a model of teaching science in play-based settings. *Research in Science Education*. https://doi.org/10.1007/s11165-017-9653-z Reprinted here with permission from the publisher.

Abstract

Eminent scientists, like Einstein, worked with theoretical contradiction, thought experiments, mental models and visualisation—all characteristics of children's play. Supporting children's play is a strength of early childhood teachers. Promising research shows a link between imagination in science and imagination in play. A case study of 3 preschool teachers and 26 children (3.6–5.9 years; mean age of 4.6 years) over 6 weeks was undertaken, generating 59.6 h of digital observations and 788 photographs of play practices. The research sought to understand (1) how imaginative play promotes scientific learning and (2) examined how teachers engaged children in scientific play. Although play pedagogy is a strength of early childhood teachers, it was found that transforming imaginary situations into scientific narratives requires different pedagogical characteristics. The study found that the building of collective scientific narratives alongside of discourses of wondering were key determinants of science learning in play-based settings. Specifically, the pedagogical principles of using a cultural device that mirrors the science experiences, creating imaginary scientific situations, collectively building scientific problem situations, and imagining the relations between observable contexts and non-observable concepts, changed everyday practices into a scientific narrative and engagement. It is argued that these unique pedagogical characteristics promote scientific narratives in play-based settings. An approach, named as *Scientific Playworlds*, is presented as a possible model for teaching science in play-based settings.

Keywords

early childhood teachers – cultural-historical – science education – Playworlds – play – affective imagination

Introduction

Despite the vast evidence showing the contribution of play to childhood learning and development, little is known about how scientific reasoning in guided imaginative play can be designed into play-based teaching programs so that preschool teachers intentionally engage young children in scientific thought in play-based settings. The study reported in this paper addresses this problem.

Many eminent scientists have revealed childhoods where thought experiments and visualisation during imaginative play feature (e.g., Rothenberg, 1979). Einstein reported spending hours playing with his toy trains and, as an adult, advocated that "Play is the highest form of research". What they appear to have in common is an exceptional cognitive capacity to visualise, imagine, model and explore theoretical contradictions for certain features of the physical world (e.g., Kass, 2003). For instance, *thought experiments* and *mental models* that give fundamentally different theoretical insights are evident in the scientific work of Michael Faraday when exploring electricity and magnetism. Albert Einstein's theory of relativity was partially derived through thought experiments. Steven Hawking used visualisation to consider big ideas in science, such as the origins of the university, and through this paved the way for new lines of scientific inquiry in science. Barbara McClintock imagined travelling down the microscope, examining the genetic structure whilst simultaneously imagining the living ecosystem of corn fields (Fox Keller, 1983). In her scientific work, she was simultaneously imagining the relations between molecular and observable contexts, changing the course of genetics research. Many of these eminent scientists comfortably engaged in theoretical contradictions, and through this created the conditions for new scientific thought (e.g., Albert Einstein when reconciling Newton's laws with relativity mechanics).

Whilst it seems intuitive that exposure to science education in the formative years (i.e., birth-five) when cognitive function is being established, can help build cognitive capabilities for scientific thought, not just for those with a genius for science enquiry but for all young children (Cook et al., 2011), little attention has been directed to studying scientific reasoning in guided imaginative play. Guided imaginative play that explores the physical world offers an ideal opportunity to teach the concepts of science (theories or laws) (Bergen, 2009). Yet, science education for the early childhood period, where imagination and creativity is commonplace in young children's play, has not yet been comprehensively investigated as an evidence-based model of teaching science for preschoolers. This is particularly surprising given the potential links between play and science inquiry. Could a play-based model of teaching science that supports the creative cognition of pre-schoolers encourage more teaching of science? Unfortunately, we cannot answer this question because very little is known about what might be an effective model of teaching science through imagination in play in play-based settings–especially for infants and toddlers, where a dearth of research exists (Sikder & Fleer, 2014).

In this paper, the findings of a case study of 26 children and 3 teachers are reported. The focus of the research was on how teachers engaged children in scientific play and how imaginative play promotes scientific learning in play-based settings. This paper begins with a brief review of the relevant background literature, followed by the conceptual framework guiding the study, the study design and then the findings and discussion. The paper concludes by outlining a cultural-historical approach to teaching early childhood science, named as a *Scientific Playworld*.

Knowledge Forms and Imagination in Science for Under 5's

Reviews of the learning of preschool science suggest two types of interrelated knowledge domains—domain-specific science learning (e.g., what children know about a concept) and domain general knowledge, such as the cognitive skills needed to understand the domain specific knowledge (e.g., process skills or scientific thinking) (Trundle & Saçkes, 2015). The former has traditionally been studied in relation to a range of science concepts, such as astronomy (Hannust & Kikas, 2007), electricity (Fleer, 1995), food (Cumming, 2003), digestion (Martins Teizeira, 2000), natural science (Venville, 2004), force (Hadzigeorgiou, 2002) and matter (Krnel et al., 2005). The latter research has focused more on determining children's abilities in how things function and work, as models for supporting everyday life (Cook et al., 2011; Gelman & Brenneman, 2004; Howitt et al., 2011). What these latter studies point to is the general ability of preschool children to engage in scientific reasoning or thinking skills (e.g., Bulunuz, 2013; Eshach & Fried, 2005; Metz, 2004). But these studies and reviews do not give insights into what might be a model of science teaching for play-based setting where scientific thought experiments and visualisations of science through play are used to support the learning of science concepts.

In contrast, there is some promising evidence of the relations between imagination in play and creative cognition in science that supports the link between visualisations of big ideas in science and play. The characteristics of curiosity (Blake & Howitt, 2012) and wonder (Hadzigeorgiou, 2001; Siry & Kremer, 2011), alongside of children imagining scientific concepts during role-play (Fleer, 2010), have been identified. What is known is that when scientific problems are introduced during children's play (Fleer, 2011) where teachers role-play scientific concepts with children (Fleer, 2014), more authentic science learning has resulted (Fleer & Pramling, 2015). But these studies do not discuss the pedagogical practices linking imagination in science and imagination in play.

Although children's natural curiosity has been studied during science concept formation (e.g., rainbows to understand concept of light refraction; Siry & Kremer, 2011), and playful approaches have been shown to help children satisfy their curiosity, we do not yet know enough about what forms of guided play enable exploration of authentic interests (Blake & Howitt, 2012) and scientific imagining (Hadzigeorgiou, 2016) of young children. The available studies point to the need for better understanding how to draw upon a pedagogy of play for supporting science teaching in early childhood settings.

Models of Teaching Science to Preschool Children

What is known about the existing teaching models of teaching science to preschool children is that the available models tend to concentrate on setting up resource rich learning environments (e.g., Zhang & Birdsall, 2016) where discovery learning is promoted (Fleer, 1995, 2009), but where many opportunities to teach science in play-based settings are lost (Tu, 2006).

It appears that early childhood teachers' models of teaching science draw upon the methods and approaches transferred from primary and secondary science education where the foundational research is based on learning environments suitable for children older than 8 years (Fleer, 2009). Teachers have difficulties with inquiry-based approaches (Fleer, 2009, 2011b), because the children have different developmental capacities, do not readily ask scientific questions that can be used as the basis for the inquiry (Fleer & Pramling, 2015) and teachers lack confidence in their knowledge of science concepts (Garbett, 2003). More needs to be known about what kinds of existing and new pedagogical practices could support science learning in play-based settings.

Whilst there are a lot of models of play in the literature (e.g., Pellegrini, 2011), conceptions about play across cultures (e.g., Göncü et al., 2007) and definitions for what is play and what is not (e.g., Lillard, 2007), there is no model of play specifically developed to support science learning. The closest possibility is an approach known as Playworlds. This approach includes the teacher in children's play (most definitions of play do not) and it foregrounds a problem scenario (as a play inquiry) as part of building a play narrative (Hakkarainen et al., 2013). There is a lot of research interest in Playworlds in Sweden (Lindqvist, 1995), Finland (Hakkarainen, 2010) and the USA (Ferholt, 2010). But this research has focused primarily on building play narratives over extended periods of time (e.g., Lindqvist, 1995) rather than focused on scientific learning of young children. However, what appears to be unique about Playworlds is that it gives a pedagogical role to the adult (see Hakkarainen et al., 2013), which actively supports imagination, and which in turn has been shown to develop children's imaginative play (Lindqvist, 1995). As such, the present study drew upon Playworlds to design and study a model of science teaching for play-based settings that featured teacher strengths in the pedagogy of play.

Conceptual Framework

The conceptual framework guiding this study is based on a cultural-historical theory for informing a strength based view of science pedagogy (Zeidler, 2016), particularly Vygotsky's (1966) conception of play for framing the unique nature of early childhood education. Vygotsky theorised play as the creation of an imaginary situation, where children change the meaning of objects and actions, and give them a new sense. Vygotsky proposed that this can be seen when a child uses a stick to act as though riding a horse. The child has changed the meaning of the stick to be a horse, and changed their actions to be a horse rider. Vygotsky's premise is that in play, children imagine and create new meaning, supported by objects, actions or words. In this study, it was thought that this cultural-historical conception of play could be used to theorise how children change the meaning of actions and objects in their play to take on a scientific meaning.

Vygotsky's conception of play alone does not theoretically explain what might be the force for the development of scientific thinking, imagination and dealing with contradiction. Other concepts were needed for understanding the scientific play of children. The study used the concepts of drama and dual positioning.

Drama-Based Play and Active Exploration of Imagination in Science

In a culturalhistorical reading of role-play, play pedagogy is psychologically connected to Vygotsky's conception of drama. The genesis of cultural development as proposed by Vygotsky (1997) suggests that when children engage in drama, every function in the cultural development of a child appears in two planes—in social relations *between people* (interpsychological level) and also *within the child* (intrapsychological level). Vygotsky (1997) proposes that it is through drama that children develop and gain different perspectives and gain new insights. At the interpsychological level, children become consciously aware or explore that which they are role-playing. Importantly, it is through drama that the feeling of "we" rather than "I" is created, as a form of social consciousness (multiple perspectives). The child actor creates on the stage infinite sensations, feelings, or images that become a visualisation of the whole theatrical performance with the audience. Children's play as a form of drama, potentially enables a collective consciousness about everyday life events, such as pretending to ride a horse, that has the potential to be directed to thinking and imagining in science. But this requires a more refined understanding of the psychology and pedagogy of play for science learning in play-based settings.

Two-Positional Perspective

Kravtsov and Kravtsova (2010) introduced the concept of a two-positional perspective in play, where the idea of audience is central for children's development. They stated that "play from the "dual (or two)-positional" perspective allows the child to better understand him/herself, as well as understanding the surrounding world" (p. 33). The child is inside the play acting out what s/he has experienced, observed or read/viewed in everyday life (e.g., nature, cooking at home, phenomenon on TV, a smart device games or in books), whilst also being able to step outside or above the play, directing how the play should take place (e.g., as we see when child changes the play).

Using the concept of a *two-positional perspective* supports the analysis of children's modelling in play and science through analysing when children visualise, model or imagine scientific concepts during play. In play, children use metacommunicative language (Bretherton, 1984), such as "Pretend I am inside the drop of water or inside the compost bin", and use a sing-song cadence at the end of a sentence to signal that they are inside the imaginary situation to their play partner (...and the worms were wriggling around [inflexion on the word around]), signalling an invitation to imagine along with them, and use conjunction words to keep the storyline going (e.g., and or then). Analysing children's metacommunicative language from a two-positional perspective gives more confidence in research about when a child is in the imaginary situation and when they are not. Metacommunicative language also has the potential to signal in the analysis particular modelling and potential thought experiments being tested in their play (e.g., wriggling worms who are exploring how a worm moves without legs). Further, teacher use and modelling of metacommunicative language specific to preschool science, such as "I wonder if...", has the potential for better understanding how play-pedagogy could consciously and systematically over time support science learning in play-based settings. But a cultural-historical study of this kind has not yet been undertaken.

A summary of the concepts that informed the study design and analysis is shown in Table 1. In keeping with a cultural-historical informed study that features a system of concepts, the content of the table is provided to show which concepts were used in this particular study.

Together, these cultural-historical concepts provided the framework for the study. What is unique about this theoretical framing is that unlike constructivist-inspired research, a culturalhistorical study does not look at the end point or cognitive result alone, but rather it also seeks to capture the process of the development of children's scientific thinking.

Study Design

The study was designed as a cultural-historical case study of one preschool site where the teachers, with support from the researchers, implemented a Playworlds approach to teaching science content to young children. The goal was to understand the pedagogical practices in the play-based setting that supported the scientific engagement of the children and teachers and the development of scientific thinking within imaginative play.

TABLE 1   An overview of the theoretical concepts guiding the study and analytical frame

Theoretical concept	Explanation of the concepts for this study
Cultural-historical conception of play (Vygotsky, 1966)	Creates an imaginary situation (adult/child) and changes the meaning of an object and/or action
Interpsychological and intrapscyhological functionoing (Vygotsky, 1997)	Play is jointly created and *later* independently enacted as the social becomes the child's personal understanding. Contradictions and dramatic events create the conditions for children's development
Play from the "dual (or two)-positional Perspective" (Kravtsov & Kravtsova, 2010)	Signals they are in the imaginary situation through words, actions or objects. Offers solutions to problem situations inside/outside of imaginary situation
Metacommunicative language (Bretherton, 1984) in collective play (Fleer, 2011)	Underscores actions or words; high inflexion at end of sentence; uses words such as "Pretend I was …", uses conjunctions to blend story lines such as "and" or "then they went…"
Cultural-historical conception of imagination in science (Vygotsky, 2004)	Evidence of thought experiments; visualisation of big ideas; engaging in theoretical contradictions; imagining the relations between observable contexts and non-observable (e.g., solar system, molecular level). Child creates models in play to show ideas, such as when role-playing, using physical materials to make something, draws upon symbols and uses digital animation

Sample

The preschool is located in an inner city suburb of Melbourne, Australia. The children live in high-rise flats or in small historic homes in the region. A mix of low and middle socioeconomic families send their children to the preschool. The centre operates from 9 until 3 each day.

The children who attend the preschool and whose families consented for their child to participate in the research include 6 Vietnamese heritage families, 6 Indian heritage families, 5 European heritage families, 3 Chinese families, 2 Ethiopian families, 1 Greek family, 1 Timorese family, 1 South Sudanese family and 1 Libyan family. Many of the families are newly arrived in Australia. The 26 children who attend the preschool are aged between 3.6 and 5.9 years (mean age of 4.6 years).

There are three staff who work in the preschool site and who participated in the research. The lead teacher holds a university degree in early childhood education, and is of European heritage origin. Another teacher is completing a degree in early childhood education. She holds a Bachelor's degree in science and has a vocational qualification in early childhood. She speaks fluent Vietnamese and is of Vietnamese heritage origin. The third teacher has a vocational qualification in early childhood and she is of Chinese/Timorese heritage origin. Two of the three teachers have over 10 years of teaching experience in early childhood education.

Procedure

Professional Development
To achieve the aims of the study, the procedure was organised to include professional development.

1. All teachers participated in professional development in their centre on a *Playworlds* approach.
2. A booklet of teaching ideas and supporting material about Playworlds was given to the teachers.
3. The brainstorming of science teaching ideas suitable for Playworlds was supported by the research team.
4. Identification of both a play narrative or story (The Magic Wishing Chair by Enid Blyton) and related science concepts (microbes and microscopic organisms) was undertaken to support the teachers. This story focuses on preschool aged children going on adventures to other imaginative lands by sitting on a magic chair. The magic chair has wings and flies the children to new adventures on different days.
5. Ongoing professional support for the science concepts was provided to the teachers.
6. Teachers implemented the *Playworlds* approach over 4 weeks during one school term, but with a focus on developing science concepts.

Video Observations
Video observations were made over the 4 weeks of implementing the *Playworld*. Two and sometimes three cameras documented the play-practices of the children and teachers during the *Playworld* activity, the general play in the outdoor area, all group times and all of the scientific investigations that

occurred either to support the *Playworld* or as a separate activity outside of the imaginary situation. A total of 69.6 h of video data were generated, and 788 photographs of play practices were documented. Nine visits to the preschool were made over 4 weeks.

Interviews

The professional development session, follow-up meetings and informal interviews in situ or held at the end of most weeks formed part of the data set. This part of the study design took place over 6 weeks. All sessions were video recorded and sessions not recorded were discussed through an interview on a subsequent day when the research team visited the site. Interviews were usually in relation to what was happening on the day of filming and what had previously taken place in the day or week when the research team had not been present. This allowed for instant capturing of teachers' perspective on what had happened in the course of implementing their program.

Analysis

In line with the theoretical approach of the study, the data analysis framework drew upon Hedegaard and Fleer (2008) cultural-historical methodology for studying young children. Three iterative analytical dimensions encompass the cultural-historical methodology used—everyday interpretations, situated interpretations and theoretical interpretations.

Everyday Interpretations

Step 1:   Data were digitally logged in their raw form with annotations and summaries of their content (e.g., *RB008*).

Step 2:   Data were tagged in relation to teachers' pedagogical practices when using a *Playworlds* approach for teaching science.

Step 3:   Data were also tagged in relation to the moments in which children imagined, appeared to exhibit behaviours and make comments related to thought experiments, and when showing behaviours or words associated with visualisation.

Step 4:   Data were also tagged for free play moments outside of the *Playworlds* teaching, and also play related investigations inside and outside of the *Playworlds*.

Situated Interpretations

Step 5:   The *everyday interpretations* (steps 1–4) across the whole data set were cut into video clips (e.g., named as *Clip 3*). These everyday interpretations were put in a digital folder focused on differing descriptors of pedagogical practices linked with imagination in science behaviour and teachers' pedagogical practices. Central here was identifying science moments across the data set.

Step 6:   Common trends or themes were identified and the folders further refined and named according to the situated practices, such as imagination in science, thought experiments, visualisation, science concepts and curiosity in science (e.g., coded as *131,113*).

Theoretical Interpretations

Step 7:   In line with the goals of the study and the theoretical concepts informing the research (Table 1), links were made between digital folders of video clips (e.g., coded to *08S*). For example, the cultural-historical conception of play was used to identify if, when and how children changed the meaning of actions and objects in their play to be scientific. Folders were digitally brought together in relation to the play practices of children and pedagogical features of the *Playworld* approach used by the teachers, but always in relation to teaching, promoting or imagining of science concepts by children, by teachers and by children and teachers together (e.g., named as *Playworlds*).

Step 8:   Representative examples of video or teacher or/and child(ren) dialogue for each of the outcomes of the theoretical interpretation were made and used to highlight some of the key pedagogical practices of the resultant *Scientific Playworld* (discussed in findings). **Steps 1–8** were iterative, because the emerging theoretical categories were used to re-analyse the full data set for frequency, type, duration and quality of pedagogical practices/imaginings. Pairing of science pedagogical practices and children's scientific imagining as evident through the play actions drove this final part of the theoretical analysis. This allowed for an understanding of how imaginative play promotes scientific learning (Research Question 1), as well as how teachers engaged children in scientific play (Research Question 2).

Findings and Discussion

The focus of the research was to understand how teachers engage children in scientific play in preschool settings. The study found a range of ways in which guided imaginative play can be designed into play-based teaching programs to intentionally engage young children in scientific thought. The major pedagogical practices for promoting imaginative scientific play were found to centre around building collective scientific imaginary situations where children and teacher could engage in shared and sustained scientific wondering.

Building Collective Scientific Imaginary Situations

Even though the literature collectively indicates that play is culturally learned (e.g., Lillard, 2007), current pedagogical practices tend to treat play as universal and natural. As a result, very little research attention has been directed to how imaginative play as a learned practice, can be explicitly introduced to support abstract learning in science. However, in this study, it was found that a key practice in play observed was the building of collective scientific imaginary situations.

Three different ways of building collective scientific imaginary situations were evident in the data. First, the teachers drew upon their practice of reading stories to create a collective imaginary situation with the children at group time. The story of the *Wishing Chair* was used to build an imaginary situation. However, the selection of the story was not random. It was important for the teachers to introduce *a story which had a structure that allowed the children to collectively go on adventures*. The story of the *Wishing Chair* created the conditions for the children to imagine themselves, going on the chair and flying to faraway lands for exploration. In line with Hakkarainen (2010), the story selection invited the children to jointly create "imaginary situations based on tales, stories and children's fiction (ideal cultural forms) which serve as the basis of adult-child joint playworlds and child initiated pretend play" (p. 79).

Second, the pedagogical strategy used by the teachers featured some kind of psychological tool to support the children's collective imaginings of going on adventures stimulated through the story of the Wishing Chair. The teachers put a chair into the space where the children sat for group time. The chair acted as a placeholder for the imaginary situation being collectively created, and this object supported all of the children to imagine the journey together. The chair helped the children to imagine the journey. This is consistent with a *Playworlds* approach. As suggested by Hakkarainen (2010), "In all playworlds some kind of psychological tools was used in transitions from classroom to imaginary playworld" (p. 79). He gives the example of the stories in the Narnia series by C.S Lewis, in particular the story of *The lion, the witch and the wardrobe* to create a *playworld*. A cardboard box was fixed to a doorframe to act as the entry into the *Playworld* of Narnia. This cardboard box mounted to the doorframe marked the boundary between the *Playworld* and the classroom. He also gives the example of the fairytale of Rumpelstiltskin. In this *Playworld*, a spell is placed on the palace, turning it upside down and making everyone walk backwards. The psychological tool used for the transition is the act of the children turning their jackets inside out, with the buttons on their backs, and walking backwards. This action by the children marks that they are in the palace–in the *Playworld*. But these children (over 6 years) were much older than the children in this study.

The wishing chair in the present study lent itself to psychologically supporting the children to transition from the preschool and into the *Playworld*. The wishing chair also physically acted as a "placeholder" for the imaginary situation being created. According to Vygotsky (2005), initially objects, then actions, and later words act as placeholders in the development of complex play. In line with Vygotsky's (1966, 2005) conception of play, the children and teachers in this study used placeholders to support the whole group to imagine together. But this practice alone did not guarantee that a scientific narrative could result or that children could imagine scientific explanations or concepts. The study found that the story of the Wishing Chair could support the building of collective scientific imaginary situation. However, it did not result in a scientific imaginary play situation being developed. But what was important was that the teachers needed to work with the familiarity of a regular story to create a *Playworld*, before they could work with building a *Scientific Playworld*. This outcome of the study was evident through their planning documentation and comments made in situ during interviews.

A third key dimension of building a collective scientific imaginary situation was the use of a range of cultural devices that more closely linked to the science that the teachers were supporting the children to learn. In this case study, the teachers were exploring the microbes in their environment through using a microscope and hand lenses to study the contents of the compost bin and also samples of pond water from the outdoor play area. Magnification was also a new concept that had to be explicitly introduced, if children were to engage with the concept of microbes. The children used hoops on the ground in the outdoor play area and magnifiers to identify a boundary and study closely the life evident within the enclosed space.

For example,

> Alex, and his teacher are in the outdoor area. They each have a magnifying glass. A hoop has marked a space on the ground. The teacher holds a large spoon which act as a digging device and also as a pointer. They have been exploring the area. Alex says, "Let me just look in the hole once more". The teacher repeats Alex's comment and invites further comment, "It is getting bigger. Is it? ". Alex responds by saying, "The hole when I look in my

magnifying glass... Don't you want to have a look? ". The teacher says, "Sure. Can I look through mine or yours? ". Alex responds, "You can look through mine. Do you see anything big?". The teacher looks closely and says, "Makes these (pause) um... rooty, planty sort of things down here look big.". Alex confirms this observation, and says, "I can see it all big". The teacher pauses and reflects, "Umm" and then says, "I can see it looking a bit bigger too". (RB 23 4)

In addition to the magnifiers, the children also used iPads for magnification. The teachers wanted the children to learn about small and microscopic organisms. The digital devices available to the children supported their explorations of the environment because they could zoom into very small organisms to see them clearly, but also to document their finds as photographs or video clips to share with each other at another time. However, having these experiences with these devices did not necessarily result in the imagining of scientific concepts. The study found that the teachers needed to build a *scientific narrative* which would allow the children to role-play being microscopic, so that they could consciously think and embody what they were experiencing. For example, the use of a fabric tunnel acted as a cultural device to support the children to imagine going down the microscope they had been using in the centre. But also, the fabric was used to support the children to imagine being a worm or a caterpillar/ butterfly (Figure 1), as the following example (Wayne, Jackie and Chantelle) illustrates:

Wayne and Jackie are standing next to Harriette the teacher. Harriette is holding the tunnel so that the children can crawl through the tunnel. The children crawl through the tunnel, laughing and smiling, and then return to Harriette to have another turn. The children continue to go through the tunnel. Harriette comments on their movements. Chantelle walks past a few times, carrying a handbag at each pass. She eventually stops and says, "What is that Harriette?". Harriette pauses, and says, "It is aaaa.... It could be a worm skin, a worm sack". Chantelle responds by saying, "That was that!". The children giggle and squeal. Harriette notices that Chantelle has moved closer, and gestures to her to have a turn. Harriette says, "Chantelle is going to have a go". The children together with Harriette explore the fabric tunnel in a new way. Harriette invites the children to stand once they are inside the tunnel. She does this many times, but on each occasion the children continue to crawl through and out of the tunnel. Harriette then takes the fabric and goes inside, standing up, and exclaiming, "I am too big for the tunnel". The children laugh and ask if they can now stand inside the tunnel. Jackie says, as he goes into fabric tunnel, "Butterfly". Harriette affirms this by saying, "A butterfly yes". Wayne shows interest and Harriette says, "You could be the butterfly and go inside it like this (models going into the fabric tunnel). If you stand up in here". Harriette then supports the children to stand inside the fabric tunnel. Jackie flaps his wings and flies around the fabric tunnel. Harriette says, "There you go. Butterfly wings are going". (RB008 131113 08S; Clip 3)

The approach adopted was discussed by the teachers with the researcher during interviews:

Teacher:	Part of that thinking and experience about what it is to be tiny, enjoyed by Wayne and Jackie who used the tube of fabric—crawling through. Howard also joined in. They often don't spend time together, so Howard was inspired to join in and that was fabulous. I am a bit of a spur of the moment person, as we did at the end of the morning with the mats and hats, and 'imagine if'. I was pleased that most of the children gave that a go.
Researcher:	…the wriggling, they were able to role play
Teacher:	To interpret that…
Researcher:	…crawling through the microscope (Fleer, 2017).

The teachers also introduced a plastic bubble (an inflated 3-m plastic bubble; as shown in Figure 2 below) to the children. The children and the teachers went inside this bubble imagining they were inside a drop of pond water that they had previously studied:

Harriette:	Imagine if this was like a drop of water
	You're inside the drop of water.
	What might you do?
Alicia:	Good.
Harriette:	Oh you are going swimming under this Alicia.
Fiona:	Swim. Good
Alicia:	Hey we go in the waterrrrrrr…..
Harriette:	Can you see outside the drop of water?
Fiona:	Yep (Fleer, 2017).

The teachers' introduction of a cultural device that closely mirrored what they were experiencing and which relied upon their imagination was an important part of the *Scientific Playworlds* approach being implemented. The

FIGURE 1   Fabric tunnels to support imagining

cultural devices mirrored the scientific investigation, and the bubble and the fabric tunnel, physically acted as a placeholder for their imaginary situation. But unlike the chair, the children's narratives in the imaginary situations were more scientific. The children's experiences with magnification of organisms in their environment enriched how they could play in the collective scientific imaginary situations. Vygotsky (2004) has postulated that the "creative activity of imagination depends directly on the richness and variety of a person's previous experience because this experience provides the material from which the products of fantasy are constructed" (pp. 14–15). It is not possible to imagine being inside a drop of pond water, if a child has not had experiences of knowing what organisms might be found there, or have had access to tools to study a drop of pond water. Further, a child does not need to directly experience everything. Vygotsky (2004) suggested that "a person's experience is broadened, because he [sic] has to imagine what he has not seen, can conceptualize something from another persons' narration and description of what he himself has never directly experienced" (p. 17). The study found that the experiences when re-presented through role-play in the bubble or after going down a fabric microscope appeared to make conscious to the children through the dramatisation of their experiences, important scientific dimensions of their everyday world—but ones not easily seen by the naked eye. This is consistent with the manner in which Barbara McClintock investigated the jumping gene. She imagined herself going down the microscope, projecting herself inside the microscope joining the chromosomes. She said, "If you want to really understand about a tumor, you've got to be a tumor" (Fox Keller, 1983, p. 202; original emphasis). Through imagination, she developed an "exceedingly strong feeling" for the oneness of things" (Fox Keller, 1983, p. 201). That is, her approach

FIGURE 2   Setting up and exploring the bubble—being inside a drop of pond water

"both promotes and is promoted by her access to the profound connectivity of all biological forms—of the cell, of the organism, of the ecosystem" (Fox Keller, 1983, p. 201), and through this, she was able to change the course of genetics research.

But these cultural devices of fabric microscope and the plastic bubble alone would not have supported the development of scientific thinking in this study. Much of science being explored is not directly observable. Many science concepts have to be imagined. Building collective scientific imaginary situations was found to support the children to develop their play, imagination and therefore their scientific understandings over time. But play is not only imaginative but also emotionally charged. Introducing scientific experiences, and using cultural devices to support the role-playing of scientific imaginings on their own, are not enough for engaging young learners in scientific thought. As such, it was found that emotionally charged situations appeared to help engage the children more in the collective scientific imaginary situations. This was the fourth important characteristic of building a collective imaginary scientific situation:

> *The children are in the outdoor are. Some of the children are holding hand lenses. The teacher faces two children Mitchell and Alex and says, "Mitchell you go and choose the log you want us to look under". Mitchell uses marching actions with his hand walks purposefully to a series of logs. The teacher and Alex follows. The teacher says, "Today might be a really good day for finding things, because..." and then in a high pitch and emotionally engaging playful voice she continues, "the ground has been made very wet with the rain". Alex says with energy, 'Because bugs LOVE rain". The children move*

around to a log that faces Mitchell, as the teacher asks, "Bugs love rain, do they?", Alex responds, "Yeah, 'cause I watched it on telly and I saw they did like rain". Mitchell says to Alex with enthusiasm, "...and they are so funny". Alex then makes grunting noises, saying with enthusiastic and forceful tone, "Let's go here, and ...". The teacher asks for helpers to push over the log, as another child, Renata joins the group. As they push the log over Alex says, "Aaarrr... I am strong!!". The teacher immediately comments in an exaggerated tone "Oooo I can see a worm. Ooo I can see another bug. O O O O. What's down here?" and at the same time Alex says with great passion, "O, Arrr". The teacher points and continues with great emotionally charged expression, "...and a slug". Mitchell says with great excitement, "I see... I see... a worm, like a 'snap!'". (RB011 131115 08PS4: Clip 1)

In the *Playworlds* literature, dramatic collisions are featured because many of the tales and stories are emotionally charged. They create some form of tension, such as being shipwrecked and encountering Captain Hook on a voyage, or meeting the wolf three times in the fairytale of the three little pigs or identifying with Wilber by feeling frightened and worried for the spider in the story of Charlotte's Web. In this study, the children conceptualised their experiences and used tools to explore the concept of magnification. Magnification was not only a challenging concept but also appeared to represent a dramatic contradiction for the children. For example, the teachers introduced to the children a giant shoe and invited the children to imagine themselves wearing the giant shoe. This created an obvious contradiction between the size of the children's feet and the giant shoe. The children were experiencing, but also imagining this contradiction.

Harriette the teacher asks, "Imagine, you were Cinderella and your foot could fit inside this shoe". Harriette holds up the large shoe and all the children gaze intently at the shoe. "Whose shoe is that?" exclaims one of the children loudly, appearing to show amazement at how large the shoe is. Harriette asks, "Do you know the story about Cinderella?" and many of the children respond "I do". Harriette briefly summarises the story of Cinderella, drawing attention to the problem scenario of finding the person who would fit into the shoe found. Harriette then asks, "Do you think we have got someone here who might fit into this shoe?". "Me", "No me" call out many of the children. Harriette asks, "Would you like to try?"... Harriette then invites the children to take off their left shoe, and then in turn they each try on the shoe and then try to walk in the shoe. Harriette then asks, "Imagine if your feet could fit in there". Harriette comments or responds in relation to the children's responses to trying on the shoe: "Imagine how big you would be if you wore this shoe" ... The children discuss where the shoe has come from, and Harriette reports that the shoe was from an American Basketball Association. She tells the children it is size 55 and then invites the children to look at their shoe size, noting many are size 3. Harriette then concludes, "So if you were big enough to fit into this shoe, I think you would be a giant". (RB008 131113 08S; Clip 3)

These moments of contradiction were observed in other scientific narratives developing over the 4 weeks observed. The drama associated with finding and observing spiders (see Fleer, 2016) and imagining how it is possible to be inside a drop of water when you are so big or drawing oneself as part of a study of microbes (Fleer, 2017) were dramatic for the children. The contradiction between being small in an adult world but being big in a microscopic world was felt and emotionally expressed when making discoveries under logs in the outdoor area. Although the contradictions are not always dramatic, they appeared and developed as part of the scientific narrative that was forming in the play-based setting in a range of different ways, such as log investigations; roleplaying being inside a fabric tunnel as a worm; being in the plastic bubble pretending to be inside a drop of water; using the digital microscope to study hair, soil, water, skin, etc.; iPads to zoom and explore for creatures; and using hand lenses exploring the compost bin.

Scientific narrative development can also be found in the unstructured play of students in secondary school. For example, Andree and Lager-Nyqvist (2013) found that play can and does support scientific learning of difficult concepts. For instance, they note that play is initiated and used as part of their practices. For instance, they found

- Different tone is used to initiate an imaginary situation where each child acts in a new role (e.g., role of witch man), partially transcending the given task of predict, measure and record. Here, the children are resistant to the existing classroom practice of a step by step procedure.
- The division of labour creates the possibility for inventing a new approach for the use of the equipment, whereby meaning is made of the science experiment by being a doctor and an assistant—role-playing as they become familiar with the microscopes.
- Students invent new rules for performing the set science experiment, such as "invents rules of fermentation (the dough has to rise) and where the wheat flour becomes a pivot to the imaginary situation" (p. 1747).

Andree and Lager-Nyqvist (2013) suggest that a collective narrative forms in the science classroom. That is, "through play, the students in these classrooms interpreted their experiences, dramatised, gave life to and transformed what they knew into lived narratives" (p. 1747). They concluded that even though the students did not follow the prescribed scientific approach, with step by step procedures, rather they played in a range of ways, their actions were never off task and then they argued that the learning was more meaningful and deeper. But young children with less-developed skills in play need support with collectively building scientific narratives in their play. The present study found that for scientific play to emerge, the teachers had to specifically build the play narrative with the help of cultural tools, such as the microscope, the hoops, hand lenses and the plastic bubble. Scientific play narrative was a learned cultural practice that the teachers needed to pedagogically support. The teachers drew upon their pedagogical strengths of interacting with children in play-based settings, but in this study with its focus on science, the teachers used particular forms of discourse to build shared and sustained wondering in the scientific imaginary situations they created.

The key feature of the program that involved wondering can be seen in the expansive example that follows: Harriette the teacher wonders with the children, but she also asks the children to imagine the different attributes of the slug. The children observe and discuss the stretching of the slugs, but also wonder what it might be like if they oozed slime from their bodies.

> *The children are looking under logs with their teacher Harriette. The children turn over a log and many organisms, including slugs, became visible. Harriette says, "We are watching the slug. Let me have a look. They are disguised in the tanbark". The children take it in turns using the hand lens. Alex says, "Look he is really getting longer". Harriette responds, "Ummm...he might have come to a stop". Mitchell in an excited tone says, "I can see slime coming out of him". The teacher thoughtfully asks, "Oh is that his slime? Gosh, imagine if you had slime that came out of your feet, or out of your fingers, everywhere you went". The children laugh. Then Harriette asks, "Do you see the white, sort of fibre bits here. Oh, if I peel that back... What do they look like under the magnifying glass?". Mitchell responds, saying, "He is getting longer". Harriette notes this: "You are right, he is getting longer". Mitchell then says to Alex, "Alex you look under it" as he hands over the hand lens to Alex. "Wow he is REALLY stretching out", says Alex. Mitchell asks, "Can I have a look?". Alex hands back the magnifying glass to Mitchell. Mitchell moves closer to the slug and says, "Let's see what they look like?" The teacher inquires, "I am interested to know what this...". Mitchell interrupts and says with great excitement at his discovery, "That slug, it got LONGER". The teacher asks, "How did it get longer?" to which Mitchell responds by saying,*

"Because it is stretching. Arrrr". Harriette wonders, "Do you get longer when you stretch?". Mitchell moves his arms up and out away from his body, as Harriette says, "Wow. Looks like you are right". "Watch this" says Alex as he also stretches out. Wow" says Harriette. Alex says," I am so long". Harriette then stretches also. Alex says, "Do you want to see how tall I am?".

The continual references to imagining and wondering by the teachers supported the building of a scientific narrative. Hadzigeorgiou (2001) puts forward the view that wonder is an emotional quality that captures an important relationship between the child and their environment and that this can be pedagogically supported in preschools by teachers. Hadzigeorgiou (2001) argues that the building of a strong conceptual base through science learning "cannot take place without the establishment of a long-term relationship between the world of science and the child. This relationship can be established only if children are helped to develop certain attitudes towards science" (p. 64). Hadzigeorgiou (2001) comments that "Wonder, in fact, gives things their meaning and reveals their significance" (p. 65). In this study, wonder was *not* something that was naturally *within* the child as a scientific way of interacting with the environment, but rather *wonder was socially produced* by the teachers through how they continually spoke about the environment, events and introduced activities.

As has been suggested by Fensham (2015), wonder has two meanings. It can be the sheer wonder of something that is the awe experienced—this was evident when the children were looking under logs at all the organisms found there. But wonder can also be a phenomenon which starts someone questioning. In this study, the teachers also created this through how they inquired in situ about things that emerged or which were specifically introduced, such as the wondering about the giant shoe and whose foot it might fit.

Scientific Playworlds: A Model of Teaching Science in Play-Based Settings

In sum, the findings of this study suggest that a *Scientific Playworld* has the potential to pedagogically support teachers to take up an intentional and dramatic role in supporting imagination in science—something they are likely to be good at doing due to their work in play-based setting and specialist training. But in this study, for *playworlds* to develop *scientific narratives*, some key pedagogical characteristics were important. The teachers needed to build a scientific narrative which would allow children to role-play scientific ideas, such as being microscopic. The role-playing allowed the children to consciously think and embody what they were experiencing. A wondering discourse was needed for broadening or widening the scope of the imaginary situations. Further, the teachers' introduction of a cultural device needed to closely mirror what the children were scientifically experiencing, so that it drove or enriched children's imaginings. In these collective scientific imaginary situations, emotionally charged situations appeared to help focus attention and engagement on the science concepts being explored. These pedagogical principles for supporting a *Scientific Playworlds approach* are shown in Table 2 below in column 2 and captured as a model in Figure 3 further.

As the goal of this study was to better understand how play-based settings, such as preschools, can support young children's scientific thinking, it was important to determine those pedagogical practices that were in tune with teachers' pedagogical strengths in promoting learning through play. Those pedagogical practices that emerged as key for the collective building of a scientific narrative and for promoting scientific learning in imaginative play are shown in column 2. They are in line with what is known about the pedagogical practices of Playworlds (shown in column 1). But they are also different enough to warrant the research attention given and summarised in column 3 and theoretically supported in column 4.

The findings of the study and the framework summarised in Table 2 are suggestive of the need to go beyond a simple statement that children learn through play, and consequently will learn science concepts through play. Further, Vygotsky's conception of play alone did not theoretically explain how the development of scientific thinking was promoted by the teachers. As such, the outcomes of this research show the need for a model of teaching science that is based on empirical evidence of how imaginative play promotes scientific learning. The framework of pedagogical practices that are shown in Table 2 are drawn from this study, and potentially act as a basis or possible foundation for a model of pedagogical practices that together create the conditions for children's scientific thinking in imaginative play contexts. Figure 3 shows the relations between the pedagogical practices that were found to iteratively support the teaching of scientific imagining, wondering and thinking in this study.

A model for the teaching of science in play-based settings is urgently needed by early childhood teachers. Scientific Playworlds which begins with the collective scientific imaginary situation, and which draws upon a cultural device that is related to the science being learned, and which invites children to go on scientific journeys, together create the dynamic imaginary scientific context. These findings are theorised and shown in the top half of the model in Figure 3.

The bottom half of the model theorises the iterative process of building the scientific narrative, where a form of drama or contradiction arises and where

TABLE 2   The key pedagogical characteristics of *Scientific Playworlds*

Pedagogical practices unique to *playworlds*	Pedagogical principles to support *Scientific Playworlds*	Examples from the data set	Theoretical concept
A story with a structure that allows the children to collectively go on adventures		Children *imagine going on adventures* inspired by the *Wishing Chair* by Enid Blyton	Playworlds (Lindqvist, 1995)
Psychological tool to support the transition from the preschool and to the imaginary situation	Cultural device that closely mirrors what the children are scientifically experiencing	*Fabric tunnel* was used for simulating science experiences and a plastic bubble for imagining being inside a drop of pond water	Playworlds (Lindqvist, 1995)
Being inside the imaginary play, taking a role	Creates an imaginary scientific situation (adult/child)	The teacher or a child changes the meaning of an object, for e.g. when using the fabric tunnel for imagining being a worm, *"It could be a worm skin, a worm sack"*.	Cultural-historical conception of play (Vygotsky, 1966)
Being deliberately in frame, setting problems up inside the imaginary play; inviting children to imagine together	Collectively building scientific narratives scenarios or problem situations	Play is jointly created *and later* independently enacted as the social becomes the child's personal understanding. *Alex in an excited tone says, "I can see slime coming out of him". The teacher thoughtfully asks, "Oh is that his slime? Gosh, imagine if you had slime that came out of your feet, or out of your fingers, everywhere you went"*. Contradictions and dramatic events create the conditions for children's development	Interpsychological and intrapscyhological functionoing (Vygotsky, 1997)
	Consciously considers scientific concepts	Signals they are in the imaginary situation through words, actions or objects, *"Imagine how big you would be if you wore this shoe"*. Offers solutions to the problem situation inside/ outside of imaginary situation, such as, *tells the children it is size 55 and then invites the children to look at their shoe size, noting many are size 3*. Harriette then concludes, *"So if you were big enough to fit into this shoe, I think you would be a giant"*.	Play from the "dual (or two)-positional perspective" (Kravtsov and Kravtsova, 2010)

(*cont.*)

TABLE 2   The key pedagogical characteristics of *Scientific Playworlds* (*cont.*)

Pedagogical practices unique to *playworlds*	Pedagogical principles to support *Scientific Playworlds*	Examples from the data set	Theoretical concept
	Imagining the relations between observable contexts and non-observable concepts	Child creates scientific models in play to show ideas, such as, when role-playing, using physical materials to make something, draws upon symbols, uses digital animation, etc. "That slug, it got LONGER". The teacher asks, "How did it get longer?" to which Mitchell responds by saying, "Because it is stretching. Arrrr". Harriette wonders, "Do you get longer when you stretch?". Mitchell moves his arms up and out away from his body, as Harriette says, "Wow. Looks like you are right". "Watch this" says Alex as he also stretches out. Wow" says Harriette. Alex says," I am SO long".	Play from the "dual (or two)-positional perspective" (Kravtsov and Kravtsova, 2010)
	Wondering: widening the scope of the imaginary situations WONDER: "I wonder what might happen if...?". IMAGINE: "Imagine if you were a...?"; DOING: "What would you do if...?" EVALUATE: "Do you think there really are...?"	Underscores actions or words through use of high inflexion at end of sentence or emotionally charged language, *You are inside the drop of water. What might you do?* *The teacher asks, "How did it get longer?" to which Mitchell responds by saying, "Because it is stretching. Arrrr". Harriette wonders, "Do you get longer when you stretch?"*	Metacommunicative language (Bretherton, 1984) in collective play (Fleer, 2011)
Dramatises concepts; creates dramatic moments and tension	Emotionally charged situations help focus scientific attention and engagement	Engaging in theoretical contradictions—e.g. magnification process—shrinking down into a drop of water; being big in a microscopic world and at the same time small in an adult world	Cultural-historical conception of imagination in science (Vygotsky, 2004)

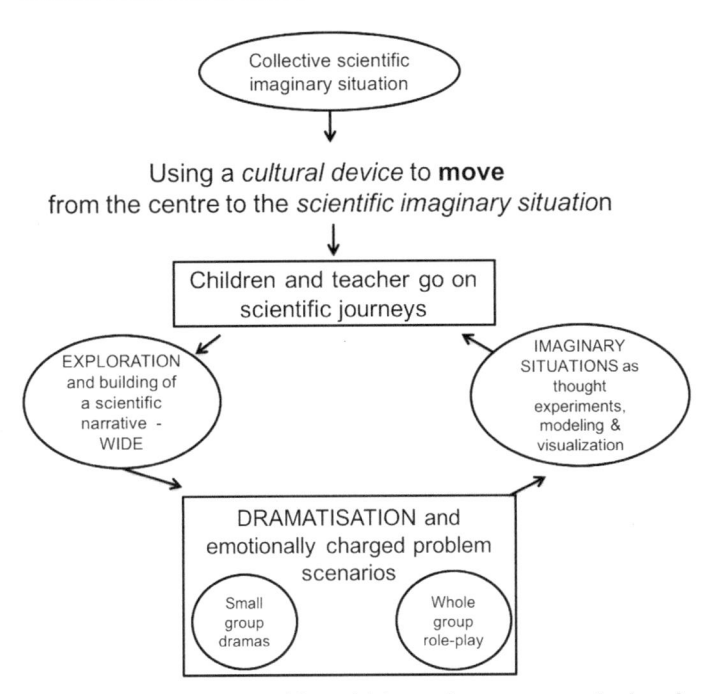

FIGURE 3   Scientific Playworlds model for teaching science in play-based settings

a scientific problem needs to be solved. This tension creates the driving force for ongoing and changing imaginary situations that this study found deepened the scientific imagining and conceptual understandings. It is theorised that it is in the imaginary scientific situations that the need for more science learning results—because of the need to solve the problem situation. In theorising the results of this study, imaginary play is the context, the motive and the narrative. But it is also the glue for holding together the science learning for the children. It is not an isolated activity, but it is ongoing activity over time that holds the children's attention and desire to keep the scientific journey going. Figure 3 brings together the findings of this study and theorises these into a model of teaching science for play-based settings.

Conclusion

This study sought to determine if and how imaginative play could promote scientific learning, as well as to identify the pedagogical strategies used by teachers to engage children in scientific play.

It was learned that the imaginary situations that were introduced using a *Playworlds* approach, combined with the scientific problems encountered, created the conditions for imagination in science. Children appeared to engage in thought experiments, when they imagined themselves being a slug trying to move along a surface. The children also used scientific narrative forms in the *Scientific Playworlds*, and engaged in mental modelling when, for example, on an adventure inside a drop of water. Finally, the dramatisation of their investigations in the compost bin or when looking at water samples from the pond in their outdoor play area created new developmental conditions for the children because they had to embody the idea of magnification and to think about a microscopic world that was not visible to the naked eye. The study found that the building of a scientific narrative, with a discourse of wondering signalled a pedagogical characteristic that turned the *Playworld* approach into a *Scientific Playworld*. Collective imagining and wondering were key, and this appeared to turn everyday events into scientific events for the children. This scientific wondering and imagining appeared to be a key characteristic of teaching science which resulted from the play-based setting and the teachers' expertise in play pedagogy. The *Scientific Playworld* approach gave a scientific structure to the teachers' pedagogical practices, and also, it supported a sustained and deepening focus on concept development over time through imagination, playfulness and wondering.

The benefit of the *Scientific Playworlds* for early childhood teachers is that it potentially gives an approach for systematically teaching science concepts in play-based settings. An approach to teaching science which utilises imagination in play is something early childhood teachers are familiar with. A pedagogical model (Scientific Playworlds) and scientific discourse (wondering and imagining) appeared to develop in the play-based setting a *scientific narrative* and *imagination in science* approach. *Scientific Playworlds* as an approach has the benefit of helping early childhood teachers to teach science because it is strength based, thus potentially supporting rather than blaming them for their lack of confidence and competence to teach science effectively (Andersson & Gullberg, 2014). The results of this study may afford more teaching of science in the early years because the pedagogical practices come from researching play-based settings (rather than drawing on models developed in non-play-based settings). However, further research is needed to determine if a *Scientific Playworlds* approach would have wider appeal and use across a broader group of early childhood teachers and contexts.

Acknowledgements

Sue March (field Leader) and the following research assistants supported the data collection process: Megan Adams, Carolina Beltrao, Selena (Yijun) Hao, and Hasnat Jahan. Special thanks to the teachers who willingly and generously gave up their time for the outcomes of this study.

Funding

The study was supported by funds from an Australian Research Council DP130101438.

References

Andersson, K., & Gullberg, A. (2014). What is science in preschool and what do teachers have to know to empower children? *Cultural Studies of Science Education, 9*(2), 275–296. doi:10.1007/s11422-012-9439-6

Andree, M., & Lager-Nyqvist, L. (2013). Spontaneous play and imagination in everyday science classroom practice. *Research in Science Education, 43*(5), 1735–1750.

Bergen, D. (2009). Play as the learning medium for future scientists, mathematicians, and engineers. American. *Journal of Play, 1*(4), 413–428.

Blake, E., & Howitt, C. (2012). Science in early learning centres: Satisfying curiosity, guided play or lost opportunities? In K. C. D. Tan & M. Kim (Eds.), *Issues and challenges in science education research: Moving forward* (pp. 281–299). Springer.

Bretherton, I. (1984). *Symbolic play: The development of social understanding*. Academic Press, Inc.

Bulunuz, M. (2013). Teaching science through play in kindergarten: Does integrated play and science instruction build understanding? *European Early Childhood Education Research Journal, 21*(2), 226–249.

Cook, C., Goodman, N. D., & Schulz, L. E. (2011). Where science starts: Spontaneous experiments in preschoolers' exploratory play. *Cognition, 120*, 341–349.

Cumming, J. (2003). Do runner beans really make you run fast? Young children learning about science-related food concepts in informal settings. *Research in Science Education, 33*(4), 483–502.

Eshach, H., & Fried, M. N. (2005). Should science be taught in early childhood? *Journal of Science Education and Technology, 14*(3), 315–336.

Fensham, P. (2015). Connoisseurs of science: A next goal for science education? In D. Corrigan, C. Buntting, J. Dillon, A. Jones, & R. Gunstone (Eds.), *The future in learning science: What's in it for the learner?* (pp. 35–59). Springer.

Ferholt, B. (2010). A synthetic-analytic method for the study of perezhivanie: Vygotsky's literary analysis applied to Playworlds. In M. C. Connery, V. P. John-Steiner, & A. Marjanovic-Shane (Eds.), *Vygotsky and creativity: A cultural-historical approach to play, meaning making, and the arts* (pp. 163–179). Peter Lang.

Fleer, M. (1995). The importance of conceptually focused teacher-child interaction in early childhood science learning. *International Journal of Science Education, 17*(3), 325–342. doi:10.1080/0950069950170305

Fleer, M. (2009). Supporting scientific conceptual consciousness or learning in a 'roundabout way' in play-based contexts. *International Journal of Science Education, 31*(8), 1069–1089. doi:10.1080/09500690801953161

Fleer, M. (2010). *Early learning and development: Cultural-historical concepts in play.* Cambridge University Press.

Fleer, M. (2011). "Conceptual play": Foregrounding imagination and cognition during concept formation in early years education. *Contemporary Issues in Early Childhood, 12*(3), 224–240.

Fleer, M. (2014). *Theorising play in the early years.* Cambridge University Press.

Fleer, M. (2016). Theorising *digital play*—a cultural-historical conceptualisation of children's engagement in imaginary digital situations, special issue on play. *Journal of International Research in Early Childhood Education, 7*(2), 75–90.

Fleer, M. (2017). Digital playworlds in an Australia context. In T. Bruce, M. Bredikyte, & P. Hakkarainen (Eds.), *Routledge handbook of play in early childhood.* Routledge Press, Taylor and Francis Group.

Fleer, M., & Pramling, N. (2015). *A cultural–historical study of children learning science: Foregrounding affective imagination in play-based settings.* Springer.

Fox Keller, E. (1983). *A feeling for the organism: Life and work of Barbara McClintock.* Freeman.

Garbett, D. (2003). Science education in early childhood teacher education: Putting forward a case to enhance student teachers' confidence and competence. *Research in Science Education, 33*(4), 467–481.

Gelman, R., & Brenneman, K. (2004). Science learning pathways for young children. *Early Childhood Education Quarterly, 19*, 150–158.

Göncü, A., Jain, J., & Tuerer, U. (2007). Children's play as cultural interpretation. In A. Göncü & S. Gaskins (Eds.), *Play and development: Evolutionary, sociocultural, and functional perspectives* (pp. 155–178). Lawrence Erlbaum.

Hadzigeorgiou, Y. (2001). The role of wonder and 'romance' in early childhood science education. *International Journal of Early Years Education, 9*(10), 63–69.

Hadzigeorgiou, Y. (2002). A study of the development of the concept of mechanical stability in preschool children. *Research in Science Education, 32*(3), 373–391.

Hadzigeorgiou, Y. (2016). *Imaginative science education: The central role of imagination in science education.* Springer International Publishing.

Hakkarainen, P. (2010). Cultural-historical methodology of the study of human development in transitions. *Cultural-Historical Psychology, 4*, 75–89.

Hakkarainen, P., Bredikyte, M., Jakkula, K., & Munter, H. (2013). Adult play guidance and children's play development in a narrative play-world. *European Early Childhood Education Research Journal, 21*(2), 213–225.

Hannust, T., & Kikas, E. (2007). Children's knowledge of astronomy and its change in the course of learning. *Early Childhood Research Quarterly, 22*, 89–104.

Hedegaard, M., & Fleer, M. (Eds.). (2008). *Studying children: A cultural-historical approach.* Open University Press.

Howitt, C., Lewis, S., & Upson, E. (2011). 'It's a mystery': A case study of implementing forensic science in preschool as scientific inquiry. *Australasian Journal of Early Childhood, 36*(3), 45–55.

Kass, L. B. (2003). Records and recollections: A new look at Barbara McClintock, Nobel-prize-winning geneticist. *Genetics, 164*(4), 1251–1260.

Kravtsov, G. G., & Kravtsova, E. E. (2010). Play in L.S. Vygotsky's nonclassical psychology. *Journal of Russian and East European Psychology, 48*(4), 25–41.

Krnel, D., Watson, R., & Glazar, S. A. (2005). The development of the concept of 'matter': A cross-age study of how children describe materials. *International Journal of Science Education, 27*(3), 367–383.

Lillard, A. (2007). Guided participation: How mothers structure and children understand pretend play. In A. Göncü & S. Gaskins (Eds.), *Play and development: Evolutionary, sociocultural, and functional perspectives* (pp. 131–153). Lawrence Erlbaum.

Lindqvist, G. (1995). The aesthetics of play: A didactic study of play and culture in preschools. (Doctoral dissertation). *Uppsala Studies in Education, 62*, 1–234. Acta Universitatis Upsaliensis.

Martins Teizeira, F. (2000). What happens to the food we eat? Children's concepts of the structure and function of the digestive system. *International Journal of Science Education, 22*(5), 507–520.

Metz, K. E. (2004). Children's understanding of scientific inquiry: Their conceptualization of uncertainty in investigations of their own design. *Cognition and Instruction, 22*(2), 219–290.

Pellegrini, A. D. (Ed.). (2011). *The Oxford handbook of the development of play.* Oxford University Press.

Rothenberg, A. (1979). Einstein's creative thinking and the general theory of relativity: A documented report. *American Journal of Psychiatry, 136*(1), 38–43.

Sikder, S., & Fleer, M. (2014). Small science: Infants and toddlers experiencing science in everyday family play. *Research in Science Education, 45*(3), 445–464. doi:10.1007/s11165-014-9431-0

Siry, C. A., & Kremer, I. (2011). Children explain the rainbow: Using young children's ideas to guide science curricula. *International Journal of Science Education and Technology, 20*(5), 643–655.

Trundle, K. C., & Saçkes, M. (2015). *Research in early childhood science education.* Springer. doi:10.1007/978-94-017-9505-0

Tu, T. (2006). Preschool science environment: What is available in a preschool classroom? *Early Childhood Education Journal, 33*(4), 245–251.

Venville, G. (2004). Young children learning about living things: A case study of conceptual change from ontological and social perspectives. *Journal of Research in Science Teaching, 41*(5), 449–480.

Vygotsky, L. S. (1966). Play and its role in the mental development of the child. *Voprosy Psikhologii, 12*(6), 62–76.

Vygotsky, L. S. (1997). The history of the development of higher mental functions. In R. W. Rieber (Ed.), *The collected works of L. S. Vygotsky* (Vol. 4). Plenum Press.

Vygotsky, L. S. (2004). Imagination and creativity in childhood. *Journal of Russian and East European Psychology, 42*(1), 7–97.

Vygotsky, L. S. (2005). Appendix: From the notes of L.S Vygotsky for lectures on the psychology of preschool children. *Journal of Russian and East European Psychology, 43*(1), 90–97.

Zeidler, D. L. (2016). STEM education: A deficit framework for the twenty first century? A sociocultural socioscientific response. *Cultural Studies of Science Education, 11*(1), 11–26. doi:10.1007/s11422-014-9578-z

Zhang, W., & Birdsall, S. (2016). Analysing early childhood educators' science pedagogy through the lens of a pedagogical content knowing framework. *Australasian Journal of Early Childhood, 41*(2), 50–58.

Paper 8: *Conceptual PlayWorlds* as a Pedagogical Intervention: Supporting the Learning and Development of the Preschool Child in Play-Based Setting

This paper originally appeared as Fleer, M. (2019). Conceptual PlayWorlds as a pedagogical intervention: Supporting the learning and development of the preschool child in play-based setting. *Obutchénie: Revista De Didática E Psicologia Pedagógica, 3*(3), 1–22. https://doi.org/10.14393/OBv3n3.a2019-51704 Reprinted here with permission from the publisher.

Universos lúdico-conceituais como uma intervenção pedagógica: dando suporte à aprendizagem e ao desenvolvimento da criança pré-escolar em contextos lúdicos

Resumo

Existe um interesse crescente em encontrar melhores maneiras de apoiar o aprendizado de conceitos em programas educativos voltados à primeira infância baseados na brincadeira. A introdução de termos como '*eduplay*' em Hong Kong, 'Brincadeira intencionada' em Cingapura e 'ensino intencional' em programas baseados em brincadeiras na Austrália sugerem que os educadores estão trabalhando de diferentes maneiras para construir novas práticas que tragam brincadeira e aprendizado em unidade para dar suporte ao desenvolvimento das crianças. Este artigo contribui para esse cenário de pesquisa ao introduzir uma intervenção pedagógica chamada Universos lúdico-conceituais (*Conceptual playworlds*). Esse modelo de prática é teorizado usando os conceitos vygotskianos de imaginação e brincadeira, e o modelo hedegaardiano de valores sociais, práticas institucionais e configurações de atividades como base para o estudo da aprendizagem de conceitos em contextos baseados em brincadeiras. O conteúdo deste artigo está situado no contexto curricular em mudança da primeira infância da região australiana, onde valores sociais para melhores resultados estão moldando práticas institucionais que criam novas demandas e condições diferentes para o desenvolvimento das crianças.

Palavras-chave

Universos lúdicos – Enfoque histórico-cultural – Imaginação – Brincadeira – Desenvolvimento infantile – Pedagogia

Abstract

There is increasing interest in finding better ways to support the learning of concepts in play-based programs in early childhood settings. The introduction of terms such as 'eduplay' in Hong Kong, 'Purposeful play' in Singapore, and 'intentional teaching' in play-based programs in Australia, suggest that educators are working in different ways to build new practices that bring play and learning together to support children's development. This paper contributes to this research landscape by introducing a pedagogical intervention called *Conceptual Playworlds*. This practice model is theorised using the Vygotskian concepts of imagination and play, and Hedegaardian model of societal values, institutional practices and activity settings as foundational for studying the learning of concepts in play-based settings. The content of this paper is situated in the changing early childhood curriculum context of the Australasian region, where social values for greater outcomes are shaping institutional practices which create new demands and different conditions for children's development.

Keywords

PlayWorlds – cultural-historical – imagination – play – child development – pedagogy

Introduction

In 2009 Australian early childhood educators were introduced to the concept of *intentional teaching* in order to foreground the importance of learning concepts in play-based settings (Australian Government, 2009). At the same time, Rao and Li (2009) pioneered the concept of *eduplay* in Hong Kong. In many different parts of the Australasian region, early childhood educators have discussed a range of pedagogical concepts to support these new societal demands. In Singapore, the Ministry of Education (2012) conceptualised the relations between play and learning as *purposeful play*. Purposeful play includes characteristics, such as, imagination, authentic contexts, collaboration, taking risks and enjoyment. China through its reforms has also seen the emergence of play in the curriculum guide for the promotion of a play-based integrated curriculum (Pan et al., 2018). However, Government has left it to the profession to formulate what this looks like in practice. Recently in Hong Kong, early childhood educators have been advised through the release of the Kindergarten Education Curriculum Guide (Curriculum Development Council, 2017), to make learning joyful through play. The expectation of teachers in Hong Kong is for a play environment to be conducive to learning, such as, "Interest corners should be set up to encourage self-directed learning in children" (p. 29), and up to 50 minutes per day should be devoted to play time in full time centres.

The Northern hemisphere has also expressed concern for the schoolification (Broström, 2017), academisation (Husa & Kinos, 2005) and formalisation (Ang, 2014) of early childhood education. What is foregrounded in the Northern hemisphere research landscape, is the study of the interface between play and pedagogy (Wood, 2014).

These reforms or curricula initiatives sit within an international context of change in early childhood education (Fleer & Van Oers, 2018). What they collectively show is a need for re-examining the relations between play and learning – empirically, theoretically and pedagogically. Consequently, the aim of this paper is to contribute to the changing practice landscape through a pedagogical intervention called *Conceptual PlayWorlds* as one approach to support the leading activity of children for play (Vygotsky, 1966), whilst at the same time recognising the need to create a personal motive for learning within play-based settings (Hedegaard, 2002). To achieve this aim, the first part of the paper introduces the central theoretical concepts underpinning a Conceptual PlayWorld. This is followed by details of intervention with examples from practice of the model being implemented in a preschool setting with children aged five years. The paper concludes by theorising the pedagogical characteristics of the intervention of Conceptual PlayWorlds in support of children's development when bringing together play, learning and development.

The Theoretical Foundations Relevant to the Cultural Age of the Preschool Child and the Problem Situation in the Australasian Region

Conceptual PlayWorlds as an intervention was originally inspired by the research of Gunilla Lindqvist (1995). Like other longstanding models of practice, such as Story Approach to Integrated Learning (SAILS) (Li & Chau, 2010) and Storytellers and Story players (Paley, 1990), Lindqvist developed a pedagogical approach that focused on children's literature. Her central finding was an approach called *play pedagogy* that featured the aesthetics of play, and which she captured in a model of practice known as playworlds. Her research was theorised from a cultural-historical perspective.

Conceptual PlayWorlds has also been theorised from a cultural-historical perspective. Specifically, the intervention model draws upon Vygotsky's conception of play (1966), development (Vygotsky, 1987, 1998) and imagination, emotions and creativity (Vygotsky, 1971, 2004). Although similar theoretical concepts have been deployed to that of Lindqvist, the focus of Conceptual PlayWorlds is on children's meaningful learning of concepts in play-based settings. In Conceptual PlayWorlds learning is in the service of the children's play. Conceptual PlayWorlds is the outcome of research into the play and learning of concepts in science (Fleer, 2017a), and for the development of executive functions in play-based programs (Fleer et al., 2017).

There are four theoretical assumptions underpinning a Conceptual PlayWorlds intervention model. First, a cultural-historical conception of play is defined as the creation of an imaginary situation, where children change the meaning of actions and objects to give them a new sense, and where children work imaginatively to create new meaning through different levels of abstraction. This can occur between children but it can also be seen when children are on their own playing imaginatively. In this Vygotskian (1966) reading, what is central psychologically for the child, is a growing conscious awareness of the world in which they live and culturally engage. It is not the biological age of the child that dominates, but rather it is the cultural practices of their community that they experience and which they contribute to, when coming to understand the roles and rules of their particular community. Children move closer to reality in play (e.g., role-playing being a mum or dad s/he acts as close as she can) because their play actions reflect what they notice and find important or interesting (e.g., caring just like dad does). At the same time, children move away from reality (build their own narratives) as they imagine and explore through their play actions abstracted concepts (pretending rather than being the mum or dad). In line with Vygotsky's (1987, 1998) conception of development, it is argued that this dialectical contradiction acts as the force for children's development.

Second, concepts to be learned are historically developed (science as a body of knowledge), culturally defined (Western science), and given meaning in everyday life through interactions with others (early childhood curriculum in action). When children use concepts in the service of their play, they have new possibilities in play and different ways of thinking (Fleer, 2017b). Vygotsky (1966) suggested that when two children who are sisters in real life, role play being sisters, they make conscious through their play actions the rules and roles associated with sisterhood. This means that play supports the child to think consciously about the concept of sisterhood. In so doing, the children's play actions deepen because they follow what might be morally expected of a sister – to act sisterly by being kind or inclusive for example. In this way, the concept of sisterhood is made conscious in play. At the same time, the concept of sisterhood is used in service of the child's play – to deepen their actions of showing how to be a sister, to follow the rules and roles of sisterhood that are important to them in their family, but also how this might be observed differently in other families. The concept of sisterhood as consciously brought into play offers more possible play scripts to imagine, to create in play action, and to conceptually and culturally explore. The concept is thereby acting in service of the children's play.

Third, play is not simply a reproduction of life (Vygotsky, 1966). Play is also a creative and imaginative production by the child. Children bring to their play insights and practices from everyday life, and in so doing are imagining and creating those actions in new ways. Children's play actions are imaginative acts which are experienced collectively in groups. Children produce new play scripts and negotiate these play scripts with their play partners. But what is different in a *Conceptual Playworld* is that play plots are introduced through the narrative of a story or through non-fiction play inquiry. In child initiated play, children generally do not follow and expand a play plot on their own. The general play literature shows that child initiated play is spontaneous and organic. Using a play plot to develop the complexity of children's play and play competence has been found in research by Lindqvist (1995) and Hakarrainen (2010) to deepen play actions, but it needs adult support. However, this is generally not a common early childhood curriculum practice in many Western and Western heritage communities. Collective play with a play plot would appear to fit well with early childhood communities who primarily use whole group teaching approaches – as is observed and reported in the literature for the Australasian region (Li et al., 2012).

Finally, a cultural-historical view of child development suggests that it is important for dramatic moments to occur that support children to think and feel more consciously about a particular phenomenon (Vygotsky, 1998).

A revolutionary view, rather than an evolutionary change in development as observed through milestones or ages and stages, underpins Vygotsky's (1998) theory of child development. In a revolutionary reading of child development, drama plays an important role for creating the dynamic tension or crisis to support development. In the context of *Conceptual Playworlds,* this means that the imaginary situations have dramatic moments that make conscious to the child particular moments, actions or ways of thinking about practice. Drama or dramatic moments are often observed in fairytales, but also in many stories (El'Koninova, 2001).

Taken together, the core theoretical concepts of emotional imagination (Vygotsky, 1971), imagination and creativity (Vygotsky, 2004), play (Vygotsky, 1966) and Vygotsky's revolutionary view of child development (1998) are the foundation for Conceptual PlayWorld developed as a result of an educational experiment for addressing the problem of greater learning outcomes for preschool children in Australia.

Educational Experiment to Support the Relations between Play and Learning in Preschool Settings

Although the curriculum project of Charlotte's Web (White & Williams, 1963) is introduced as an example from practice in the next section, the work has come from expansive research into the relations between play and learning in Australian preschool settings (Fleer, 2017a, 2017b).

The story of Charlotte's Web introduces moral dilemma of culling the runt of a litter of pigs, which upsets Fern the 8-year-old girl who lives on the farm. Children live the emotional moments with the characters in the story and imagine the plot unfolding. In this story, further tension is created because Charlotte the spider becomes a special friend to the runt in the litter –Wilbur the pig. But spiders are often feared by children. The contradiction in the story emotionally connects with children's lives in different ways, making conscious to children the importance of spiders in the ecosystem. The drama in the story becomes the foundation for the Conceptual PlayWorld (see www.monash.edu/conceptual-playworld) that is played by the children, and this drama when relived by the children in play, contributes productively to the children's development, learning and play actions.

In the research, two teachers over two years, were followed as they implemented a series of playworlds (Fleer, 2016). However, unlike previous research into playworlds, the focus of attention for the curriculum development centered on how to introduce to children in personally meaningful ways the learning of science and technology concepts (Fleer, 2017a). The curriculum project foregrounded in this paper for discussing play and children's development, was collaboratively developed between the participants and the research team using the core concepts from cultural-historical theory. Although the data and the analysis also followed how children entered into the activity settings of the Conceptual PlayWorld, that is not the focus for this paper.

The curriculum context included a total of 6 Conceptual PlayWorlds that were progressively developed as an educational experiment (Hedegaard, 2008) over two years (50 sessions over 2 years). The two teachers who co-taught the PlayWorlds (Rebecca and Oriana) had extensive teaching experience and the lead teacher (Rebecca) had studied cultural-historical theory and the play-worlds literature generally. The teachers were familiar with the Vygotskian concepts of imagination (Vygotsky, 2004) and drama as a form of crisis in child development (Vygotsky, 1998), and Vygotsky's conception of play (Vygotsky, 1966). The focus of the ongoing professional learning and the educational experiment (Hedegaard, 2008) was on how to create motivating conditions for the productive development of play that would lead to conceptual learning of scientific, technological and engineering concepts (Fleer, 2017a). The data generated included the documentation of the professional learning, digital video observations (152.3 hours) of the teaching practices, interviews of the teachers in situ and during the professional learning (32.5 hours), digital photographs, and children's drawings and designs. This constituted a significant body of data that were analysed using Hedegaard's (2014) model of development, which centres on the societal values, institutional practices and the personal perspective of the teachers and children as part of developing a motive orientation for learning. Hedegaard (2014) foregrounds the activity setting within the practices of the institution "where the relations between institutional objectives and the demands from the institutional practice can be studied in relation to a person's motives and the demands in the setting that are placed on both other people and materials" (p. 189). Activity settings was an important construct used in the analysis of the institutional practices developed through the educational experiment. The core Vygotskian concepts discussed in this paper were also used to analyse the curriculum, especially in relation to how imagination in play and imagination in learning were interrelated in the Conceptual PlayWorlds.

Conceptualising a Conceptual PlayWorld Intervention

A main outcome of the research for creating motivating conditions for learning concepts in play was a Conceptual PlayWorld (Fleer, 2018). The Conceptual PlayWorlds is an intervention for realising learning outcomes in play-based settings in contexts where greater outcomes are expected at the societal level through the demand for changing the institutional practices of preschool settings. The outcomes of the research have generated a set of interrelated pedagogical characteristics for embedding learning experiences into play-based programs, but in ways that serve the children's play and support of the development of personally meaningful concepts. The curriculum example of *Charlotte's Web* is presented to illustrate the pedagogical practices of the intervention model that was an outcome of solving the problem of the new societal demand of introducing conceptual learning in play-based settings in Australia.

Conceptual PlayWorld Story as the Activity Setting for Creating the Imaginary Situation

In line with Vygotskian conception of crisis as a developmental condition, the story acts as the centre piece for initiating and developing an imaginary situation with the children that is emotionally charged. Different to spontaneous play where the story line may not be known to all the children, using a story book means that the characters and the plot are collectively known and understood when children imagine together. For example, in the story of *Charlotte's Web* the story unfolds over the chapters of the book. Importantly the drama begins early and engages the children quickly and moves them into the imaginary situation of the smallest piglet in the litter being potentially killed. The story plot is dramatic and emotional. The story creates a dynamic tension, builds empathy and introducing a problem situation to the children: How to save Wilbur the pig? The problem situation emerges in each chapter, but in different ways, with new characters and contexts – thus deepening the possibilities for the children's play. The activity setting of the PlayWorld creates the imaginary situation, as was identified in the research and captured here as conversation between Rebecca and Oriana.

Rebecca:	And we found over the various playworlds that if you can choose a story where you can really develop empathy with the characters that's one of the most important things for the children to then be engaged to help solve problems with the characters from the story. And particularly, we've found, animals.
Oriana:	Yes, that's right.
Rebecca:	Stories with animals have been particularly successful.
Oriana:	So it was that connection to the character, and having that emotional connection as well, and being able to respond and feel an investment, I think, an emotional investment to the story was really important for us.

The societal demands for increased learning outcomes for play-based settings in the Australian context means that the story selection must be considered in relation to the concepts to be learned. This is a different approach to previous playworlds where play development through narratives is fore- grounded (Hakkarainen, 2010). In the Conceptual PlayWorld intervention, the educators plan the concept and its relation to the story and play plot and this changes their relations with children.

> And sometimes the children are still, they're very keen to be involved but they're perhaps not ready to go really deep with the conceptual knowledge, so often they'll just sit in one of our laps, or they might be on our hip, so they'll be playing. They might be very happy to play the characters in the story, but they may need more support and experience it literally with you when exploring something like a concept about the ecosystem. But you can say, "Let's be the rain together," or, "Let's be the sunshine together," and so you can, with the child, help them to enter the play if they're feeling unsure. Whereas the other children will be completely leading it. (Rebecca)

In this example of the story of *Charlotte's Web,* concepts such as ecosystem are learned when studying spiders in the environment, but the motive orientation for learning these concepts is developed through the story and the children's play. The anatomy of the spider is studied when children become curious about how a spider spins a web. Friendship and the exploration of emotions and emotion regulation are possible when being the different characters at different chapters in the story – such as Wilbur the pig being lonely and not having a friend; or empathising with Fern when she learns that the runt of the litter might be culled. Concepts are emotionally imaginative and children are motivated to learn concept to build the story plot. Ultimately, the concept to be learned must serve to enrich the children's play. That is, the motive orientation draws upon the children's leading activity for play (Vygotsky, 1966) or dominating motive, and uses it as a stimulating motive for learning (Hedegaard, 2002). The latter is introduced by the teacher through the story line and problem situation of how to help Wilbur. It is when the conditions change through the introduction of the problem to be solved, that this creates a new demand which can have a developmental effect. Hedegaard and Chaiklin (2005) have said, "development is understood as a result of the demands created in the social situation of development, which arises from the interaction between the children's motives and the adults demands associated with the practice in which they are engaged" (p. 64).

Designing a Conceptual PlayWorld Space – Activity Setting Where Children and Teachers Collectively Change the Meaning of Actions and Objects to Give Them a New Sense

The imaginary situation as discussed by Vygotsky (1966) is where children change the meaning of objects and actions to give them a new sense of the situation. The teacher draws upon this conception of play when designing the PlayWorld space to generate a collective imaginary play situation.

> I think when planning the physical play space it took a little bit of prac-tise for us to realise that you do actually need a designated area where you can go and be play partners with the children, and that can be quite open-ended (Rebecca).

> So perhaps we were thinking about, will the children be bored with that situation, or will they not enjoy going through that particular space again, but we found that that was something that was quite successful. They enjoyed going through the tunnel, or through the gate, all those particular things were almost something that was reassuring for them that they were about to reenter into that play space and be really comfortable knowing that it was safe to immerse themselves in the play with their teachers as well. (Oriana)

In the story of *Charlotte's Web* the educators used the outdoor area as Mr and Mrs Zuckerman's farm. Changing the meaning of the objects already in the outdoor space is done through imagination. The tressel becomes a pig sty, the fort acts as a barn, where Charlotte the spider spins her web, and tunnels become pathways for Templeton the rat to scurry down to find food in differ-ent locations (or potentially different PlayWorlds for the children to go down and imagine being in, such as the Fairground). It is through the teachers and children collectively entering into the same imaginary situation that children are supported in their play to change the meaning of actions and objects. In this sense, the story and the imaginary situation of the scene for the story creates new conditions for children's development. This is in contrast to the developmental view that children's play is teacher-free, a commonly held view, based on a maturational view of play development.

Collectively Entering and Exiting the Conceptual PlayWorld Space – Collective Transition into and out of the Activity Setting

In line with a cultural-historical concept of child development, in a Concep-tual PlayWorld we see children and teachers visit the imaginary space multiple times over an extended period as the story unfolds and as new problem situations arise. Teachers support children to collectively go into imaginary situations by signalling the entrance and exit into the space. For example, in the story of *Charlotte's Web* the teacher puts up a sign on the gate: "Mr and Mrs Zuckerman's Farm" and this signals to the children that they are about to enter a collective imaginary situation. At this moment, the children and the teachers talk about what character they will be before entering. Then as they go through the gate, they transform into the character. This might mean there are a lot of spiders or many piglets, but it can also be that children with support of the teacher act out being different parts of the ecosystem – such as the annoying flies. A sign on the back of the gate, such as, "Please close the gate as you leave the farm" signals that the children are leaving the imaginary situation. Rebecca explains how she initially signalled the entry and exit into the imaginary play:

> So with Charlotte's Web, we would line up on the log, and it's such a beautiful way to enter play. One of the things that we found particularly valuable about our play world experiences was that it involves the whole group, so it's a really effective pedagogical tool to be able to include every child in the group. And so part of that is that you all need to be in the same imaginary space, so in this situation that was Charlotte's Web, it was Zuckerman's Farm, it was the barn. So we would line up on the log and the children would choose their characters, and sometimes two people wanted to be Wilbur, that's fine, some days everyone's a spider, some days … It really doesn't matter as long as we're getting into that space as a collective. And as the teacher I would always choose a character, so depending on what we had planned for that day's experience. So for example if we were introducing a new character I might be the rat that day, or I might be part of the ecosystem, so I might be the sunshine that day. So it was a good way to get the children into the right head space where we're all imagining similar things. (Rebecca)

The collective entry into the Conceptual PlayWorld actively supports the creation of an imaginary situation because the teacher physically signals entry and exist of the established story plot. There is a collective Conceptual PlayWorld and this is in contrast to children in free play settings who must independently negotiate their own entry into as imaginary play situation. The intervention actively supports children with their play development, because the teacher is sensitive to their zone of proximal development, creating the conditions in support of the next development period that children are proximally demonstrating at that moment in the play. As play is children's leading activity at the preschool age, the children have a strong motive orientation towards entering into complex play. In the Conceptual PlayWorld this is amplified through the collective story and imaginary situation that they enter and exist with support of their teacher.

Planning the Play Inquiry or Problem Scenario – Changing the Actions within the Activity Setting

Hedegaard has argued that the societal values are reflected in the institutional practices, such as play-based program in preschool and a more formal learning program in school. The dynamic between societal values and educational practices in preschools is exemplified in the Australasian region where learning concepts has become increasingly important, thus creating a new developmental crisis in the preschool age period. Traditionally, transitions from one institution to another, such as from preschool to school, has been shown to create these kinds of developmental conditions for children, where the social position of the child (Bozhovich, 2009) changes to that of a school child, and the institutional practices change to become more oriented towards the learning of concepts (Hedegaard & Fleer, 2013). The new demands placed on teachers and children in the preschool setting for more learning outcomes is resolved through the intervention of a Conceptual PlayWorld. The Conceptual PlayWorld space supports the development of concepts, such as learning about the anatomy of spiders when exploring how spiders spin their web, or the role a spider has in an ecosystem. Planning the concepts to be learned in service of the children's play is key aspect of the Conceptual PlayWorld so that children become oriented towards learning in the activity settings of the preschool – but in ways that are personally meaningful.

Thinking through how the concept can enrich the children's play in the imaginary situation can add complexity to the children's play actions, whilst at the same time meeting curriculum objectives. Oriana foregrounds this new practice need.

> It was always a lot of fun thinking about the problem and how we were about to go about it. So when we were thinking of the story of Charlotte's Web and the particular problem, that took a little while to think really carefully of how, again when we're thinking about the play worlds approach and how emotionally invested the children were, we wanted them to, we wanted that important hook. So we thought long and hard about this. Again, coming in as a character, as Farmer Zuckerman, I was able to just completely think of this problem with the children. And the beauty of that is that the children were able to completely connect with

that character, and then we knew we could really take them on board in terms of being able to develop that concept. So being able to be really clear again about that concept helped us to plan very carefully about how that actual problem would be presented through the character with the children so that we could immerse them in it with us and together, and really hear the child's voice in that problem. (Oriana)

In the story of *Charlotte's Web* Oriana uses the character of Farmer Zuckerman to raise a problem "There are so many flies on the farm. They are really annoying". These scenarios lend themselves to the problem situation or play inquiry of how to be rid of flies. This play inquiry gives the possibility for learning about the ecosystem. But it also expands the play by introducing more characters to role play the scientific processes through the imaginary situation, such as being spiders being eaten. Further, when the children and the teachers are out of the imaginary situation, they do research that they can take back to Farmer Zuckerman next time they visit the farm. For instance, making a movie of the ecosystem of the farm on a digital device, or a report on how spiders spin webs, are examples of meaningful learning that can help Farmer Zuckerman deal with the fly problem.

Problem scenarios that relate to the story plot or extend it, such as learning how spiders can help reduce the number of flies on the farm, become stimulating motives for children's learning (Hedegaard, 2002). Learning of concepts gives more content to the children's play. For example, this is seen through children and teachers acting out the important role of spiders in the ecosystem (Charlotte can help), learning about the spider's anatomy to better understand how Charlotte actually spin her web (anatomy), and then more accurately acting out spinning webs (embodying concepts) as learning tasks that have become personally meaningful to children (Fleer, 2011). Learning enriches the play of the children in the imaginary situation, at the same time as affording meaningful and joyful learning of concepts as detailed in early childhood curricula. This is different to the playworld of Lindqvist (1995) and Hakkarainen (2010) because the societal values for greater learning outcomes for preschool children in Australia has created new demands upon teachers and children to find ways to orient children to learning as their leading activity in the preschool period. This has created the new need for an intervention that orients children to learning whilst at the same time recognises their leading activity for play as part of their cultural developmental trajectory. Learning as the new leading activity appears to be positioned in policy (Grieshaber, 2016) and in practice (Edwards et al., 2010; Fleer, 2011; Wong & Fleer, 2013) in Australia.

Planning Interactions to Build Conceptual Learning in the Activity Setting

Different to previous research into playworlds which has focused on the development of play narratives through teachers partnering with children, is how Conceptual PlayWorlds positions teachers to plan their interactions as dynamic pairs. Inspired by Kravtsov and Kravtsova's (2010) concept of pair pedagogy, Conceptual PlayWorlds assigns different roles to each of the pairs of teachers when in the imaginary situation. Having two teachers in the imaginary situation is important because one teacher can be inquiring along with the children (equally present), whilst the other teacher can suggest ways to find out how to solve the play problem (model to the children). The teachers plan and enact different but complementary roles. For instance, to be above the children, to be equal with the children, to be below the children, and to be in a primordial we position with the children. Planning for this relation is important because the relations between the teacher and the children change, as explained by Rebecca:

> Yeah, so something that was different for us, we'd always been fortunate enough to have the opportunity to team teach, but I wouldn't say that we work together in terms of planning our subject positioning - how we related to each other and the children. So really consciously thinking about how to support certain children, how to enable other children to be leaders. So for example, each week we would plan a play episode and if we felt there was a child who needed to be challenged we thought very carefully about how we could position them in a certain way so that they could be an expert and inform the group. There were other children who needed a bit more help, so for example in Charlotte's Web we had one child who needed a bit of a confidence boost, so we gave him the very special role of being the seed inside the apple because it all grew from there, and he was thrilled to have that very important role in the play (Rebecca).

Subject positioning of the teachers in relation to the children is dynamically enacted. In the Conceptual PlayWorld of *Charlotte's Web* one teacher is present with the children (equal), acting out being a character in the story, watching all the flies buzzing around being annoying. The other teacher who is in role as Mrs Zuckerman can tell the children about her problem and ask for help. The teacher who is present with the children can say "Yes we can help" or "I am ready to help" so as to inspire and collectively problem solve with the children. The children in turn can lead the play, as is evidenced when they introduce new ideas into the collective imaginary situation, such as "Let's be spiders. We can catch all the flies to help". The approach is different to team teaching or to having a team which includes a teacher and an assistant in the traditional roles seen in many preschool settings. Rather, in a Conceptual PlayWorld the roles are carefully planned so that there are opportunities to extend the play in character, to manage the children in character, and to introduce problem situations to deepen the learning, which in turn enriches the play of the children. The children can spin webs when role playing, because they now know about this. They can invite others into the play, and draw on scientific knowledge and give scientific meaning in their play to the objects they use, such as when string becomes a web. The roles are not scripted. But the position of each teacher is carefully planned to support a play narrative. Together this creates a dynamic interactional context that progresses the play, because children have more concepts to introduce into their play and teachers meaningfully supports children to work with these concepts to solve the problem situation (Fleer, 2017a; 2017b).

New Practice Traditions for Teachers

Taken together, the pedagogical characteristics discussed above of a Conceptual PlayWorld as an intervention, support preschool teachers with the central problem of introducing concepts into play-based settings. Theoretically, a Conceptual PlayWorld changes how teachers conceptualise their practice. That is, teachers are in the same situation, but change the meaning of the objects and their actions to give them a new sense. In the traditional preschool environment, the practice traditions with their activity settings of group time, snack time, sleep time, free play time inside and outdoor are maintained. However, in PlayWorlds, teachers and children collectively change the meaning of this physical space and imagine new play situations. Specifically, new activity settings are created that are collectively shared.

Broadly, there are two activity settings that together make up a Conceptual PlayWorld – the activity setting of the imaginary situation of the storyline; and the activity setting where children are researching problems. The transition is a fuzzy zone between these, because the entering and exiting into the Conceptual PlayWorld is supported by the teacher through a cultural device acting as a border (e.g., log, farm gate), and it is here that children can flicker (El'Koninova, 2001) between an imaginary play situation of the story line and the conceptual research situation in support of the imaginary play. This is a new practice tradition for teachers. The flickering is a marker for teachers of children's agency, but it is also an important characteristic of personal meaning making of concepts to support play. It is the teachers who support children to enter into the imaginary situation, and who help change the meaning of actions and objects as a collective. This activity setting is imagined but collectively understood. Teachers draw upon children's motive orientation to play as the driving force for maintaining the collective imaginary situations. Hakkarainen (2010) has also shown that the teachers role in the play is a fundamental characteristic of a successful playworld.

Another change in the practice tradition of the teachers is planning and implementing Conceptual PlayWorld so that both teachers and children enter into the different activity settings of the Conceptual PlayWorld in ways that are motivating for both play and learning. Hedegaard (2002) has argued that a stimulating motive is planned by teachers to orient children towards learning. Her research has focused on schools, where the practice tradition is for learning discipline concepts. Inspired by Hedegaard's (2014) concept of motives for realising new societal demands for greater learning outcomes in preschools, Conceptual PlayWorlds was developed with teachers as a new practice tradition. Hedegaard (2014, p. 188) has argued that, "how actions in activities are nested within institutional practices" have a significant effect on "broader cultural expectations and traditions" and teachers in a Conceptual PlayWorld explored "motives within practices" that could be directed towards reflecting the "broader traditions" for greater learning outcomes, but in ways that support children's "personal motives" for the learning of concepts in service of their play. A new practice motive was generated and this motive is captured in a Conceptual PlayWorld through action of personally meaningful inquiries that are in service of children's play. This means the leading activity of children to play is maintained, but the actions and motives are oriented towards learning concepts. Hedegaard (2014) has said, "children's learning and development take place through their engagement in activities in specific institutional practices that are in turn influenced by motives and demands from other practices" (p. 188). The aim of preschool practice in this Australian context has changed to include an emphasis on learning outcomes associated with school knowledge. But rather than to duplicate the practice traditions of schooling in the preschool sector, the educational experiment drew upon the leading activity of the preschool child to play as the stimulating motive to change the orientation of children towards learning concepts. New demands were made upon the children by the teachers. But also, the societal demand for greater learning outcomes put demands upon the teachers to develop new institutional practices to support learning in play-based settings. The Conceptual PlayWorld created motivating conditions for the children, but also the teachers to meaningfully support children's learning. The core model of development that underpins the new practice tradition focused on the drama in the collectively imagined situation and its resolution. The new practice tradition supported a new motive orientation towards learning whilst maintaining children's motive orientation to play. The new actions to solve problem situations in support of the drama in the imaginary situations were captured in practice as a collective, but also teachers were sensitive to the flickering between a motive to play and a motive to learn. The latter was indicative of children's transitioning as a dynamic fuzzy zone within a repetition of practices. This is line with Vygotsky's skipping metaphor in his revolutionary view of child development and which captures the dynamic between environment and person observed by teachers in Conceptual PlayWorlds.

Conclusion

In this paper the pedagogical characteristics of a Conceptual PlayWorld model has been theorised using cultural-historical concepts and illustrated through the practice example of *Charlotte's Web*. What is different to previous models of practice, is how teachers in role with children, collectively enter into the imaginary situation together. Teacher planning of interactions as a pedagogical pair in the imaginary situation is also new. When dramatic stories are read or told, and children enter into these imaginary play situations with their teachers, who have planned problem situations, learning and play is enriched. Learning concepts in this model of Conceptual PlayWorld is always in the service of the children's play. In these dramatic and emotionally charged imaginary play situations, both children and adults experience joyful and playful learning (Fleer, 2018). The intervention model was presented to illustrate one way to address the new societal need in Australia for learning subject based concepts, but in ways that maintain the practice tradition of a play-based program in early childhood education for the Australasian region.

Acknowledgements

Sincere gratitude to the Australian Research Council for supporting the original research (ARC DP 140101131) through funding research assistance of Sue March and the two teachers for the intensive work needed in the educational experiment, and to the school and families for kindly agreeing to video record the children experiencing the *Conceptual Playworld* of Charlotte's Web.

References

Ang, L. (2014). Preschool or prep school? Rethinking the role of early years education. *Contemporary Issues in Early Childhood, 14*(2), 185–199. doi:10.2304/ciec.2014.15.2.185

Australian Government. *The early years learning framework of Australia.* Department of Education, Employment and Workplace Relations for the Council of Australian Governments. ACT, 2009.

Bozhovich, L. I. (2009). The social situation of child development. *Journal of Russian and East European Psychology, 47*(4), 59–86. doi:10.2753/RPO1061-0405470403. https://doi.org/10.2753/rpo1061-0405470403

Broström, S. (2017). A dynamic learning concept in early years education: A possible way to prevent schoolification. *International Journal of Early Years Education, 25*(1), 3–15. doi:10.1080/09669760.2016.1270196. https://doi.org/10.1080/09669760.2016.1270196

Curriculum Development Council. (2017). *Kindergarten education curriculum guide.* Education Bureau, HKSAR.

Edwards, S., Cutter-Mackenzie, A., & Hunt, E. (2010). Framing play for learning: Professional reflections on the role of open-ended play in early childhood education. In L. Brooker & S. Edwards (org.). *Engaging play* (pp. 136–151). Open University Press. https://doi.org/10.1007/978-3-319-03740-0_2

El'Koninova, L. I. (2001). The object orientation of children's play in the context of understanding imaginary space — Time in play and stories. *Journal of Russian and East European Psychology, 39*(2), 30–51. https://doi.org/10.2753/rpo1061-0405390230

Fleer, M. (2011). Kindergartens in cognitive times: Imagination as a dialectical relation between play and learning. *International Journal of Early Childhood, 43*(3), 245–259.

Fleer, M. (2017a). Scientific playworlds: A model of teaching science in play-based settings. *Research in Science Education, 22.* doi:10.1007/s11165-017-9653-z. https://doi.org/10.1007/s13158-011-0044-8

Fleer, M. (2017b). Digital playworlds in an Australia context. In T. Bruce, M. Bredikyte, & P. Hakkarainen (Ed.), *Routledge handbook of play in early childhood* (pp. 289–304). Routledge. https://doi.org/10.4324/9781315735290-27

Fleer, M. (2016). Theorising digital play—a cultural-historical conceptualisation of children's engagement in imaginary digital situations, Special Issue on play. *Journal of International Research in Early Childhood Education, 7*(2), 75–90. https://doi.org/10.1017/cbo9781107282131.006

Fleer, M. (2018). Conceptual playworlds: The role of imagination in play and imagination in learning. *Early Years, 13.* doi:10.1080/09575146.2018.1549024. https://doi.org/10.1080/09575146.2018.1549024

Fleer, M., & Van Oers, B. (2018). International trends in research: Redressing the north-south balance in what matters for early childhood education research. In M. Fleer

& B. Van Oers (Ed.), *International handbook on early childhood education* (vol. 1, pp. 1–31). Springer. https://doi.org/10.1007/978-94-024-0927-7_1

Fleer, M., Veresov, N., & Walker, S. (2017). Re-conceptualizing executive functions as social activity in children's playworlds. *Learning, Culture and Social Interaction, 14,* 1–11. https://doi.org/10.1016/j.lcsi.2017.04.003

Grieshaber, S. (2016). Play and policy in early childhood education in the Asia Pacific region. *Asia-Pacific Journal of Research in Early Childhood Education, 10*(2), 7–28. https://doi.org/10.17206/apjrece.2016.10.2.7

Hakkarainen, P. (2010). Cultural-historical methodology of the study of human development in transitions. *Cultural-Historical Psychology, 4,* 75–89.

Hedegaard, M. (2002). *Learning and child development.* Aarhus University Press.

Hedegaard, M. (2008). The educational experiment. In M. Hedegaard & M. Fleer (Ed.), *Studying children: A cultural-historical approach* (pp. 181–201). Open University Press.

Hedegaard, M. (2014). The significance of demands and motives across practices in children's learning and development: An analysis of learning in home and school. *Learning, Culture and Social Interaction, 3,* 188–194. https://doi.org/10.1016/j.lcsi.2014.02.008

Hedegaard, M., & Chaiklin, S. (2005). *Radical-local teaching and learning.* Aarhus University Press.

Hedegaard, M., & Fleer, M. (2013). *Play, leaning and children's development: Everyday life in families and transition to school.* Cambridge University Press. https://doi.org/10.1017/cbo9781139236744

Husa, S., & Kinos, J. (2005). Academisation of early childhood education. *Scandinavian Journal of Educational Research, 49*(2), 133–141. doi:10.1080/0031380500048865. https://doi.org/10.1080/0031383050048865

Kravtsov, G. G., & Kravtsova, E. E. (2010). Play in L.S. Vygotsky's nonclassical psychology. *Journal of Russian and Easter European Psychology, 48*(4), 25–41. https://doi.org/10.2753/rpo1061-0405480403

Li, H., & Chau, L. (2010). Story Approach to Integrated learning (SAILS): A postmodernism curriculum for Hong Kong kindergartens. In L. E. Kattington (Ed.), *Handbook of curriculum development* (pp. 329–346). Nova Science Publishers.

Li, H., Rao, N., & Tse, S. K. (2012). Adapting Western pedagogies for Chinese literacy instruction: Case studies of Hong Kong, Shenzhen, and Singapore preschools. *Early Education and Development, 23*(4), 603–621. doi:10.1080/10409289.2010.536441. https://doi.org/10.1080/10409289.2010.536441

Lindqvist, G. (1995). *The aesthetics of play: A didactic study of play and culture in preschools.* Gotab.

Ministry of Education Singapore. (2012). *Nurturing early learners: A curriculum framework for kindergartens in Singapore.* Ministry of Education.

Paley, V. P. (1990). *The boy who would be a helicopter: The uses of storytelling in the classroom.* Harvard University Press.

Pan, Y., Wang, X., & Li, L. (2018). Early childhood education and development in China. In M. Fleer & B. van Oers (Ed.), *International handbook of early childhood education* (vol. 1, pp. 599–622). Springer. https://doi.org/10.1007/978-94-024-0927-7_28

Rao, N., & Li, H. (2009). "Eduplay": Beliefs and Practices related to play and learning in Chinese kindergartens. In I. Pramling Samuelsson & M. Fleer (Ed.), *Play and learning in early childhood settings: International perspectives* (pp. 97–116). Springer. doi:10.1007/978-1-4020-8498-0. https://doi.org/10.1007/978-1-4020-8498-0_5

Vygotsky, L. S. (1966). Play and its role in the mental development of the child. *Voprosy psikhologii, 12*(6), 62–76.

Vygotsky, L. S. (1971). *The psychology of art.* M.I.T. Press.

Vygotsky, L. S. (1987). *The collected works of L.S. Vygotsky, Vol. 1, Problems of general psychology* (R. W. Rieber & A. S. Carton, Eds.; N. Minick, Trans.). Plenum Press. https://doi.org/10.1017/s0142716400008341

Vygotsky, L. S. (1998). *The collected works of L.S. Vygotsky, Vol. 5,* Child Psychology (M. J. Hall, Trans.; R. W. Rieber, Ed. English translation). Kluwer Academic and Plenum Publishers.

Vygotsky, L. S. (2004). Imagination and creativity in childhood. *Journal of Russian and East European Psychology, 42*(1), 7–97.

White, E., & Williams, G. (1963). *Charlotte's web.* Puffin Books/Hamish Hamilton.

Wong, P., & Fleer, M. (2013). The development of learning as the leading activity for Hong Kong immigrant families in Australia. *International Research in Early Childhood Education, 4*(1), 18–34.

Wood, E. (2014). Play-pedagogy interface in contemporary debates. In L. Brooker, M. Blaise, & S. Edwards (Ed.), *The Sage handbook of play and learning in early childhood* (pp. 145–156). Sage. https://doi.org/10.4135/9781473907850.n15

Conceptual PlayLab for Early Childhood STEM

Australian Research Council Laureate Fellowship Scheme

Abstract

This chapter gives details on the research being taken forward through the Australian Research Council Laureate Fellowship Scheme. The previous research in this volume comes together in this chapter to showcase how research in early childhood education STEM can be systematically taken to scale. The place of social media underpins how the research is brought into the community. Rather than be accompanied with a published journal paper, this chapter is anchored in a series of social media links that tell the story of research translation for making a difference to early childhood science teaching in Australia and elsewhere. Social media holds few geographical boundaries and speaks to the next generation of teachers and researchers.

Keywords

diversity – social media – Facebook – imagination – STEM

∙ ∙ ∙

We now have research which shows a link between imagination in STEM and imagination in play (Fleer, 2018). But limited large scale research attention and funding has traditionally been directed to this area. The previous chapters have shown that over a period of 20 years, a corpus of research following a cultural-historical perspective has identified that incrementally, we can say something unique about how imagination in play and imagination in STEM is dialectically formed in play-based settings.

But thanks to the ARC, the ARC Laureate Fellowship provided the basis for establishing Australia's first programmatic study of:

1. STEM concept formation of infants, toddlers and pre-schoolers,
2. contributing conditions of family pedagogy supporting STEM learning at home, and
3. a national evidenced-based model of intentional teaching of STEM for play-based settings.

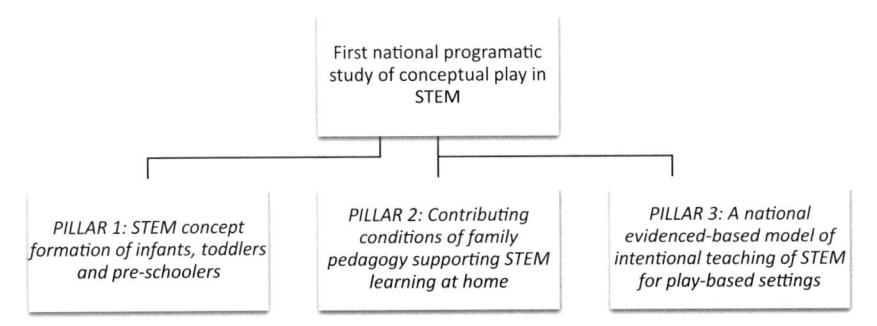

FIGURE 5.1   Programmatic study leading to an International Centre of Excellence in play-based STEM learning

The program of research is made up of these three pillars (Figure 5.1) to build Australia's research capacity in early childhood STEM, culminating in a national cultural-historically informed baseline and impact study of a play-based STEM model known as STEM Playworlds, pioneering methodological innovations in researching concept formation of infants, toddlers and pre-schoolers from diverse settings (SES, gender, CALD, geography), including the development of an innovative digital imagination in STEM scale, drawing upon the latest advances in early childhood STEM app development.

But how could this go to scale, and bring with it the teachers and the community?

Lara says, "Have you thought about using *Twitter*?". I respond instantly with a "No way. I don't have the time to learn how to do that. I am too old". She smiles.

1   **Engaging with Social Media – Making and Curating Content**

We are in a small country town in Western Australia. Our role is to prepare a video that will be used the following year when the Laureate Programmatic research is launched. Lara is the Communications Strategist at Monash University, Faculty of Education, and has the most amazing skills with the translation of research. Bas is the film maker and extraordinarily creative. I am apparently 'the talent' and they want to capture my story. After 3 days of filming, sharing meals together, being up before dawn so we get the blue hour for the best filming, journeying around the places I taught, visiting where I grew up and went to school, Lara had finally convinced me to try.

Building the Twitter feed, generating content for a private closed book for teachers, and creating a website loaded with resources and working papers

Conceptual PlayWorld website
Download our free app
TeachSpace article
Lens article
Newsletter link
Working papers on website: https://www.monash.edu/education/research/
projects/conceptual-playlab/publications
PlayLab shares practices (Facebook)
Educators share their PlayWorlds (Facebook)

Working papers: https://www.monash.edu/education/research/projects/
conceptual-playlab/publications

Conceptual PlayLab research website
YouTube channel

FIGURE 5.2   Resource bank

were all needed for the launch. We were six months out from the launch of the Laureate Fellowship programmatic research. Lara said, "When we launch, people will go looking and need to find engaging contact. You have to build it now".

Social media is critical for bringing forward the findings. Social media is the engine that moves the content into the community. Through social media, a spiral of research and community engagement can pioneer a new generation of early childhood science education researchers. Just what I hoped I could achieve through the Kathleen Fitzpatrick award. But I didn't know how significant social media would be then.

2   Video Productions

I am packing my bag ready for the big trip to WA. Lara and I touch base on the phone. She casually says, "Oh by the way. I promised the school you would do a PD session with the teachers on your Conceptual PlayWorld model. I said you would show them how in the centre".

Panic sets in. How can I deliver in a morning a full Conceptual PlayWorld that normally takes a term?

In true academic spirit, I go through the five characteristics and plan how I might deliver a Conceptual PlayWorld for the intentional teaching of STEM to

FIGURE 5.3   Social media launch of the self-paced online Professional Development for teachers (Photo by Lara McKinley)

children I do not know. How might I enlist the staff into a process they had not yet experienced – all whist being filmed, as part of creating the video for the launch in April.

But this experience did more than give me credibility in being able to use the model, it inspired me into conceptualising a new way of thinking about the implementation. I invented the 'pop-up Conceptual PlayWorld" and used it thereafter to engage educators who were new to the approach and wanted to just put a 'toe in the water'.

I was so lost in the moment of the Conceptual PlayWorld of Rosie's Walk by Pat Hutchins, that I didn't even notice I was being filmed – nor were the staff and children alert to this either. Bas the filmmaker brought the content together, as well as many other Conceptual PlayWorlds he filmed thereafter, almost as a Hollywood production! It was just magical.

At the launch of the programmatic research Lara kindly tells my daughter Freya who is at the launch to support me (*Launch video*), along with my mother and sister, "You have to get your mum to stop calling it *The Twitter*". I was still catching up, learning a whole new social media language.

Lara was right. The stats speak for themselves – 1.3K Facebook community and a 4.5K Twitter following. What was the content they were all looking for by following the work of our Conceptual PlayLab community?

3   Halfway through the Five-Year Period of Funding

Halfway through the life of the research and Lara initiates and strategically plans a social media launch of our online self-paced PD for teachers. Who would have thought? Back in Mt Barker before we began our journey, I would never have dreamt that recruitment of research participants for one of our key research pillars would be through social media. Whilst we had targeted 3K participants across Australia for the life the research project, we had engaged 1K teachers after one month. If the literature into successful early childhood teachers' PD is right, then anticipate successful outcomes. But that is for another chapter in the journey.

Reference

Fleer, M. (2018). *Conceptual playworlds: Foregrounding imagination and creativity as foundational for children's learning.* Monash University Working Paper. https://www.monash.edu/education/research/projects/conceptual-playlab/publications

Agentic STEM Practices

From Role-Playing "As If" Engineer/Scientist to Imagining This as a Career

Abstract

This chapter explicitly brings into focus the concept of imagination, and the future imagining and moral imagining that Jennifer Vadeboncour has introduced into the literature. There is a dual goal. The first goal is how early childhood educators resource their professional development of a Conceptual PlayWorld for the intentional teaching of STEM through the psychological function of imagination. The second goal is oriented to bringing forward girls' imagining that STEM is for them and imagining a career in STEM. This chapter bookends the volume and solves the problem of how to bring STEM concepts into children's play. This chapter also paves the way for a new research agenda centred on researching STEM within the field by early childhood education researchers working in collaboration with teachers who draw on different assumptions than those from outside of the field, and who take forward new thinking as we go into the future.

Keywords

engineering – gender – teacher confidence – teacher competence – imagination – engineering conceptual PlayWorld – Family Day Care – museums – discovery centres

•••

After 30 years of scholarship that brought together early childhood education and science education through a deep connection with the Collected Works of L.S. Vygotsky (1987, 1993, 1997a, 1997b, 1998, 1999), this final chapter answers the question of how to bring science concepts into children's play, and sets the stage for a new agenda. But first, this chapter begins by a metaphorical visit to the Monash Conceptual PlayLab.

I am sitting in the Conceptual PlayLab surrounded by a diverse group of scholars who make up our research team and early childhood colleagues from the School of Educational Psychology and Counselling. Looking around the PlayLab I consider how exciting it is that I have finally created a space in which rich conversations about theory, research and practice have become the norm. It was not always like that. When I first arrived at Monash the Dean at the time charged me with developing a research culture on the campus.

Back then – I sat in the tea area and listened, I observed the work practices of my colleagues, and I considered the paper trail associated with teaching and researching in one of the largest universities in Australia. I also walked the corridors of the Peninsula campus each day, and checked in on how everyone was going, and importantly set up a monthly research sharing session.

In the tea area of the Peninsula campus, the conversations were centred on how time consuming it was to be marking student work and the lack of resources for reducing teaching loads. No one knew what each other was researching. Few of the staff in early childhood education had PhDs, and most were publishing irregularly. Our staffing profile was primarily middle-class women who were passionate about their field, and wanted to engage in more research, but the context didn't make it easy. However, that progressively changed. Could the goal of the Discipline Review of Mathematics and Science Education (Department of Education, Employment and Training, 1989) to support the scholarship of early education academics have been achieved after all?

Sitting in the PlayLab now the staff are culturally diverse, everyone who is not a student has a PhD, and everyone has a strong research profile and publication record – some even have a Twitter handle. My colleagues engage in contract research and have funds to resource international conference attendance, and grow their libraries and minds to support their activities. Everyone is time poor. That has not changed in 20 years. But the conversations have.

It is exciting to be part of a collective that has studied cultural-historical theory, has used the system of concepts to analyse their data, and who have each contributed to highbrow conferences, impactful journals, and highly prestigious books. We have a common language. Important for this agenda has been the faculty visiting scholar program.

I recall Professor Anne Edwards from the University of Oxford, saying, "I have been here for a few weeks as your visiting scholar. But I have never been in your office". Anne was our second visiting scholar. Our research group had hosted her visit. She said, "You have looked after me so well, what I can I do for you?". I replied, "If one of our early career colleagues knocks on your door, please spend some time with them". I only recall too well how hard it was for an ECR to forge and resource an international network and to reap the benefits of being in close quarters with top thinkers (Chapter 2). The visiting scholar program offered a way that the best scholars in my field, like Anne Edwards, could connect with our group. We seemed to have no difficulties attracting them to Monash. They all wanted to come.

Over the years, students and staff went on mass to key international conferences to share their research. Major planning went into preparing the most engaging abstracts, symposia and posters. This was not a private affair. We workshopped. We had a strategy. We had within group mentoring. We were a critical mass of cultural-historical researchers. We were being noticed. Over the years I have had many conversations with international colleagues who envied our group, because many cultural-historical scholars were sprinkled around the universities, and only had ISCAR as their conceptual home in which to share and stretch their thinking with others.

1   Mentoring in the Academy …

Fast forward to Oxford. I am sitting in a study adjacent to Anne Edwards' office. We are both working on two major projects. One is a festschrift to honour the work of Mariane Hedegaard and the other is a special issue of Learning, Culture and Social Interaction. We bring together the recent presentations given in Copenhagen. Both projects came out of the retirement symposia to celebrate the life work of Mariane Hedegaard.

I brought into the PlayLab over 2 decades of being theoretically mentored – this mentoring came from working on research projects with Mariane Hedegaard and the more recent collaborations with Anne Edwards through using her ground-breaking concepts of common knowledge, knowledge of each other's motive orientation, relational agency, and relational expertise (Edwards, 2012).

2   Building the Legacy and Circling Back …

While there were many moments in which mentoring happened, the memory of sitting in Valda Kirkwood's office with a fellow PhD student each Friday afternoon (Chapter 1) was most significant. In this office the problems in science education were discussed. It was also the space in which concepts from cultural-historical theory were shared. And significantly, the interface between constructivism in science education and cultural-historical theory that was emerging in my thesis through the analysis of my data, propelled me forward. The relations between play and learning science concepts sat within this space. I did not know it then, but the PECSTEP Professional Development (PD) model that Valda co-designed with Margaret and Tim, showed me that early childhood teachers could engage in science, could teach science concepts, and could think and act scientifically in play-based settings. With the right model to build confidence and competence, and the credit assumption about early childhood teachers, the vision was set for the future.

3   Where Are We at Now?

With 3K teachers to engage in a Conceptual PlayWorld in STEM as part of my programmatic research, it was now time to design a PD program for effective practice change. In bringing together the literature on PD it became evident that there were three key drivers (Table 6.1) that have been shown to be most impactful for early childhood teacher development.

The key drivers of a multimodal program, with an outside expert, the use of a cultural tool to support new practices, and enough time to experience practice change, set the stage for designing a PD with maximum flexibility. The PlayLab team organised multimodal delivery, as well as fully face-to-face delivery. With our credit model in mind, we learned how imagination for teachers was as important as imagination for children (Fleer, Fragkiadaki, & Rai, 2021).

We learned that an iterative process of *imagination and creativity in professional practice* emerged. We identified that during the PD program the teachers began imagining the new practices and collectively problem solved – through multiple imaginings – how to bring into their practices the characteristics of a Conceptual PlayWorld. We had not come across this previously in the literature. The teachers imagined 'as if' in a mature form of a Conceptual PlayWorld. They put forward solutions through mini role-playing. There was a distributed collective imagining of a Conceptual PlayWorld. Teacher gesturing in these mini performances of the new practice, appeared as thought experiments in action. We observed miniature dramatizations of practices. We had not seen reference to this kind of PD practice in the literature. Our research found that imagination as a psychological function resourced teacher learning.

We determined from our research that the problems identified in Chapter 1, of teacher confidence and competence being the problem of why early childhood teachers did not teach science, was the wrong assumption. Rather, what we learned was that we had to look at teacher knowledge of STEM differently (Fleer, Fragkiadaki, & Rai, 2022). Table 6.2 shows how teacher knowledge of STEM develops over time – not in relation to a worry about the STEM concept, but rather, in relation to identifying a credible problem that sets the stage for children's inquiries as part of the Conceptual PlayWorld.

TABLE 6.1   Characteristics and concepts as background for the design of PD (Fleer,
                Fragkiadaki & Rai, 2022)

Characteristic identified in the literature specific to early childhood teachers	Cultural-historical concepts used in PD studies generally relevant to the characteristics and closest to Vygotsky's conception of development	References
1. online professional learning community with an outsider supporting professional inquiries for a flexible model of practice change in early childhood settings	The dialectical relations between everyday and scientific concepts in practice (Vygotsky, 1987) Higher mental functions: Relations between inter and intra psychological functioning (Vygotsky, 1987) Collective/individual tensions Communities of practice	Eun (2008, 2011) Shabani (2016)
2. use of cultural tools for bringing forward possible contradictions and illuminating teacher motives for PD	The relations between mature and real forms of development The Zone of Proximal Development Apprenticeship in thinking – legitimate peripheral participation (Lave & Wenger, 1991)	Johnson et al., (2020) Grimmett (2014) Shi (2017) Tasker et al., (2010) Brown & Mowry (2017) Ellis (2007)
	Drama and contradiction for creating conditions for development Perezhivanie – affect and intellect Consciousness as a double move – theory into practice and practice into theory Relations between everyday and scientific concept formation	Grimmett (2014) Hoffman-Kipp et al., (2003)
3. recognition of the unique practice context of early childhood teachers	Vygotsky's (1966) conception of play as a psychological function of the preschool child Social situation of development (Vygotsky, 1994)	Edwards et al. (2019)
	Relations between motives and motivation (Hedegaard, 2014)	Nuttall et al. (2015)

TABLE 6.2   Solving the theoretical problem associated with STEM learning in children's play

Dialectical relations	Theoretical problem period 1	Theoretical problem period 2	Theoretical problem period 3	Theoretical problem period 4
Teacher motives	What STEM concepts could be used with the narrative of the chosen book?	What was the STEM knowledge needed?	What was the essence of the STEM concept?	Was the STEM problem credible to the children?
Children's motives as motivating conditions for teachers	Moving from the book to generating the narrative that brings forward STEM play and problems to be solved.	Dialectical relations between everyday knowledge and scientific knowledge	Modelling: Children generate a model to capture the essence of STEM concept	Motivating conditions for children to want to solve the problem.

The educational experiment involved teachers and researchers working with a theoretical problem. This created a different kind of context for teachers' planning and pedagogy. What dominated their weekly planning and evaluation of the children's learning and their pedagogical practices, was not a problem of practice. But rather, the theoretical problem of how to meaningfully bring STEM concepts into children's play at the same time as distilling the big ideas in STEM as credible concepts for children's learning, and the development of their play. While this was an ongoing point of crisis for the teachers, it was found, like Edwards et al. (2019), that the drama of the problem gave motivating conditions for their development. That is, the teachers viewed the same practice situation differently at different points over time. The teachers entered into the theoretical problem differently, as their own social situation of development was changing.

How to bring science concepts into children's play was solved through the educational experiment. We learned that the recurrent demands of practice were met with theoretical thinking about play and STEM concepts by teachers. It was found that the theoretical problem appeared to create new developmental conditions for teachers, and the educational experiment brought changes in the dominating motives of the teachers from practice to theoretical thinking. The studies over time determined that the source of development for the teachers was found to be the theoretical problem. Therefore, teacher transformation has to be conceptualised not as a simple problem of practice change, but as a mature form of theoretical thinking by early childhood teachers about play and STEM concepts. The significance of bringing teachers into a theoretical problem (Chapter 4) creates the conditions that act as a source of teacher development.

We also learned that the narrative of the story provides the glue for fusing children's ongoing experiences of the science in a Conceptual PlayWorld (Fleer, Fragkiadaki, & Rai, 2022). The narrative of the story makes the science personally meaningful for children. Books with drama matter because the excitement of going on adventures, where problems arise, is what propels learning in play forward. We identified that story selection was not so much about choosing a book focused on a science concept, such as, "Light", but rather to find a book that created the possibility for many adventures, such as "Spooky old tree" – with the light, stick and rope – the little bears go over great sleeping bear.[1]

But just as I had thought the research question had finally been resolved, the new knowledge domain of engineering emerged as an area of study in play-based settings. Whilst engineering in preschools is common in north America, it is relatively new for Australian preschool teachers. Table 6.3 summarises what is known about engineering in play-based settings. A limited number of studies are showcased in this table. But the content of these papers takes us full circle back to Chapter 1 where the problem lies with the teacher.

A critical review of this literature through the lens of what counts as engineering knowledge shows that what is known about preschool engineering has primarily been guided by practices from only some engineering professions, such as civil engineering. There are many engineering professions, and we need to know about how these forms of engineering knowledge could be considered as valued forms of knowledges for STEM. The literature shows that knowledge construction is based on both pre-defined and emergent categories set by engineers. Research has tended to focus mostly on constructing (e.g., blocks). Gendered engineering knowledge has also been identified, suggesting only partial understandings of engineering education is currently evident.

Engineering teaching knowledge is being constructed primarily by engineers who show through their research that early childhood teachers (1) don't use the language of engineering when talking to children in the block area, and (2) demonstrate a lack of confidence and competence of engineering knowledge. The solution is to fix up the problem through professional development to teach educators engineering principles and the engineering processes. This echoes the longstanding literature into teacher confidence and competence in science, where the same research problem and conclusion emerged year after year without systemic change. The view is that we give early childhood teachers the knowledge they need, and then more engineering will happen in play-based settings.

TABLE 6.3   Research papers oriented to engineering for play-based settings

Bagiati, A. (2011). *Early engineering: A developmentally appropriate curriculum for young children* [Doctoral thesis, Purdue University]. ProQuest Dissertations and Thesis.

Bagiati, A., & Evangelou, D. (2016). Practicing engineering while building with blocks: Identifying engineering thinking. *European Early Childhood Education Research Journal, 24*(1), 67–85. https://doi.org/https://doi.org/10.1080/1350293X.2015.1120521

Bagiati, A., & Evangelou, D. (2015). Engineering curriculum in the preschool classroom: the teacher's experience. *European Early Childhood Education Research Journal, 23*(1), 112–128. https://doi.org/https://doi.org/10.1080/1350293X.2014.991099

Bairaktarova, D., Evangelou, D., Bagiati, A., & Brophy, S. (2011). Early engineering in young children's exploratory play with tangible materials. *Children Youth and Environments, 21*(2), 212–235. https://www.jstor.org/stable/10.7721/chilyoutenvi.21.2.0212

Beat, K. (1991). Design it, build it, use it: Girls and construction kits. In N. Browne (Ed.), *Science and technology in the early years. An equality opportunities approach* (pp. 77–90). Open University Press.

Bergen, D. (2009). Play as the learning medium for future scientists, mathematicians, and engineers. *American Journal of Play, 1*(4), 413–428. https://eric.ed.gov/?id=EJ1069001

Briseno Sandoval, L. M. (2015). *Science Technology Engineering and Math (STEM) Education MUST Begin in Early Childhood Education: A Systematic Analysis of Washington State Guidelines Used to Gauge the Development and Learning of Young Learners* [Master thesis, University of Washington]. http://hdl.handle.net/1773/33769

Brophy, S., & Evangelou, D. (2007). Precursors to engineering thinking (PET) project: Intentional Designs with Experimental Artifacts (IDEA). Proceedings of the 2007 Annual Conference & Exposition, Honolulu, Hawaii.

Browne, N. (1991). *Science and technology in the early years. An equal opportunity approach.* Milton Keynes: Open University Press

Capobianco, B. M., Diefes-dux, H. A., Mena, I., & Weller, J. (2011). What is an engineer? Implications of elementary school student conceptions for engineering education. *Journal of engineering education, 100*(2), 304–328. https://doi.org/https://doi.org/10.1002/j.2168-9830.2011.tb00015.x

English, L. D. (2016). STEM education K-12: Perspectives on integration. *International Journal of STEM Education, 3*(1), 1–8. https:// doi.org/10.1186/s40594-016-0036-1.

English, L., & Moore, T. (2018). *Early engineering learning.* Springer.

Fleer, M. (2019). When preschool girls engineer: Future imaginings of being and becoming an engineer. *Learning, Culture and Social Interaction*, 100372. https://doi.org/10.1016/j.lcsi.2019.100372

Fleer, M. (2020). Studying the relations between motives and motivation – How young children develop a motive orientation for collective engineering play. *Learning, Culture and Social Interaction, 24.* https://doi.org/10.1016/j.lcsi.2019.100355

Forbes, M. H., Sullivan, J. F., & Carlson, D. W. (2018). Ascertaining the Impact of P–12 Engineering Education Initiatives: Student Impact through Teacher Impact. *Journal of Pre-College Engineering Education Research (J-PEER), 8*(1), 4. https://docs.lib.purdue.edu/jpeer/vol8/iss1/4/

(cont.)

TABLE 6.3   Research papers oriented to engineering for play-based settings *(cont.)*

Gold, Z. S. (2014). *Preschoolers' physical, social, and engineering play behaviors: Differences in gender and play environment* [Master thesis, Purdue University]. ProQuest Dissertations and Thesis.

Gold, Z. S. (2017). *Engineering play: Exploring associations with executive function, mathematical ability, and spatial ability in preschool* [Doctoral thesis, Purdue University]. ProQuest Dissertations and Thesis.

Gold, Z. S., Elicker, J., Choi, J. Y., Anderson, T., & Brophy, S. P. (2015). Preschoolers' engineering play behaviors: Differences in gender and play context. *Children, Youth and Environments, 25*(3), 1–21. https://doi.org/https://doi.org/10.7721/chilyoutenvi.25.3.0001

Gold, Z. S., Elicker, J., Bairaktarova, D., & Evangelou, D. (2017). Preschool engineering play behaviors (PEPB). Purdue University.

Hallström, J., Elvstrand, H., & Hellberg, K. (2015). Gender and technology in free play in Swedish early childhood education. *International Journal of Technology and Design Education, 25*(2), 137–149. https://doi.org/https://doi.org/10.1007/s10798-014-9274-z

Kelly, A. (1987). *Why girls don't do science.* Open University Press.

Lyon, E. (1991). The role of the Nursery School in developing a non-sexist approach to science and technology. In N. Browne (Ed.), *Science and technology in the early years. An equality opportunities approach* (pp. 67–76). Open University Press.

Lippard, C. N., Lamm, M. H., & Riley, K. L. (2017). Engineering thinking in prekindergarten children: A systematic literature review. *Journal of engineering education, 106*(3), 454–474. https://doi.org/10.1002/jee.20174

Lippard, C., Lamm, M. H., Tank, K. M., & Choi, J. Y. (2019). Pre-engineering thinking and the engineering habits of mind in preschool classroom. *Early Childhood Education Journal, 47*(2), 187–198. https://doi.org/10.1007/s10643-018-0898-6

Lippard, C. N., Riley, K. L., & Lamm, M. H. (2018). Encouraging the development of engineering habits of Mind in Prekindergarten Learners. In L. English & T. Moore (Eds.), *Early engineering learning* (pp. 19–36). Springer.

Little, A. J., & León de la Barra, B. A. (2009). Attracting girls to science, engineering and technology: An Australian perspective. *European Journal of Engineering Education, 34*(5), 439–445. https://doi.org/10.1080/03043790903137585

Malone, K. L., Tiarani, V., Irving, K. E., Kajfez, R., Lin, H., Giasi, T., & Edmiston, B. W. (2018). Engineering Design Challenges in Early Childhood Education: Effects on Student Cognition and Interest. *European Journal of STEM Education, 3*(3), 11. https://doi.org/10.20897/ejsteme/3871

Moore, L. Tank, T., & English, L. (2018). Engineering in the early grades: Harnessing children's natural ways of thinking. In L. English, and T. Moore (Eds.). *Early engineering learning* (pp. 9–18). Springer.

Mulvey, K. L., Miller, B., & Rizzardi, V. (2017). Gender and engineering aptitude: Is the color of science, technology, engineering, and math materials related to children's performance? *Journal of Experimental Child Psychology, 160*, 119–126. https://doi.org/10.1016/j.jecp.2017.03.006

(cont.)

TABLE 6.3   Research papers oriented to engineering for play-based settings (*cont.*)

Pantoya, M. L., Aguirre-Munoz, Z., & Hunt, E. M. (2015). Developing an engineering identity in early childhood. *American Journal of Engineering Education, 6*(2), 61–68. https://eric.ed.gov/?id=EJ1083229

Park, M.-H., Dimitrov, D. M., Patterson, L. G., & Park, D.-Y. (2017). Early childhood teachers' beliefs about readiness for teaching science, technology, engineering, and mathematics. *Journal of Early Childhood Research, 15*(3), 275–291. https://doi.org/10.1177/1476718X15614040

Penuel, W. R. (2016). Studying science and engineering learning in practice. *Cultural Studies of Science Education, 11*(1), 89–104. https://doi.org/10.1007/s11422-014-9632-x

Savinskaya, O. (2017). Gender equality in preschool STEM programs as a factor determining Russia's successful technological development. *Russian Education & Society, 59*(3–4), 206–216. https://doi.org/10.1080/10609393.2017.1399758

Tank, K. M., Rynearson, A. M., & Moore, T. J. (2018). Examining Student and Teacher Talk within Engineering Design in Kindergarten. *European Journal of STEM Education, 3*(3), 10. https://doi.org/10.20897/ejsteme/3870

Thorshag, K., & Holmqvist, M. (2019). Pre-school children's expressed technological volition during construction play. *International Journal of Technology and Design Education, 29*(5), 987–998. https://doi.org/10.1007/s10798-018-9481-0

Torres-Crespo, M. N., Kraatz, E., & Pallansch, L. (2014). From Fearing STEM to Playing with It: The Natural Integration of STEM into the Preschool Classroom. *SRATE Journal, 23*(2), 8–16. https://eric.ed.gov/?id=EJ1044758

Wyvill, B. (1991). Science INSET and equal opportunities in the early years. In N. Browne (Ed.), *Science and technology in the early years. An equality opportunities approach* ((pp. 117–129). Open University Press.

Zucker, T. A., Williams, J. M., Bell, E. R., Assel, M. A., Landry, S. H., Monsegue-Bailey, P., Crawford, A., & Bhavsar, V. (2016). Validation of a brief, screening measure of low-income pre-kindergarteners' science and engineering knowledge. *Early Childhood Research Quarterly, 36*, 345–357. https://doi.org/10.1016/j.ecresq.2015.12.018

This swings back to the problem of blaming the victim as discussed in Chapter 1 – it is the preschool teacher's fault for not having engineering knowledge, and the solution is to fix the teacher (Fleer, 2020).

4   Future Imagining in Engineering

Governments worry about the supply chain of female engineers. The existing research on this is mixed.

What is different when preschool girls engineer? How can the science education community bring in the future imaginings of being and becoming an engineer?

It is important to study how girls become oriented towards or imagine themselves being and becoming an engineer when in preschool. Play is the leading activity of the preschool child. Imaginary play gives scope for imagining 'as if' you are an engineer. Paper 9 studies engineering practice during free play time, and the results suggest that, simply playing at being an engineer was not enough to realise a possible future imagining by girls to do engineering.

4.1   *Paper 9: When Preschool Girls Engineer: Future Imaginings of Being and Becoming an Engineer*

What did we learn?

First the study found a strong motive for engineering through how all the children quickly occupied the space and sought to access the resources within the activity setting. Girls were as interested as boys in the new practice tradition of engineering in the preschool.

Second, the study found that the engineering activity setting was difficult for girls to enter when there were so many children seeking to engage with the resources. The girls held back. The boys pushed forward.

Third, the repeated attempts by girls to enter the engineering space failed. Girls were progressively presented with a future imagining of civil engineering as something that was not for them. Rather, it seemed the engineering activity setting was for boys. The boys were regularly named 'as if' they were engineers, despite the girls being present. The girls were made to feel invisible.

The new engineering activity setting privileges engineering actions and imaginings as children act 'as if' they are engineers. How confident girls feel in the new activity setting has been shown in the general literature to be problematic for STEM. Research associated with preschoolers constructing (see Hallström et al., 2015) shows girls acting as helpers. This research also shows gendered differences emerging, such as, girls construct to play, rather than to build. But if girls only have periphery access or have unencumbered access once the building work is completed, then different ways of playing will emerge. Differences in the engineering actions of boys and girls could be because of access rather than differences between girls' and boys' ways of playing 'as if' engineers.

5   Engineering PlayWorlds

Maybe a way of resolving girls access to engineering is to think about the problem differently, and from collaborations between early childhood teachers and researchers to generate new scholarly knowledge of engineering pedagogy in

FIGURE 6.1   Active engagement begins early – creating the motive for engineering through an
              Engineering PlayWorld (Photo by Lara McKinley)

order to shape the future directions for the teaching of STEM. The educational
experiment (see Hedegaard, 2008) brought forward new ways of being and
becoming engineers through an Engineering PlayWorld (Fleer, 2020).

The new model of practice was built from within the field of early childhood education by teachers and early childhood education researchers. Could
this new model of practice solve the problem identified by the engineers who
were researching (Table 6.3) in play-based settings?

6   Looking Forward

The next step is to bring the PlayLab scholarly team into an ARC Australian Centre of Excellence. Moving from a Conceptual PlayLab to a Centre of
Excellence will set the stage for cementing into the foundations of Australian research early childhood STEM education and creating the pathways for
generations of researchers from within the field of early childhood education.

Studying complexity in STEM is still needed. This is where the solutions
to problems are not yet known or imagined – as opposed to known concepts
found in a textbook. This could create motivating conditions and could inspire
children and youth, along with their families into not just valuing the place of
STEM in everyday life, but also motivating children into STEM careers.

A life course approach in which scientists/engineers, STEM education
researchers, and STEM communicators in the community (with installations,

citizen science apps, embodied light and sound virtual labs) work together, could become the blueprint for the new labs of the future.

Rather than community-university doorways and well-trodden pathways as boundaries, virtual interactive spaces could bring the community into the lab. Imagining STEM concepts not directly observable and imagining STEM concepts/principles not yet invented takes a whole community. But it also takes a step wise change in how we conceptualise the boundaries of research.

Even if an ARC Centre for Excellence funding proposal is not successful, we would have learned the processes and a new generation of researchers would have the skillset to go again in the future.

What we do know because of the ARC Laureate Fellowship scheme, is that play is the leading activity of the preschool child, and play matures through a Conceptual PlayWorld. We know that imaginary play is the source of a child's development, and this begins in infancy as a form of togetherness that transforms into collective imaginary play. Importantly, imagination as a psychological function is cultural rather than biologically predetermined process, and educators have a key role in supporting its development from birth to eight years. Finally, studying children's STEM conceptual development demands a particular kind of research expertise that must come from within a profession that understands play-based settings. A Centre of Excellence that honours, celebrates and goes forward with this unique skill set, is the legacy needed for the future.

Note

1 https://www.youtube.com/watch?v=IZ936HXchCM

References

Brown, C. P., & Mowry, B. (2017). "I wanted to know how they perceived jail": Studying how one early educator brought her students' worlds into her standardized teaching context. *Early Childhood Education Journal, 45*(2), 163–173. https://doi.org/10.1007/s10643-016-0776-z

Department of Employment, Education and Training. (1989). *Discipline review of teacher education in mathematics and science, Report and Recommendation.* Australian Government Publishing Service.

Edwards, A., Chan, J., & Tan, D. (2019). Motive orientation and the exercise of agency: Responding to recurrent demands in practices. In A. Edwards, M. Fleer, & L. Bøttcher

(Eds.), *Cultural-historical approaches to studying learning and development societal, institutional and personal perspectives* (pp. 201–214). Springer Nature.

Edwards, A. (2012). The role of common knowledge in achieving collaboration across practices. *Learning, Culture and Social Interaction, 1*(1), 22–32. https://doi.org/10.1016/j.lcsi.2012.03.003

Ellis, V. (2007). Taking subject knowledge seriously: From professional knowledge recipes to complex conceptualizations of teacher development. *The Curriculum Journal, 18*(4), 447–462. https://doi.org/10.1080/09585170701687902

Eun, B. (2008). Making connections: Grounding professional development in the developmental theories of Vygotsky. *The Teacher Educator, 43*(2), 134–155. https://doi.org/10.1080/08878730701838934

Eun, B. (2011). A Vygotskian theory-based professional development: Implications for culturally diverse classrooms. *Professional Development in Education, 37*(3), 319–333. https://doi.org/10.1080/19415257.2010.527761

Fleer, M. (2020). Engineering playworld—A model of practice to support children to collectively design, imagine and think using engineering concepts. *Research in Science Education,* 1–16. https://doi.org/10.1007/s11165-020-09970-6

Fleer, M., Fragkiadaki, G., & Rai, P. (2021). Collective imagination as a source of professional practice change: A cultural-historical study of early childhood teacher professional development in the motivated conditions of a Conceptual PlayWorld. *Teaching and Teacher Education, 106*, 103455. https://doi.org/10.1016/j.tate.2021.103455

Fleer, M., Fragkiadaki, G., & Rai, P. (2022). The dialectical relation of real and digital conceptual playworlds in family day care. *International Journal of Early Years Education.* https://doi.org/10.1080/09669760.2022.2041406

Grimmett, H. (2014). *The practice of teachers' professional development: A cultural-historical approach.* Sense Publishers.

Hallström, J., Elvstrand, H., & Hellberg, K. (2015). Gender and technology in free play in Swedish early childhood education. *International Journal of Technology and Design Education, 25*(2), 137–149. https://doi.org/10.1007/s10798-014-9274-z

Hedegaard, M. (2014). The significance of demands and motives across practices in children's learning and development: An analysis of learning in home and school. *Learning, Culture and Social Interaction, 3*(3), 188–194. https://doi.org/10.1016/j.lcsi.2014.02.008

Hoffman-Kipp, P., Artiles, A. J., & López-Torres, L. (2003). Beyond reflection: Teacher learning as praxis. *Theory into practice, 42*(3), 248–254. https://doi.org/10.1207/s15430421tip4203_12

Johnston, K., Hadley, F., & Waniganayake, M. (2020). Practitioner inquiry as a professional learning strategy to support technology integration in early learning centres: Building understanding through Rogoff's planes of analysis. *Professional Development in Education, 46*(1), 49–64. https://doi.org/10.1080/19415257.2019.1647871

Lave, J., & Wenger, E. (1991). *Situated learning.* Cambridge University Press. https://doi.org/10.1017/CBO9780511815355

Nuttall, J., Edwards, S., Mantilla, A., Grieshaber, S., & Wood, E. (2015). The role of motive objects in early childhood teacher development concerning children's digital play and play-based learning in early childhood curricula. *Professional Development in Education, 41*(2), 222–235. https://doi.org/10.1080/19415257.2014.990579

Shabani, K. (2016). Applications of Vygotsky's sociocultural approach for teachers' professional development. *Cogent education, 3*(1), 1252177. https://doi.org/10.1080/2331186X.2016.1252177

Shi, H. (2017). The theoretical interpretation of EFL teacher's professional development from the perspective of sociocultural theory. *Theory and Practice in Language Studies, 7*(11), 1059–1064. https://doi.org/10.17507/tpls.0711.14

Tasker, T., Johnson, K. E., & Davis, T. S. (2010). A sociocultural analysis of teacher talk in inquiry-based professional development. *Language Teaching Research, 14*(2), 129–140. https://doi.org/10.1177/1362168809353871

Vygotsky, L. S. (1966). Play and its role in the mental development of the child. *Voprosy Psikhologii, 12*(6), 62–76. https://doi.org/https://doi.org/10.2753/RPO1061-040505036

Vygotsky, L. S. (1987). *The collected works of L. S. Vygotsky: Problems of general psychology* (N. Minick, Trans.; R. W. Rieber & A. S. Carton, Eds. 1987 ed., Vol. 1). Plenum Press.

Vygotsky, L. S. (1993). *The collected works of LS Vygotsky: The fundamentals of defectology* (J. E. Knox & C. B. Stevens, Trans.; R. W. Rieber & A. S. Carton, Eds. Vol. 2). Springer Science & Business Media.

Vygotsky, L. S. (1994). The problem of the environment (T. Prout, Trans.). In R. van der Veer & J. Valsiner (Eds.), *The Vygotsky reader* (pp. 338–354). Blackwell.

Vygotsky, L. S. (1997a). *The collected works of LS Vygotsky: Problems of the theory and history of psychology* (R. Van der Veer, Trans.; R. W. Rieber & J. Wollock, Eds. Vol. 3). Springer Science & Business Media.

Vygotsky, L. S. (1997b). *The collected works of L. S. Vygotsky: The history of the development of higher mental functions* (M. J. Hall, Trans.; R. W. Rieber, Ed. Vol. 4). Plenum Press.

Vygotsky, L. S. (1998). *The collected works of L.S. Vygotsky: Child Psychology* (M. J. Hall, Trans.; R. W. Rieber, Ed. Vol. 5). Plenum Press.

Vygotsky, L. S. (1999). *The collected works of L. S. Vygotsky: Scientific legacy* (M. J. Hall, Trans.; R. W. Rieber, Ed. Vol. 6). Springer Science & Business Media.

Paper 9: When Preschool Girls Engineer: Future Imaginings of Being and Becoming an Engineer

This paper originally appeared as Fleer, M. (2019). When preschool girls engineer: Future imaginings of being and becoming an engineer. *Learning, Culture and Social Interaction*, 100372. https://doi.org/10.1016/j.lcsi.2019.100372 Reprinted here with permission from the publisher.

Abstract

Not a lot is known about how preschool teachers engage children in the future imaginings of engineering. What is known has primarily come from Northern American contexts, where the positive affordances for engineering education in preschools have been noted. What we do not know, is how the pedagogical practice invites girls into engineering activity settings in preschools, and if and how they are positioned to imagine a future self in engineering. The central problem reported is centered on how girls become oriented towards or imagine themselves being and becoming an engineer when in preschool. The study examined how children develop a motive orientation to engineering practices when teachers create motivating conditions in engineering education over 5.4 weeks (27.3 h digital observations) for 31 children (aged 3.4–5.5 years; mean age of 4.4 years). The study found that rather than a future imagining of engineering by children during free play time, the girls had difficulties with access to the engineering activity setting, and therefore had limited possibilities for acting 'as if' they were engineers.

Keywords

preschool – engineering education – cultural-historical – gender – STEM

Introduction

Concerns for the low number of girls and women engaged in engineering have been repeatedly reported by Governments across the Western world for over a decade (Kaspura, 2017) and even longer by researchers (Vrceli & Kirshnan, 2008; Whyte, 1986). Calls for action at the beginning of the pipeline have recently emerged (Australian Academy of Science, 2019), generating a new societal need for quality preschool engineering education in some countries (Early Childhood STEM Working Group, 2017; McClure et al., 2017). In response to this, some researchers have investigated the affordances for engineering education within preschools (Briseno, 2015) and others have worked with educators to realise new goals for preschool engineering practice (Fleer, under review, 2020). Despite this, there is still only a limited amount of research into the practices of engineering within preschools (Lippard, Riley, & Lamm, 2018). We simply do not know enough about this new cultural practice for young children, and particularly for girls.

What we do know, is that it is girls who opt out of engineering education, contributing to the dismal statistic of only 12% of engineers being women in many Western countries (Kaspura, 2017). We also know that communities are increasingly interested in supporting girls and women in engineering and STEM more broadly (Blickenstaff, 2005; Moroz, 2015). But we do not yet know when or how disengagement in engineering begins for girls. Therefore, it is timely to investigate how girls enter into, are shaped by, and shape the engineering activity settings at the beginning of the pipeline.

The central problem of this paper is on understanding how girls become oriented towards or imagine themselves being and becoming an engineer when in play-based settings where engineering education is promoted as a new activity setting during free play time. To achieve this goal, the paper begins with a review of the relevant literature into preschool girls' engineering and a brief historical overview of the models of practice available to support girls in STEM education. This is followed by the theoretical framework driving the research, the study design, findings and a discussion of what was learned from a study that followed one girl as she experienced engineering education over 5.4 weeks in her preschool.

Preschool Engineering Education

What is known about preschool engineering has primarily come from studies in the north American context, where there has been a longer tradition for introducing engineering education into preschools. Research has identified 3 broad understandings about the nature of the new practice tradition within play-based settings. First, this research shows that preschools give many opportunities for engineering practice because the play materials and the practice tradition for play, collectively afford what Lippard, Lamm, Tank, and Choi (2018) call pre-engineering thinking. For instance, in their study of 9 preschools over 3 mornings using an early engineering observation tool, Lippard,

Riley, and Lamm (2018) identified system thinking, collaboration, communication, and ethical considerations. These were found to occur most frequently in the block areas in the classrooms, with some also observed in the dramatic play area, and with art, manipulatives and sensory materials. However, gendered interactions or differences were not studied or reported, even though block building in preschools is frequently dominated by boys (Bagiati & Evangelou, 2016). This is an important gap in our understandings of the possible engineering affordances.

Second, and related to Lippard, Riley, and Lamm (2018) findings, is Bagiati and Evangelou's (2016) study which focused on the play materials and play practices found in preschools. Their research was an observational study of free play in the block area only. Eighteen children aged 3–5 were digitally observed over four months in order to identify precursors to engineering behaviour that might involve a *design process model* during block building. The findings show that during free play with block building a precursor to engineering thinking was evident, and this included goal setting, design and implementation, communication, verbal declarations when identifying and testing, and the ability to replicate constructions. Relevant to the focus of this paper, is that they noted that over the 4 months of data gathering, that it was the boys who were consistently block building. But, specific findings relating to gendered interactions or analysis of why or how it was that it was primarily the boys in the block area were not given. In an earlier study by Bagiati (2011) which followed a similar study design, only boys' engineering practices were reported. In summary, these researchers of preschool engineering appear to have drawn on categories of engineering thinking and practice that align with what matters in the engineering profession, and in so doing seem to have been oriented primarily towards more obvious areas of the preschool for block construction, where boys have been shown to dominate. This means that the findings may well be specific to boys only, leaving a gap in understanding about how girls may or may not engage in engineering practices in other areas of the preschool.

Third, of the limited preschool engineering literature that goes beyond block building, this work shows that most have not differentiated between boys' and girls' experiences of engineering education. For instance, Bairaktarova, Evangelou, Bagiati, and Brophy (2011) examined precursors to engineering more broadly by examining children's behaviours with tangibles in open, semistructured and structured materials. They argued that tangibles are already part of the Froebelian Kindergarten, where manipulating tangibles in the sandbox, puzzles, water table, painting, and construction kits are common place. Bairaktarova et al. (2011) suggest that these tangibles give contexts for studying existing engineering thinking of children. In their study of 18 children over

4 months during free play time using digital video techniques, they found that children asked more goal oriented questions when using structured materials and semi structured materials; and when using open tangibles, they encourage exploration and creativity, stating "artifacts do in fact facilitate children's engagement with engineering ideas" (p. 231).

When taken together, the findings of the literature that looks for engineering affordances within the common Froebelian structure of a kindergarten in US contexts, gives evidence of the genuine possibilities for advancing engineering education in preschools. However, this literature has not yet examined if there are differences in how girls enter into the different activity settings within the preschools, where engineering precursors or thinking are being developed.

Finally, there have only been a few studies that explicitly examine differences in gender behaviours during preschool engineering play within preschools. Gold (2014) investigated how 68 children aged 3–5 years played with loose parts and blocks in three settings – an imagination playground, a traditional playground and a dramatic play area across 4 preschools. Using a check list proforma of categories of engineering play, social play and physical play by observers, he documented over 3.5 months boys' and girls' behaviours. Whilst gender differences were reported for girls, noting they engage more positively in social play, no differences were found in gross and fine motor skills and stability play. Further, although more engineering thinking play was found in the imagination playground, no differences in the frequency of engineering play was reported in relation to gender. Unfortunately, the details of how the girls and boys entered into, shaped or were shaped by the activity settings, were not reported.

In another study of preschoolers' engineering play behaviours, Gold, Elicker, Choi, Anderson, and Brophy (2015) also did not find differences in behaviours of girls and boys, but reported that there was a small difference in boys' engineering discourse, as boys explained how things work more frequently than girls. In their study of 66 preschool children in the same 3 contexts and study design procedure described by Gold (2014), they noted that children tended to play in same gender groups, but no gender differences in engineering behaviours were found – similar goal-setting, planning, designing, construction and communication play goals and results were noted. They argued that "the results of this study at least suggest the possibility that interest in engineering could be recognized and fostered in both boys and girls during the preschool years" (p. 16).

In stark contrast to Gold (2014) in the US, is a study by Hallström, Elvstrand, and Hellberg (2015) who studied free play preschool settings in Sweden specifically in relation to gender and construction technology (Lego, wooden blocks, model making, sand, water) both indoors and outdoors. Even though the study did not focus on engineering per se but rather construction activities, the activity settings were similar to those studied by Bagiati (2011), Bagiati and Evangelou's (2016), Bairaktarova et al. (2011), Gold (2014), and Gold et al. (2015) and therefore the results are relevant to this paper. In following 38 children aged 3–6 years across 2 preschool departments during free play time over 9 sessions of 2–6 h, it was found that what the children played with during free play time was gendered, particularly for the 5–6 years. It was reported that boys played with cars, making roads whilst the girls played with animals. The boys were found to construct more than the girls. The behaviours of the boys showed they concentrated on stability with blocks, breaking apart and mending road systems when using cars. The girls built fences for their animals, and once complete, created play narratives rather than adjusting or pulling down and re-building fences. Hallström et al. (2015) also found that girls and boys showed differences in their orientation and approach to technology. Girls appear to distance themselves from experimentation, such as when making a model of a volcano and then using baking powder to simulate an eruption, or when in the block area passing blocks to boys to support their build, rather than building themselves. They concluded that girls design and build with a purpose for playing, suggesting building is an auxiliary activity, whilst for boys the process of building is the focus. Further, boys tend to use technical language in the process of building, aligning with the findings of Gold et al. (2015) who noted how boys explain their constructions more than girls.

Overall, Hallström et al. (2015) argue that, "The pedagogical problem that girls and boys learn to approach and handle technology differently remains, however, thereby confirming rather than dissolving gender boundaries." (p. 147). They suggest that in free play settings, gender differences are reinforced, and that future research should look into how this situation and gendered orientation to technology has arisen. Therefore, further research is needed into understanding how preschool girls enter into, are shaped by, and shape the engineering activity settings. Because of the limited amount of research into preschool engineering, we now turn to the broader gender and STEM literature to identify possible interventions over time and to conceptualise these models in relation to the future imaginings of engineering for girls.

Broader Educational Models on Changing STEM Engagement

In the broader literature on girls' participation in STEM it has been noted that over time, waves of challenges and solutions have been researched and theorised (Alloway, 1995). We have seen an additive model (Harding, 1987), a feminist epistemology (women have different experiences and these can contribute to knowledge generation that is currently absent) (Bleier, 1986; Harding, 1986; Harding & Sutoris, 1987; Rose, 1986), a distinction model (Harding, 1987), an alternative pathway model (Smail, 1987), a restructuring model (Harding, 1987) and a re-positioning model (Kelly, 1987a). More recently, the literature has focused more on the need for role models in engineering (Moroz, 2015), whilst also making visible the everyday practices of women and girls in STEM where a myriad of microaggressions are experienced (Grossman & Porche, 2014). Problems persist (Morgan, Farkas, Hillemeier, & Maczuga, 2016), and therefore it is important to briefly review what is known about these models to help guide the present study and to theorise how these models could be drawn upon for supporting the being and becoming of an engineer in the future.

In the early 1980s we learned a great deal about gender and STEM (at that time it was referenced mostly as science and/or technology). What was learned is worthy of re-visiting in the context of the engineering literature for play-based settings because the historical context can inform the contemporary research need of engineering education, where only 12% of the profession are women (see Kaspura, 2017). In the additive model, it is claimed that we include or add into STEM programs content that is more likely to engage girls and women (Smail, 1987), as the contemporary research of Mulvey, Miller, and Rizzardi (2017) show when researching (and problematizing) the foundational thinking associated with changing the colour of the resources to appeal more to girls to engage in engineering. Their research found that it was unhelpful for both girls and boys to do this. The distinction model is about redesigning STEM programs to be girl-only programs (Bentley & Watts, 1987), so that girls do not need to compete for resources (Kelly, 1987a), and can access equipment and materials needed for genuine participation in STEM. But subsequent research has theorised this also as unhelpful because it blames the victim and asks them to deal with the societal issues surrounding why so few women go into engineering. Related to this has been a compensatory model (Stage, Kreinberg, Eccles, & Becker, 1987), where girls are specifically taught to use equipment and to learn fundamental STEM concepts to catch up to the boys' skill set in STEM. This also blames the victim and asks them to 'catch up', rather than re-thinking how pedagogical practices should change. Some researchers have argued that boys are thought to have had in their free play activities more experiences of using objects and construction kits in their play (Beat, 1991) and this was also shown by Hallström et al. (2015) in engineering play. This aligns with the idea of a feminist epistemology, where women's different experiences and interests are drawn upon to re-design the nature of knowledge in STEM so that it goes beyond a masculinised construction (Kelly, 1987b). This view opens up new imaginings for engineering education that could be taken forward.

Others have captured the waves of theorising the problems and solutions in STEM and gender as framed within a biological difference argument set within a sociological frame. These can be summarised as girls' lack of academic preparation for STEM fields, girls poor attitudes and a lack of positive STEM experience in childhood; the absence of female role models in STEM, science curricula irrelevant to many girls, pedagogical practices in science favours males, the 'chilly climate' that exists for girls/women in science classes, the cultural pressure for girls and women to conform to traditional gender roles, and the inherent masculine worldview of scientific epistemology already mentioned (see Blickenstaff, 2005; Vrcejh & Krishnan, 2008). However, biological arguments have and continue to be questioned because they lack a new imagining of engineering education. In the longstanding research of Smail (1987), she has shown that through early gendered interactions, girls' develop interests later in schooling that become increasingly centered on nurturing whilst boys interest appear to be more instrumental and analytical. In presenting the outcomes as an unhelpful binary of boys' interests in rules, machines, fairness and justice, hierarchy and competition, analytical thought and inanimate things, and girls' interests as geared to relationships, people, pragmatism, networks and cooperation, aesthetics and the nurturing of living things, she advocates for curriculum adjustment to be more girl-friendly in order to make science more appealing to girls. But how children during the early childhood period develop these imaginings of what they should be interested in, that is their motive orientations, is not taken up in these models.

In summary, research into girl-friendly engineering has revealed that additive models (Harding, 1987) for increasing the participation of girls is problematic (see Mulvey et al., 2017). Research into girl-friendly engineering, also suggests that this focus maintains existing societal structures, practices and ways of learning STEM. Girls-only STEM as also a compensatory program, is simply designed as a catch up for girls to boys' skill set and does not change the underlying reason for the differences in STEM capability. In both theoretical models (additive and compensatory), the problem and the solution appear to be the responsibility of girls. These models do not support the contemporary need for changing practices to support girls imagining of being and becoming an engineer in the future.

Contemporary thinking in relation to gender and STEM appears to draw upon what Grossman and Porche (2014) have named as micoagressions and this offers some guidance for the study reported in this paper. It is through brief, but regular negative and subtle messaging during everyday interactions, that girls begin to doubt or question their place within engineering – imagining it as not for them. Grossman and Porche (2014) in capturing gendered interactions between humans under this umbrella term, make visible small but significant acts of aggression towards girls and women in STEM. A more nuanced conception shows both microassults and microinsults that can be helpful for analysis of imagining being and acting as an engineer within preschool. The former aims to explicitly attack a person's group identity, such as being a girl, or harm them through name calling, such as girls don't do engineering because it is not lady like. The former also involves discriminatory action, such as creating policies or allocating resources differently for girls and boys in engineering, or through some form of avoidance, such as deliberately not engaging girls in engineering. These are conscious acts of microaggressions by the perpetrators to another person. In contrast, microinsults are often unconsciously delivered by the perpetrator. These are known broadly in the literature as *unconscious bias*, and can be expressed through conveying a stereotypical image of a group identity, such as expressing surprise when meeting a woman who is an engineer, or always referring to engineers with the male pronoun, or though referencing women in engineering as 'women engineers' as though it is a separate category or societal anomaly. Unconscious bias expressed through day to day interactions, can feel like rudeness or an attack on a person's identity, even though the perpetrator is unaware of their insensitivity when they deliver a microinsult. These can contribute to how girls or boys may imagine their place in engineering activities within the preschool.

Directly relevant to this paper, Moroz (2015) in writing about these concerns for the field of engineering suggest that both microassults and micoroinsults accumulate, and over time girls and women in engineering experience a form of microinvalidation. That is, girls and women feel excluded, negated, and denied access to engineering. Even though their experience in engineering is less valued or their right to be involved in engineering is questioned, the negative interactions may be perceived as an irrational overreaction by the perpetrators or the victims themselves. Therefore, it is becoming increasingly important to determine when and how these reported micoragressions first begin in education and if they can help researchers interested in knowing about when girls engage, but also begin to disengage from engineering as something not for them. Understanding this, can help with a better conceptualisation of how girls begin to imagine themselves in, or excluded from, engineering practices in the preschool (or indeed a future engineering profession). This latter conceptual model was drawn upon to analyse the practices and the activity settings of the preschool where engineering was being introduced to children.

Imagining

In order to address the central problem of the study reported in this paper, it is important to elucidate four fundamental and interrelated theoretical concepts. First, if we are to understand how the environment can act as a source for the future imagining of the child to be an engineer, then it becomes significant to theorise the environment of the child as something "possible to achieve at the end and as a result of the developmental process, [which] is already available in the environment from the very beginning" (Vygotsky, 1994, pp. 347–348). That is, if we wish a child to imagine themselves as an engineer in the future, then the developmental conditions must not only be present, but should be exerting "an influence on the very first steps in the child's development" (Vygotsky, 1994, p. 348). This is not a linear progression, but a qualitative relation between the ideal form and real form of the child's development (Vygotsky, 1994). This suggests that preschool teachers introduce into kindergartens new practices and a new engineering activity setting that goes beyond existing Froebelian designed kindergartens.

Second, Vygotsky (1994) argued that as "time goes by, the child begins to understand more and more" (Vygotsky, 1994, p. 346) as evidenced through the child's changing relations to the same social situation. This is captured through the concept of the *social situation of development* (Vygotsky, 1994), where the cultural age period orients children to their environment differently. For preschool children, which is the focus of this paper, Vygotsky (1966) theorised that the leading activity of the child is to play, and children correspondingly approach the environment through their play. This means that children create imaginary situations, where they change the meaning of objects and actions to give them a new sense, as we see when a child puts on a hard hat, lifts blocks and builds bridges, imagining a role of being a civil engineer. In this theorisation, play gives a contradictory context in which the "child operates with meaning severed from objects and actions [imagination], but [who is] in real action with real objects" (Vygotsky, 1966, p. 13). To engage in the imagining of being an engineer, requires a new kind of future imagining by the adults who organise the preschool environments in support of children's play.

Third, to support this new need, the conception of *future imagining* introduced by Bottcher and Dammeyer (2016) is helpful because it draws attention to the "present interpretations of the child's abilities and future imaginings of the child's potential" ("organise developmental support in which ideas about potentials are tested, revised and actively turned into developmental trajectories" p. 186). In these *future imaginings* of a child, they have noted in their research that adults (p. 186). This is more than an ideal form of development which Vygotsky (1994) has conceptualised as already present in the child's environment. But rather it is about developmental trajectories and associated pathways, not yet available to the child in their present environment, or not yet imagined as needed. They are pathways that must be created, and which require a new form of future imagining that is specific for the developmental trajectory of specific children. This conception of *future imagining* has resonance with a STEM field concerned with wanting a different kind of future for girls and women than is currently available (Kaspura, 2017).

Finally, and related to the theoretical problem of the *future imagining* of engineering possibilities for girls, is the concept of *moral imagining* as introduced by Vadeboncoeur (2019). She explains this as a moral compass of how children are engaged in playful situations with each other, in how they self-direct in relation to others, and how play narratives are jointly developed within the different contexts they inhabit. This concept offers a cultural-historical conception of what the sociological and general psychological literature has reported on microaggressions (Moroz, 2015). Moral imagining goes one step further, because it captures "a relational sensibility of imagining, creating and acting together that is oriented towards a shared future" (Vadeboncoeur, 2019, p. 227). The core idea of imagining a shared future may open up possibilities for studying disruptions or trajectories in the context of engineering (e.g., leaky pipelines or pathways as has been described by Vrceli & Kirshnan, 2008). How different developmental opportunities are *morally imagined* by girls and boys in engineering can support a more nuanced analysis. It is in how children self-direct *in relation to each other within engineering activity settings*, that future imaginings in engineering could emerge. Rather than a binary of different pathways, or a *compensatory or additive model* to catch girls up as reviewed above, *moral imagining* is relationally understood and therefore could be relationally conceptualised in practice at both the institutional and personal levels within the current societal values and need (Hedegaard, 2019) for more girls and women in engineering in Australia.

Study Design

The study design was guided by Hedegaard's (2019) model of societal, institutional, and personal framing, where practices and activity settings foreground in research the demands children meet and their motives. By following children's participation in the activity settings, it becomes possible to interpret the developmental conditions. Through following how one child Rita enters into the activity setting of engineering over a period of 5.4 weeks we see how the activity setting creates new demands on children and how the children in turn meet these demands, as well as contribute to the activity setting.

Preschool Setting and Institutional Practices

The traditional kindergarten designed by Froebel includes a broad range of activity settings. Indoors we see activity settings, such as the home corner, the block area, the book corner and in the outdoor we see activity settings of the sandpit, water trolley and climbing equipment. The practice tradition is for teachers to set up instructional moments during circle time when all the children participate together with the teacher, or free play time where children can choose to participate in small group activities with or without the teacher, such as table top activities, home corner area, and the block area.

In this preschool, the teachers created an additional activity setting that children could participate in during free play time. New conditions for children's development through introducing an engineering area within the traditional Froebelian structure of a kindergarten were created. An analysis of the new practice tradition can be found in Author (under review).

Activity Setting

The engineering activity setting was located close by the block area and the home corner, but also this space was surrounded by tables where props, a digital device, and construction and drawing were possible. The focus of the engineering activity setting was on implementing an engineering program on civil engineering. The content of the engineering was bridge building. The social purpose for engineering was building a bridge for the set design of the popular fairytale of the 3 Billy Goats Gruff. The idea was to make a digital movie of this fairytale using a hand-held digital device and MyCreate app. The digital practices are not included in the analysis discussed in this paper. Children are free to come and go into the engineering activity setting.

Engineering Intervention

The engineering program was centered on reading, re-telling, and watching YouTube videos over time, the story of the 3 Billy Goats Gruff at circle time, followed by making available to the children during free play time, the new activity setting of building a bridge for the 3 billy goats to cross, and for the re-enactment of the fairytale during free play time by interested children, where they could also make a digital movie of the story. The main teacher took interested children into the engineering activity setting and introduced the challenge of how to build a bridge for role-playing the story of the 3 Billy Goats

Gruff. The teachers regularly visited this activity setting to offer support as needed, staying for between 2 and 10 min at a time.

Participants

Rita (aged 4.1 years) is the focus of this paper. She is part of a group of 31 children (aged 3.4–5.5 years; mean age of 4.4 years) and 5 teachers (3 Indian Australian, 1 Sri Lankan Australia, and 1 European Australian heritage background). She is one of 18 girls and 13 boys who regularly attend the centre. She appeared interested in the engineering activity setting, and along with five other girls, who opted to go into this area in order to participate in the engineering program. She was selected as the focus of the study and its analysis because she chose to stay in the engineering activity setting for the duration of the engineering program – spending most of the free play time in the engineering activity setting. After the initial introduction, the frequency and duration of the other girls' participation in the engineering activity setting was brief.

Australia is a culturally diverse community. In this study the children were from a range of cultural heritage backgrounds, including Anglo/Australian 15; Euro/Australian 2; Chinese/Australian 2; Japanese/Australian 1; Zimbabwe/Australian 1; Indian 2; Indonesian 1; Italian/Chinese 1; Mongolian 1; Vietnamese 1; Mauritian 1; Papua New Guinea 2; Saudi Arabia 1.

The teachers held post-secondary or degree qualification in early childhood education and had cultural heritage of Indian Australian (3), Sri Lankan Australia, and European Australian.

Data Gathering

The overall data that were generated centred on digital observations (27.3 h), photographs of practices (336), and interviews of the teachers (2.5 h). Data collection took place over 8 visits (5.4 weeks) with each period lasting 2–5 h. To achieve a holistic study of both the practices and the activity setting, two cameras were used to capture what was taking place in the engineering space. One hand-held camera followed Rita as she entered into the activity setting, as well as capturing the children/teachers around her. This enabled close-up observations of the children's and teachers' interactions. The second camera was mounted on a tripod and placed near each of the relevant activity settings associated with the bridge building and role play, plus group time and other engineering related activity settings planned or emerging over the observation period. Together, the practice of moving cameras and following children gave a holistic sense of the activity settings (Hedegaard, 2019), as well as its location within the overall practice tradition of the kindergarten. As engineering was a new practice tradition it was important to go beyond the specific engineering space and to also capture the practice traditions of for example, group time, and the transition between activity settings (Hedegaard, 2014).

Analysis

For the purposes of the gender analysis, it was important to draw upon a holistic analytical framework (Hedegaard, 2014) where the societal values and expectations for more women in the engineering professions has arisen, the institutional practices to introduce engineering education in preschool, and person's motive orientation towards engineering within the engineering activity setting could be dynamically examined. This complex cultural-historical dynamic framed how the analysis was undertaken, because examining future imaginings of girls in engineering requires strong theoretical constructs for understanding the practices and the activity settings of the preschool. This is different to previous preschool engineering research that uses a proforma of looking for engineering behaviour and thinking through a check list or through digital data analysis, where frequencies are reported on who is participating. Closer to Hallström et al. (2015), this study was interested in how children were participating in the new engineering activity setting.

Through following how one child meets the demands of the activity setting, such as making a bridge to re-tell the story of the 3 Billy Goats, and contributes to this new activity setting by adding or waiting to build with blocks, gives insights into how the new conditions could create developmental moments for the focus child. For example, the engineering activity setting places new demands on Rita, because she has to build a bridge that will support the 3 billy goats. How this is negotiated with other children, can give insights into how Rita imagines the activity setting as a place for her to be involved in, and thereby how engineering is something that she imagines she can do and be later in life. Hedegaard (2012) has captured this dynamic as following the motivated actions of the child (e.g., persistently present), which in turn acts as a construct for determining possible interpretations of future imaginings (re-entering the activity setting).

In order to achieve this holistic interpretation, the digital data needed to be logged, coded and stored as tagged raw digital data. Files were then copied and analysed using Hedegaard's conception of a common sense interpretation, situated practice interpretation, and a thematic/theoretical interpretation (Hedegaard & Fleer, 2008). In a common sense interpretation, video files are tagged as moments of gendered interactions and these are related to what is already known from the literature (e.g., access to resources). In a situated practice interpretation video data were viewed many times, with the task of slicing single situated practices into a series of interrelated clips, but these were always tagged in relation to the raw data (i.e., holistic interpretation). For example, multiple examples of how boys and girls access resources were copied and put into a folder marked as "access to resources". This could be a 5 min clip of a girl trying to access the bridge in order to place a block on it or a 3 s video clip of a girl being pushed away from the bridge. In this digital process of a situated interpretation, data folders of gendered interactions are created where a sense of density emerges.

Finally, in a thematic/theoretical interpretation, the digital data were revisited in relation to the whole data set, but with the view to coding and nuancing of the interpretations. In this final phase of the iterative process, a conceptual synthesis and theorisation of the data categorisation takes place and it is here where the theoretical concepts underpinning the study are deployed. The Hedegaardian concepts of demands and motives were used in relation to the societal values, institutional practices and the engineering activity settings where microaggressions in the context of the theoretical construct of future moral imaginings in order to understand the patterns of gendered interactions that emerged, as well as what was categorised in relation to what is known from the literature (such as, access). Because the literature was limited, the study needed to also develop new categories, such as, identifying clusters of clips associated with engineering motive for girls. However, as will be reported in the next section, these moment did not exist or were compromised because of the moral imagining and associated unconscious bias of the teachers. Consequently, this paper only reports details of the microinvalidations within the holistic context of practices and activity settings.

Results and Discussion

An overall summary of the activity settings for the new engineering practice is shown in Table 1, alongside of Vignettes 1–8 taken from the digital observations to illustrate how Rita enters into these activity settings. In Column 1 the activity settings listed are related to the focus of the engineering theme, and in Column 2 a summary of the motivating conditions created by the teachers is presented. This table is a backdrop for the detailed vignettes that follow. It gives a holistic frame to the organisation and interpretation of data.

The engineering activity setting is new in the centre, and this places new demands on the children as the teachers orient them to an engineering motive (Author, 2019) as they role play (engineering area), hear the fairytale of the 3 Billy Goats Gruff and discuss engineering actions (circle time), embody the story and the engineering in the outdoor area as they prepare the bridge and

TABLE 1   Summary of activity settings that Rita enters into within the preschool setting
related to being and becoming an engineer

Activity setting	Motivating conditions for imagining being and becoming an engineer (examples only)
Circle time (CF1–13)	The teacher reads 3 Billy Goats Gruff fairytale and explains the story from the point of emotions (e.g. scared of troll, happy to have the green grass) and activities, such as bridge making (CF1). Teacher reads the story then she shows the pictorial story in the YouTube video to children. She divides children into 2 groups and asks one group to go to the engineering area and the other group to make horns for the goats (CF5)
Engineering area (CF1–6; CF9–11)	*Building:* They make a wooden bridge then they add rocks. They also set the dry leaves one side and green grass another side of the bridge (CF1). *Role-play:* Children experience the story scenario in the engineering area. They act out the story using the propos and the bridge they made in the engineering area (CF3). *Movie making of 3 Billy Goats Gruff (CF9–11):* Teacher shows the slowmation movie to J and he is very interested to make the movie. Then they go to the studio again to make the movie. J makes the full movie with the help of teacher and research assistant. Then A and K come and join with them to make the movie (CV9).
Sports Buzz (CF3)	Children experience how racing heart beat feels whilst engaged in sports buzz activities. Educator talks to a few children about the body parts specifically the heart; what happened after the sports buzz activities and linking it to the goats in the story. What they might have experienced when their heart beats faster when they encountered the Troll and ran over the bridge towards the grass.
Music (CF5)	The music lady arrives with musical instrument and does circle time with children. She sings song and children follow her. She introduces balloon for discussing how our lungs works and how do we breathe. Teachers linked how goats huff and puff in the story and what happen to their lungs. Children are excited and curious on these activities and provide their full attention on science activities (CF5).
Outdoor play equipment/area	Teacher guides children to role play of the three billy goats gruff on climbing equipment. They set up the bridge and grass. Some children do the role play. After some times, the teacher was not there and they lose their interest and moves to go for other play activities (CF5).
Planting seeds outside (CF7–8)	Teacher takes printed picture of grass growing. Children prepare the tray with soil, plants grass seeds, water with help. Discuss need for quality soil, water and sun for growing grass. Links to 3 billy goats gruff and grass are made (CF7).

role-play (outdoors), and as they explore emotions in relation to the fairytale and associated physiological response to fear, effort, etc. (Sports Buzz; Music).

In order to understand how the new activity setting of engineering creates new imaginings about role-playing and being and becoming an engineer (Vignettes 1–8), we examine how the children enter into this new practice tradition within the engineering activity setting in the preschool, through following the demands and motives of one child, Rita. Importantly, we also examine if and how a shared motive to act 'as if' engineers emerges in the activity setting, where the imaginary play of building a bridge for the 3 Billy Goals Gruff is featured. In line with Vygotsky (1966), Vadeboncoeur (2019) has said, "A shared motive may enable a common vision, a shared purpose and, perhaps for the participants a 'general enterprise'" (p. 244). Relevant to a shared future imagining in engineering, is the view that "'as if' by playing they are relating, imagining future relationships with others" (p. 244). But to achieve this kind of imagining, Vadeboncoeur (2019) says, "to feel one's way into a role, imagining worlds that have not been experienced as possible worlds, and sympathizing with others in ways that foster collective action towards possible social future – in these ways imaginative play may be said to leave both collective and individual traces on children who play" (p. 244). The activity settings (Column 1) and the motivating conditions found there (Column 2), were designed by the teachers to create these possibilities.

Who Can Be in the Engineering Space Contributes to the Future Imagining of Engineering as a Profession

How Rita enters into the new activity setting of engineering a bridge for the 3 Billy Goats Gruff is introduced in Vignette 1. Rita is one of the longstanding engineers who stays in the activity setting for most of the free play time for engineering (Table 1). The engineering activity setting is popular with the children. The teacher invites the children into the space, as engineers who are going to build a bridge for the 3 Billy Goats Gruff. In Vignette 1 is an observation made directly after circle time (CF1), and where the children are first introduced to Engineering. Initially a large group of children go into the area with the teacher, including Rita. There are more children than can comfortably work on bridge building, so the teacher asks those who really want to engineer to stay.

> **Vignette 1:** Rita enters into the new activity setting – Who dominates the engineering space?
>
> Seven children are now in the engineering area and the teacher looks to the boys and asks, "Can anyone remember what did the trolls have to

cross?". One boy calls, "The bridge". The teacher moves out of the engineering area and gathers together a range of props and places them near the bridge building area. Rita who has remained in the engineering area, looks intently into the box. Two girls and one boy join her and look at the props. The teacher directs her gaze to the four boys on her left and says, "Let's start everyone". Signalling with her hands, she says, "This is the bridge". The teacher has inadvertently positioned her back to the girls and creates a physical barrier between the girls behind her near the props, and the boys in front of her. It is the boys who now have the front position in the engineering build area.

Rita and the other two girls stand at the back behind the teacher. The teacher can see the bridge building from above and the boys can see it directly in front of them. The girls have partial sight of the engineering building area.

Along with 2 other girls, Rita continues to observe from the side, and does not move into the building area.

We know from the theorisation of Vygotsky (1966) that role-play draws upon children's experiences. The narrative productions of children at play are not replications, but are meaning making actions of 'as if' scenarios. The story reading of the 3 Billy Goats Gruff and the invitation by the teacher to build a bridge and role-play is a motivating condition for introducing engineering. It is full of possible imagining for Rita 'as if' she is an engineer. However, as Vignette 1 shows, Rita has no opportunity to be close to the engineering space because first, the teacher has positioned her body in a way that directs her gaze at the boys standing close to the engineering area, which could affirm their right to the space and to act 'as if' engineers.

Second, the teacher does not engage or create a space for Rita and the other two girls to enter into the main build area. Having her back to them could suggest and signal a lack of expectation of girls to engineer. Whilst it is not possible to determine at this moment how this action is interpreted by the girls, later observations over the observation period show that one of the original 3 girls remained in the engineering space – suggesting their initial enthusiasm and expectation for building a bridge in the engineering activity setting was not realised. Vadeboncoeur (2019) has argued that "imagining in play is central for participants to begin to recognize their own actions in the world as potentially agentic, as well as to recognize that particular social futures are shaped in the present" (p. 231). Rita's future imagining of being and becoming an engineer is being shaped at this first social moment of roleplaying being an engineer and building the bridge for the 3 Billy Goats Gruff. The space and Rita's inability to easily access the building area, makes it difficult to act 'as if' she is an engineer. Her social imagining in this moment appears to be compromising her imagining of being and the future becoming, of an engineer. Longstanding research into access to STEM resources has been shown to be difficult for girls because boys tend to claim the space and resources before girls (Kelly, 1987a). In Vignette 1 the teacher did not notice that it was only boys who were at the front of the engineering build area, or that her own positioning made it difficult for Rita to enter into the action zone for building. A different kind of positioning by the teacher and including the girls in her gaze as she discussed engineering the bridge, could have changed this first social encounter of engineering for Rita.

Vignette 1 illustrates the way Rita tries to enter into the engineering activity setting. In Vignettes 2–7 we see how Rita who is now in the activity setting, meets the new engineering demands. Her motive orientation to act 'as if' she is an engineer is evident. But what is shown again is how her "social futures are shaped in the present" (Vadeboncoeur, 2019, p. 231) and her imagining of being an engineer continues to be compromised. In Vignette 2 the general enterprise of role-playing being engineers building a bridge for the 3 Billy Goats Gruff is featured. The original group of boys and Rita are still in similar positions to that described in Vignette 1. However, an additional 5 boys move past the teacher and position themselves directly behind the 4 boys who are standing in front of the build area and who are building the right pillar of the bridge. One boy Nathan is standing close to the teacher, and this boy pushes against the wall of boys. The teacher notices, and as Vignette 2 shows, she gives him access to the build area.

> **Vignette 2:** Who is given space to engineer? Making space for Nathan but not for Rita
>
> Oliva, Grey and Bryce are directly in front of the bridge construction. They have been working on the bridge building for some time now. Most of the other children have left, except Rita, who has been standing close by waiting for an opportunity to add more tape to the construction, but because 3 boys are taking the prime bridge building space it is difficult to move in. She tries several times, but each attempt to position herself into the space is aborted because Oliva physically pushes her back or does not give her space to enter. Oliva also previously pushed the other boys. On this occasion, the teacher notices, as Nathan tries to move in, and is forced back by Oliva. The teacher who has been at the back of the space cutting masking tape says, "Oliva use your words. Oliva, Nathan is trying to get in here". The teacher taps Oliva as she speaks to him, and leans forward and lowers herself to make direct eye contact with him, and then says,

"Nathan has decided to put the grass along here. On this bit (pointing)".
This opens up a space and Nathan moves into place with his grass and
contributes to the creation of the set. Meanwhile Rita is observing from
a distance, and more boys join, seeming to notice the teacher's intervention. Five boys push forward behind Oliva, leaving no space for Rita.

Vignette 2 suggests that there is a shared motive for engineering play, but
the ethical and moral behaviour to play as a collective enterprise by all the children in the area, as has been so eloquently discussed by Vadeboncoeur (2019)
as being key for future imagining of being together, on this occasion appears
to be working against Rita, and presumably the other girls who have left the
engineering area. First, although there is a shared engineering motive, the
engineering area becomes a formidable space to enter because the children in
the front were pushed by the children at the back. Many of the children at the
back eventually moved away, because any attempt to break into the engineering area by those children was difficult, as Vignette 2 shows.

Second, Oliva dominates the engineering space and the teacher notices
this and tries to work out solutions for giving other children opportunities
to construct. The example shows expert teacher positioning of Nathan into
the engineering space that is respectful of both Oliva and Nathan. However,
Rita appears to be invisible. Rita is not supported or positioned to enter into
the engineering space even though she has been patiently waiting. How the
teacher opens up a space for Nathan and does not notice ongoing problems
with access for Rita, has been consistently reported in the literature for girls
who seek to be involved in STEM activity settings (Hallström et al., 2015).

The imagining of this activity setting as an engineering space by Rita over
the data collection period appears to be a contested space. The boys and the
teacher create challenging conditions for Rita, because although she is in the
space, she is also ignored or pushed back from the bridge, which is the site of
engineering action. The less assertive boys are supported by the teacher, as the
example of Nathan shows, but similar equity of access is not afforded to Rita
by the teacher. The imagining of being or becoming an engineer in the new
activity setting is supported for the boys. For Rita, she has limited possibilities
to act 'as if' she is an engineer. The engineering activity setting and being and
becoming an engineer could therefore be imagined as a space for boys only. In
play, Vygotsky (1966) has argued that children's motives to be together in social
relations means acts of negotiation for realising a shared collective imaginary
situation can shape children's behaviours. However, Rita seems to be invisible
within the new activity setting and does not have the same teacher support
for negotiating her way into the action zone. For Rita, the moral compass of

imagining being and becoming an engineer, has swung towards Nathan being supported to act 'as if' he has a right to be in the engineering space, and he is shown how to negotiate this with Oliva. But for Rita, she is not socially supported within the engineering activity setting to engineer.

Who Is Positioned to Be the Engineer Contributes to the Future Imagining of Engineering as a Profession

Engineering is new area of learning for preschool teachers in Australia, and this means that educators interested in this curriculum need to create new practices to support the future imagining of engineering for preschool children. We already know from the research of Capobianco, Diefes-Dux, Mena, and Weller (2011), that when children aged 6 and 9 year are asked about what is an engineer, their responses suggest they do not know. The teachers in our study created motivating conditions to support children's future imagining of the engineering profession through organising in the centre (Table 1) opportunities for acting 'as if' they are civil engineers building and role-playing to test their construction. The teachers thoughtfully embedded explanations of engineering within the new activity setting, as Vignette 3 below shows, but how this was taken up and imagined by the other children is shown in Vignettes 4 and 5, with specific focus on the girls in Vignette 6. Together, these examples show how teachers are seeking to build a relational history of future imagining of being and becoming an engineer through role-play.

Vignette 3: Head engineers have more authority

There are 2 girls and 4 boys in the engineering activity setting. Although the boys are in front of the bridge, the girls are actively involved from time to time placing tape on to the structure – but mostly to the left side of the bridge where there is less engineering activity by the boys. The teacher appears to have deemed that there is a problem with the bridge, and calls the head engineer to undertake an inspection. She says, "Oliva are you my head engineer? Oliva do you know what an engineer is?". He does not respond. "He designs the bridge. Right. Oliva, my head engineer can you come along". The teacher holds out her arm to signal to Oliva which direction to walk. She invites Oliva to stand back from the bridge and asks all the children to get out of the way, stating: "Can we all stand back a bit, so our head engineer can have a look". She then reinforces compliance by foregrounding Andrea's immediate action by saying, "Thanks Andrea, that's beautiful". At this moment, all the girls leave the area near the bridge and go to the back or go on to another activity, and the boys all move forward again to the bridge. The teacher continues to try and move the boys back. She gives up and moves forward and discusses that there is a problem, signalling to the other end of the bridge by pointing, suggesting something is missing.

Later in the bridge building the teacher re-introduced the idea of what is an engineer to more of the children, but in this example, only the boys are present. As before, she draws attention to engineering by positioning the children as they are working on the bridge engaged in engineering practices.

> **Vignette 4:** Engineer Number 1, 2, 3, 4
> There are six boys who are working in the engineering space. The girls have left. The teacher drops her body to the same level as the children and she says as she taps each child, "Engineer Number 1, Engineer Number 2, Number 3, Number 4 and 5" and then she points to a child further away, and says, "Number 6". This child says, "I am number 6". He changes his mind and says, "I want to be Number 5". The teacher nods and says, "Ok you can be Number 5". The child smiles and stretches tall, as though very proud of this new social position in the group.

The labelling of children as engineers appears to be important. The children notice the labelling of being an engineer, being a head engineer or Number 1 engineer, as this appears to be accorded a great deal of status, as Vignette 5 shows:

> **Vignette 5:** Why are you the Number 1 engineer?
> Later in the engineering construction work Rita, Bryce and Oliva are working on the bridge. Bryce points to the bridge span and says twice to Oliva, "Look Number one". Oliva does not respond. Rita looks but does not respond, as the comments are not directed to her. Then Bryce says pointing to the two strips over the span of the bridge "2 over one", "2 over 1, Number 1". Oliva looks but does not comment.
> Bryce asks Oliva, "Why are you number 1 Oliva?". Oliva says, because "The teacher says I am".

What these examples show is that boys become positioned as engineers and are named as Number 1 or 2 engineer or Head engineer. Vignette 3 showed that Rita was not given this status, yet Oliva who dominated the use of the space and resources was given the status of the head engineer and Number 1 engineer. Vignette 5 shows how children do notice and wonder why. Once again, Rita is not recognized by the teachers as an engineer, but rather she is invisible as a engineer. The messaging from the teacher centres on the boys as engineers, and this creates conditions for Rita that validate the boys' presence and status as an engineer. This suggests that for Rita that it is boys who are being imagined as being and becoming an engineer by the teachers and by each other. How Rita could imagine herself as being and becoming an engineer in this social context of validating the boys and ignoring her, would be working against the narrative developing in the preschool.

It is also difficult for teachers to create conditions for the girls as the engineering practices continued in the preschool (Table 1), because the girls left the engineering space and only returned for brief periods. It was only Rita who persisted and stayed. When the teachers did notice this on one occasion, she tried to solve the problem by calling for the girls to be in the engineering activity setting. In Vignette 6 it shows how Rita is accorded the status of an engineer, but she and the position is referenced as a 'girl engineer'. This labelling of gender did not occur for the boys throughout the observation period.

> **Vignette 6:** Girl engineers or girls in engineering?
>
> Rita is still in the engineering activity setting. Teacher 1 asks, "So how many *girl engineers* have we got?". Teacher 2 answers, "One only". Consequently, Teacher 2 calls out across the neighbouring area, "Come on girls". With no response from the girls, she then moves across the centre calling out, "Where are the *girl engineers?*".

Is it possible that in calling the girls – *girl engineers* – that this suggest to them that the default mode is that Number 1 engineer or Head engineer should be a boy? Is it possible that boys in *engineering* is the default mode, and the anomaly is the girls – hence being named as a '*girl engineer*'. Imagining being and becoming an engineer in the context of the practices and narratives illustrated in Vignettes 1 to 6, suggest that it is difficult to realise a future imagining as an engineer for Rita, even though she shows a strong motive to build. The "relational sensibility of imagining" and acting together with the other boys who were being oriented to engineering, appeared to not provide "a shared future" (Vadeboncoeur, 2019, p. 227) of engineering for both girls and boys.

Do the Different Activity Settings Give Different Kinds of Authority to Children?

On the same day as the engineering activity setting was first introduced to the children, Rita was observed going in the home corner. In this different activity setting which was not the focus of the study, we see a very different kind of interaction, but one that is nevertheless linked with gender, as Vignette 7 shows.

> **Vignette 7:** Rita has some authority in the home corner
>
> Rita is standing in the engineering space, and steps forward towards the home corner. As she does, she notices 2 boys in the home corner and runs across calling assertively, "Hey, this is our house". Harry leaves but Jackson resists and continues to play with the cups and saucers on the floor. He looks up and says, "This is our house". Rita puts her hands on her hips and assertively says, "This is our house first!". Jackson responds by saying, "But you got Shadow House". Rita emphatically says, "No" as she rocks a trolley back and forth. Jackson looks up again and says forcefully, "Yes" implying she already has a house. Rita offers a suggestion to Jackson in order to negotiate a shared play narrative within the home corner, "Let's make an ice-cream".

There are two interesting things to notice about Rita's interaction in the home corner. First, Rita commands a real sense of presence in this activity setting. She appears to be speaking from a position of authority. Her hand gesturing signal that she is in control of the space. This was also observed when Rita participated in other non-engineering activity settings. Second, she appears to negotiate with Jackson when he resists her authority, and offers a new play narrative. Both situations demonstrate that this activity setting is a space that she can inhabit with some authority. Her assertive gesturing, lies in stark contrast to how she appears to engage in the engineering activity setting, where she seems much more pensive. Vignette 8 further illustrates this, because she does not show the same level of conviction or resistance when her access to resources is violated in the new engineering activity setting.

> **Vignette 8:** Rita's right to resources is violated
>
> Rita is working on the bridge, but has left a distance between herself and the left end of the bridge. The boys mostly worked on the right end. Rita has tape and is securing blocks together, in anticipation of joining them on to the left end of the bridge, so that both ends have a support and the span is then horizontal. The boys primarily stick rocks to the bridge using tape.
>
> Rita finishes the sticking and takes the plastic goat and begins a narrative, "And he bumped on his head". She calls with great excitement to the teacher who is observing, "Hey teacher M, he bumped on his face".

She places her hands to her mouth and laughs. The teacher says, "What was he saying?". Rita responds, "He bumped on his head". She continues to interact with the teacher in relation to the narrative she is developing with the prop. Oliva and Bryce who have been sticking tape to the bridge look to Rita and to the teacher. They seem interested in her narrative.

Bryce resumes sticking rocks and layering the tape and calls out to the teacher, "We need one more on here". At this moment, Oliva moves close to Rita, whilst still holding a block and tape in his hand, he pushes closely against Rita, and takes the plastic goat out of her hand.

Bryce continues to talk to the teacher about needing more tape, whilst Oliva goes back to sticking tape. He keeps a hold of the goat.

Rita puts her hands together in front of her. She rubs her hands together nervously. She reacts as though violated. She steps backwards as though wishing to avoid further assaults. The teacher continues to talk to Bryce and does not seem notice that Rita no longer has the prop for narrating her story.

Drawing on the concept of moral imagining it is possible to see that Oliva's moral compass creates a different kind of space for play for Rita, but also earlier we saw this when he engaged with Nathan (Vignette 2). The "relational sensibility of imagining, creating and acting together that is oriented towards a shared future" (Vadeboncoeur, 2019, p. 227) in Vignette 8 does not auger well for Rita as an engineer in this moment, across the observation period and potentially into the future.

In the home corner Rita resists and shows authority, and this suggests that this space is a place she can inhabit. Her actions within the home corner are different to the new engineering activity setting where space, resources and any sense of engineering being for her, seem to be seriously compromised. In the home corner her moral compass is to negotiate and to realise a shared narrative with Jackson, as an orientation that is moving towards a shared future (Vadeboncoeur, 2019). This is the antithesis of Oliva's interactions with her. But in the engineering space, Rita continually experienced new demands where the moral compass oriented her away from a shared future with the others for becoming an engineer (Vadeboncoeur, 2019). Rita was excluded, her being negated, and she was continually denied access to the new engineering experience. It is possible that through brief, but regular negative and subtle messaging during everyday engineering interactions, that Rita could begin to doubt or question her place within engineering. When these doubts accumulate over time, the engineering experience for Rita (Table 1) could possibly not create a motive orientation towards being or becoming an engineer.

Discussion

In this paper, the motives and demands associated with building future imaginings of being and becoming an engineer for Rita was shown across eight vignettes within the context of the new practice tradition and activity settings of the preschool (Table 1). As a new practice tradition in Australia, the teachers sought to create motivating conditions which could orient children to acting 'as if' they are engineers.

Seen through the perspective of Rita, this study found how the new activity setting of engineering, and the motivating conditions for engineering practice during free play time, suggested that, these on their own were not enough to realise a possible future imagining for girls to do engineering. Not only did the girls stop going to the engineering space, but Rita was left to negotiate with the boys how to share in the enterprise of acting 'as if' they were engineers with a common project. That is, the goal of bridge building for the Billy Goats Gruff, could not be actioned by Rita because the demands on the space and resources by the other children prevented her from easily accessing the engineering area. Overall, how the results can be understood centre around four areas.

First, what the first set of Vignettes (Vignettes 1–2) showed was a strong motive for engineering through how the children quickly occupied the space and sought to access the resources within the activity setting. However, it was primarily the boys who entered into the new practice tradition in the preschool. The results show that they were able to role-play 'as if' they were engineers building the bridge. In contrast Rita stayed on the periphery. Later when the bridge had been constructed, it was mostly the girls who had access to the space and they 'used the bridge' for role-playing. The blocks were taped onto shape (shown in Vignette 8), and thereby semipermanent, giving no further suggestions for changing the bridge design. Therefore, acting 'as if' engineers was no longer a possibility (Table 1). This suggests that how the program and the activity setting for engineering were planned and implemented in the preschool gave girls limited opportunities to role play 'as if engineers' in the new activity setting. Therefore, it can be argued that developing girls' competence in bridge design and construction were in this particular study rather limited.

Second, the engineering activity setting was difficult to enter when there were so many children seeking to engage with the resources. Rita's efforts (Vignette 1) to enter into the action zone and act 'as if' she was an engineer created new demands on her. But surprisingly, the demands were in relation to entering the space rather than for building engineering competence. The social enterprise of playing with others on the common goal of engineering a bridge for the 3 Billy Goats Gruff could be seen. Rita did not negotiate the space with the other players (Vignette 2). The teacher noticed Nathan, and helped him with the social negotiation for collectively entering into the civil engineering area. But the teacher did not give support to Rita with how to socially negotiate her place within the collective imaginary play.

Third, the second set of Vignettes (Vignettes 3 and 6) revealed how the moral compass for Rita progressively presented a future imagining of civil engineering as something that was not for her, but an activity setting for boys, who were named 'as if' they were engineers, despite Rita being present. She was not imagined 'as if' she was an engineer by the teacher. Therefore, this suggests that who is positioned to be the engineer, could contribute to the future imagining of engineering as a profession by young children.

Fourth, the new activity setting privileges engineering actions and imaginings as children act 'as if' they are engineers. How confident girls feel in the new activity setting has been shown in the general literature to be problematic for STEM (Grossman & Porche, 2014). The level of confidence and competence across activity settings in this study (Vignette 7–8) appeared to suggest that Rita wanted to role-play and be in the engineering activity setting. However, the results suggest a different kind of action by Rita to the other children. Is it possible that the social demands within the activity setting, particularly in relation to how other children appeared to violate Rita's efforts to engineer (Vignette 8), could contribute to her timid reactions, or could she bring with her a set of gendered interactions related to using blocks? Without further research, this is difficult to answer. The differences in Rita's actions across activity settings points to an area already linked to the outcomes of research associated with preschool constructing (see Hallström et al., 2015) where girls act as helpers, and girls construct to play, rather than to build. But if girls only have periphery access (Vignette 1) or have unencumbered access once the building work is completed (Table 1), then different ways of playing will emerge. These differences could be because of access rather than differences between girls' and boys' ways of playing 'as if' engineers. However, further research is needed to determine this.

Conclusion

Beginning in early childhood, this paper focused on preschool engineering practices with a view to better understanding how girls' future imagining of being an engineer could be supported. As a new area of learning in Australia for preschools children, there is the possibility to develop a new kind of future imagining for girls, and to change the current concerns for a lack of representation of women in engineering. But the expected outcome was not realised because this study showed that even in preschool, girls experience difficulties as early as four years of age (Grossman & Porche, 2014).

What was learned from this study centered on three major outcomes. First, in free play time it was found that the girls did not stay in the engineering area, only one girl persisted. The study showed that it was boys who primarily used the engineering area. This could contribute negatively to girls' future imagining of engineering as a profession. If only boys are noticed in the engineering area, as an unconscious bias on the part of the teachers, then this can incrementally signal to girls that this new area in the preschool is a *boy's only space*. This is consistent with the longstanding models of practice in STEM reviewed previously.

Second, the children noticed who was positioned by the teachers to be an engineer, and as the vignettes showed, they asked why? When teachers position only the boys as a head engineer or named them as engineers and do not notice the girls who were with them in the area, this contributes to a future imagining of *engineering as a profession that is for males only*. When teachers do notice that there are no girls in the engineering area, then inviting them into the area is important. But when they are named as 'girl engineers' and called into the space in this way, this contributes to the unconscious bias towards girls in engineering, because it becomes a microaggression when only girls are named as 'girl engineers' and boys are named 'as engineers'.

Finally, the outcomes of the study suggest, that like the literature on secondary students participation and engagement in STEM, preschool children's interactional patterns are brought into the centre and dominant ways of interacting emerge during free play time. Children's sense of authority in particular areas of the preschool were found in this study, and it was noted through the example of Rita, that she assumed authority in the home corner where she took control of the play narrative and had a voice in relation to who should be in this area. This level of authority by Rita was not found in the new activity setting of the engineering area, suggesting some form of prior gendering. Further research is needed in determining how the different activity settings give different kinds of authority to children, as well as how new activity settings for STEM should be created and introduced to children, so that girls can find a place in engineering, and can imagine a possible future in being and becoming an engineer.

In playing 'as if' they are engineers, the children changed how they acted in the new activity setting of civil engineering. Not only do the children negotiate the storyline in the imaginary situation as Vygotsky (1966) has argued, changing the meaning of their action (being engineers) and objects (blocks as resources for bridge building), but they are producing their own narrative about what it means to be in an engineering profession. As previous research has shown, there are many engineering possibilities in preschools. But if building with blocks is transformed to give new and meaningful possibilities for engineering, it is also important for the future imagining of engineering for girls, to be pedagogical developed to give access to girls, and allow them to experience acting 'as if' they are engineers in preschool.

In conclusion, it can be argued that this study has shown through one girl's experience how girls become alienated from engineering resources/spaces and experience a form of engineering invisibility. More needs to be known about how engineering as a profession and a practice could better invite preschool girls, and position them to incrementally imagine themselves as having a future career in STEM. Just at a time when societies are worried about the under representation of woman and girls in STEM (Régner, Thinus-Blanc, Netter, Schmader, & Huguet, 2019), there is a real need for moving towards building dissidents and disruption to the established narratives of STEM not being for girls, so that a new future imagining of girls in engineering can be realised. Normalising girls 'as if' they are future engineers in preschool play also needs a new imagining of the practice traditions of preschools to support the engineering activity settings that are now emerging.

Funding

This work was supported by the Australian Research Council: [DP130101438] and [DP140101131] for data collection, and [FL180100161] for subsequent analysis.

Acknowledgements

Special thanks to Shukla Sikder (field leader), and to the research assistants Sue March, Selena (Yijun) Hao, Anamika Devi, Omar Sulaymani, Kulsum Chishti Yonzon and Ainslie Holland (data organisation). Australian Research Council Discovery Grant [DP130101438 and DP140101131] for supporting the foundational research and [FL180100161] for data analysis and writing of this paper.

References

Alloway, N. (1995). *Foundation stones: The construction of gender in early childhood.* Curriculum Corporation.

Australian Academy of Science. (2019). *Women in STEM decadal plan*. Australian Academy of Science.

Author (2019a), (in press).

Bagiati, A. (2011). *Early engineering: A developmentally appropriate curriculum for young children* [Unpublished doctoral dissertation]. Purdue University.

Bagiati, A., & Evangelou, D. (2016). Practicing engineering while building with blocks: Identifying engineering thinking. *European Early Childhood Education Research Journal, 24,* 67–85. https://doi.org/10.1080/1350293X.2015.1120521

Bairaktarova, D., Evangelou, D., Bagiati, A., & Brophy, S. (2011). Early engineering in young children's exploratory play with tangible materials. *Children, Youth and Environments, 21*(2), 212–235.

Beat, K. (1991). Design it, build it, use it: Girls and construction kits. In N. Browne (Ed.), *Science and technology in the early years: An equality opportunities approach* (pp. 77–90). Open University Press.

Bentley, D., & Watts, M. (1987). Courting the positive virtues: A case for feminist science. In A. Kelly (Ed.), *Science for girls* (pp. 89–98). Open University Press.

Bleier, R. (Ed.). (1986). *Feminist approaches to science*. Pergamon Press.

Blickenstaff, J. C. (2005). Women and science careers: Leaky pipeline of gender filters? *Gender and Education, 17*(4), 369–386. https://doi.org/10.1080/09540250500145072

Bottcher, L., & Dammeyer, J. (2016). *Development and learning of young children with disabilities: A Vygoskian perspective*. Springer International Publishing.

Brieseno, L. M. (2015). *Science Technology Engineering and Maths (STEM) Education must begin in early childhood education: A systematic analysis of Washington State Guidelines use dot gauge the development and learning of young learners* (Unpublished MEd thesis). University of Washington.

Capobianco, B. B., Diefes-Dux, H. A., Mena, I., & Weller, J. (2011). What is an engineer? Implications of elementary school student conceptions for engineering education. *Journal of Engineering Education, 100*(2), 304–328.

Early Childhood STEM Working Group. (2017). *Early STEM matters: Providing high-quality STEM experiences for all young learners: A policy report*. University of Chicago, Erikson Institute. Retrieved August 2, 2019, from http://ecstem.uchicago.edu

Fleer, M. (2019). *Engineering PlayWorld – supporting children to collectively design, imagine and think using engineering concepts*. Research in Science Education.

Fleer, M. (2020). Studying the relations between motives and motivation – How young children develop a motive orientation for collective engineering play. *Learning, Culture and Social Interaction, 24*. https://doi.org/10.1016/j.lcsi2019.100355

Gold, Z. S. (2014). *Preschoolers' physical, social, and engineering play behaviors: Differences in gender and play environment* (Master Thesis), Purdue University. https://search.proquest.com/docview/1651208002?accountid=12528

Gold, Z. S., Elicker, J., Choi, J. Y., Anderson, T., & Brophy, S. P. (2015). Preschoolers' engineering play behaviors: Differences in gender and play context. *Children, Youth and Environments, 25*, 1–21. https://doi.org/10.7721/chilyoutenvi.25.3.0001

Grossman, J. M., & Porche, M. V. (2014). Perceived gender and racial/ethnic barriers to STEM success. *Urban Education, 49*(6), 698–727. https://doi.org/10.1177/0042085913481364

Hallström, J., Elvstrand, H., & Hellberg, K. (2015). Gender and technology in free play in Swedish early childhood education. *International Journal of Technology and Design Education, 25*, 137–149. https://doi.org/10.1007/s10798-014-9274-z

Harding, J., & Sutoris, M. (1987). An object relations account of the differential involvement of boys and girls in science and technology. In A. Kelly (Ed.). *Science for girls* (pp. 24–36). Open University Press.

Harding, S. (1986). *The science question in feminism.* Cornell University Press.

Harding, S. (1987). *Feminism and methodology: Social science issues.* Open University Press.

Hedegaard, M. (2012). Analyzing children's learning and development in everyday settings from a cultural-historical wholeness approach. *Mind Culture and Activity, 19*, 127–138.

Hedegaard, M. (2014). The significance of demands and motives across practices in children's learning and development: An analysis of learning in home and school. *Learning, Social Interaction and Culture, 3*, 188–194.

Hedegaard, M. (2019) (in press). Children's perspectives and institutional practices as keys in a wholeness approach to children's social situations of development. *Learning, Social Interaction and Culture.*

Hedegaard, M., & Fleer, M. (2008). *Studying children: A cultural-historical approach.* Open University Press.

Kaspura, A. (2017). *The engineering profession: A statistical overview.* Engineers Australia.

Kelly, A. (1987a). Why girls don't do science. In A. Kelly (Ed.), *Science for girls* (pp. 12–17). Open University Press.

Kelly, A. (1987b). The construction of masculine science. In A. Kelly (Ed.), *Science for girls* (pp. 68–77). Open University Press.

Lippard, C. N., Lamm, M. H., Tank, K. M., & Choi, J. Y. (2018). Pre-engineering thinking and the engineering habits of mind in preschool classroom. *Early Childhood Education Journal, 1–12.* https://doi.org/10.1007/s10643-018-0898-6

Lippard, C. N., Riley, K. L., & Lamm, M. H. (2018). Encouraging the development of engineering habits of Mindin prekindergarten learners. In L. English, & T. Moore (Eds.), *Early engineering learning* (pp. 19–36). Springer.

McClure, E. R., Guernsey, L., Clements, D. H., Bales, S. N., Nichols, J., Kendall-Taylor, N., & Levine, M. H. (2017). STEM starts early: Grounding science, technology, engineering, and math education in early childhood. *Joan Ganz Cooney center at sesame work-shop.* https://eric.ed.gov/?id=ED574402

Morgan, P. L., Farkas, G., Hillemeier, M. M., & Maczuga, S. (2016). Science achievement gaps begin very early, persist, and are largely explained by modifiable factors. *Educational Researcher, 45*(1), 18–35. https://doi.org/10.3102/0013189X16633182

Moroz, S. (2015). Microaggressions: Gender and microaggressions. In R. Parker, J. Pelletier, & E. Croft (Eds.). *WWEST's gender diversity in STEM: A briefing on women in science and engineering* (pp. 2–5).

Mulvey, K. L., Miller, B., & Rizzardi, V. (2017). Gender and engineering aptitude: Is the color of science, technology, engineering, and math materials related to children's performance? *Journal of Experimental Child Psychology, 160*, 119–126. https://doi.org/10.1016/j.jecp.2017.03.006

Régner, I., Thinus-Blanc, C., Netter, N., Schmader, T., & Huguet, P. (2019). Committees with implicit biases promote fewer women when they do not believe gender bias exists. *Nature Human Behaviour.* https://doi.org/10.1038/s41562-019-0686-3

Rose, H. (1986). Beyond masculinist realities: A feminist epistemology for the sciences. In R. Bleier (Ed.), *Feminist approaches to science* (pp. 57–76). Pergamon Press.

Smail, B. (1987). Organising the curriculum to fit girls' interests. In A. Kelly (Ed.), *Science for girls* (pp. 80–88). Open University Press.

Stage, E. K., Kreinberg, N., Eccles, J., & Becker, J. R. (1987). Increasing the participation and achievement of girls and women in mathematics, science and engineering. In A. Kelly (Ed.), *Science for girls* (pp. 119–133). Open University Press.

Vadeboncoeur, J. A. (2019). Moral imagining through transitions within, between and from imaginative play: Changing demands as developmental opportunities. In A. Edwards, M. Fleer, & L. Bottcher (Eds.). *Cultural-historical approaches to studying learning and development: Societal, institutional and personal perspectives* (pp. 227–246). Springer Nature Singapore Pte Ltd.

Vrcejh, Z., & Krishnan, S. (2008). Gender differences in students attitudes towards engineering and academic careers. *Australasian Journal of Engineering Education 14*(2), 43–56.

Vygotsky, L. S. (1966). Play and its role in the mental development of the child. *Voprosy Psikhologii, 12*(6), 62–76.

Vygotsky, L. S. (1994). The problem of the environment. In J. Valsiner & R. van der Veer (Eds.), *The Vygotsky reader* (pp. 347–348). Blackwell.

Whyte, J. B. (1986). Starting early: Girls and engineering. *European Journal of Engineering Education, 11*(3), 271–279. https://doi.org/10.1080/03043798608939308

Index